Circle of Fire
The Indian War of 1865

Circle of Fire
The Indian War of 1865

John D. McDermott

STACKPOLE
BOOKS

Published by
STACKPOLE BOOKS
5067 Ritter Road
Mechanicsburg, PA 17055
www.stackpolebooks.com

Printed in the United States of America

10 9 8 7 6 5 4 3 2 1

FIRST EDITION

Library of Congress Cataloging-in-Publication Data

McDermott, John D. (John Dishon)
  Circle of fire : the Indian war of 1865 / by John D. McDermott.— 1st ed.
    p. cm.
  Includes bibliographical references and index.
  ISBN 0-8117-0061-5
  1. Indians of North America—Wars—1862–1865. 2. Indians of North
America—Great Plains—Wars. 3. Indians of North America—Government
relations—1789-1869. 4. Fort Caspar (Wyo.)—History. 5. Fort Laramie
National Historic Site (Wyo.)—History. 6. United States—Politics and
government—1861–1865. I. Title.
  E83.863 .M35 2003
  973.7—dc21

2002156351

In the case of the Indians, traditional hostility, which teaches the settler's offspring from the cradle to "hate an Ingin as he hates pisen," is added to an instinct of aggression which has swept the red man from his Atlantic hunting-grounds to the Pacific, and, now surrounding him on that side, and all sides, seems to enclose him like . . . a contracting circle of fire.

—"The Indians," *Army and Navy Journal,* August 5, 1865, 793.

To Sharon

CONTENTS

Illustrations   xi

Maps   xiii

Acknowledgments   xv

Chapter One: Context   1

Chapter Two: Julesburg   15

Chapter Three: Mud Springs and Rush Creek   35

Chapter Four: Hanging of the Chiefs   46

Chapter Five: Fouts's Fiasco and Moonlight's Mistake   65

Chapter Six: The Battles of Platte Bridge and Red Buttes   86

Chapter Seven: Connor Strikes Back   100

Chapter Eight: The Sawyers Expedition   120

Chapter Nine: Cole and Walker   129

Chapter Ten: Rescue and Reversal   137

Chapter Eleven: Prospects   145

Chapter Twelve: Spotted Tail's Daughter   153

Chapter Thirteen: Conclusions   158

Epilogue   171

Endnotes   177

Bibliography   249

Index   271

ILLUSTRATIONS

Maj. Gen. John Pope 11

Maj. Gen. Grenville M. Dodge 11

Col. John M. Chivington 14

Col. Thomas Moonlight 61

Hanging of the Chiefs 63

Capt. William Fouts 71

Platte Bridge Station 87

1st Lt. Henry Bretney 89

Maj. Martin Anderson 90

Commissary Sgt. Amos Custard 92

James Bridger 102

Spotted Tail 155

George Bent 175

MAPS

The Indian War of 1865   4

The Indian War of 1865: The First Stage   19

Avengers' Campsites, December 1864 to February 1865   20

The Indian War of 1865: The Second Stage   52

Fouts's Fiasco and Moonlight's Mistake: June 3 and June 17, 1865   72

The Powder River Expedition   101

ACKNOWLEDGMENTS

MANY HAVE CONTRIBUTED TO THIS STUDY BY ASSISTING IN RESEARCH. I express my gratitude to the National Archives, especially to Michael Meier, Michael Pilgrim, Todd Butler, and Robert Kvasnicka; the Library of Congress, especially to Marilyn Ibach; the National Anthropological Archives of the Smithsonian Institution; the Department of the Interior Library; the U.S. Army Military Service Institute, Carlisle, Pennsylvania, especially to David Keough and Kathy Olson; the Nebraska State Historical Society, especially to James Potter; the South Dakota State Historical Society, especially to Nancy Tystad Koupal; the North Dakota State Historical Society, especially to Janet Daley; former director Ramon Powers and the staff of the Kansas State Historical Society; the Colorado State Historical Society, especially to David Halaas; the Iowa State Historical Society; the Montana State Historical Society, especially to former employee Charles E. Rankin; the Ohio State Historical Society; the Missouri State Historical Society; and the Bureau of Land Management District Office, Casper, Wyoming, especially to Jude Carino. I also thank the staffs of Fort Laramie National Historic Site, especially Sandra Lowry; Little Bighorn Battlefield National Monument; the Denver Public Library, Denver, Colorado, especially Lisa Backman; the Casper Community College Library, Casper, Wyoming, especially Kevin Anderson; the Wyoming State Archives, Cheyenne, Wyoming, especially Ann Nelson and Cindy Brown; and the American Heritage Center, Laramie, Wyoming, especially Rick Ewig.

Other special collections used include those of the Bieneicke Library, Yale University, New Haven, Connecticut; the Brigham Young University Library, Provo, Utah; the Highland County Public Library, Hillsboro, Ohio; the West Virginia University Library, Charlestown, West Virginia; the Natrona County Public Library, Casper, Wyoming; the Sheridan County Fulmer Library, Sheridan, Wyoming; the Johnson County Public Library, Buffalo, Wyoming; the Pioneer Museum, Douglas, Wyoming; the

Rawlins County Public Library, Pierre, South Dakota; the Southwest Museum, Los Angeles, California; the Newberry Library, Chicago, Illinois; the St. Charles Historical Society, St. Charles, Missouri; and the Colorado State University Library, Fort Collins, Colorado.

Special thanks go to Richard Young, supervisor at Fort Caspar; South Pass historic site experts Craig Bromley of the Bureau of Land Management, Lander Office, and Todd Guenther, Pioneer Museum, Lander; Dean Knudsen, curator of Scotts Bluff National Monument; Mr. and Mrs. Charles Cape and their son Scott and Leon "Bud" Gillespie for their assistance in my study of the battles of Mud Springs and Rush Creek; Susan Badger Doyle of Pendelton, Oregon, for her knowledge of the Bozeman Trail; and Jeff Broom, Denver, Colorado, who assisted with gathering data for maps. Special thanks also go to my friends and associates who have shared the same interests, exchanged information, and provided invaluable insights over the years: Paul L. Hedren, Douglas C. McChristian, and Neil C. Mangum of the National Park Service; R. Eli Paul of Overland Park, Kansas; Thomas R. Buecker, curator at Fort Robinson, Nebraska; James S. Hutchins of Vienna, Virginia; and Michael P. Musick of the National Archives. I am especially indebted to Jerome A. Greene of the National Park Service, my friend of many moons, who read the entire manuscript and offered valuable suggestions. Finally, I thank my son, James D. McDermott, of Arlington, Virginia, who assisted with research.

Chapter 3 of this book appeared in a slightly different version in the summer 1996 issue of *Nebraska History*. Permission to use that material is gratefully acknowledged. I also thank the Fort Caspar Museum, Casper, Wyoming, for the funding that resulted in my book *Frontier Crossroads: The History of Fort Casper and the Upper Platte Crossing* (1996), which covers some of the material treated in this book in either expanded or condensed form.

J. D. M.
Rapid City, South Dakota

CHAPTER ONE

Context

THE LAND

IN 1857 CORNELIUS CONWAY WENT WEST TO UTAH. IN THE NORTH Platte River Valley in present-day Nebraska, he marveled at the wonders of nature. Traveling parallel to the sandstone formations that stood on the south bank of the river, he saw a succession of grand and beautiful views that he likened to sepulchral graveyards, stern old fortresses, temples of old "cities of the fairy world dropped down from the heavens," and towers reminiscent of the unfinished Babel of Shinar.[1] Others also commented on the rough beauty and power of the landscape, seeing within it, as did young Lieutenant "Link" Ware in 1865, "the handiwork of the Almighty."[2]

To many who roamed the Northern Plains in the nineteenth century, the land seemed without end, a vast ocean of grass, whipped by wind, pelted by rain, and beaten down by hail. To others farther west, it was an arid panorama, with mile upon mile of sagebrush, coloring the land a faded blue-green, inedible to horses and pungent in the hot sun. British adventurer Richard Burton felt the land's isolation and barrenness. In 1860, he wrote: "You see, as it were, the ends of the earth and look around in vain for some object upon which the eye may rest."[3] Traveling the Oregon Trail in a stagecoach about the same time, Mark Twain remarked on the "limitless panoramas of bewildering perspective" and "the blue distance of a world that knew no lords but us."[4] Robert Louis Stevenson saw it as "spacious vacancy" where one could see the whole arch of heaven.[5]

For those used to woods and few open spaces, it was a stark and inimical land. In a letter written to his aunt in April 1865, Ohioan Caspar Collins called his duty station near Sweetwater Bridge, Wyoming, "one of the most desolate regions of the American Continent, the natural penitentiary of the United States."[6] A traveler who visited Fort Laramie in 1857 believed that living there was exile and that a man might die without the world finding out about it for six months.[7] In this lonely vastness and in little clusters of buildings and people that sometimes broke the monotony of the plains, the Indian War of 1865 came to life, grew and festered, and finally succumbed at year's end in the snows of winter.

The causes of the war grew out of the pressure exerted by emigrants on the land and its inhabitants. Eighteen forty-three was the first year of significant westward migration into the nation's midsection, along the Oregon Trail, and in the succeeding quarter century, thousands of covered wagons followed the Great Platte River Road across present-day Nebraska and Wyoming, eventually separating to head for Oregon, Utah, and California. The trails traversed land roamed by the Northern Plains Indians, principally the Sioux, Cheyennes, and Arapahos. As emigration grew, conflict occurred. Travel on the road increased to several thousand wagons a year by the late 1840s. This disrupted the game supply and antagonized the Indians, leading to a growing number of raids and fights.[8] In response, the federal government ordered three military posts built to guard the Oregon-California-Mormon Trail: Fort Kearny (1848) in Nebraska, Fort Laramie (1849) in Wyoming, and Fort Hall (1849) in Idaho.

In 1865, traveler Charles Young described the Oregon Trail across western Nebraska from Fort Kearny for 400 miles up the Platte River Valley as one vast rolling plain. No vegetation could be seen except for a coarse, luxuriant growth of grass in the valley near the river and beyond the bluffs. In spots that were not bare grew the prickly pear cactus and short crisp grass of light color and two varieties—the nutritious bunch and buffalo grasses, upon which cattle thrived and grew fat.[9]

The North Platte River Road was smooth and hard. A visitor noted that the stage company had a stable every ten or fifteen miles placed along it, and every other ten or fifteen miles an eating house. This was often connected with a ranch whose owner lived by selling hay to the trains of emigrants or freighters. Every 50 or 100 miles was a blacksmith shop and often a military outpost with one or two companies of troops.

As far as Mr. Bowles from Springfield, Massachusetts, was concerned, the food at the ranch houses was very good. The staples were bacon, eggs, hot biscuits, green tea, and coffee. Occasionally beef was the main course, and most ranches served canned fruits and vegetables about half the time. The fare for breakfast, lunch, or dinner was always the same and cost $2. A well-stocked ranch and a man with business acumen to run it could make a very good living. It was reported in November 1865 that one ranch owner located near Julesburg, Colorado, made close to $25,000. Soldiers were good customers, spending much of their pay on whiskey, which sold for fifty cents a glass.[10] Some of the ranchmen were honest, but others stepped over the line, trading worn-out cattle that had been doctored to pilgrims, dealing in stolen livestock, and selling the vilest type of whiskey to all comers.[11]

Because of the scarcity of wood, proprietors often made their houses and barns of sod, piled layer upon layer and sealed between and over with a claylike mud. The military used the same material for its small forts and for fences around cattle and horse yards. Men cut the sod in lengths of two to four feet. Laid grass side down, they were about four inches thick and eighteen inches wide. Side walls were either single or double width, usually reaching six feet in height, with the end walls tapering upward. From a long pole placed from peak to peak, the roof took shape, usually being constructed with a combination of poles, branches, twigs, and sod and covered with sand or clay or whatever else was available. Some forts had an inside lining of skins or thick cloth. Floors were usually compacted soil. The completed structure was an efficient fortification, impenetrable by bullets and impervious to fire, and many of them became bunkers in the opening phases of the conflict.[12]

As travelers moved westward to northwestern Nebraska and central and southern Wyoming, the landscape began to change. One observer described the scene in the spring of 1865:

> As the prairie grew more barren, the prickly pear and the sage became plenty in their tough unfruitfulness; the road was marked more frequently with the dead carcasse of oxen and horses—scarcely ever were we out of sight of their bleaching bones; occasionally the pathos of a human grave gave a deeper touch to our thoughts of death upon the Plains. . . . . All the water of this region and the Plains has the savor of alkali or sulphur in it, but not to an unhealthy degree.[13]

One other area played an important part in the Indian War of 1865. Although remote from the field of battle, it was an irritant to the Sioux and their allies. They viewed it as a forerunner of pressures to come and another intrusion that impacted game and threatened subsistence. The place was southwestern Montana, its ravines and gulches alive with miners searching for precious metals.

Gold had been discovered in the region as early as 1852, but not until the strike at Bannock in 1862 did fields attract much attention. Montana Territory was carved out of eastern Idaho in 1864; Virginia City, its capital, yielded $30 million worth of dust and nuggets during its first years. Gold

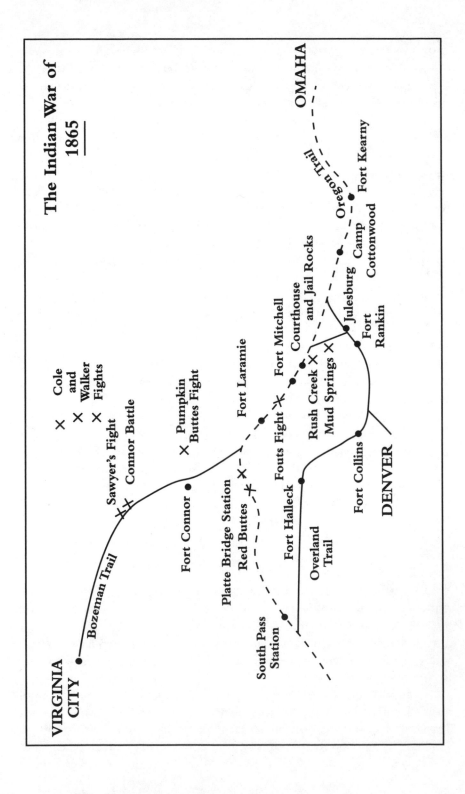

The Indian War of
1865

VIRGINIA CITY

Bozeman Trail

Sawyer's Fight
Connor Battle

Fort Connor

Pumpkin Buttes Fight

Platte Bridge Station
Red Buttes

Fort Laramie

South Pass Station

Fort Halleck

Overland Trail

Fouts Fight

Fort Mitchell

Courthouse and Jail Rocks

Rush Creek
Mud Springs

Julesburg

Fort Rankin

Fort Collins

DENVER

Camp Cottonwood

Fort Kearny

Oregon Trail

OMAHA

Cole and Walker Fights

continued to pour out of Montana in 1865. When the steamer *Marcella* docked in Sioux City in late July, it unloaded $200,000 worth of Montana gold dust.[14]

Initially, gold seekers traveled to Montana by two routes. Some took a steamboat up the Missouri River to Fort Benton in north-central Montana and then traveled west by wagon. Others followed the Oregon Trail to Fort Hall, Idaho. There they turned north and eventually east to reach the gold fields. Taking the water route still meant a 300 mile trip overland through Indian country after reaching the head of navigation, and the Oregon Trail cutoff required two crossings of the Continental Divide.

Because of the circuitous routes, entrepreneurs began considering shortcuts. Jim Bridger, the famous mountain man and scout, whose geographical knowledge of the region was unrivaled, was one of the first trailblazers. In 1864, he cut a trail north from the Oregon Trail that paralleled the west side of the Big Horn Mountains and then circled west up the valley of the Yellowstone and pushed over the low Bridger range into the Gallatin Valley. Bridger led his first train out in the spring of 1864, reaching Virginia City about July 8. It was roughly 510 miles from Red Buttes to Virginia City, requiring thirty-four days travel at 15 miles a day. The trail, however, was never popular.[15]

The adventurous could see that the most direct route was one that left the Oregon Trail at Fort Laramie and cut due northwest, winding through Powder River Country and paralleling the east side of the Big Horn Mountains. Indians and their ancestors had used this general route for centuries, following well-worn game trails. The Sioux had fought hard to wrest this area from the Crows, and it was one of the finest hunting grounds left on the Northern Plains and one of the few still remaining in Indian hands. No white man was welcome here.[16]

In 1859 a government expedition mapped the territory, indicating political and military interest in the Powder River Country. Capt. William Raynolds, the expedition leader, prophesied that land fronting the Big Horns would become an important thoroughfare for white settlers.[17] The first men to blaze a trail were John M. Bozeman and John M. Jacobs during the spring and summer of 1863. Wagon trains successfully followed the route in the summer of 1864. Led by Bozeman, the first train left Richard's Bridge on the Upper North Platte about June 18, arriving in Virginia City on July 29. This route was about 535 miles, or thirty-six days travel at 15 miles a day.[18] The *Montana Post* reported that the Big Horn route saved 700 miles of travel, allowing emigrants starting in the spring to reach the diggings in the middle of the mining season. The newspaper also noted that grass along the route would feed thousands of teams, the water was abundant, and the game was sufficient to supply an army.[19]

Finally, the exploration of another road in Powder River Country in 1865 would bring violent reaction. The so-called Niobrara-Virginia City Wagon Road was to follow the Niobrara River westward, turning north to the Powder River to join the Bozeman Trail to Virginia City. The Yankton *Dakotaian* printed a table of distances from Sioux City via Yankton to Virginia City that totaled 849 miles. Again the road intruded into the hunting grounds of the Sioux and their allies, prompting reprisals.[20]

THE INDIANS

Fighting the U.S. Army and white settlers in the Indian War of 1865 were three tribes: the Sioux, Cheyennes, and Arapahos. The latter two had divided into northern and southern groups. Circumstances dictated that they come together for one last time to fight the whites.

The Fort Laramie Treaty of September 17, 1851, had generally acknowledged the lands occupied by each of them. The document described the boundaries of Sioux territory as commencing at the mouth of the White Earth River on the Missouri River, proceeding in a southwesterly direction to the forks of the Platte River, then up the north fork of the Platte River to a point known as the Red Buttes or where the road leaves the river, then along the Black Hills to the headwaters of Heart River, then down Heart River to its mouth, and then down the Missouri River to the place of beginning. The boundaries of the territory of the Cheyenne and Arapaho began at the Red Buttes or the place where the road leaves the north fork of the Platte River, proceeded up the north fork of the Platte River to its source, then along the main range of the Rocky Mountains to the headwaters of the Arkansas River, then down the Arkansas River to the crossing of the Santa Fe Trail, then in a northwesterly direction to the forks of the Platte River, and then up the Platte River to the place of beginning. The treaty also reached formal agreement concerning travel through the area. In return for an annual payment of $50,000 in merchandise, domestic animals, and agricultural implements, the Indians guaranteed whites safe passage and acknowledged the permanence of military posts in their homeland.[21]

Allied against the three tribes were a number of other smaller groups: the Crows, Shoshonis, Pawnees, and Winnebagos. Small groups of the last two served as scouts and auxiliaries to the army.

Information concerning the numbers of people in these various tribes was scanty at best. In September 1865, Maj. Gen. Grenville Dodge stated that the number of warring Indians on the plains was 25,000.[22] This appears highly inflated. According to an article published in the *New York Times,* the total Indian population in the United States and territories numbered between 320,000 and 350,000. Citing the Indian Office as the source, the reporter gave figures for the Plains Sioux (5,600), the Arapahos (3,000), and the Cheyennes (2,800), which totaled 11,400.[23] Other estimates were similar.[24] While the figures may be inaccurate, they do convey the government's best intelligence for the Arapahos, the Cheyennes, and two bands of Sioux— Red Cloud's Oglalas, and Spotted Tail's Brules.[25]

In the years immediately preceding 1865, the army had been involved in several Indian campaigns that affected the conflict to come, either by eliminating possible allies or by subduing tribes that might have kept some of the military's fighting force busy elsewhere. One of these was the so-called Minnesota Uprising of 1862 involving the Eastern or Santee Sioux. Rebelling against reservation life, poor food, and Indian agent graft, the Santees killed more than 500 white settlers in thirty-eight days. The final toll was 650 civilians dead, and more than 100 soldiers and an unknown number of Dakota killed. On December 26, 1862, at Mankato, Minnesota, thirty-eight warriors convicted of murder or rape were hanged. For three years after the end of fighting in Minnesota, troops roamed the Dakota prairie in search of "renegade" Indians. Henry Sibley led an expedition in the summer of 1863, and Alfred Sully did the same that year and the next. Thus, the focus was in the country west of Minnesota, mostly in what is now North Dakota. Perhaps the most significant victory was Sully's when he attacked the Sioux camp at Killdeer Mountain on July 28, destroying 1,600 lodges and killing as many as 150 Sioux.

Although the campaigns were in the end inconclusive, many of the most warlike Sioux began congregating in the north, away from white routes of travel and commerce, and they were not engaged in the war that broke out in Colorado and then spread to Wyoming and southern Montana. There is a definite connection, however, between what happened in Minnesota and the Indian War of 1865. Knowledge of what occurred spread through all the Sioux, Cheyenne, and Arapaho camps and helped fire resentment against whites. Through March 1864 the Indians near Denver showed no trace of aggressive resistance. Only when contact with their Dakota allies brought the war spirit to them did any of the Cheyennes or Arapahos take hostile action. The Report of the Commissioner of Indian Affairs in 1864 listed contact with emissaries from the north as the only known cause of Indian unrest.[26]

In a series of battles and skirmishes in 1863, Gen. Patrick Edward Connor and his California Volunteers soundly defeated the Western

Shoshonis, eliminating a long-standing threat to travel along western trails. Most devastating was the attack on a village on Bear River, near present-day Preston, Idaho; Connor's troops killed 263 men, women, and children. Government officials followed these encounters with treaty agreements that brought a peace that lasted for several years.

The Utes in present-day southern Colorado and south-central Wyoming had also been a problem. In February 1863, the Grand River and Uinta Utes began raiding the mail line west of Fort Halleck. By June, apparently as many as 600 to 1,000 Utes were participating. Early in July, Kansas troops from Fort Halleck met about 250 Utes in a battle that resulted in sixty Indians killed or wounded. This victory, coupled with General Connor's peace negotiations and new overtures from the Colorado Indian superintendency, ended the Ute and Shoshoni threat to the Fort Halleck division of the mail line. From then on, it was the Sioux, Northern Cheyennes, and Arapahos who constituted the problem in that locality and in the region. And it would be General Connor who would subdue them.

THE U.S. ARMY

The U.S. Army troops that confronted the Plains Indians were not regular career soldiers. They were men who had joined state regiments to fight Confederates in the Civil War. Indian problems and the necessity for keeping transportation and communication systems open had sent some of these volunteer troops far from their eastern homes. These included troops from Ohio and West Virginia. Others were closer by—from Iowa, Missouri, Nebraska, and Kansas—but they were eager to return home and did not wish to be delayed by frontier service. First to arrive were volunteer troops from Ohio.[27] On May 30, 1862, Col. William Collins reached Fort Laramie with Companies A, B, C, and D of the 1st Battalion, 6th Ohio Volunteer Cavalry, having traveled 700 miles from Fort Leavenworth.[28] Finally, there were the Galvanized Yankees, regiments of Southerners who had been captured in the East and pledged allegiance to the Union. In return for their freedom, they agreed to serve in the volunteers until the war was over.

As the Civil War got under way, a new challenge presented itself for troops stationed in the West: in the late fall of 1861, the transcontinental telegraph went into operation. The Pacific Telegraph Company, a subsidary of Western Union, built the system through what is now Nebraska and Wyoming. Enacted on June 16, 1860, the authorizing statute called for a line running from Omaha to Salt Lake City, much of it following the Oregon Trail. Workmen also built a line east from Carson City, Nevada, the wires joining on October 24. Eastern manufacturers sent galvanized iron wire and glass insulators by wagon to Omaha, Nebraska, and by ship around Cape Horn to San Francisco. Men cut poles where they found them along the way.[29]

Government officials believed that it was crucial to maintain close communication with the West, and the telegraph made this possible. The precious minerals of the territories were important in fueling the war effort, and President Lincoln knew that in order to keep political loyalty of frontier states, he had to protect transportation and communication routes and guarantee the safety of burgeoning communities.

Because the lines were powered by storage batteries, telegraphic relay stations had to be constructed every fifty to seventy-five miles. Each had quarters for a telegraph operator and one or more repairmen. Shortly after the line opened, a traveler described the station at Rocky Ridge as a ranch built of quaking aspen logs covered with a dirt roof and constructed in the shape of the letter L, its longest side running north and south. Visitors found three rooms in this part and two in the section running east and west. A telegraph room sported glass windows. Other stations were similar.[30]

To protect the telegraph line between Fort Laramie and Fort Bridger, the army sent detachments of troops to man small outposts, usually from twenty-five to fifty miles apart. Going west from Fort Laramie were Horseshoe Creek Station, La Bonte Station (Camp Marshall), La Prelle Station, Deer Creek Station, Platte Bridge Station (later Fort Caspar), Sweetwater Station, Three Crossings Station, Rocky Ridge Station (St. Mary's), and South Pass Station (Burnt Ranch). The distance between South Pass Station and Fort Laramie was 283 miles. It is not clear, but other sites may have been occupied for short periods. these subposts becoming the front lines. On the move between them were those who repaired the telegraph lines, working daily to keep them operating. This grouping of tiny military subposts completed the army's presence in the Rocky Mountain West. One soldier likened them to beads strung on a thread.[31]

On July 11, 1862, because of the large number of Indian raids in Nebraska and Wyoming, the postmaster general directed mail carriers to move their travel routes to the Overland Trail via South Platte, LaPorte, Virginia Dale, and Bridger Pass. The move required constructing twenty-three new stations.[32] Troops still had to protect telegraph lines and guard settlers who used the Oregon Trail; consequently, many former stage buildings and compounds became military outposts and relay stations.

THE COMMAND STRUCTURE

As the Civil War drew to an end and military leaders began looking westward, they saw a new challenge, one difficult and complex in its own way. For one thing, there was the space involved. The land mass was twice the size of that covered in the Civil War. The extent of the country made the success of expeditions difficult.[33] Then there were supplies to be toted, as well as troops to be transported. The rough ground and extremes of climate slowed caravans and weakened livestock and men. It was a full-time job, and yet the nation needed the military to deal with Reconstruction in the South and the French threat in Mexico, as well as guard the country's borders.[34]

The army's role in the West in 1865 was twofold: to protect succeeding waves of trail emigrants, miners, and settlers from actual or threatened attack by Indians and other unfriendly parties, and to protect and extend lines of transportation and communication linking East and West and points in between. The organizational structure for doing this was centered in two military departments. On September 2, 1862, the army created the Department of the Northwest. In December 1864, it included the states of Wisconsin, Iowa, and Minnesota and the territories of Dakota and Montana. Maj. Gen. John Pope commanded the department at Milwaukee.

Born in Louisville, Kentucky, on March 16, 1823, Pope graduated from the U.S. Military Academy in 1842. His first assignment was with the topographical engineers. Prior to the Mexican War, he had surveyed the northeast boundary between the United States and Canada. In the war with Mexico he fought in the battles of Monterey and Buena Vista, receiving the brevets of first lieutenant and captain. Just prior to the Civil War, he served on lighthouse duty. He commanded the Army of the Mississippi, and with Admiral Foote took New Madrid in 1862. That same year, he made major general of volunteers and brigadier general in the regular army. Placed in charge of the Army of Virginia, he took a very active part in all of his command's engagements. Pope was a favorite of Gen. Ulysses S. Grant and would soon receive more responsibility.

The other jurisdictional unit of importance was the Department of Kansas commanded by Maj. Gen. Samuel R. Curtis, with headquarters at Fort Leavenworth. It included the state of Kansas and the territories of Colorado and Nebraska.[35]

SOME REASONS

Early in the twentieth century, a former soldier of the 11th Kansas Cavalry tried to explain the reasons for Indian hostility in 1865. Sgt. Stephen Fairfield remembered that whites had previously discovered precious metals in the mountains beyond the plains and that thousands of gold seekers had rushed through Indian country, killing and destroying the game. He wrote, "Long trains of wagons were winding their way over the plains, the mysterious telegraph wires were stretching across their hunting grounds to the

Maj. Gen. John Pope
*The overall commander of troops
on the frontier, Pope had his own
ideas concerning Indian policy.*
NATIONAL ARCHIVES

**Maj. Gen.
Grenville M. Dodge**
*As commander of the Department
of the Missouri, Dodge struggled
against difficulties to organize a
campaign against the Sioux,
Cheyennes, and Arapahos in
1865.* NATIONAL ARCHIVES

mountains, engineers were surveying a route for a track for the iron horse, and all without saying as much as 'By your leave' to the Indians. Knowing that their game would soon be gone, that their hunting grounds taken from them, and that they themselves would soon be without a country, they had resorted to arms to defend their way of life and themselves."[36]

But there was a more immediate reason that grew out of the culminating battle of 1864 between Coloradans and the Plains Indians. Hostilities began on April 9, when a detachment of Colorado volunteers attacked a guiltless band of Cheyennes in retaliation for recent cattle theft. Three days later, troops fired upon Cheyenne Dog Soldiers on their way north to help the Sioux fight the Crows. The next week Indian raiders killed a Denver rancher, and a campaign was organized to punish the offenders. On April 22, a detachment of the 1st Colorado Volunteer Cavalry skirmished with Cheyennes at Fremont Orchard on the South Platte, about sixty miles northeast of Denver. The encounter engendered fears that a general uprising of Plains Indian tribes was imminent.[37]

The war continued to spread as warriors found isolated families and undermanned wagon trains. At the start of summer, the Minniconjous of Two Kettle's band, numbering from 300 to 400, began depredations along the Oregon Trail. On July 12 they attacked the Larimer wagon train, killing four men and carrying off Mrs. Fanny Kelley. The next day, Col. William O. Collins ordered Lt. John A. Brown and two companies to pursue. The soldiers reached Cheyenne Fork before making camp on July 19. When visiting a nearby spring for water, Brown and thirteen others walked into an ambush. The Sioux wounded Brown, but his men thought he had been killed and fled. A morning search party found Brown still alive, but he died the next day. The men buried him near the spring that now carries his name.[38]

On August 20, a Nebraska family suffered a similar fate. Lt. Henry Palmer was leading sixty Galvanized Yankees of the 11th Ohio Volunteer Cavalry to Fort Kearny when he came upon the aftermath of Cheyennes raiding in the valley of the Little Blue River. The first stop was the ranch of the Eubank family, where the men found the bodies of three children, ranging in age from three to seven years old. They had been swung by the heels against the log cabin until their heads disintegrated. About fifteen rods away, they found the naked corpse of the hired girl, staked out on the prairie, tied by her hands and feet, her body full of arrows and horribly mangled. Close by was the body of Mr. Eubank, his whiskers cut off and body mutilated. A search revealed that the wife was missing.

The scene was especially shocking for Palmer, since he had known the family, meeting them in the spring of 1864. He remembered Mrs. Eubank as a fine-looking woman, possessing youth, beauty, and strength, just married, with bright hopes for the future. The ranch was a stage stop, and Mrs. Eubank cooked for the passengers. He remembered that her log cabin was unlike any in his experience: a cotton cloth hid the dirt roof, giving the interior a clean, tidy look; a plain carpet covered the rough board floor; and real china dishes appeared on the table. Was she dead, he wondered, or perhaps a captive?[39]

At the Spring Ranch, the same story of death and ruin was replayed. Before the raiding along the Little Blue River and Plumb Creek stopped, fifty-one settlers were dead, nine were wounded, and seven women and children were captured. In addition to Lucinda Eubank, Laura Roper and Nancy Morton also later wrote of their captivity. From August 15 to September 24, the road to Denver was completely closed, the mail being sent via Panama and San Francisco.[40]

The ultimate act came on November 29, 1864, when Col. John M. Chivington, an erstwhile Methodist minister recently from Nebraska, led a savage attack of the 3rd Colorado Cavalry on a village of Black Kettle, White Antelope, Sand Hill, and One Eye, camped at Sand Creek in west-central Colorado. Troops completely surprised this band of Southern Cheyennes and some Arapahos in a dawn raid, the Indians believing themselves under the protection of the military at Fort Lyon. The order was to take no prisoners, and the carnage that followed shocked even some of the most hardened Indian haters. When the fighting ended, 163 were dead—53 men and 110 women. The troops later displayed scalps and severed genitals to cheering crowds in Denver. When news of the butchery reached the East, condemnation followed, and officials held several investigations. Chivington escaped recrimination by resigning his commission.[41]

At the Cheyenne camp on the Smoky Hill, survivors gathered in council. They decided to ask their allies, the Sioux and Northern Arapahos, to join with them in a war of vengeance. Invitations went to the Sioux on the Solomon Fork and then to the Northern Arapaho camp. A large village soon assembled. Leading the Cheyennes were Leg-in-the-Water, Little Robe, and a reluctant Black Kettle. Other chiefs were Lean Bear, White Antelope, Little Wolf, Left Hand, and Tall Bear. Foremost among the Cheyenne Dog Soldiers, who assumed a leadership role, were Tall Bull, White Horse, and Bull Bear.[42] The half-Cheyenne sons of William Bent, George and Charles Bent, pledged their support. Joining the coalition were Spotted Tail's and Pawnee Killer's Sioux, as well as Northern Arapahos under Little Raven, Storm, and Big Mouth.[43]

At the same time, some Southern Cheyenne, Northern Arapaho, and Oglala Sioux warriors journeyed north to the headwaters of the Powder

Col. John M. Chivington
*The attack by Colonel Chivington
and his Colorado Volunteers on
Black Kettle's village on November
28, 1864, led to retaliation that
kept troops busy in Colorado,
Nebraska, Wyoming, and
Montana.* DENVER PUBLIC LIBRARY

River to inform the Oglalas, Minniconjous, and Sans Arcs Sioux and the
Northern Cheyennes living there of the killing.[44] Soon these tribes planned
vengeance, joining their tribesmen in the south in one last united campaign. Northern and Southern Cheyennes, separated for several decades by
circumstances of geography and trade, came together for one last time. The
western Sioux, just beginning to feel the pressure of white encroachment in
the north, joined the warpath, bringing large numbers of fierce fighters to
the battleground.[45]

The conflict extended westward from the settlements bordering on the
Missouri River in Nebraska and Kansas. In its early phases it affected Den-
ver, then a new and brash mining center. Its first battlegrounds were the
North Platte River Road, cutting across present-day Nebraska heading for
Fort Laramie and points west, and the South Platte River Road, leaving the
Oregon Trail at Julesburg and running south into Denver. The Indian War
of 1865 was about to begin.

CHAPTER TWO

Julesburg

THE FIRST TARGET FOR THE AVENGERS WAS JULESBURG, COLORADO, established in the late 1850s by Jules Beni[1] and a home station on the Overland Stage line.[2] Ben Holladay's Overland Stage had daily carriers leaving Denver for Atchison, Kansas, in the east and Salt Lake City in the west, and Julesburg was a supply point for travelers and transporters going both ways. The line also advertised the carrying of gold dust, with a charge of 1 to 1½ percent per $100, and promised meals at sixty-five cents, Concord coaches, teams of six large horses, and protection, courtesy, and respect for its passengers. One source reported that Holladay had 2,000 horses and mules and $2 million invested in property between Atchison and Salt Lake City.[3]

Those going north from Denver to connect with the main east-west route along the North Platte River, the much-traveled Oregon Trail, reached Julesburg after 180 miles. The last two-thirds of the route paralleled the South Platte. At Julesburg two roads stretched north to join the Oregon Trail. The northeastern connector was Cottonwood Springs, near present-day North Platte, Nebraska. The northwest route, which followed Lodgepole Creek, joined near Court House Rock. Shown on a map, the three roads formed a triangle, with Julesburg at its southern apex.

The roads had been created because of the Colorado gold rush in 1858 and the need for access to the burgeoning city of Denver. Those leaving Julesburg for Court House Rock had to ford the South Platte, the site of which became known as the Upper or California Crossing. Julesburg was also an important station of the Pacific Telegraph that connected Denver with Fort Laramie and points west. As a center for communications and a jumping off place for the Colorado goldfields or westward migration to Oregon, California, Utah, and Montana Territory, Julesburg was one of the most important travel points in the region.[4]

Besides an impressive cedar log stage station, the settlement of Julesburg included a telegraph office, blacksmith shop, warehouse for corn storage, stable for fifty horses, large corral, billiard saloon, ample boarding house for travelers, and a few other buildings. Protecting the east side of the station was a sod breastwork with holes fashioned to shoot through. A decided disadvantage was the lack of trees in the area, the closest source of good timber being from 70 to 100 miles in any direction. The only other disadvantage was a topographical one. A few miles east of Julesburg an arroyo came in from the south, and the hills of the plateau protruded north to the riverbed, cutting off sight of the valley. This was called the Devil's Dive. Passing this, travelers reached open country and could see where they were going.[5]

Less than a mile west of town on the south side of the river opposite the mouth of Lodgepole Creek was Fort Rankin, a one-company post established on paper on May 19, 1864, but not activated until late summer. Present proprietors were the officers and men of Company F of the 7th Iowa Volunteer Cavalry. Commanding was twenty-seven-year-old Capt. Nicholas J. O'Brien, a native-born Irishman. A printer by trade, he had enlisted at the beginning of the Civil War, serving initially as a sergeant in the 5th Wisconsin Battery, where he became a skilled artilleryman. He was commissioned a lieutenant in the spring of 1865 and was promoted to command Company F of the 7th Iowa Volunteer Cavalry on May 15. A friend described him as always alert and so energetic that he had to be doing or saying something at all times.[6] The first lieutenant was John S. Brewer, a gray-haired and gray-whiskered man who said he was forty-five years of age. His immediate subordinate characterized him as "a very gentlemanly, placid old man, without the slightest particle of military instinct or habit."[7]

The second lieutenant was twenty-three-year-old Eugene F. Ware. Born in Hartford, Connecticut, he was well educated for his time, having received instruction in Latin, Greek, and French, and studied German with a private tutor. Ware enlisted as a private in Company E, 1st Iowa Volunteer Infantry, eight days after the firing on Fort Sumter. After serving in several other regiments and participating in the battle of Pea Ridge, he joined the 7th Iowa in February 1863. He became a second lieutenant on September 4, 1863. Gifted with great powers of observation and a felicitous pen, he would later write of his experiences in *The Indian War of 1864,* one of the best reminiscences of frontier army life produced in the nineteenth century. Ware had earned the nickname "Lincoln" or "Link" because he was tall and slim, weighing 150 pounds and standing six feet tall.[8]

Completing the officer contingent was Acting Assistant Surgeon Joel F. Wisely. According to Ware, the doctor was thoroughly devoted to his patients and immersed in the practice of his art to the extent that he only wished to talk about medicine. Wisely had one peculiar physical aspect, his nose. He was a Cyrano whose protuberance was grotesque. Ware called it a combination of a beak and snout. The appendage earned the surgeon the name of Dr. Nosely. The doctor had the responsibility for caring for the sick at two other little posts as well.[9] The mission of Company F was to guard the road east to Cottonwood Springs. Colorado volunteers patrolled the road between Julesburg and Denver.

Company F had arrived at Julesburg on September 4. Because of the lateness of the year, O'Brien received permission to purchase quarters for the troops. The best property available was the ranch complex owned by Samuel D. Bancroft one mile west of town. It consisted of a one-story adobe house, a storeroom, and an unfinished sod corral. Bancroft wanted $3,500 for the property, but O'Brien offered $3,000, which he accepted. Soldiers were soon at work enlarging and strengthening their new post, dubbed Fort Rankin, using sod cut from the river bottom in one- by three-foot slabs.[10] To complete the work, they obtained cedar poles from distant Cottonwood Canyon and cut-lumber for doors and windows from Denver. Built inside the sod corral were a company quarters and a large stable, 30 by 140 feet. A good water well and a stock well in the rear made the compound self-sufficient.[11]

Everything was peaceful until the morning of January 7. The night before, the Sand Creek avengers had made camp among the hills south of Julesburg, taking care to keep their presence unknown. Indian guards prevented ambitious young men from slipping away during the night. Hours before dawn, the camp stirred with men and women making preparations, the women cooking and the men painting themselves and donning raiments of war. Throwing off their white garb, George and Charlie Bent dressed as Cheyennes, intending to take part in the fighting to come. The main body, about 1,000 strong, kept among the bluffs that lined the South Platte, about three or four miles south of the river. The chiefs had decided to try to draw the soldiers out of Camp Rankin.[12] The headmen chose Big Crow, chief of the Crooked Lance Society, to lead the decoys. He selected seven men, five Cheyenne Indians, including Starving Elk and Old Crow, and two Sioux.[13] A gully ran northeast out of their hiding place in the sand hills, crossed bottomlands east of the stage station, and entered the Platte River below the fort. Concealed in the ravine, the party drew close to the post, where they discovered some soldiers outside walking. Shouting and yelling, the warriors charged. Within a short time a bugle blew, and dashing from the stockade came Captain O'Brien and a detachment.

Captain O'Brien led a small force of thirty-seven men, the rest of his troops being out on patrol or escort duty. As the men advanced, the decoys retreated, drawing the soldiers toward Devil's Dive and the place of ambush. As the troops neared, however, some of the young warriors could wait no longer and rode out to fight, thus giving away the stratagem. At this point, the officer and his men were about 300 yards from the stockade.[14] In a reminiscence, O'Brien remembered that he and his men suddenly faced "a horde of war-painted horsemen who rode with superb disregard of danger, filling the air with fiendish shrieks and yells." Realizing that he had nearly led his men into a trap, O'Brien ordered his bugler to sound retreat, utilizing his howitzer to cover the withdrawal. The bugler, Alanson Hanchett, did not make it, however, his horse falling on him in the retreat, where Cheyennes found and killed him. During the engagement, the officer observed an Indian upon a hill nearest the post directing his followers by signals, employing at times a looking glass and at other times a buffalo robe.[15]

The ensuing fighting was close, so close in fact that Pvt. James Cannon was able to use his jammed carbine as an effective club. Several times the men had to fight their way through superior numbers. In the withdrawal, the soldiers were forced to leave their dead and some of their injured behind. One of the retreating enlisted men received an unusual wound, being shot in the hip with an arrow that had incorporated within it a nine-inch section of frying pan handle. The missive pierced the pelvis, defying removal until a comrade later used a blacksmith's pincers to help wrench it free. Killed in the retreat were four noncommissioned officers and ten enlisted men of Company F and a young recruit, John M. Pierce, who had been previously sworn in but who had not been officially enrolled because of the lack of an enlistment form. As O'Brien maneuvered his men toward the fort, many warriors headed for Julesburg with new prey in mind.[16]

About the time that the troops were nearing the stockade, the westbound stage came hurrying up the road. Warriors killed an escort in the desperate run to the settlement, but the driver, arrows sticking in his heavy buffalo coat, brought the coach to the doors of the station. The driver, his passenger, and the employees left in town began running as hard as they could for Camp Rankin, reaching it shortly before the return of the retreating troops.[17]

When he reached the fort, O'Brien rolled out one of the new Parrott guns. The officer's three previous years of service with the artillery stood him in good stead; he knew what he was about. To lure the raiders closer, he used less powder than normal in his first few shots so that the shells fell short, encouraging the Indians to move closer. After they did so, O'Brien

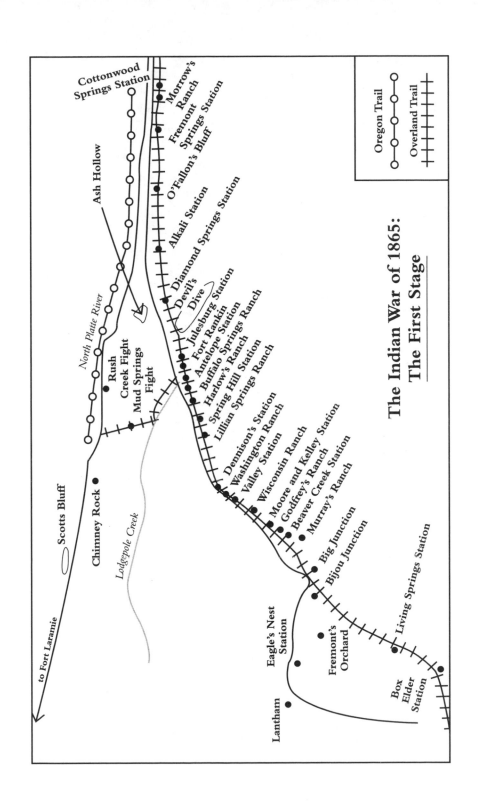

The Indian War of 1865:
The First Stage

Oregon Trail

Overland Trail

Cottonwood
Springs Station

Morrow's
Ranch

Fremont
Springs Station

O'Fallon's
Bluff

Ash Hollow

Alkali Station

Diamond Springs Station

North Platte River

Devil's
Dive

Diamond

Julesburg Station

Fort Rankin

Rush
Creek Fight

Antelope Station

Buffalo Springs Ranch

Mud Springs
Fight

Harlow's Ranch

Spring Hill Station

Lillian Springs Ranch

Dennison's Station

Washington Station

Valley Station

Wisconsin Ranch

Scotts Bluff

Chimney Rock

Moore and Kelley Station

Godfrey's Ranch

Beaver Creek Station

Lodgepole Creek

Murray's Ranch

Big Junction

Bijou Junction

to Fort Laramie

Eagle's Nest
Station

Living Springs Station

Fremont's
Orchard

Box
Elder
Station

Lantham

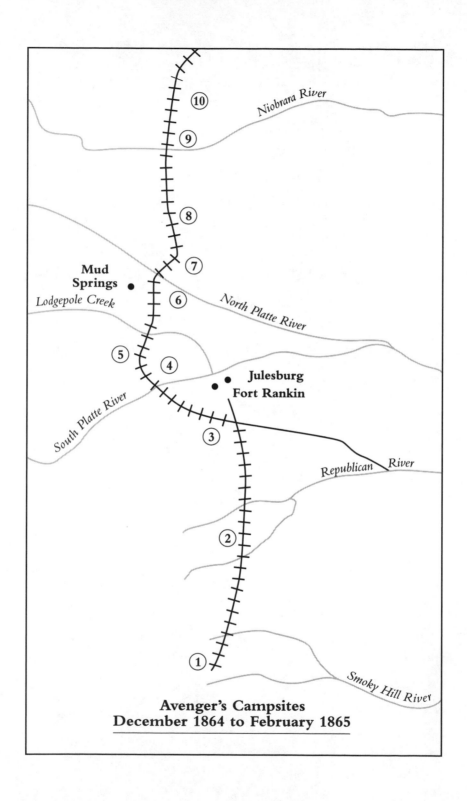

Niobrara River

⑩

⑨

⑧

⑦

⑥

Mud
Springs •

Lodgepole Creek

North Platte River

⑤ ④

• • Julesburg
Fort Rankin

South Platte River

③

Republican River

②

①

Smoky Hill River

**Avenger's Campsites
December 1864 to February 1865**

scored a direct hit, apparently killing several warriors and sending the rest scurrying for safety. This concluded the battle for all intents and purposes, most of the Indians leaving to join in the pillaging at Julesburg, with a few remaining to keep the soldiers from leaving the fort.[18]

At Julesburg, the Sioux and Cheyennes smashed windows and doors and splintered furniture in the buildings. From the warehouse and blacksmith shop they took clothing, corn, harnesses, and other supplies and provisions. The Indians found well-filled shelves in the general store owned by Green Thompson, for the shopkeeper carried on a thriving business at the junction with travelers, freighters, and ranchers. In cleaning out the store, the Indians carted away sugar, flour, bacon, and other meats, the Indian women loading their travois for the trip back to Cherry Creek. Of special interest was a box filled with watches, the raiders pushing and shoving to claim one of the fascinating objects. Bolts of bright-colored cloth provided amusement, as warriors tied the cloth to their bodies and sped across the valley on their ponies, the bolts unfurling behind them. Participants tried to get close enough to one another to trod on the cloth and pull it to the ground. The government later paid the widow of Thompson $20,000 for goods lost in the raid.[19]

At the boarding house, George Bent and his compatriots found warm food on the table for the day's stage passengers, prepared by Mrs. Edwin Haymaker. After eating, one of the unexpected arrivals took the sugar bowl and tied it to his belt where it dangled as he rode away. Stage agent Richard Quinn reported the loss of seven sacks of mail. Found in one of the pouches was a package containing a new major's uniform, which became the property of the Bents. In the mail station, Indians finding bottles not to be liquor decided to empty them on the floor. The spreading nitric acid burned through moccasins and sent them hopping.[20]

The single passenger in the stage that had arrived during the attack was a U.S. paymaster on his way to pay the Colorado troops. In escaping to the fort, he carried one box of money with him, leaving the other in the coach. When looters found and opened the big tin container, they were disappointed to find nothing but strips of green paper. Chopping one bundle into pieces with a tomahawk, they tossed the fragments into the air, amused to see the wind catch the shreds of green and hurry them away. George Bent arrived in time to secure some of the bills, but the box was soon empty. The paymaster sent out soldiers to look for the money later, but they found only a few dollars scattered on the prairie.[21]

Two mountain howitzers helped to hold the Indians at bay during the rest of the day, and the war party withdrew late in the afternoon, moving south with their plunder. The avengers had dispatched nineteen whites, killing fourteen soldiers and five civilians. Some of the warriors wanted to set fire to the buildings at Julesburg, but the chiefs said no; they might want to come back some other time to get provisions. The next morning, soldiers recovered the bodies of their comrades. They were badly mutilated, with fingers, ears, and toes cut off, their mouths filled with powder and ignited. The troops reported fifty-six Sioux and Cheyennes killed but were not sure, since the victors carried off their dead. A smiling George Bent declared many years later that not a single warrior had lost his life.[22] Bent also recalled that because of the loads of plunder, it took the tribesmen and their allies three days to return to the camp on Cherry Creek. Once there, they danced and feasted, the Cheyennes who had been mourning joining in for the first time.[23]

On January 8, O'Brien had his scouts out, and having rescued the telegraphic equipment before the sacking of the telegraph office, he was able to wire Gen. Robert Mitchell the latest intelligence:

My scout just in reports an Indian village 10 or 15 miles south of White Man's Fork. He supposed he was within six miles of the village. The Indians that I fought yesterday were seen by my scout on White Man's Fork, about 60 miles south of here. Indians attacked Dennison's Ranch at the same time I was fighting them. They killed 4 and wounded 7 white men. The force on the Republican is not less than 4,000 warriors; this the report of my scouts and Jewitt [Jewett], also 50 of my best men.[24]

Mitchell in turn wrote his superior, Maj. Gen. Samuel Curtis, the commander of the Department of Kansas. Reporting on the raid on Julesburg, Mitchell declared that the numerous posts needed to be concentrated, some of them being too weak to withstand heavy odds. "Either give me power to act as I deem best," he wrote, "or direct what I should do; while we are corresponding the Indians are masters of the Overland Road and immediate action is imperative."[25] In exploring the countryside, station employees at Julesburg recovered the treasure trunk taken from the stage coach and a small amount of money.

The fighting at Julesburg was not the only action on the South Platte on January 7. That same morning a man named Cross started out from the American Ranch with a wagon load of passengers. At the halfway point to Valley Station, about forty to seventy Indians suddenly appeared, firing arrows at the wagon and trying to force the team off the road. First grazed in the face by an arrow, Cross had his arm shattered at the elbow by a rifle shot delivered at close range by a member of the party. The killing of the wheel horses finally brought the wagon to a halt, the passengers lying down to protect themselves. One passenger had already been killed. The party succeeded in running to the riverbank, using their guns as clubs, since none of them were loaded. They made their way to Valley Station, where Cross's arm was amputated. Another group in the same area, including Messrs. Marsh, Edwards, and McCullough, fought from their wagon and lost one man and had several wounded.[26]

About this time, Little Bear and Touching Cloud and a number of other Cheyenne came upon two discharged soldiers riding in a wagon. After the raiders killed them, they found two scalps in a valise. They were at once recognized as those of White Leaf and Little Wolf or Little Coyote, the son of Two Thighs, the first because of the woman's unusually light hair and the second because of the warrior's habit of wearing a distinctive little shell in his hair, which remained attached. Upon discovery of the trophies and their identification, the Cheyennes cut the bodies of the dead into pieces. This was the first certain revenge for Sand Creek.[27]

On Sunday, January 8, men left Valley Station to look for those attacked the day before near Dennison's Ranch. They found that the post's train from Denver had lost one man, named Andrews, and five men had been severely wounded. The party also suffered two horses killed, and their wagons had been burned. Andrews's body was horribly mutilated, with his arms and legs cut off and arrows in his eyes. Marsh's train had one man and a mule killed, two slightly wounded, and one wagon destroyed. The Haynes party had three men killed and four wagons burned. Of the group, seven men were missing. Clark's, Keith's, and Cook's trains, which had been heading east, also suffered, losing a total of four men.[28]

The commander of the District of Colorado in Denver sent the following report to his superiors in the Department of the Plains on January 11: "The Indians have attacked Julesburg, Valley Station, and several other points on the Overland Route, murdered men women and children just as they come, burned trains and houses, driven off stage and other stock so that the Overland Route is shut off, and here I am without a man to throw on either track or even to defend the ranches with."[29] On January 14, the *New York Times* reported that the overland mail to California had been suspended until General Curtis could disperse the hostile Indians on the plains.[30] The *Rocky Mountain News* later reported that eighty bags of mail destined for Kansas and Julesburg had to be returned to New York because the Indians held an area extending about 500 miles along the overland mail route. The mail had to be sent via the isthmus route.[31]

Some of the early reports of the Julesburg raid were not kind to the troops at Fort Rankin. The Central City, Colorado, *Miner's Register* reported that the soldiers involved were an Ohio regiment "consistently represented as a band of rebels and thieves, who have constantly annoyed the emigration, without affording the least protection. If we mistake not, they have shown themselves cowards as well."[32] The *Rocky Mountain News* came to their defense, however, noting that the editor of the *Register* was "prone to judge others by himself," and referring to the fight as "one of the terrible and gallant actions of the war." Instead of abuse, the *News* declared, "the remnants of that devoted little band deserve the united thanks of the people of Colorado and the Legislative Assembly."[33]

On January 10, O'Brien received orders to place Camp Rankin in charge of invalids, dismounted men, and any civilians he could find and proceed with all available force to join Gen. Robert Mitchell at Cottonwood Springs for an Indian campaign.[34] Company F reached Cottonwood Springs on the evening of January 14. On January 15, Mitchell's command drew up in line. Present were 640 cavalry, men from the 7th Iowa, 1st Nebraska Veteran Volunteer Cavalry, and Companys B and C of the 1st Nebraska Militia (mounted). Loaded into 100 mule wagons were tents, rations, other supplies, and corn for the animals. Also included in the expedition were fifty extra horses and armament consisting of four 12-pounder mountain howitzers and two light 3-inch Parrott guns. Col. Robert R. Livingston was second in command, and Captain O'Brien served as chief of artillery. The scouts were Joe Jewett, Charley Elliston, and Leon Palladay.[35]

During the next twelve days, the column moved south from Morrow's Ranch (about fifteen miles west of Camp Cottonwood) to the Medicine River, west to the Stinking Water, and south to the Republican, before heading north and east to the original point of departure, a half circle some 360 miles in length. While the troops saw smoke signals and a few Indians observing their progress from a distance, the only real contact came when some Sioux and Cheyennes raced through the night camp of an advance scouting party, shooting off firearms and pulling up tent pegs without inflicting or receiving casualties. On January 19, at a place near the Republican River that Mitchell called Big Timber, they found signs of a large village, probably that just abandoned four days earlier by the Cheyennes and their allies.[36]

In the meantime, rumors ran rampant in Denver and other settlements. Especially susceptible, Denver was a wide-open town of about 5,000 souls where, as one visitor put it, "Every fifth house appears to be a bar, whiskey-shop, or lager-beer saloon; every tenth house appears to be either a brothel or a gaming house—very often both."[37] According to one observer, Denver was the home to "lawbreakers of every kind and from every land, to men of culture and refinement."[38] Here tales ran fast with strong drink. Exasperated at the stories heard, a writer for the *Rocky Mountain News* explained that he had discovered the real truth:

> The Indians under Big Smoky and Old Gassy, are to attack Denver tonight at seventeen minutes before eight o'clock to-morrow forenoon; or failing in this, by reason of their transportation not coming to time, the attack will be made at twenty-three minutes past ten o'clock this evening.
>
> The forces under Big Smoky number 7,893 warriors, consisting of Comanches, Apaches, Kiowas, Shawnees, Ogallallahs, Pottawattamies, Black feet and Cheyennes, (most of them friendly) the latter led by Black Kettle, who has obtained a furlough from down below for that purpose. The main body of the enemy will advance from the west, crossing the Platte on a foot-log near Camp Weld, pushing boldly across the peninsula they will lay pontoons across Cherry Creek just outside the fortifications and attempt to storm the formidable defences erected last summer. Succeeding in this, our own guns will be turned upon the doomed city and men, women and children will be put to the sword.[39]

Col. Thomas Moonlight, the new commander of the District of Colorado, did not help matters by publishing a notice in the newspapers in which he explained that he had received daily reports of men wearing the uniform of the United States who were visiting ranches, appropriating stock, and arresting citizens in the name of the government. Calling them thieves and murderers, he warned citizens against them and requested information regarding them. Moonlight also rescinded the order that prohibited citizens from carrying arms in Denver, stating that "Surrounded as this Territory now is by hostile Indians, it is but right that every man should be prepared to defend his home."[40] In response to the raiding along the South Platte, the governor of Colorado called for six companies of volunteer militia to patrol the road. Moonlight indicated that he would furnish guns, munitions, horse equipment, rations, forage, transportation, and camp and garrison equipage. Volunteers had to supply horses, blankets, revolvers, and clothing.[41] On the night of January 17, when the aurora borealis appeared on the northern horizon between 9:00 and 10:00 P.M., some imagined it to be a conflagration started by the Indians in the valley of the Platte or the Cache la Poudre.[42]

Moonlight fanned the fires of anxiety again on January 27, when he published the following:

I have just received a private letter from the commanding officer of Fort Lyon (not knowing that he was in my command) informing me that according to the most reliable accounts, the following tribes of Indians are concentrated on the head waters of the Smoky Hill, and that they contemplate an attack upon Denver City, and surrounding country,—viz: Cheyennes, Arapahos, Sioux, Kiowas and Comanches. I make this statement for the information of the people, and that they may see the necessity for an immediate organization, such as is now going on; and also that they may not be lulled into security of position. It is not necessary that these facts should cause an undue excitement, but it is necessary or, at least prudent, that we should be prepared.

Yours, truly,
T. Moonlight
Colonel Commanding[43]

Meanwhile, the real foe on General Mitchell's late January march turned out to be the weather. On the night of January 22, the reading was 22 degrees below zero. That night everyone kept in motion, not daring to go to sleep. Before the journey was over, many had suffered frostbitten ears and fingers.[44]

One night around the campfire, General Mitchell shared his unique solution to the Indian problem, recorded by Lieutenant Ware. "It is a well-known fact," he said, "that it costs a million dollars a year to keep a cavalry regiment in the field. It takes in my district, from Omaha to South Pass, three regiments of cavalry; that is to say, three million dollars a year. This is outside the loss of productive labor and loss of men by death and disease. I would put the Indians on reservations, dress them up in broadcloth, feed them on fried oysters, and furnish them money to play poker with, and all the tobacco and whisky they wanted, and then I will be a million dollars ahead of the game in my little district every year."[45]

Mitchell was very disappointed that he had not been able to discover the Indians' location, but he did find evidence that led him to believe that the Sioux and Cheyennes were crossing the Platte and heading north to Powder River country. The expedition had not resulted in the death of a single raider, but ended in the disablement of not less than fifty soldiers from frozen limbs or other injuries. Mitchell himself froze a toe. The commander noted, however, that "not a murmur was heard from any one." Also, the expedition had ruined 100 horses, and six wagons had to be abandoned. As he rode down Cottonwood Canyon on January 26 at the end of the trip, the general was heard to mutter, "Well what more could we do? What more could we do?" Mitchell told Lieutenant Ware that he would rather go down south and be shot to death than to stay up north and fight Indians and be frozen to death.[46] Upon returning to his desk, Mitchell wrote a letter requesting either a reassignment to fight in the South or the acceptance of his resignation.[47]

At the same time, Mitchell learned that in his absence, the Sioux and Cheyennes had started a new campaign. At Camp Cottonwood, he received a telegram stating that Indians were raiding everywhere, burning stage stations between Julesburg and Valley Station, stopping all travel. He learned that the Beaver Creek stage station had been burned and Godfrey's Ranch had been attacked on January 14. The latter had several solid buildings into which the owner, Holan Godfrey, two of his herders, and some others retreated and survived, while the Indians drove off his cattle and horses. Godfrey inflicted enough damage to earn the name "Old Wicked" from his Indian attackers, and thereafter, his ranch was known as Fort Wicked.[48] On that same day, raiders torched Wisconsin Ranch, fifty-six miles west of Camp Rankin, and killed a woman and two children. On January 15, the avengers burned Morrison's American Ranch, killing eight whites and carrying off Mrs. Morrison and her child.[49] Telegraph operator J. W. Ford was one of those who found the bodies and reported all burned to a cinder, calling it the most horrible sight that he had ever seen.[50] On January 18 the Indians menaced Valley Station, but the seventy soldiers on duty there kept them from making an attack. The troops did not feel, however, that they had sufficient numbers to pursue. On January 25 Gittrell's Ranch was burned. At Valley Station, the men could see signal fires burning every night in every direction.[51]

While Captain O'Brien remained to consult with General Mitchell, Lieutenant Brewer and most of Company F left for Fort Rankin.[52] Mitchell's response to this new development was to put into effect a plan that he had formulated over the past week: if he couldn't subdue the marauders himself, perhaps a fast-moving fire could. On the morning of January 27, the sky was clear with a strong wind blowing from the north, so Mitchell cleared the telegraph line and wired instructions to all posts between Fort Kearny and Denver to fire the grass at sundown. His subordinates carried out his command on schedule, so that a 300-mile line of fire rose in the fading twilight. Post commanders employed different methods for setting the fire. At Julesburg, soldiers prepared lighted bales of hay bound with chains, using horses and ropes to drag the blazing bundles over the prairie. Three days later, the fire had reached the Arkansas River, some of it finally running down into the Texas panhandle before extinguishing.[53]

Mitchell's main objective in setting the fire was to deprive raiders of forage for their ponies and drive all game out of the region, reducing their subsistence.[54] In this he succeeded; however, the fire had little immediate effect, except perhaps to deepen the hate the Sioux and Cheyennes already had for the whites. On the day of the burning, some Sioux and Cheyenne raiders attacked Washington's Ranch and burned Lillian Springs Ranch.[55]

Mostly Mitchell's fire was ineffective because the majority of the Indians were no longer where they used to be. After returning to the camp on Cherry Creek after the attack on Julesburg, the chiefs had decided to travel north to Powder River to join the Northern Cheyennes and the Oglalas.[56] On January 15, they moved to the stream known as White Butte Creek, about halfway between the South Fork of the Republican and the South Fork of the Platte.[57] Black Kettle and his eighty lodges of Southern Cheyennes parted company with the main body on January 26. He had decided to join the Kiowas, Comanches, and Little Raven's Southern Arapahos south of the Arkansas.[58] While the women, children, and old people traveled north, large war parties ranged up and down the South Platte, leaving devastation in their wake. The Cheyennes began fifty miles west of Julesburg, the Sioux forty miles east, and the Arapahos raided in between.[59]

On January 27, the Cheyennes under George Bent began their depredations at the American Ranch, where they ran off 100 head and then burned 100 tons of hay belonging to the soldiers at nearby Valley Station. Cavalry under Lt. J. J. Kennedy from the little post fought a skirmish with the raiders and, after a twenty-mile pursuit, recaptured some of the stolen stock. Troops estimated they had killed between ten and twenty of the raiders. At the same time, warriors with the main village attacked Harlow's Ranch, about twenty-three miles west of Julesburg, where there was an emigrants' store. Burning the buildings, including a four-room house, they killed three white men, and a Sioux, Cut Belly, took a woman prisoner. The store yielded a large supply of liquor. During the drinking spree that followed, an inebriated Cheyenne shot in the head and fatally wounded an Arapaho. Five miles east was Spring Hill Station, which the raiders set afire.[60]

The next target was Ackley's or Gillette's Ranch, within twelve miles of Julesburg. There Oglalas under Two Face and some Northern Cheyennes attacked freighters on their way to Central City, Colorado, in their overnight camp. They destroyed an ox train of sixteen wagons belonging to James H. Southerland and H. M. Foster & Company, the entrepreneurs suffering loss of quantities of flour, bacon, ham, codfish, and mackerel, as well as jugs of molasses syrup, buffalo robes, camp fixtures, nails, and other goods. After the attack, the freighters fled to Gillette's Ranch, where they were joined by the fleeing William Harlow and wife. At night, the party crawled to the river in an attempt to reach Fort Rankin. The river was ice-covered, with many small islands on which bunches of willows grew. These afforded enough shelter to cover their retreat, and they were able to reach the fort about daybreak. On January 29, the raiders also burned Antelope Stage Station and Buffalo Springs Ranch, both within a half hour ride from Fort Rankin.[61]

Later in the day, after the swift attack along the line, the main party went into camp on the left bank of the South Platte, across from Harlow's Ranch, where they would remain until February 2. There they enjoyed fresh beef, new clothing, dress goods, hardware of all kinds, and myriad foodstuffs, with even candied citron to tease the pallet. The camp spread out for some distance, the three tribes camping separately but near one another, their drums pounding out the joy of victory. In summarizing the raid, Bent noted that three Sioux Indians had been killed in an attack on one of the wagon trains and declared that he had never seen so much plunder in an Indian village.[62]

As reports came in, the Omaha *Nebraska Republican* called for more troops, declaring, "The plains, from Julesburg west, for more than one hundred miles, are red with the blood of murdered men, women, and children—ranches are in ashes—stock all driven off—the country utterly desolate. . . . The truth is a gigantic Indian war is upon us."[63] In Denver a rumor that 300 warriors approached from the south soon grew to 3,000, causing the editor of the *Rocky Mountain News* to remark how "astonishing it was that Indians 'increase and multiply.'"[64]

On the morning of February 2, the camp broke up and continued north. Since the Sioux knew the country best, they led. First went an advance guard to search for troops on the North Platte. A second group stayed behind to warn the people if soldiers should come from that direction. Moving across the prairie, the travelers cut a swath a mile wide. Women and boys drove the extra ponies and herds of captured cattle. When the trek began, a large war party of the three tribes turned toward Julesburg once again, this time to finish what they had begun.[65]

On the morning of January 29, O'Brien, Ware, and a small escort, with nineteen wagons, left Camp Cottonwood for Julesburg. Ware had been detailed as aide-de-camp to Mitchell, and his task was to report on conditions and immediately wire his superior. The party reached John A. Morrow's Ranch late in the day, where they supped on antelope hearts, beaver tails, and champagne provided by their host. Jack Morrow had been there since 1858. He had married an Indian woman, had a number of children, and had good relations with his wife's tribe.[66] In the meantime, Lieutenant Brewer, acting commander at Fort Rankin, learned that Indians had been reported in force in the vicinity, and he decided to send an escort of thirty men to meet O'Brien and his group. This left only fifteen men inside Fort Rankin.[67]

On January 30, O'Brien's detachment reached Alkali Station guarded by Capt. John Murphy and Company A of the 7th Iowa Cavalry. Murphy had detained a westbound stage for safety reasons, which held two stage company officials, Andrew Hughes and a man named Clift, the division manager. They were trying to get the line reopened. Captain Murphy added to their escort so that it totaled ten men and provided increased protection in the form of a mountain howitzer. Hughes and Clift also joined the group.[68]

Two days later, at midmorning on February 2, O'Brien's little party reached Dick Cleve's Ranch, an hour's ride from Camp Rankin. There they discovered a number of plainsmen preparing to defend themselves. On the other side of the river a few Indians were rounding up Cleve's cattle herd, preparatory to driving them off. While the plainsmen did not fear the results of an attack, they suggested that Mrs. Cleve go with O'Brien to the fort, which she reluctantly agreed to do. Also joining the party was John Kay, the telegrapher from Alkali Station, who was traveling to Julesburg to see why his line had gone dead. To help out, O'Brien left four of his men, feeling confident with his howitzer in tow.[69]

It was near noon when O'Brien's party reached the Devil's Dive arroyo, about three miles from Julesburg. Years later, O'Brien recalled the scene:

> From the summit of the hill above Devil's Dive, where the main part of the first battle was fought, I could see smoke rising above the intervening rise of land and I moved cautiously across to where I could see through my field glasses that the stage station was burning, causing the column of smoke we had observed. Indians covered the area in all directions, circling their horses around the station and other burning buildings at close range. They were circling the fort also, but at a much wider range remembering their first experience with howitzers in the stockade.[70]

Some witnesses later claimed that between 1,500 and 2,000 warriors participated in this second attack on Julesburg, which had begun about 10:00 A.M. The little force at Fort Rankin had fired on the attackers but could not drive them away. O'Brien's decision was to run the gauntlet to the post. Hazy weather and a northwest wind that blew a pall of smoke from the burning buildings in their direction covered their approach. After corralling the wagons, O'Brien had the howitzer loaded with canister, and one of the soldiers carried a friction primer, in order to fire the gun from horseback. O'Brien instructed Ware to carry the field glasses and ride in front, followed by four cavalrymen. O'Brien followed with the gun squad. Bringing up the rear was the stagecoach, pulled by four horses. The driver occupied the box in front, while Hughes and Clift rode on top, and Mrs. Cleve kept inside. The stage station, built from the logs from Jack Morrow's canyon, burned with a fierce heat as the group approached Julesburg. Mrs. Cleve asked O'Brien for a revolver, declaring, "I am going to have a part in this fight." The captain handed her one, which she made good use of, firing first out of one window, then out of the other, as the stage sped toward the little settlement. O'Brien later commented, "Mrs. Cleve was the bravest woman I ever saw."[71]

O'Brien had determined to make the Indians believe that his command was but the advance guard of a large force of cavalry, the smoke, haze, and the lay of the land favoring this ruse. Soon the little caravan came into full view of the pillagers, who were busily carrying off sacks of corn and flour, loading their ponies with goods to send across the river on a sanded strip of ice about six feet wide. O'Brien ordered the howitzer discharged, and the warriors that had gathered before them drew back, temporarily opening the way. Down the road they sped, shooting, shouting, and calling on the phantom army they hoped the raiders would believe was following close behind. O'Brien ordered the men to draw their sabers.

About 200 yards farther, a group of riders moved directly in front to bar the way. At Fort Rankin, Lieutenant Brewer could see their predicament and opened up with the howitzer, firing shells into the clumps of horsemen. O'Brien then ordered another blast from his howitzer, catching the Indians in a cross fire. Not knowing what was coming behind or what the smoke concealed, the warriors moved aside. Not daring to charge, they hovered on the flanks, as the mounted party, followed by the coach, moved at full speed toward the post and safety. Hughes and Clift maintained the fast pace, keeping the horses on the run. Both yelled much and fired often, causing the warriors to move aside, and to O'Brien they seemed filled with hilarity.

All arrived safely. Looking back over the years, O'Brien still felt a sense of awe at their success, as if he had participated in a miracle. Lieutenant

Brewer, Chief of Scouts Charles Elliston, and the rest of the defenders rejoiced in the coming of the late arrivals, not only for their own sake but for the added firepower they represented. Augmenting the little military force were a dozen or more ranchers, travelers, and citizens of Julesburg who had fled to the post when the attack began, including E. D. Bulen, the co-owner of the closest ranch to Julesburg. Two miles from Fort Rankin, the G. D. Connelly & E. D. Bulen Ranch provided hay needed by travelers for their animals, as much of the grass in the region had been burned in numerous raids. Also at Fort Rankin were Philo Holcomb and S. R. Smith, who ran the Pacific Telegraph office, which they had moved to the post after the raid on January 7.[72]

While respect for the cannon had kept the raiders at a distance from the fort, the soldiers believed that an attack was imminent. Compared to a hive of disturbed bees by O'Brien, Indian raiders swirled about the post, but the defenders noticed that many began slipping away to Julesburg to secure remaining grain, clothing, and other supplies before all perished in the flames. Especially desirable were shelled bags of corn found in the warehouse, which the raiders packed on their ponies.[73] Observing the tumultuous scene was Noble Ware, who took care of horses at Fort Rankin and whose wife was a cook for officers. Ware sketched the burning of Julesburg and later created a large painting of the event, which he presented to the Colorado Historical Society in 1933.[74] While Julesburg burned, the raiders appropriated stock owned by Abraham T. Litchfield a few miles distant, killing several herders in the process.[75]

By evening it was over. Carrying their booty across the South Platte, the Indians divided into three parties, the largest remaining to camp on the bank opposite Fort Rankin, near present-day Ovid, Colorado, while a group of Cheyennes and Arapahos continued to raid upriver, and a large party of Sioux sought new action in the opposite direction.[76] Those who stayed in camp on the bank of the South Platte arranged downed telegraph poles into a huge pile for a victory fire and began a night of feasting and dancing. In the meantime, O'Brien prepared for the possibility of a night assault on the stockade. Mounting one of the howitzers on the roof of the stable, he stationed soldiers at strategic points along the walls of the fort. Climbing atop an eighty-ton haystack at the northwest corner of the post, O'Brien and Lieutenant Ware peered through field glasses to watch the war dance in progress—the circling, ground stamping, gesturing figures illuminated in firelight. Burrowing deep into the hay for protection from the cold, the officers prepared for a long vigil.[77]

At midnight, the defenders carried out their own patriotic ritual. The men raised a pole bearing a tattered American flag, topped with an Indian arrow that pointed west. Buried at the foot of it was a document signed by all within the walls of the post. It read:

This pole is erected by Phil Holcomb and S. R. Smith, operators for the Pacific Telegraph Line, and Joel F. Wisely, Surgeon, U.S. Army—twenty-six days after the bloody conflict of January 7, 1865, between 1200 Cheyenne warriors and forty brave boys of the 7th Iowa Cavalry under command of Capt. N. J. O'Brien. On this occasion, the telegraph office and hospital at the mail station were totally destroyed and both institutions re-established at this post. The lives of fifteen soldiers and five citizens were lost during this terrible raid, and their remains interred nearby. With a fervent prayer for the success of the Union cause, and shouts for victory to our arms—we raise this humble memorial, high in the free air.[78]

Eventually, in the wee hours, the drumbeat stopped, revelry ceased, fires died down, and smoke drifted lazily across the river upon the chill breeze. When dawn broke, besieged sought signs of besiegers, but there were none: all was quiet on the north bank. Soon thereafter, O'Brien, Lieutenant Ware, and a squad of cavalrymen moved across the river to find the camp deserted. Conspicuous were great numbers of broken bottles scattered around the ashes of the campfire and the heads of 156 cattle that had been slaughtered for the night's feast. As they rode upriver toward Gillette's Ranch, the men were surprised to see the prairie dotted with spots of white flour, droppings from sacks that had burst open in hard riding. They represented all that remained of 600 sacks of flour that had been part of the load in the wagons owned by H. M. Foster & Company captured on January 28. At the ranch, the soldiers found the ground scorched but twenty-four wagons filled with mining equipment untouched. On one of the large-rimmed wheels the admonition "GO TO HELL" had been written in charcoal.[79] O'Brien and a detachment visited Ackley's Ranch, where they found everything destroyed, except a pile of codfish, which they appropriated for use at the fort.[80]

Desolation marked the scene at Julesburg. The buildings were smoldering ruins. What telegraph wires remained were down. Telegraph poles had been cut down and the line rendered inoperative for ten miles toward Denver and thirty-four miles toward Fort Laramie. The men described the wire as twisted and tangled inextricably and the poles cut off at the ground. New poles had to be hauled from Cottonwood Springs, 134 miles distant. The Sioux and Cheyennes had secured or destroyed 3,500 sacks of corn and run off 1,000 heads of stock. Some of the freighters were able to put out a fire that was consuming a huge pile of corn belonging to the stage station. For a reward, many of them received enough smoky corn to feed their animals and start them on their way back to Denver. Ben Holladay estimated $115,000 in damages.[81]

As a result of the attack on Julesburg and associated raiding, the army limited travel along the road, permitting only caravans of 100 wagons or more to proceed, accompanied by troops. The approach of Col. R. R. Livingston from Cottonwood Springs with a detachment of Companies F and K of the 1st Nebraska Cavalry, numbering about 300 men, had caused the quick departure of the Indians during the early hours of February 2. Livingston had seen Julesburg ablaze from Alkali Station and had wired Mitchell: "For God's sake get me troops—what in the name of God means this apathy?"[82] Livingston reached Fort Rankin about 4:00 A.M., missing the Indian exodus by a few hours. Scouts examining one of the Indian campsites estimated 800 lodges.[83]

Word of the sacking and burning of Julesburg reached Denver in a few days. Colonel Moonlight reacted by declaring martial law in the city, which included closing of all business houses, and Acting Governor Samuel Elbert called for six companies of militia to be raised from Arapahoe, Gilpin, Clear Creek, Jefferson, Boulder, and Larimer Counties.[84] Major General Curtis responded by ordering the establishment of a regular post with troops and supplies at Valley Station.[85] Joining the hysteria, the Omaha *Nebraska Republican* shrieked, "The sober truth is a gigantic Indian war is upon us," while the *Oskaloosa* (Kansas) *Independent* calmly reminded its readers that the army needed to protect the miners, whose supplies were being cut off, so that they would be able to continue to produce the wealth that the nation so sorely needed.[86]

The height of feeling in the Colorado mining settlements reached its apex on the evening of February 9, when Colonel Moonlight addressed the citizens of Central City. In an inflammatory speech, he reminded his listeners that "nits make lice" and that he planned to wage war against all ages and sexes. The Central City *Miner's Register* applauded the remarks, declaring that "extermination is their final doom, and we do not care how much it is hastened."[87] The citizens did have one piece of good news. On February 1, Joseph Bissonette and Jules Ecoffey had been able to ransom Nancy Morton from her captors, delivering her safe and sound to the commanding officer at Fort Laramie.[88]

CHAPTER THREE

Mud Springs and Rush Creek

FOLLOWING THE ATTACK ON JULESBURG, THE CHEYENNES AND SIOUX decided to move north to the Tongue and Powder River areas. On the road between the North and South Platte Rivers, there were two telegraph stations, one at Lodgepole Creek and one at Mud Springs.[1] On February 3, the advance party began appearing in great numbers on Lodgepole Creek, quickly destroying the buildings there. The telegraph operator was absent, and when he returned to see his station in flames, he quickly left for Mud Springs.[2]

Wagons loaded with booty slowed the movements of the Indian party. Warriors used long rawhide and twisted buffalo hair lariats to secure wagons to their ponies, but the vehicles swayed back and forth as they moved over the rough ground.[3] Tipi poles cut a swath a mile wide. Warriors finally left the wagons, fastening their plunder on ponies' backs. The next day found them at Mud Springs.

Travelers headed for Oregon and California began using Mud Springs in the mid-1850s. When reaching the forks of the Platte River, some emigrants continued to follow the South Platte to Julesburg before heading north to Court House Rock. This route, although twenty-five miles longer, avoided the rough country at Ash Hollow and the alkali flats. For those coming from the south, the so-called Jules cutoff was a more direct route to Fort Laramie. In use as early as 1854, the road moved northwest, parallel to Lodgepole Creek, and then turned due north at present-day Sidney, Nebraska, to cross the plains. The first stop was Mud Springs, the only water on the trail between Lodgepole Creek and the North Platte. By the Laramie road, Mud Springs was seventy miles from Fort Rankin. In 1860, the Pony Express established a home station there,[4] and in 1861, it became a station for the transcontinental telegraph, becoming operative on July 15.[5] Richard Burton, who visited the springs in 1860, stated that it took its name from "a little run of water in a black miry hollow."[6]

Surrounded by hills and knolls cut by gullies, the little outpost at Mud Springs was impossible to defend. Attackers could reach positions where they could not be observed or routed by cavalry charge. In the late summer of 1864, the army had decided to station troops there to protect the emigrant trail and the telegraph from Indian attack. General Mitchell had ordered establishment of military garrisons of varying size at Julesburg, Mud Springs, Ficklin's Springs, and Scott's Bluff.[7] Only a dozen or so troops normally watched after things at Mud Springs. Caspar Collins drew a ground plan of the outpost in 1864 showing two log buildings. The first measured thirty-five by sixteen feet, with a telegraph office and squad room nearly dividing the building in half. The second was labeled a stable and measured forty by twenty feet.[8]

Living at Mud Springs Station on February 4 were the telegraph operator, Martin Hogan, and nine soldiers. According to one of the enlisted men, Winfield S. Davis of Company H, 11th Ohio, the place was located in "god forsaken country." He went on to say that the only amusements were playing cards and fighting Indians, and the only variation in diet was to have bread and coffee for one meal and coffee and bread for the next.[9] Also at Mud Springs were four stock herders for Creighton & Hoel, whose ranch was on Pumpkin Creek about four miles away. Warriors took stock from the corral in the first attack. Missing were one mule and three horses belonging to the government and ten or fifteen ponies and horses owned by Creighton & Hoel.[10] The raiders also appropriated the cowpunchers' nearby cattle herd.[11]

District Commander William O. Collins learned about the attack by telegraph at about 4:00 P.M. Saturday, February 4.[12] He immediately ordered a relief party from Fort Mitchell. Composed of 1st Lt. William Ellsworth and thirty-six men of Company H, 11th Ohio Volunteer Cavalry, the men rode through the night, covering the fifty miles to reach Mud Springs by daylight the next morning. At 7:00 P.M., on the evening of February 4, Collins led his own force out of Fort Laramie. The troops numbered 120 men, consisting of a detachment of Company D, 7th Iowa Cavalry, officered by Capt. William D. Fouts and Lt. Dudley L. Haywood; another detailed from Company I, 11th Ohio Volunteer Cavalry, under command of Capt. Jacob F. Apt and Lts. Theodore B. Harlan and John R. Moloney; and a third unit formed from Companies A, B, C, and D of the

1st Battalion, 11th Ohio, led by lst Lt. Robert F. Patton and 2nd Lt. John V. Herriman. Traveling all night, Collins's command reached Fort Mitchell about 11:00 A.M. on February 5. Here the men rested and refreshed themselves and their mounts. About 7:00 P.M., they resumed the march, Collins and twenty-five men hurrying ahead of the main column, which followed under the command of Capt. William Fouts of the 7th Iowa.[13]

Ellsworth's detachment from Fort Mitchell reached Mud Springs in the early hours of February 5.[14] Before drawing close, Ellsworth ordered the bugler to sound a call to let the besieged know that help was at hand. David Peck of Company H reported the happy reunion: "When . . . the doors were thrown open, an old soldier named [William] Idlet cried for joy. The boys knew that it was the intention of the Indians to crawl up around the building in the night, and if a head appeared it would be sure death."[15] Just before daylight, a group of young warriors made a successful raid on the corral and the new bunch of animals now held there. As horse and mules departed, their pursuers did their best to touch them with whip or bow, thus establishing ownership, which the rest recognized.[16]

At daylight, sixteen of the relief party ascended a bluff in the rear of the station to prevent the Indians from getting too close. The men had fired several rounds at the raiders as they galloped from one bluff to another, when suddenly about 500 warriors rose up behind the creek bank and opened fire. One participant described the barrage as like a "shower of hail stone."[17] In the face of the intense fire, the soldiers received the order to retreat. As the men formed to go back, two brothers, standing on either side of David Peck, were hit. One received a shoulder wound that dropped and stunned him, but he was soon up and running. Peck, who had been bringing up the rear, opened the station door to let him in. Upon entering, the man collapsed. His comrades placed him in a bunk, where he eventually received medical attention from Assistant Surgeon Zeigler, who arrived a few hours later. The other brother had been shot in the hip, the ball lodging in his groin, making it difficult for him to move. Peck reported that while the defenders in the station looked on helplessly, they "could see the Indians jumping up, waving their scalping knives and yelling like demons" in anticipation of the kill.[18]

The wounded man lay near a depression and had the strength to roll himself over into it and draw his revolver. In the meantime, Sgt. William Hall, a veteran who had seen service on the frontier and who had recently reenlisted in the company, volunteered to rescue the man.[19] According to Peck, Hall "took off his revolver belt and hung it on a peg, as unconcerned as though he was going to his supper." Officers tried to dissuade him, as the mission appeared suicidal, but Hall opened the door, moved quickly to the man, placed him on his shoulder, and brought him safely into the house without mishap. Peck later mused, "I think the hand of Providence was surely manifested there."[20] Hall's efforts went for naught, however, as the man later succumbed and found a resting place under a mound on the plains. The other brother survived. At dusk, the raiders withdrew, and the men rested.

As daylight broke over the winter scene on the morning of February 6, Col. William O. Collins and his command from Fort Laramie came struggling in. Having marched for two nights and a day in bitter cold with no sleep and but little rest, the troops were debilitated, and many of the them had their ears and feet badly frozen. As the reinforcements arrived, Cheyenne and Sioux warriors swarmed over the bluffs in all directions, laying down a desultory fire in an effort to pick off some of the new arrivals before they reached the compound.[21]

Collins estimated that the number of warriors engaged that day was from 500 to 1,000, with the latter probably a truer figure.[22] He declared that the raiders were armed with rifles and revolvers and bows and arrows, that they had plenty of ammunition (minié balls were common), and that they were bold and brave. He noted that the Indians generally shot too high, else his command should have suffered many more casualties. He also saw that many of the attackers rode American horses and believed that there were white men or Mexicans among them.[23] Some enlisted men of the 11th Ohio reported seeing a white man with long red hair and whiskers carrying a flag representing the Lone Star of Texas or, as one of them put it, "a secesh flag." He rode a sorrel horse with a bob tail which seemed to have the fleetness of the wind.[24]

After arriving, Collins's troops hastily formed a corral out of four wagons, securing their stock. The Indians made several desperate attempts during the day to stampede the horses and mules to get them out of the corral. The were not successful, however, as heavy fire from the soldiers' Spencers turned them back. During the day, Collins telegraphed Fort Laramie to send an artillery piece, in order to dislodge warriors from their sheltered positions in the many gullies and ravines.

As fighting progressed, there evolved what Collins was later to call a game of bo-peep. In his report to his superiors, Collins explained as follows:

> We found it necessary to imitate the Indians, get under banks and creep up to favorable position, watch for an Indian's head, and shoot the moment it was shown and pop down at the flash of his

gun. The men got quite handy at this game and soon made any ground occupied by Indians too hot for them. It was common to see a soldier and an Indian playing bo-peep in this manner for half an hour at a time.[25]

At one point, 200 warriors gathered behind a hill and in its ravines, where they could come within seventy-five yards of the station buildings. From this proximity, they sent a shower of arrows that fell into the corral at an angle of about forty-five degrees, wounding many animals. The destruction dictated quick action, and Collins ordered two parties, one afoot and one mounted, to clear the area. The rush was successful, and the men took possession of the hill and dug a rifle pit on its highest point, ending the threat from that quarter.

After about four hours of fighting, troops began to move warriors back in every direction, and the Sioux and Cheyennes finally left the battlefield. The chiefs decided to relocate their village in the high country at the head of Brown's Creek, on the north side of the North Platte River. After resting their ponies for four or five days, they planned to begin the difficult march through the sand hills to the Black Hills. That night spirited Sioux and Cheyenne warriors danced under a full moon.[26] George Bent remembered that none of his kinsman had been killed that day.[27]

On February 6, Collins's troops had seven wounded, three of them seriously, and the Indians had killed a few mules and some horses.[28] Collins believed that Indian losses numbered about thirty, but explained that he could not be certain because the attackers immediately carried off their dead and wounded. He noted that some warriors tied themselves to their mounts so that in case of death or disablement, their horses would carry them away. After dark, Collins sent out a party to repair the telegraph line to Fort Laramie. This was done by taking wire from downed poles to the east. During the night, the command fortified the compound and made plans to take the offensive. This was possible because of the arrival under cover of darkness of Lt. William Brown and about fifty men of the 11th Ohio towing a 12-pounder mountain howitzer.[29] Brown and his men had made the trip from Fort Laramie in thirty-four hours, including stops.

On February 7, Collins sent out a scouting party to determine the Indians' whereabouts, and the next morning troops moved forward: the decision had been made to try to catch the Cheyennes and their allies. As Pvt. George Nelson remembered, "Catching them was an easy enough matter, but we had a terribly hard time letting them go."[30] Collins divided his command, numbering 185 men, into four squadrons. First in line was the 3rd Squadron, followed by the field piece, the 4th Squadron, the wagon train, the 2nd squadron, and, bringing up the rear, the 1st squadron. Captain Fouts and his men stayed behind to guard the station. The pursuing party moved rapidly, scouts out in front and rear and on the flanks. No Indians were in sight, but the whole country showed evidence of travel, its surface inscribed by passing travois. The trails appeared to concentrate and point to Rush Creek, about fifteen miles distant.[31]

Scouts found that the avengers abandoned camp about ten miles out, located in a sheltered valley that opened toward the North Platte River. Protected by rocky precipices, the camping place had good grass and clear water, its source being what the scouts called Rock Creek Springs. Evidence indicated that the camp had been recently abandoned and that its inhabitants had been there about three days in great numbers. The village had covered several miles, and scattered everywhere were flour sacks, quantities of codfish, and the spoils from ranches and trains. Empty oyster, meat, and fruit cans were plentiful, and over 100 beef cattle had been slaughtered to feed the multitude. The column continued to follow the broad road made by thousands of travois and tipi poles. In a few miles, the men reached the valley of the North Platte River near the mouth of Rush Creek.[32] As they approached the river, they saw Indian horsemen on the other side grazing their stock. Nowhere to be seen were women, children, dogs, and tipis, for the Cheyenne and Sioux camp was beyond the bluffs about five miles north.[33]

As troops neared the frozen river bed, they saw warriors riding out from the hills to meet them. One observer estimated that Indians outnumbered soldiers fifty to one. Looking through his field glass, Collins guessed that 2,000 Cheyennes and Sioux were in his front. The Cheyennes and Sioux crossed the frozen river at points above and below the command to surround it on every side. The riders came in such numbers that one volunteer remembered that at times the ice on the river was literally black with them.[34]

From the high bluffs on the opposite side of the river, another person looked through field glasses. George Bent remembered the scene:

> On the south side of the river I saw a train of white-topped wagons moving along the road under an escort of cavalry, and toward this train the Indians were hurrying, looking like a swarm of little black ants, crawling across the river on the ice . . . I could see that there were four groups or companies of [calvary] escorting the wagons. I watched them move on until they reached the stream on

whose head our camp had stood the day before, and here in the angle formed by the junction of the creek with the river, they halted, corralled the wagons, and began to prepare to fight.[35]

For a moment, Lieutenant Brown's double-shot howitzer held the charging warriors back, a few effective shots scattering those who had compacted in crossing. But they soon regrouped, and troops barely had time to corral the train before the warriors were upon them.[36] Quickly the troops dug in, easily scooping out the sandy soil and throwing it up in front to make a wall. By the time the battle commenced, the breastworks were well under way. In his report Collins described the action:

> The position chosen was the best we could get but there were many little sand ridges and hollows under cover of which they could approach us. A very great change had come over the men however and they were now cool, had confidence in their officers, obeyed orders, and went to work with a will. Sharpshooters were pushed out to the hillock commanding the camp occupied and rifles pits dug upon them. The Indians are the best skirmishers in the world. We were not strong enough to charge or scatter. It was necessary to be prudent and at first take the defensive. They dashed up very boldly but soon fell back from our bullets and resorted to their old game of skulking and sharpshooting. At this they were well met by our men.[37]

At one point, the Cheyennes and Sioux reached a little knoll about 400 yards from the breastworks, taking cover in a long, low gulch, where the sagebrush had grown tall and fallen dead grass provided good cover. Warriors carried one another to the spot, two mounting a single horse, one of them slipping off while the other raced through the gully. Since the place commanded the volunteers' position, it had to be taken. To this end, Collins detailed sixteen mounted men, part from the detachment of Company D, 7th Iowa Cavalry, and part from a detachment of the 1st Battalion of the 11th Ohio. Orders were to charge at full speed with revolvers in hand, clear out the Indians, and return immediately. Placed in command was Lt. Robert Patton of the 11th Ohio.[38] Patton gave the command "Forward," and into the nest they went pell-mell, the Cheyennes and Sioux running out just as rapidly. The Cheyenne youngster Yellow Nose was shot in the breast but was able to make his escape flattened on the back of his pony.[39]

After emptying the two revolvers that each carried, the attacking party began to return to the breastworks. In the meantime, 150 to 200 Cheyenne and Sioux who occupied the rising ground beyond the contested hillock swarmed down to save their companions, engaging the soldiers in a short hand-to-hand fight. From the breastworks, the volunteers delivered a thunderous volley, checking the Indian advance and enabling the charging squad to scramble back to safety.[40] According to military participants, many warriors were killed and wounded in this charge. In the foray, the volunteers lost two men: Pvt. John A. Harris of Company D, 7th Iowa Cavalry, and Pvt. William H. Hartshorn of Company C, 11th Ohio. Both had been on the frontier more than three years and were valued fighters.[41]

What happened to Hartshorn was not uncommon in the Indian wars. He rode a horse that was unruly, the animal always running away at the first opportunity. He was asked not to ride the horse but declined another mount. In the charge, true to its nature, Hartshorn's horse bolted, the Indians opening a way to let him through.[42] Witnesses said that Hartshorn hit his horse by the side of the head, trying to turn him around, but the warriors enveloped him before he could gain control. Later, a small party went out and brought in Harris's body, the mission being accomplished soon enough to keep the warriors from scalping him or taking his arms or clothing. The men were not successful in reaching Hartshorn's remains. Military casualties for the day, besides the two men killed, included nine wounded.[43]

At the end of the day, as the Cheyennes and Sioux withdrew across the North Platte, Collins detailed men to water the horses and mules on Rush Creek. By mistake, some of the men started toward the North Platte, where on the ice lay the body of a warrior killed during the day's fighting. Seeing the approach of the volunteers, the Cheyennes and Sioux came streaming back. Collins had recall sounded, and troops hurried back. In the morning the body was gone.[44]

During the predawn hours of February 9, the troops solidified their positions. At sunrise, while they were eating, they saw about 400 mounted warriors come over the bluffs. The riders crossed the river, and a few shots were exchanged, but soon the horsemen withdrew, recrossed the river, and headed rapidly north. About this time, the troops observed a few Indians standing on a bluff, about a quarter mile away, apparently interested in some object. Lieutenant Brown ordered a gunner to double-shot the howitzer, and the ensuing blast sent the last of the Indians on their way. A party of twenty went up to where the Indians had last been seen. There lay the body of Private Hartshorn, the head crushed, one arm cut off at the shoulder, one hand amputated, both legs severed at the knee, the breast cut open, and the heart gone. One eyewitness counted ninety-seven arrows in the body, another ninety-eight. Soldiers placed the bodies of Harris and Hartshorn in a wagon for later burial at Fort Laramie.[45]

At this point, the battle at Rush Creek ended. In his report, Collins stated that continued pursuit would have been "injudicious and useless," because the large numbers of Cheyennes and Sioux could compel his small force to corral and fight whenever they pleased. "This war party of Indians has rarely been equalled in size," Collins declared, noting that the assemblage included Cheyennes, Oglala and Brule Sioux, presumably a few Kiowas and Arapahos, and perhaps some straggling Apaches and Comanches. He remembered that the size of the ensemble was so large that he could see the smoke of their fires by day and the light in the sky by night for at least fifty miles as they went north. Although he did not say so, Collins had another reason for not pursuing: his troops were in no condition to continue—the main body had marched nearly 400 miles in ten days, much of it by night, suffering greatly from the cold, and the men had been two days and nights on a diet of hardtack and raw flesh. They had also lost significant numbers of horses and mules to their adversaries.[46]

Collins left the battlefield about 2:00 P.M. on February 10. Moving up the North Platte River about fifteen miles, he divided his command, sending Lieutenant Brown and the 11th Ohio back to Fort Laramie, which had been left with an insufficient garrison, and then setting out with the remainder, about ninety-five men, for Mud Springs. Collins proceeded to Lodgepole Creek, where he encountered Capt. John Wilcox of the 7th Iowa, who had a party out to repair the telegraph line. Initially mistaking the riders for Indians, Collins had corralled his wagon train and made ready for battle.[47]

Lodgepole Creek Station had been torched, and below that point and Mud Springs, fifteen miles of the line had been destroyed.[48] To the east, the havoc was even greater. Collins later commented: "The Indians had evidently good teachers and did their work well. They have got over their superstitious idea that it is bad medicine to touch the Telegraph."[49] On February 11, Collins started his return to Fort Laramie, via Fort Mitchell, reaching his command post on February 14.

Collins's first chore was to make out his report of the expedition. He stated his own losses as three killed, sixteen wounded, and seven disabled from frostbite suffered during his night marches. He estimated the total Indian loss in all engagements to be between 100 and 150, which varied markedly from George Bent's later recounting of no dead and two wounded—the Cheyenne Yellow Nose and a Sioux.[50]

In writing of the Cheyennes and Sioux, Collins stated his belief that they had gone to the Powder River country and might be expected to continue depredations along the North Platte until severely punished. "They are well armed and mounted," he wrote, [and] "have many rifled muskets and plenty of ammunition including minnie cartridges with ounce balls, [and] are full of venom and bent on revenge for the loss of their people south." Then, in a prophetic statement, he added, "The posts on the Platte especially Deer Creek and Platte Bridge will be in immediate danger."[51] In concluding his report, Collins noted that he was about to leave the service after three years and wished to make his final recommendations concerning Indian policy. His solution was to send troops into the heart of the Plains Indians' buffalo country and hold forts there until the trouble was over. The best place to keep them, he declared, was in the north, toward the main Missouri, so that other areas, notably the Black Hills, the Big Horn Mountains, and the Yellowstone country, could be opened up for mining and agriculture.[52]

One of the first to spread the news of Collins's victory back East was the colonel's son, Caspar. In a letter written to his mother, published in the Columbus, Ohio, *High Land Weekly News*, Caspar wrote:

I suppose you have heard of the fight father had with the Indians. It was the largest Indian battle, and fought at the greatest odds, of any event fought in this country. It has turned out that he killed a great many more than were reported, as the Indians themselves own to fifty or more dying of their wounds, which makes about two hundred placed hors du combat by a little more than half that number of the "terrible eleventh," with a loss of only two killed and fifteen or so wounded. Two of the wounded have since died.[53]

William Collins's performance was open to question in later years. Writing in the *National Tribune* on January 30, 1890, Pvt. George Rowan of Company D, 7th Iowa Cavalry, recalled that "Although Colonel Collins was a good man, yet as a soldier and as an officer, he was a mere cipher with shoulder straps." Rowan recounted that when the command reached the North Platte on February 8, Collins wanted to cross the river and take the fight to the Cheyennes and Sioux. If he had done so, Rowan declared, "the greatest slaughter that ever occurred in the West would have taken place (the Custer massacre not excepted)." According to Rowan, however, all the commissioned officers of the command earnestly advised and finally persuaded the colonel to fall back to a commanding position on the banks of Rush Creek. After the fighting began, Rowan continued, it was the skill of Lieutenant Brown with the howitzer that saved the day, not the leadership of Collins.[54] Additionally, the charge led by Lieutenant Patton was not something Collins had initiated; rather, he had approved the request of his subordinate to do so.[55] George Nelson agreed with Rowan that if Collins had acted upon his original impulse to cross the North Platte River, all of them would have been killed.[56] Francis M. Drake of Company B of the 11th Ohio, writing in the *National Tribune* in 1898, gave Collins his approval for what happened later, however, crediting the colonel with good management of the forces in the two-day battle.[57] An anonymous enlisted man also lauded Collins in a letter to the *Rocky Mountain News,* stating that the colonel had proved himself to be "a man of pluck and courage." According to the writer, Collins "had laid off his straps and went into the fight with as much coolness as the hero of a hundred battles," passing among the men and encouraging them to take sure aim and not waste any ammunition.[58]

What were the long-range consequences of the engagements at Mud Springs and Rush Creek? First, neither side suffered major setbacks. The military defended the routes of communication and transportation that it believed most important to the nation's interest, and the Cheyenne and Sioux continued on their intended course to Powder River. Second, in the case of the military, the campaign had the effect of boosting morale. The exaggerated reports of Indian casualties indicated that the troops had dealt the Cheyennes and Sioux a severe blow, giving a much-needed lift in spirit after Julesburg. From the enlisted man who toasted Collins and his men in the February 21 issue of the *Rocky Mountains News*—"All honor to Col. Collins and his brave men; long may they live to chastise the blood thirsty and thieving red devils on the West"—to the paper's editor, who the next day used irony to make his point—"The World stands aghast! The Sun is darkened! The Moon turned to blood! Dreary storms sweep o'er the Earth. The future is dark and dreary. Col. Collins, a veteran whose locks are silvered by the snows of many winters, has wantonly slaughtered some scores or hundreds of 'inoffensive,' 'friendly,' 'pacific noble red men'"—Indian fighters and haters had their day.[59]

Furthermore, neither side won a significant victory, since the fighting continued in the months ahead. Even before Collins returned to Fort Laramie, the Plains Indian raiders were at it again. On February 13 at La Prelle Creek, west of Fort Laramie, the men of Company G, 11th Ohio, skirmished with Sioux warriors, losing their commander, Capt. Levi M. Rinehart. Finally, in the fighting of February 1865, the troops had gained new respect for their foe. As George Nelson put it, "They were well armed, well mounted, cunning and brave; in fact, they fought like old warriors from away back."[60]

CHAPTER FOUR

Hanging of the Chiefs

ON JANUARY 30, 1865, THE U.S. ARMY COMPLETED A MAJOR REORGAN-
ization of its western hierarchy, due in part to the changing regional situation. Abolished was the Department of Kansas. Its responsibilities were
added to those of the Department of the Missouri, headed by Maj. Gen.
Grenville M. Dodge, a position he had held since December 9, 1864.
Smart, forceful, and efficient, Dodge had a degree in civil engineering from
Norwich University, Vermont. Born in Danvers, Massachusetts, on April
12, 1831, he had moved to Iowa after graduation, settling at Council Bluffs.
On July 8, 1861, he entered the service as colonel of the 4th Iowa Volun-
teer Infantry. Distinguishing himself at the battle of Pea Ridge, Arkansas, in
March 1862, he was promoted to brigadier general of volunteers. His skill
in swiftly rebuilding bridges and railroads that had been destroyed by Confederate forces brought him praise from General Sherman. Promoted to
major general on July 7, 1864, he had commanded a corps in the Atlanta
Campaign.[1] When knowledge of Dodge's additional duties became known,
Central City's *Miner's Register* lauded the move, noting that gone were "the
imbeciles who have so long subsisted upon Uncle Sam's grub, without ren-
dering any return therefor but violence done to peaceable citizens."[2]

The Departments of the Missouri and the Northwest were placed
under the control of the Military Division of the Missouri, a newly established office commanded by Maj. Gen. John Pope, who arrived at his St.
Louis headquarters on February 5. Pope and Dodge had identical views on
Indian policy and other military matters, and together they made plans to
free the plains of Indian attacks. Dodge expressed his views about the
Indian problem in a letter to Pope:

> In my opinion there is but one way to effectually terminate these
> Indian troubles, to push our cavalry into the heart of their country

from all directions, to punish them whenever and wherever we find them, and force them to respect our power and to sue for peace. Then let the military authorities make informal treaties with them for a cessation of hostilities.[3]

Succeeding Pope as the commander of the Department of the Northwest was Maj. Gen. Samuel R. Curtis, who had been serving as the commander of the Department of Kansas. Initially, defending Chivington, Curtis had lost the respect of his superiors as he had been unable bring a halt to depredations in his region. His removal from that area was at his own request. On March 21, oversight for Indian Territory was transferred from the Department of Arkansas to the Military Division of the Missouri. General Pope now controlled all of the Great Plains region except that in the Department of New Mexico.[4]

When word reached federal officials in Washington of resumed raiding by the Plains Indians, they began to act. In a communication to Secretary of War Edward M. Stanton, Secretary of Interior J. P. Usher reminded his colleague that engineers surveying the right-of-way of the Union Pacific Railroad had to be protected from Indian raids. He recommended that Brig. Gen. Patrick E. Connor, conqueror of the Western Shoshonis, undertake the task. Secretary of War Stanton had already received a letter from Ben Holladay, urging Connor's reassignment. Holladay declared that Connor's "familiarity with Indian warfare, prompt and efficient protection to the Western line, and wholesome dread of the savages of his name, point to him above all others as the man for the work of punishing these marauders."[5] Consequently, in the fall of 1864 Connor received orders from Maj. Gen. Henry W. Halleck, army chief of staff, to protect the overland route between Salt Lake City and Fort Kearny without regard to department lines. When Connor suggested that he be given control of the whole route, Halleck replied that no changes were contemplated. In cases where parts of different commands acted together, the ranking officer would take charge as provided in army regulations.[6]

On November 5, Connor and his aide took the stage for Denver, arriving on November 13. After studying the situation, Connor returned to Salt Lake and prepared his report. In it, he noted that he found only a few troops in the vicinity of Denver that could cooperate with his command and that he could not transport his command across the mountains at present without ruining about two-thirds of his horses. His superiors agreed and shelved the plan.

When raiding began in January, Connor was again seen as the man of the hour; the Colorado legislature implored the president to create a new department for the plains with Connor in charge. Early in 1865, Connor had submitted a plan for the protection of the overland route to General Halleck, who in turn forwarded it to Major General Pope, who found it acceptable. In his letter to Halleck, Pope remarked that "I found on all hands much confidence reposed in General Connor, and a very strong and general wish that he should be placed in charge of the protection arrangements for the whole region."[7]

In response, Connor received orders to meet Department Commander Dodge in Denver on February 27 to discuss a new administrative structure. After deliberations with Connor, Dodge established the District of the Plains on March 28, comprising what had been the Districts of Colorado, Nebraska, and Utah. With Connor in command, the new District of the Plains included Utah, Colorado, Nebraska, and Wyoming, with headquarters at Denver.[8]

Patrick Edward Connor was an excellent choice to command on the plains. Born near the lakes of Killarny in Ireland on St. Patrick's Day, March 17, 1820, he had emigrated with his parents to New York City. After service in the Seminole and Mexican Wars, he traveled to California in 1850, becoming involved in mining ventures. He received a commission as colonel of the 3rd California Infantry at the beginning of the Civil War. After commanding Benecia Barracks on San Francisco Bay from November 20, 1861, to May 26, 1862, he received orders to march his troops to Utah. He reached Salt Lake on October 20, 1862, and went into Camp Douglas nearby on the same day. After his successful campaign against the Western Shoshonis in the Bear River region, he was promoted to brigadier general on March 29, 1863. He became commander of the District of Utah in October. Blunt, forceful, and focused, he had a record of victories in Indian battles, and he was unforgiving and relentless in pursuit. One of the men who served under him in 1865 described him as a "quiet, unpretentious, untrained, taciturn, little Irishman, who had risen from the ranks, looked upon his duties as those of a proconsul with unlimited administration, or rather, originative powers, or as a soldier-citizen with unlimited opportunity and power of good." A contemporary described him as a polished gentleman of medium size with sandy hair, blue eyes, a slightly Roman nose, and very square shoulders. His Indian foes called him Red Chief because of his red whiskers.[9]

The new commander divided his district into four subunits. The first was the south subdistrict, commanded by Colonel and Bvt. Brig. Gen. Guy V. Henry, with offices in Denver. It included the Territory of Colorado (but excluded the post of Julesburg) and Fort Halleck in Dakota Territory.

The east subdistrict comprised the Territory of Nebraska. Commanding was Col. Robert Livingston, with headquarters at Fort Kearny. The north subdistrict, commanded by Colonel Thomas Moonlight, included all that portion of Dakota Territory (excepting Fort Halleck), lying west of the twenty-seventh degree of longitude and the post at Julesburg, with head-quarters at Fort Laramie. Finally, Connor created the west subdistrict, which included all of Utah, with Lt. Col. Milo George commanding at Camp Douglas.[10]

In February 1865, Generals Pope and Dodge had begun to formulate a plan for an expedition in force against the Sioux, Cheyennes, and Arapa-hos. Their plan was to strike in the early spring before the grass was up and Indian ponies had regained their vigor. Brig. Gen. James Ford was the choice to lead a campaign on the Southern Plains, while Connor and Gen. Alfred Sully would march from the south and southeast into Powder River country to hit villages believed to be in the neighborhood of the Big Horn Mountains and north of the Black Hills. At the time that Pope and Dodge planned the campaign, 52,000 troops were available for duty in the Division of the Missouri, and Dodge needed 5,000 to guard existing stations and protect wagon trains.[11]

Already, troops to help carry out the plan had been ordered west. They were two regiments of recycled Confederate prisoners. These men had been captured in battles in Georgia and Tennessee and chose freedom in service to the Union.[12] These Galvanized Yankees had received their orders in late February. The newly formed Colorado militia had begun to take the field as well. Companies A and B of the 1st Regiment Colorado Mounted Militia, 120 men, began operations near the end of February. Their job was to police the road between Denver and Julesburg.[13]

Also ordered west was the 11th Kansas Volunteer Cavalry. Leaving Fort Riley on February 16, it arrived at Fort Kearny on March 4. There the regiment received its final complement of horses and departed for Lodge-pole Creek. New orders sent the regiment to Mud Springs and then on to Fort Laramie.[14] The Kansans were not happy, however, having nearly com-pleted their terms of service. The situation evidenced one of the difficulties in dealing with the Indian problem: those who served on the frontier were volunteer troops, and three-year enlistments were running out for many units. Thus, to mount any kind of a campaign, Dodge and Connor had to find and use troops whose enlistments expired later in the year. The 11th Kansas was one such regiment.

Organized during the summer of 1862 by Chief Justice Thomas Ewing, Jr., the 11th Kansas was one of the last units to enter the war. It consisted mostly of teenagers and older family men who were shop owners, clerks, or farmers, prompting one state military history to call the regiment "the most truly Kansan" of all. Its first action occurred on October 20, when the 11th helped to defeat a Confederate force near old Fort Wayne, Indiana. Prior to marching west, the men had been skirmishing with Quantrill and Price in Missouri. When the 11th Ohio, which had been guarding the Oregon Trail through Wyoming, began retiring its companies, Connor ordered the 11th Kansas forward.[15]

Also called to enter the fray was the 16th Kansas Cavalry, stationed at Fort Leavenworth. Organized in 1863, the 16th would arrive later and form one of the three large units that marched north and west to the Powder River. While part of the regiment had participated in the battle of the Big Blue near Westport, Missouri, most of it had seen little action. Within a few months of mustering out, these reluctant warriors took more than two months to march from Fort Leavenworth to Fort Kearny, causing General Mitchell to caustically remark that its rate of progress was the most miraculous event of the war.[16]

Finally, the initial plan included the Pawnee Scouts. Company A, Pawnee Scouts, commanded by Capt. Frank North, arrived at Fort Kearny during the last week in February. The Omaha *Nebraska Republican* remarked on their improved situation and soldierly demeanor:

> These men seem to be greatly improved since their transformation from the ill-clad, poorly fed, roving Pawnees, to the well-cared for position of a soldier. Their appearance generally has elicited some commendatory remarks. They are obedient and ever ready to do the duties required of them. It is certainly to be desired that all prejudice may be withdrawn from them, and a chance given them to show their ability and aptitude to become citizens in common with a more highly favored race.[17]

On February 24, Colonel Livingston returned to Fort Kearny and immediately sent a detachment of twenty-five men from Company A of the Pawnee Scouts under Lieutenant Small to scout north to the Niobrara River. Livingston also prohibited wagons from leaving Fort Kearny unless they were in organized bands. On February 26, a government train of 130 wagons, loaded chiefly with corn, left for Julesburg, escorted by Company D, 1st Battalion, 2nd Nebraska Cavalry. Flooding east of Fort Kearny made operations difficult, a number of roads and trails being closed. At Atchison, Kansas, the trains of the newly reorganized Butterfield Overland Express began to move again. Reported on hand at the Atchison warehouse were four million pounds of freight waiting for transit to Colorado, Utah, and Montana. By the end of February, all was quiet along the Platte route past Julesburg.[18]

Amidst the feeling of relief that the avengers had moved on, and that the army was mobilizing to pursue them, came the thrilling news of the end of the Civil War. In Denver citizens decided to celebrate with a grand illumination. From bank to barbershop, from hotel to hovel, from one end of the city to the other, thousands of lamps and candles dispelled the night. One observer likened the city to one brilliant chandelier. Roman candles sparkled for the sake of Union glory from the offices of Capt. John C. Anderson and elsewhere on Larimer Street. A military parade, led by the 1st Colorado Regimental Band, marched through town to the Denver Theatre, where Colonel Moonlight, Colonel Chivington, and others gave speeches. Pistol shots punctuated patriotic outpourings, and champagne flowed freely in every saloon. The Union had survived, and Denver was safe again.[19]

The belief that the war party had moved northwest from Julesburg and headed for the Black Hills was correct. As the caravan neared the Hills, Brule Indians under Spotted Tail and Pawnee Killer moved still farther west, while the Southern Cheyennes headed north for the villages of the Oglala Sioux and Northern Cheyennes on the Powder River.[20]

As the avenging warriors moved north at a leisurely pace, the scene of action shifted west. The activities of the Cheyennes and the Sioux in Colorado and Nebraska had inspired other bands and subdivisions to respond in kind. Strung out along the Oregon-California Trail in Wyoming were the men of the 11th Ohio Volunteer Cavalry, which had come west in 1864. It was now their turn to feel the might of Plains Indians on the warpath. In addition to guarding routes of transportation, these troops also had the job of maintaining the Pacific Telegraph, which came up from Julesburg, via Lodgepole Creek. The major post in the region was Fort Laramie, activated in 1849 and the scene of the Great Treaty of 1851. Eight miles southeast on August 19, 1854, a small detachment of infantry from Fort Laramie led by the young hot spur 2nd Lt. John Grattan had died in a fight with several thousand Brule Sioux, an event that marked the beginning of concerted conflict.

West of Fort Laramie were a number of tiny garrisons, each about twenty to fifty miles apart, guarding a telegraph office, and subject to constant raiding.[21] In order to protect the stations, the army eventually sent troops to all these places between 1862 and 1864, developing a compound of varying size at each. Also, from time to time other troops spent a few days or weeks at other spots along the main route as a part of duty in

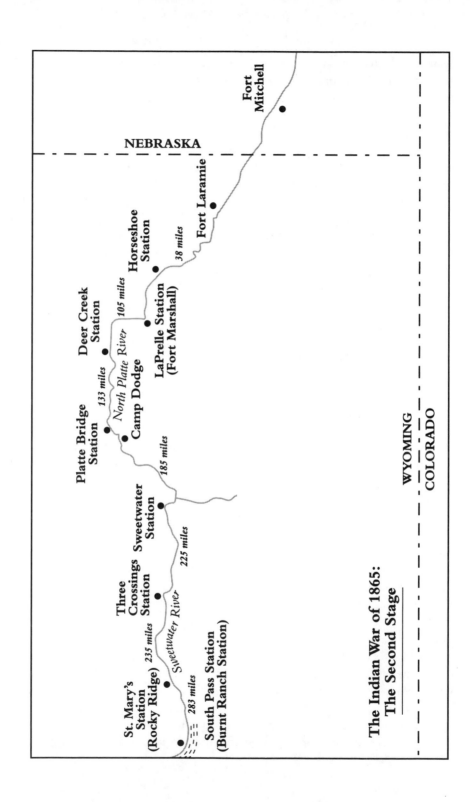

Fort Mitchell

NEBRASKA

Horseshoe Station

Fort Laramie

38 miles

Deer Creek Station

North Platte River

105 miles

LaPrelle Station (Fort Marshall)

133 miles

Platte Bridge Station

Camp Dodge

185 miles

Sweetwater Station

225 miles

Three Crossings Station

Sweetwater River

235 miles

St. Mary's Station (Rocky Ridge)

283 miles

South Pass Station (Burnt Ranch Station)

WYOMING

COLORADO

The Indian War of 1865:
The Second Stage

patrolling the road and repairing the line. Some of these fixed outposts were tiny, with a force varying from five to twenty enlisted men, while others, especially after 1864, grew to house a company or more. In a reminiscence, Stephen H. Fairfield of the 11th Kansas remembered that most of the smaller garrisons had log stockades with portholes for defense. Drawings by Lt. Caspar Collins show that compounds were usually square. The enclosure at La Bonte, for example, measured about 100 by 100 feet, and that at Deer Creek about 75 by 75 feet.[22]

Fighting began in the west on February 13, when Company G of the 11th Ohio engaged Sioux warriors near La Prelle Creek. Capt. Levi M. Rinehart was killed in the skirmishing. Succeeding him in command of the company was 1st Lt. Henry Bretney. Born in Springfield, Ohio, in 1840, Bretney had attended Wittenburg College, planning a college teaching career. He could write and speak French and German.[23] John Lafferty, a private in his company, recalled that when at Camp Dennison, Ohio, Bretney proved himself a splendid runner who could outjump anyone: "there was not a stouter or more robust man in our Regiment."[24]

James Patton, another enlisted man, remembered Bretney's leadership and compassion:

> [He was] always kind and looking after the welfare of his men; always ready to share their hardships and dangers; never shirking any duty, however hazardous; never saying "go" but "come on boys." While discreet, he knew no such word as fear, and was a man among men, and generally loved by all the privates soldiers of the Regiment, but envied by some of the officers of the Regiment for his popularity amongst the common soldiers. He would always help anyone who was sick or in distress. Gave up his private room, to me at Sweet Water when I was wounded, and personally watched over me until I was past the critical point; gave and put on me his cotton shirts when I was lying wounded, as woolen shirts were not good for me. This was in June, 1865.

Patton also remembered Bretney's gray horse, "Old Comanche," calling the animal "a race horse indeed."[25]

Caspar Wever Collins was the junior officer of Company G. The son of William O. Collins, the commander of the 11th Ohio, he was born at Hillsboro, Ohio, on September 30, 1844. Trained as a civil engineer, he was an accomplished mapmaker.[26] Collins came west with his father in the summer of 1862, participating in every expedition, acting as clerk, engineer, and draftsman. While in the West, he learned to speak Sioux fluently. Having obtained a commission as a 2nd lieutenant in Company G, 11th Ohio, on June 30, he joined his father's regiment at Fort Laramie on October 17, 1863. His company protected the telegraph line from Horseshoe Creek Station to South Pass Station.[27] In personal appearance, some described him as boyish, slight, and delicate. Others characterized him has slender, medium in height, and rather ordinary in appearance. He sported crisp sideburns. All agreed that he was an expert horseman, efficient hunter, and good poker player.[28]

Company G was soon to experience the difficulties of service on the Oregon Trail. In a reminiscence, John Lafferty recalled the hard duty:

> We were often out all night on marches and raids, and would have to lie on the ground with our saddles for pillows and no protection from the rains and cold. We also had to haul feed for our horses for several miles in the winter and this was awfully hard on all of us. And some of our boys were badly frozen and a few lost their hands and feet.[29]

On March 8 near Poison Creek, Arapahos attacked Pvts. William T. Kame and Philip W. Rhodes of Company G when they were driving a wagon from Platte Bridge to Sweetwater Station. In a running fight, they killed Rhodes, but Kame kept on driving his team, returning the raiders' fire until dark. Taking a horse from the wagon, Kame hurried to Sweetwater Station, reaching there at midnight.[30] Outpost commander Caspar Collins wired the news to Bretney at Platte Bridge. At the same time, he sent a party to pursue the Indians and recover Rhodes's body. Bretney did the same. C. B. Cook remembered that Bretney's night march was "the worst thing I ever was in" and remarked that "the only way we could keep from being lost was by keeping sight of the man and horse ahead of us." After finding Rhodes's frozen body, the detachment returned to Platte Bridge.[31]

On March 28, 1865, 11th Ohio troops skirmished with Indians at Camp Marshall. The following day, newspapers finally reported some good news: General Mitchell had captured 150 lodges of Sioux and 90 Arapahos about 150 miles north of Fort Laramie. One source estimated the number of prisoners at 1,440 persons. Central City's *Miner's Register* cautioned their captors to beware of treating them too well, reminding its readers of one of Aesop's fables, where a farmer found a snake in the field that had been chilled through and nearly frozen. The farmer placed the reptile in his bosom, but when the snake regained its vitality, it bit its benefactor and caused his death. In completing the analogy, the newspaper remarked, "The Indians have never been known to keep their pledges of peace, when it better suited their notions to go to war."[32]

In truth, the Indians were heading for Fort Laramie to make peace. Included in the group were Little Thunder and Spotted Tail's sixty lodges of Southern Brules and Swift Bear's Corn Band. They had planned to join the long-standing camp of friendly Brules and Oglalas, known in some circles as the Laramie Loafers. For many years, these Lakota had camped near Fort Laramie, intermarried with whites, and raised half-blood offspring. The Oglala Old Smoke, a fat and jovial chieftain and a great friend of the whites, had been the camp's leader, but he died in 1864 and Big Mouth took his place. Scorned by their wild brethren in the north, these Indians were more aware of the power of the whites and their overwhelming numbers and, consequently, realized the ultimate futility of war. The newcomers reached Fort Laramie on April 14.[33]

Immediately, the army found an important use for some of the warriors. Between thirty and forty of the young men joined a newly created scouting unit. Formed into two squads and supplied with a small amount of ammunition, muskets and revolvers, and a uniform consisting of an old-style dragoon cap and jacket, they served as an intelligence arm in the immediate vicinity, reporting the comings and goings of nonmilitary personnel and Indians to their commander, a white scout named Charles Elliston. He had married a Sioux woman and lived in the Indian camp near the post.[34]

While the fighting continued in March and April, a changing of the guard was taking place. On April 1, Companies A, B, C, and D of the 11th Ohio were mustered out at Omaha, Nebraska, and the 11th Kansas was on its way to Fort Laramie. The new regiment arrived on April 9, led by Col. Thomas Moonlight, formerly the head of the District of Colorado and the new commander of the north subdistrict of the Plains, now headquartered at the post. Moonlight was to take center stage for the next several months in the Indian War of 1865.

A veteran of many campaigns, Thomas Moonlight was an ambitious man, a politician, and a forceful orator. A Scottish emigrant at the age of thirteen, he had served as an enlisted man in the Seminole War and as an orderly sergeant and chief commissary clerk at Fort Leavenworth before leaving the service in 1859 to farm in Kansas. He raised a battery of artillery at the beginning of the Civil War and became its captain. In September 1862, he received his commission as lieutenant colonel of the 11th Kansas Infantry, the unit later becoming the 11th Kansas Cavalry. He brought with him a reputation for fondness of strong drink. While commander of the District of Colorado, Moonlight was noted for issuing organizational orders of various kinds and making inflammatory speeches to local citizenry. Now he found himself close to the front lines in the burgeoning war in the west.[35]

The trip to Fort Laramie in winter did not endear General Connor to the troops of the 11th Kansas and was but the first incident in what was to be a mutually distasteful relationship. In his history of the 11th Kansas, published in the *Leavenworth Daily Conservative* eight months later, Moonlight railed at his treatment: "My regiment crossed the Plains in dead of winter, suffering horribly from the cold. About three hundred men marched all the way on foot, having not received horses. This, I presume, was a reward of merit for their gallantry and devotion during the border campaign. I look upon it as the greatest outrage that was perpetuated on any regiment."[36]

After reaching Fort Laramie on April 9, the troops made camp nearby. About 4:00 P.M. the next day, the volunteers learned of Lee's surrender. The result was unbridled celebration and a sleepless night. As Charles Waring put it, "Officers and men lost control of themselves and did many foolish things."[37] When the men reached Deer Creek on April 14, they learned of Lincoln's assassination. According to Waring, some men wept and others raged beyond all reason, calling upon their officers to lead them South to "clean out the whole country."[38] While his regiment marched farther west, Moonlight remained at Fort Laramie, where he assumed command of the north subdistrict of the Plains on April 26.[39]

On April 19, the 11th Kansas reached the Upper Platte Crossing and Platte Bridge Station. About six miles south, in the foothills of the Laramie range, Lt. Col. Preston Plumb established regimental headquarters, giving it the name Camp Dodge. The job of the 11th Kansas was to patrol the road between Fort Laramie and Platte Bridge, stationing detachments at Horse Shoe Creek, La Bonte, Deer Creek, and other places. Company G of the 11th Ohio continued to provide major service west of Platte Bridge, aided by other units, including Galvanized Yankees.[40] Companies H and I of the 11th Kansas eventually went to Sweetwater Station, and then detachments from these companies went on farther west to Rocky Ridge and Three Crossings. The troops were mostly on foot, the men having lost many of their mounts in Indian raids along the trails.[41]

As spring blossomed, raiding became more frequent. On April 21, Pvt. John Donjon of the 11th Ohio lost his life in a fight with Indians on La Prelle Creek, and the new Kansas troops had their first skirmish shortly thereafter. The *Denver News* reported on April 25 that a few days before, a large body of Indians had attacked Major Adams of the 11th Kansas and a detachment of thirty men twenty miles north of Deer Creek. Troops killed ten and captured six ponies, losing five horses killed. On April 23, Pvt. L. E. Timmons died in an exchange of fire with a party of Indians at Camp Marshall.[42]

While this was going on, an execution took place at Fort Laramie. The victim was Big Crow, a Cheyenne Indian who had been arrested on February 9 and charged with being a murderer and spy. He had been identified as one of the leaders of the band of Cheyennes that had warred on settlers on the Little Blue the preceding fall. Incriminating evidence was the scalp of a white woman tied to his belt.[43] When 11th Ohio troops returned from their battles with the Sioux and Cheyennes at Mud Springs and Rush Creek on February 14, they were in an unforgiving mood, and when they learned that Big Crow was in the guard house, the men acted. Rushing into the building, they lassoed the Indian with a lariat and dragged him outside. He had been fixed with a leg chain and iron ball, and some of the men pulled on this, while others yanked on the rope in another direction. Hearing the commotion, Colonel Collins appeared and, working his way in among the mob, drew his sword and sliced the rope, the men pulling on it going down in a heap. Order was restored, and Big Crow returned to his cell.[44] On April 24, however, the Cheyenne's luck ran out. On April 22, the commanding officer at Fort Laramie, Lt. Col. William Baumer, received this telegram from General Connor: "Take Big Crow to the place where soldier was killed yesterday, erect a high gallows, hang him in chains and leave the body suspended."[45] This was about a mile and a half west of the post.

When the time came to transport the prisoner to the gallows, Big Crow began singing his death song. When they arrived at the scaffold, chains were placed about his neck and his hands tied with rope in front of him. When the wagon pulled away, Big Crow was able to grab the chain, and with his great strength hoist himself up to the crosspiece.[46] There he sat, while his captors decided what to do. Some wanted to shoot him, but the orders said hanging. Finally, a powerfully built young soldier climbed up the chain and grabbed the Indian, both falling to the ground.[47] This time there was no reprieve. Big Crow was hanged with the ball and chain that had manacled him still attached to his leg, and it was not long before the body decayed sufficiently so that the weight of the ball pulled off the limb, and there the grisly remains stayed as a warning to others.[48]

Early in May, Colonel Moonlight took his first offensive initiative. On May 3 he led an expedition to find a camp of 300 lodges of Cheyennes who had been raiding west of Fort Laramie, which he believed to be located in the Wind River Valley. His force consisted of 500 cavalry from the 11th Kansas, 11th Ohio, and 7th Iowa. Included in the group were Lieutenant Bretney and twenty men of Company G. Snow and cold weather made the journey difficult. According to a member of Company K, 11th Ohio, at one point Moonlight mistook a herd of antelope for a large party of Indians. Instead of attacking with his own regiment, he ordered Bretney's poorly mounted detachment forward. This incident increased the bad feelings developing between the 11th Ohio and the 11th Kansas that would surface during the battle of Platte Bridge about three months later.

Moonlight's expedition reached Wind River on May 12, but the scouts, who included Jim Bridger, could not find a trace of recent Indian activity. They did find some old trails indicating movement toward Powder River. The expedition returned a week later empty-handed.[49] One 11th Ohio soldier remembered the expedition as the time "when he [Moonlight] was hunting for them in opposite direction where their trail led."[50] However, the Sioux and Cheyennes followed the colonel closely on his return and made their presence known by raids at many stations along the line.

Depredations also continued along the Oregon Trail in Nebraska. On May 12, twenty-five Indians attacked a squad of Company H, 1st Nebraska Veteran Cavalry, near Gillman's Ranch, fifteen miles east of Cottonwood Springs. Despite being wounded in the thigh and shoulder, Pvt. Frances W. Lohans kept the attackers at bay, preserving the property in his charge. The bodies of three Indians were later recovered. Lohans received the Medal of Honor for his gallantry on this occasion.[51] On the same day Indians attacked four soldiers in a wagon near Smith's station, twenty-five miles west of Cottonwood, killing Sergeant Creighton of Company A, 1st Battalion, Nebraska Veteran Cavalry.[52]

After returning to Fort Laramie on May 23, Moonlight wrote a report of his fruitless foray. In it he simply noted that he had been too late to catch the Cheyennes, whom he believed had gone north, and then made a recommendation. He stated that "It is no . . . use to attempt to do . . . anything unless an expedition is started, striking Powder River about one hundred miles north of where I was, that is north of here and west where a large and strong fort should be built. . . . The Cheyenne[s] and Sioux who are with them will number about (4000) four thousand fighting men. No time to be lost in making campaign but horses are in a poor condition, having had no corn for a month."[53]

On May 11, General Connor took steps to deal with trouble along the 400 miles of the Overland mail route from Camp Collins to Green River, Wyoming. He sent five companies of the 11th Kansas under Lieutenant Colonel Plumb to Fort Halleck to reopen the road, using cavalry mounts to pull mail stages and soldiers as drivers.[54] While important in keeping routes of communication open, this move left the little force guarding the Oregon Trail and the Pacific Telegraph short-handed.

The success of the Sioux and their allies in raiding along the Oregon Trail and elsewhere prompted young men of other tribes not normally inimical to whites to share in the hostilities. One such example occurred in Nebraska on the Little Blue River on May 18. About 2:00 P.M., fifteen to twenty Indians attacked eighteen men of the 3rd U.S. Volunteers (Galvanized Yankees) riding in a wagon two miles east of Elm Creek Station. The men were en route to Fort Kearny from Fort Leavenworth. They were unarmed, having been in the hospital. The warriors killed two men and wounded six. Pvt. John Twyman received three blows from a U.S. saber and lost his scalp but survived. Two or three Indians were dressed in old government pantaloons, others in buckskin leggins. One had a revolver, and it was he who killed one of the enlisted men. When the soldier begged for his life, the warrior responded, "God d—n you, I'll give you quarter," and shot him dead. One of the Indians identified himself as Cheyenne, but the soldiers believed them to be Pawnees, several having roaches, and subsequent investigations proved this to be true.[55]

The stage driver decided to wait an extra day before leaving Elk Creek Station, and on May 20 the coach left at daylight. A few miles out, near Liberty Farm, twenty-five Pawnees suddenly emerged from the bluffs and charged the coach. While the horses were running at full speed, Willie Kehler and two other men got on top of the coach and kept up a continuous fire. The attackers fired between 200 and 300 arrows without effect. One Indian was killed, which Kehler accomplished with his heavy rifle. In about six or seven miles they reached their next stop and continued to Denver without incident.[56]

In late May, the Sioux and Cheyennes seemed to be everywhere, attacking the army's little outposts guarding the trail west of Fort Laramie. On May 20, 1865, large numbers of Indians skirmished with troops at Three Crossings, losing one warrior. The defenders were in danger of being overrun, and only the last-minute dramatic arrival of troops from other stations saved them.[57] On May 21, warriors appeared at Deer Creek. Second Lt. William B. Godfrey and three men of the 11th Kansas exchanged shots with about twenty-five warriors three miles above Deer Creek Station, killing two.[58] In their nearby work camp, Sergeant Smythe and six men withstood an attack of fifty warriors, killing three. At the same time, 200 Indians captured the soldiers' horse herd. On May 24, three warriors tried to run off the herd at Sweetwater Station, losing one man.

The next day, Indians attacked the Green River stage station, driving off the stock.[59]

While this was taking place, General Connor arrived at Fort Kearny. With him were Senator Schyler Colfax, Lieutenant Governor Bross of Illinois, representing the *Chicago Tribune,* and A. D. Richardson of the *New York Tribune.* The men were on a tour of the plains, headed eventually for California. Connor and his party received an eleven-gun salute upon arrival. The men were pleased to find shelter, having just passed through a hail storm whose stones were the size of Hickory nuts. The dignitaries departed later in the day.[60]

On May 26, at Fort Laramie, Colonel Moonlight retaliated for Indian depredations and mistreatment of a white woman by hanging the Oglala Sioux chiefs Two Face and Black Foot. On May 15, Charles Elliston's Indian scouts had discovered a group of Sioux camped about ten miles east of Fort Laramie. This turned out to be Two Face's band of Oglalas. Discovered among them was Lucinda Eubank and her small daughter. They had been kidnapped by the Cheyennes in raids along the Little Blue in August the year before. Mrs. Eubank was nearly naked and in wretched condition, having just been pulled across the North Platte with a rope.

While some of the band initially fled, Elliston's men captured most after several days. They confined Two Face in the guardhouse. On May 24, guided by information garnered from Mrs. Eubank, the Indian scouts also captured Black Foot's band of Oglalas. Located about 100 miles northwest on Snake Fork, this camp contained Chief Black Foot, 4 warriors, 17 women, and 51 children. The men joined Two Face in the guardhouse, making a total of six imprisoned.[61] Discovered in the Indians' remuda were three U.S. horses, six U.S. mules, and five unbranded mules believed stolen. Two Face had $220 in bills, and others had denominations totaling $50. These went to Mrs. Eubank.[62]

Mrs. Eubank's story was a grim one indeed. Although Two Face had purchased the woman and her daughter from her Cheyenne captors as a friendly gesture, he and his followers had mistreated her, compelling her "to toil and labor as their squaw, resorting to some instances in lashes."[63] Furthermore, she had been forced to have relations first with an old Cheyenne chief and later with Black Foot.[64] When she arrived at Fort Laramie, Henry Palmer was at the post. To him she looked twenty years older. In his reminiscence, he graphically described her condition:

Her hair was streaked with gray, her face gave evidence of suffering, and her back, as shown to General Conner [*sic*] and myself,

Col. Thomas Moonlight
*Orator, egoist, and incompetent,
Moonlight commanded the North
Sub-District of the Plains, soon
earning the ire of Patrick Connor
and an early mustering out.*

was a mass of raw sores from her neck to her waist, where she had been whipped and beaten by Two Face's squaws. The sores had not been permitted to heal and were a sight most sickening to behold. The poor woman was crushed in spirit and almost a maniac. I sent an escort with her and her companion, Miss Laura Roper, with an ambulance to Julesburg, where they were placed upon a coach and returned to the east.[65]

From what information he had, Moonlight deduced that Two Face was the leader of the Indians that had raided on the Little Blue and had captured Mrs. Eubank. Informants also told him that Black Foot was a principal in the Mud Springs and Rush Creek battles.[66] Acting upon his beliefs, Moonlight decided to make a statement by hanging the two chiefs. On May 25, Moonlight issued Special Order No. 11:

The Indian Chiefs Two Face and Black Foot of the Sioux nation Oglala tribe, now in confinement at this post will be hung [*sic*] tomorrow at 2 P.M. as an example to all Indians of like character, and in retaliation for the many wrongs and outrages they have committed on the white man. Abundant and satisfactory proof of which has been furnished at these Headquarters; viz., murdering white men, women, and children, keeping white women prisoners and treating them like brutes, stealing government property and inciting the Sioux and Cheyennes to make war on the whites.

The commanding officer of Fort Laramie is charged with the execution of this order and see it properly and promptly carried out. The execution will be conducted in a sober soldierly manner and the bodies will be left hanging as a warning to them. No citizens or soldiers or Indians will be permitted to visit or touch the dead bodies without permission from this headquarters or that of this post.[67]

One who did not agree with Moonlight's plan was the Fort Laramie post trader, Col. William Bullock. Fearing repercussions, Bullock called upon the commander to deliver a strong protest. Upon receiving Bullock and hearing his objections, Moonlight replied, "Well, Colonel, you think there will be a massacre: Let me tell you there will be two Indians who will not take part in it. Good day, sir."[68]

Men rose early on the morning of May 26: there was much to do before the hanging. Soldiers polished their weapons, their arms and sabers catching the sun. The post band "discoursed some beautiful strain," and at 1:30 P.M., the men formed in columns to march to the place of execution. The escort brought the chiefs out of the guardhouse. Their arms were tied behind them at the elbows and in front at the wrists, and ropes also encircled their knees and ankles. At 1:40, the line moved forward, the band playing the "Dead March in Saul," the chiefs riding in an army wagon. Soldiers had constructed the gallows from three pieces of heavy timber, two upright with a crossbar on top. Dangling down were two lengths of chain. The chiefs maintained their composure to the end. As the hangmen fastened the chains around their necks, the warriors began to speak in Sioux, saying "Meah washts" ("I am brave"). They declared that they had killed many whites and that they would kill more if they could, but now they had to leave that work to their brothers. The wagon, which served as the launching platform, moved forward, and it was over.[69]

Moonlight reported the hanging to his superiors in a letter to Acting Asst. Adj. Gen. George Price of the District of the Plains. In it he noted that "both of the chiefs openly boasted that they had killed white men and that they would do it again if let loose." Thus, he wrote, he had decided

Hanging of the Chiefs

This sketch by an unknown artist, shows the hanging of Sioux chiefs at Fort Laramie on May 26, 1865.

"to tie them by the neck with trace chains, suspended from a beam of wood, and leave them there without any foothold."[70] One Fort Laramie observer reported that all the Indians camping near the post were in bad humor and the men were sticking close to the fort.[71]

By the end of May, the Sioux and Cheyennes had effectively controlled the North Platte River Road in Wyoming, just as they had immobilized traffic around Julesburg and south to Denver in January and February. Connor's decision to send five companies south in early May may have helped to stabilize that region, but it left troops guarding the Oregon Trail through Wyoming without many resources. Although more units marched west, they were not in sufficient number to make a difference, and before the situation would get better from their standpoint, it would get worse.

CHAPTER FIVE

Fouts's Fiasco and Moonlight's Mistake

CONNOR ORDERED DISTRICT HEADQUARTERS MOVED TO JULESBURG, where he arrived on May 4 and then left immediately for St. Louis to confer with General Dodge. On his way east, Connor noted the great shortage of corn along the route and that Canadian horses recently purchased for the army were utterly worthless.[1]

On May 30, Connor issued a circular to the commissioned officers stationed in the District of the Plains. In it, he gave voice to a number of concerns. Foremost was the problem of respect.

> The General Commanding the District takes this opportunity to say, that he has for some time noticed, with regret and decided disapprobation, a disposition on the part of some of the officers of the command, to indulge in a spirit of scandal, and comment on the act of their fellow officers. Slander and backbiting, whether relating to inferiors or superiors in rank, are, not only distinguishing marks of ungentlemanly conduct, but indicative of a want of sense, breeding and decency, even where indulged in by civilians, but when such a spirit pervades, to any extent, in a camp of soldiers, where gentlemen, in the highest sense of the term, are supposed to be wearing the insignia of their country's honor, it cannot be too strongly reprobated. Not only does it degrade the cloth worn by the soldiers of the country, but its demoralizing effect on the enlisted men, is both marked and detrimental. Quarreling and bickering among commissioned officers, from whatever cause, are the prolific source of some of the evils which afflict a camp, and

promote to an alarming extent insubordination among enlisted men.

Connor went on to point out that such disrespect was in violation of the letter of army regulations and would not be tolerated. Those having serious questions regarding the conduct of an officer had recourse to prefer charges against him. Furthermore, he cautioned his subordinates about contracting personal debt and fraternizing with enlisted men. He instructed them to be circumspect in deportment, giving proper attention to their uniforms, and asked them to be prompt in their dealings.[2]

Soon after, he issued another circular setting forth his policy in Indian campaigns:

> Officers commanding expeditions ordered out will not leave a trail after once striking it until they have overtaken and punished the Indians. Hostile Indians will be pursued and punished without reference to sub-district lines. The war must be prosecuted with the utmost vigor and energy. By this means only can we expect a lasting and beneficial peace. Parleys will not be held with the Indians. They must first be severely chastised and given to understand that punishments and not presents as heretofore, will in future be meted out to them for their crimes. By such a course alone can we hope for a peace of any duration. They have massacred our men, women and children, burned, stolen and otherwise destroyed our country, and committed outrages upon innocent women which sicken the soul and crush the pleadings of mercy. They are now to feel that by good conduct only can they be saved from annihilation, before we will listen to any terms with them. No outrages will be perpetuated upon their women and children, neither will they be killed.[3]

The *Rocky Mountain News* lauded Connor's circular, calling it "the best document that has blessed our eyesight for many a day . . . full of that good, hard, practical sense."[4]

The hard line laid down by Connor in this and earlier pronouncements probably affected Moonlight's actions concerning the captors of Lucinda Eubank. The death of the chiefs, however, did not seem to affect the depredations of the Sioux and Cheyennes. If anything, it may have inspired them to greater efforts. On the day of the execution, warriors tried to capture the herd at Sweetwater Station. Forty-eight hours later, about 150

Indians burned the Rocky Ridge compound. The five 11th Ohio enlisted men stationed there sought cover in a nearby dugout. When two of the men tried to enter the cave at the same time, they found themselves wedged and immobile. A great deal of frantic digging finally freed them. The raiders fired the buildings, and eventually flames reached a store of black powder. The explosions that followed caused the Indians to withdraw, but not before Pvt. Bruce Vandoren wounded one warrior in the leg.[5]

Before he left the station when the attack began, Pvt. Chavil St. Clair grabbed a telegraph key and some wire. After the Indians left, he was able to contact Fort Bridger, and he and his comrades went on to South Pass Station.[6] In his telegraphic message, St. Clair noted that because they had been separated from their ammunition, the detachment had been unable to respond effectively. Upon hearing this, Colonel Moonlight called it a "convenient excuse." In a telegram to his adjutant on June 3, he expressed his repugnance concerning the behavior of all those guarding this line, singling out officers for special censure. "Every officer who has had stock taken from him by Indians unless in extreme cases," he ranted, "should be dismissed from the service." He noted, however, that none of the men in his own regiment, the 11th Kansas, had lost stock, and they had killed several Indians. The only other regiment along the Oregon Trail in large numbers was the 11th Ohio, and Moonlight made still more enemies.[7]

Lieutenant Bretney and eight men of the 11th Ohio soon arrived from Platte Bridge to begin reconstruction of the outpost at Rocky Ridge.[8] There they found a company of the 1st Nevada from Fort Bridger already at work. General Connor named the new compound St. Mary's Station.[9]

The raiding continued unabated during the last days of May. On May 28, thirty Indians stole four horses and two mules from soldiers at Sweetwater Station. They also ran off army stock at the sawmill at Laramie Peak and skirmished with troops at Pole Creek. On the same day, sixty warriors attacked Elkhorn Station, dispatching one man of Company E, 11th Ohio.[10]

On May 29, warriors twice engaged a wagon train traveling between Platte Bridge Station and Fort Laramie, killing one of the men in the party. About 5:00 P.M. the next day, 300 warriors harassed Three Crossings Station, destroying telegraph wire. Ninety troops came to the rescue, reaching the outpost at 9:30 P.M.[11] Because of the gravity of the situation, General Connor directed soldiers at Fort Rankin near Julesburg to prohibit emigrant travel beyond that point, allowing only the military and government contractors to use the route. The rest were told to continue south on the Overland Mail route.[12] In response to the attacks, the commanding officer at Platte Bridge improved security at Platte Bridge Station, stationing a noncommissioned officer at Richard's Bridge as a lookout, hidden during the day in the house on the south side of the river. He also increased the number of men protecting the night herd to ten.[13]

At 3:00 P.M. on June 3, ten warriors opened fire on troops at Platte Bridge Station from the opposite or south bank of the North Platte River.[14] Fire from a mountain howitzer caused the raiders to seek cover beyond the bluffs. A twenty-one-man detachment under Colonel Plumb caught the fleeing party after a five-mile run.[15] In the skirmish that followed, the volunteer troops killed an Indian pony and wounded two warriors. Disaster almost occurred, however, when a number of men on the best horses drew far in advance of the rest, and Indians turned on them.[16] At the same time, other warriors began to appear here and there. The timely arrival of twenty men from Companies A and F of the 11th Kansas from Camp Dodge saved the day for this group. Six or seven others, however, rode into an ambush that resulted in the deaths of Pvt. William T. Bonwell, Company F, 11th Kansas, and Pvt. Tilman Stahlnecker, Company G, 11th Ohio.[17] Troops found Bonwell's body the next day, scalped, minus fingers, and otherwise mutilated. In his report, Plumb claimed one Indian killed and four to six wounded.[18]

While troops skirmished with the Sioux and Cheyennes in late spring, Platte Bridge Station lost its oldest resident. On June 6, the builder of the bridge, Louis Guinard, disappeared without a trace. Several months' later, however, one of the man's high-top boots surfaced in the river. It contained part of a man's leg and foot. The finder presented the vestige to Guinard's Shoshoni widow, who hung the boot on the wall where it became a sort of miniature scaffold for her dearly departed.[19]

Action shifted south to the Overland route. On June 2, the Sioux killed two emigrants near Willow Creek, stripping them and filling their bodies full of arrows.[20] At daylight on the morning of June 8, about 100 Indians attacked Sage Creek Station. Defending it were Cpl. W. H. Caldwell and four enlisted men, Pvts. George Bodine, Perry Stewart, Orlando Ducket, and William Wilson, all of Company K, 11th Ohio. Two civilians were also present. After an hour of severe fighting, with ammunition running low, the men left the compound on horseback. Warriors immediately surrounded them, however, and they had to fight their way through, heading for Pine Grove Station. In the skirmish, the raiders killed Bodine and Stewart, captured Ducket, and wounded Corporal Caldwell and Private Wilson. Reaching Pine Grove Station, Caldwell and Wilson joined troops retreating to Sulphur Spring Station, where, reinforced, they retraced their route. They found the bodies of Bodine, Stewart, and one civilian lying in the road, horribly mutilated. No trace of Ducket or the other civilian was ever found. When the detachment reached Sage Creek, they found the station a smoking ruin.[21] During the next two weeks, Indians concentrated their efforts on acquiring horses. The Overland Stage Company lost eighty-seven heads between the Cherokee and Sulphur Springs Stations. Local sources identified the Arapaho as the guilty parties.[22]

On June 9, trouble was reported in the Yellowstone River Valley. The agent of the Missouri River and Rocky Mountain Wagon Road Company, M. Courtright, left Yellowstone canyon on May 15. His job was to take two ferryboats down the Yellowstone River to the crossing of Clark's Fork and the Bozeman crossing of the Big Horn. With him were Colonel Smith of the 14th Wisconsin, D. Shrike, J. Donnelly, and Scout Mitch Bouyer. When the party reached the junction of the Bozeman and Bridger lines on June 9, about 100 Sioux warriors appeared. The Indians first appeared friendly and dismounted, but after a short talk, the chief drove the horses away, and the Sioux opened up, killing Colonel Smith in the first fire. Wounded in the hip, Bouyer shouted to his companions to head for the brush. Securing cover, the men crossed the creek and moved up a ravine, never stopping for thirty-six hours until they reached Snow Mountain. Leaving Bouyer with rifle and ammunition, the others set out for Yellowstone Canyon, about thirty-five miles away. They reached their destination on June 13; Bouyer arrived twenty-eight hours later.[23] Raiding in the north country continued in mid-June as Indians killed N. W. Burrows and ten men below Fort Benton.[24]

Early in June, military leaders turned their attention to the friendly Indians that had been camped near Fort Laramie. Some estimated that there were 1,500 Sioux in residence after the southern Brules and Oglalas arrived in April. At first the Indians camped near James Bordeaux's Ranch, about eight miles east of the post. A trader in the region for nearly three decades, Bordeaux had married a Brule woman and kept cordial relations with the tribe.[25]

Early in the spring of 1865, officials ordered the camp reestablished about eight or nine miles up Cherry Creek. The village remained there about two months, the Indians having difficulty finding enough to eat. The army provided the ever-expanding group with condemned rations, and cattle from Bordeaux's herd were sacrificed. As summer neared, the Oglalas received word to return to the vicinity of Fort Laramie and the Brules to return to Bordeaux's Ranch. In early June, Secretary of War Stanton decided that the Sioux should be transferred to Fort Kearny, where they would be out of the firing line, and tribesmen would be made to put in a crop to provide for their support until the Office of Indian Affairs assumed responsibility.[26] On Sunday, June 4, in a farewell gesture, the Indians entertained the officers with a dog feast. Will Young attended and wrote this in his journal: "At 2 o'clock I, with the other officers, went to a dog feast and ate some dog, oysters, fresh peaches and drank some coffee. I could not tell the taste of dog from any other kind of meat; it was quite a delicacy, though I would not care to make a regular thing of such feasts."[27]

Put in charge of the move was Louis Rubideaux, who obtained transportation and provisions. Colonel Moonlight invited white men who had intermarried with the Indians to go with them, and several took advantage of the offer, including early inhabitants James Bordeaux, Gemenier P. Beauvais, Sefroy Iott, and Leon Pallady. The traders had considerable stock with them, which they drove together at the head of the caravan.[28] On June 11, the Sioux left the area. Soon an escort consisting of four officers and 135 cavalrymen of the 7th Iowa Cavalry and Elliston's uniformed Indian police joined the party, and Capt. William D. Fouts took command, with Rubideaux acting as interpreter.[29]

Born in 1816, William Davenport Fouts was an ordained Methodist episcopal minister and a circuit rider in Illinois until 1857, when he moved his family to Iowa, settling at Albia. He had entered military service as an officer of Company D, 7th Iowa Volunteer Cavalry, on April 28, 1863. He had commanded Fort Kearny for six weeks in the spring of 1864 and Fort Laramie from December 29, 1864, to January 10, 1865. His wife, Charity, and two younger children traveled with him, riding in one of the wagons. Also in the party were the family of one of his subordinates, 1st Lt. J. H. Triggs, and Lucinda Eubank. Also present were the four Indians from Black Foot's band who had been confined in the guardhouse, including Thunder Bear, Yellow Bear, and Calico. Still wearing ball and chain, three of them had been allowed to ride horseback, while the fourth had such a swollen foot that he received permission to travel in a wagon.[30]

For some unknown reason, Fouts had allowed the Indians to keep their weapons but had not allowed troops forming the rear guard to have any ammunition.[31] During the day's journey, some of the young men raced their horses back and forth, which Fouts finally ordered stopped. The first night the caravan made it past Bordeaux's old trading post, and on the second night it camped at a place called Thick Ears. The group spent the night of June 13 camped at the site of the Fort Laramie Treaty of 1851 on Horse Creek, about two miles below its mouth on the North Platte River and twelve miles west of Fort Mitchell. Here troops camped down beyond the east bank and the Indians on the west side.[32]

That night the Sioux held a dog feast and secret council. All of the warriors present, about 400, attended. The men decided they would rather

Capt. William D. Fouts
Captain Fouts lost his life at Horse Creek when Indians being moved to Nebraska rebelled.

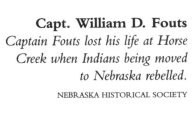

NEBRASKA HISTORICAL SOCIETY

die than go to Fort Kearny to exist in a starving condition and live close to their Pawnee enemies. The more determined planned to make a break for it in the morning, crossing the North Platte and heading north to the Black Hills. The men chose Black Wolf to find a favorable place for crossing. During the night, he and a few others marked a ford by fixing long sticks that showed above the water so that the fugitives could follow them from one side to the other. Resentment continued to heighten as some of the soldiers took Indian women into their beds.[33]

When the troops marched out the next day, the Indians were slow to follow. Returning to investigate, Fouts found a quarrel in progress between peace and war factions.[34] Suddenly, the Brule chief White Thunder fired at Fouts. The captain died instantly, one bullet hitting him in the heart and another in the head. Using a pickax, the attackers tore off the upper part of his head and plunged the tool into his chest. Warriors also killed Standing Elk and three other chiefs who had not wanted to join the revolt. All of the remaining Sioux, including the Indian police, headed for the North Platte. Lt. John Wilcox came back on the run with the 7th Iowa, but the warriors advanced so aggressively that he ordered his command to take a defensive posture behind their wagons. When the rear guard arrived, Wilcox found

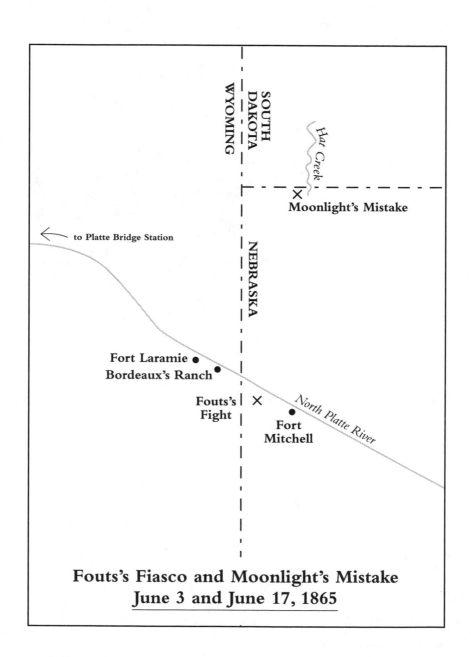

WYOMING

SOUTH
DAKOTA

Hat Creek

✕
Moonlight's Mistake

NEBRASKA

← **to Platte Bridge Station**

Fort Laramie ●
Bordeaux's Ranch ●

Fouts's ✕
Fight

North Platte River

●
**Fort
Mitchell**

Fouts's Fiasco and Moonlight's Mistake
June 3 and June 17, 1865

that Fouts had refused them cartridges. Wilcox was able to put together a force of seventy men mounted on serviceable horses and began pursuit.[35]

When pursuers reached the Platte, Indians were already crossing. Indian ponies had been trained to manage rivers in flood season, and all members of the tribe knew how to swim, so the crossing was accomplished with a minimum of difficulty. A skirmish followed. In the fighting at the river, Wilcox reported a loss of four killed and four wounded and estimated that thirty Sioux were slain. The troops did not attempt to make the crossing, their horses being unused to the task and many of the men being unable to swim. Returning to the campsite, troops recovered Fouts's mutilated body. Wilcox accompanied the whites with Indian families to Fort Mitchell, and afterwards they all returned to Fort Laramie. Bordeaux and the other traders lost their herd of about 400 animals to the Sioux.[36]

Moonlight learned of the disaster on the afternoon of June 14. He quickly gathered a force of 234 California, Ohio, and Kansas Cavalry and set out to recapture the fugitives. After crossing the North Platte, he pursued with such haste that in three days, 103 men had to turn back with spent horses. On the morning of the seventeenth, on Dead Man's Fork of Hat Creek in the far northwestern corner of present-day Nebraska, 120 miles east-northeast of Fort Laramie, 200 Sioux surprised Moonlight and his command during a rest break, stampeding seventy-five horses, about half of which they were able to recover. The horses lost on the march were some of the best in the region. Destroying many saddles and other now useless accouterments, the men returned to Fort Laramie, most of them, including Colonel Moonlight, on foot. In a reminiscence, L. W. Emmons, corporal of Company L, 11th Kansas, remembered that the California troops blamed Moonlight for losing their horses. The mutterings and threats reached such proportions that Emmons feared that his commander might be "plugged in the back by some fool Californian."[37]

One of the California Volunteers later wrote an account of the outing that appeared in the *Rocky Mountain News:*

> The morning of the fifth day had found us about one hundred and forty miles from the Fort, without any grub and nary an Indian. We started and traveled about ten miles, when Moonlight halted to rest in a deep ravine, the banks of which were about sixty feet high on each side, and not more than eighty yards wide from the top of one bank to the other. He ordered us to turn all our horses loose, neglecting to put a picket guard out and stubbornly refused to do so, although Captains Brown and Conrad earnestly entreated him

to put one out, he having kept up to that time a guard twenty-five strong every day.

The consequence was, that, by the time we had turned the horses loose and laid down to rest our ears were greeted with the yells of the Indians from every side. You can bet your life that the California boys were not long in coming to time, and with a yell, and firing as they went, made a rush up the hill at the painted devils, who, not being used to such a reception, scattered in all directions, while Moonlight and the rest of his gang (with a few exceptions) skulked away under the trees, and were as much astonished at our way of fighting as the Indians were.

In about half an hour they had got out of reach of danger with about a dozen of them killed, shot mostly at long range, while we had but one man wounded in the head. As near as could be judged there were five hundred Indians. In the meantime they had stampeded our horses, of which they got seventy head, our two companies losing thirty head. The only order that Moonlight was heard to give during the fight, was "rally around me men," and there he stood with a pistol in each hand and his mouth wide open, the rest of his officers in imitation.

It was through the exertions of Captains Conrad and Brown, and about eight of the men who had caught their horses at the commencement, that many of the horses were saved at all. With many a curse upon Moonlight, we started on our way back, half the company on horseback and half on foot, with not a mouthful of grub, but some beef, which we had to eat without salt; but the next day we met rations sent to us from the Fort, which brought us in all safe after being out eight days.[38]

The California officers also let it be known that Moonlight had been drinking constantly.[39]

In the meantime, General Connor was growing irritable. In a letter of June 15 to General Dodge, he wrote, "Everything appears to work unfavorable, owing to the failure of corn contractors, and incompetence of some of my subordinates."[40] Of the subordinates referred to, Moonlight was first in line; Connor was highly critical of the colonel's handling of his duties. In another letter to General Dodge, he pointed out that his subordinate had allowed the Sioux to keep their weapons for the journey to Fort Kearny, making it possible for them to escape. When Connor received word of Moonlight's failed expedition, he moved quickly. On June 20, he wrote Dodge that because of Moonlight's recent "unfortunate" dealings with Indians, he had relieved him from command of the north subdistrict.[41] On July 7, Connor informed Dodge that he had ordered Moonlight to Fort Kearny to be mustered out, his administration having been "a series of blunders."[42] Apparently not satisfied with dismissal by mail, Connor met Moonlight at Court House Rock and told him exactly why he had ordered him mustered out.[43]

On June 22, Connor transferred his headquarters to Fort Laramie to make arrangements for the forthcoming campaign.[44] In the meantime, ranking officials in the army had been continuing to plan a concerted movement against the Plains Indians. The plans, however, had changed considerably. Bad weather, flooding, and lack of cavalry horses had complicated things, but the overriding cause for delay was the failure to obtain supplies on time. General Ford's foray on the Southern Plains had ended in failure as men under his command served out their enlistments and Congress initiated a peace effort that caused him to delay an offensive. Just at the time he received new instructions to proceed, Ford was mustered out. Gen. J. B. Sanborn, commanding the District of the Upper Arkansas, replaced Ford as the commander of the expedition. Two separate, small and light columns were to move up the Republican and Smoky Hills Forks of the Arkansas River, respectively. Their mission was to keep the country between the Platte and the Arkansas River free from Indians and to aid in keeping the great Overland routes unobstructed.[45]

In May, chance circumstances affected the campaign planned for the Northern Plains. Early in the month a group of sixteen Santee Sioux began raiding as far south as Mankato, and Minnesota was in a panic, believing the actions signaled a large-scale outbreak. As a result, Sully received new orders to move from Fort Rice on Indians believed to be concentrated at Devil's Lake, leaving Connor to deal with the Sioux and their allies on Powder River.

Concurrently, politicians were lobbying for a new peace effort. On the same day that Fouts died, General Pope sent a letter to Lieutenant General Grant commenting on a request by Governor Newton Edmunds of Dakota Territory to negotiate a new treaty with the Sioux. Pope recommended more force rather than more coddling, declaring that the Sioux had been on the warpath in that region and only recently attacked Fort Rice. "What have they done to entitle them to presents and annuities," he asked, "unless . . . the violation of former treaties and the murder of whites are to be thus compensated?" Secretary of the Interior James Harlan agreed with Pope, and plans for Connor's campaign on Powder River continued. On July 22,

Harlan issued a circular to the Superintendent of Indian Affairs and all Indian agents in which he stated that in future dealings with hostile tribes, the Interior Department would subordinate its actions to the policy of the Department of War. At the moment, this meant that Indian superintendents and agents were to make no deliveries of money and goods to warring bands or have any intercourse with them, except as directed by the military. Harlan also instructed them not to provide information about these activities to the public or to public sources.[46]

Governor Edmunds, however, was not dissuaded. He was able to amend the Indian Appropriations Act for $20,000 to obtain funds to negotiate peace agreements with the Upper Missouri Sioux. As finally constituted, the presidentially appointed treaty commission consisted of Governor Edmunds, Edward B. Taylor (superintendent for the northern superintendency), Major General Curtis, Brigadier General Sibley, Henry H. Reed of Iowa, and Owen Guernsey of Wisconsin. Captain Ruth served as secretary of the commission and R. B. Hill as reporter.

When Edmunds applied for a military escort for his commission, Pope said no, remarking that "there are no Sioux Indians in Dakota Territory with whom it is judicious to make such treaties of peace as you propose."[47] Pope had his own ideas of Indian treaties, and he proposed what he called explicit understandings. Executed by the military and the tribe involved, the treaty would simply require that the Indians keep the peace. If they did not, the army would march through the Indians' country and establish military posts therein. As a natural consequence, their game would be driven off or killed. No presents or annuities would be used as bribes. Pope, however, was preempting the power of Congress, and his ideas went nowhere.[48] However, Edmunds's success did not stop the planned reprisals, and both efforts proceeded their separate ways, pointing out once again difficulties in the divided system of Indian control.

At the same time, yet another peace effort was under way. This one, spearheaded by Senator James Doolittle of Wisconsin, chairman of the Committee on Indian Affairs, was to investigate the "condition of Indian tribes and their treatment by the civil and military authorities of the United States." Prompted by national reaction to the Sand Creek Massacre, this joint congressional committee included Senator LaFayette S. Foster of Connecticut, the new president of the Senate, as chairman; Representative Lewis W. Ross, Democratic member from southern Illinois; and Congressman Higbee. In order to ensure consideration of the army viewpoint, Pope was able to arrange for Maj. Gen. Alexander McCook to accompany the committee.[49] Again, this did not affect the proposed campaign; however, one might expect possible meddling in the future.

To augment Connor's Powder River expedition forces, Dodge had been able to obtain the services of the 2nd Missouri Light Artillery (equipped as cavalry) and the 12th Missouri Cavalry. Commanded by Col. Nelson Cole, this force had orders to march to Loup Fork to receive instructions from Connor. Cole's advance party reached Omaha by steamer on June 18, and his full command moved out on July 1.[50]

Born on November 18, 1833, at Rhinebeck, New York, Nelson Cole grew up in the business world. After building a sugar refinery for Gen. Narisco Lopez in 1854, he had settled in St. Louis. In April, he recruited a company of the 5th Missouri Volunteer Infantry and became its captain. After service in the battle of Wilson's Creek and other engagements, he became lieutenant colonel of the 2nd Missouri Artillery on September 12, 1863, and colonel on March 15, 1864.[51]

In mid-June, reacting to the conditions of war on the plains, General Connor repositioned some of his troops. On June 11, he ordered Lieutenant Colonel Plumb and Companies A, B, F, L, and M of the 11th Kansas to Fort Halleck, where they arrived on June 24. Their task was to reopen the southern mail and stage route. To protect the west end of the line, Connor sent troops from Fort Collins to Green River, the men traveling about 400 miles. Initially, soldiers handled the mail coaches.[52]

As it finally worked out, the Powder River expedition involved about 2,500 men divided into three commands. The plan called for Nelson Cole, with the 12th Missouri Cavalry and the 2nd Missouri Light Artillery, to move along the east and north sides of the Black Hills and then turn west. Lt. Col. Samuel Walker, who commanded six companies of 16th Kansas Cavalry and a detachment of the 15th, had orders to travel directly north from Fort Laramie. Cole and Walker were to join forces somewhere beyond the headwaters of the Cheyenne River. Connor chose to march northwest from Fort Laramie along the eastern flanks of the Big Horn Mountains. He planned to rendezvous with Cole and Walker at the north end of the Panther Mountains in the vicinity of the Rosebud River on September 1.[53]

Samuel Walker commanded the 16th Kansas in the absence of Col. Werter Davis. Born on October 19, 1822, in Franklin County, Pennsylvania, Walker had begun his military career in 1855 as a member of the Free State (Kansas) Volunteers. In 1861 he became captain of Company F of the 1st Kansas Volunteer Infantry, later serving as a major in the 5th Kansas Volunteer Cavalry and becoming lieutenant colonel of the 16th on October 18, 1864.[54] To get everything in readiness for an early departure, General Dodge had ordered Walker's regiment from Fort Leavenworth to Fort Kearny in the dead of winter.[55]

West of Fort Laramie, the raiding continued. On June 17, three warriors surprised Pvt. Silas Henshaw of Company A, 11th Kansas, as he gathered wood about 200 yards from Deer Creek Station. Three arrow wounds proved fatal. Three days later, from forty to seventy-five Arapahos attacked a detachment from Sweetwater Station while they were repairing the telegraph line. Killed was telegraph operator Edgar M. Gwynn. According to one eyewitness, he had been scalped, his hands had been cut off at the wrists, and his heart and liver had been removed.

On June 26, about 300 Cheyennes and Arapahos surprised Lt. W. Y. Drew and twenty-five men from Company I of the 11th Kansas as they worked on the telegraph line near Red Buttes. Expending from thirty-five to sixty rounds of ammunition per man, the troops made it back to Platte Bridge in six miles of hard fighting. Six of the men suffered wounds. Sgt. Isaac Pennock marveled at the way the Indians handled their horses, guiding them by a careening motion of the body from one side to the other and the pressure of the leg. He named them "among, if not the best horsemen in the world."[56] The action near Platte Bridge, however, did not deter migration. On June 28, Major Mackey at Platte Bridge reported that 147 wagons had passed on their way north.[57]

On June 27, the army instituted another reorganization. Abolished was the old Military Division of the Missouri. Created in its place was the Military Division of the Mississippi, with headquarters at St. Louis. Commanding the division was Civil War hero Maj. Gen. William T. Sherman. Under him, General Pope commanded the newly established Department of the Missouri. It encompassed the states of Wisconsin, Minnesota, Iowa, Missouri, and Kansas, and the territories of Nebraska, Dakota, and Montana. Added later were the territories of Colorado, Utah, and New Mexico. This included most of Pope's previous domain, except Illinois, Indiana, and Indian Territory. Dodge was made commander of forces in the field, except for those under General Sully.[58]

On June 30, Connor and staff arrived at Fort Laramie from Julesburg. He was ready to take command of the expedition. He had completed his journey with Senator Colfax and his party, which ended in a banquet in Denver in early June, and he was ready to move.[59] His appearance at Fort Laramie was a signal for military pomp. One observer reported that "a good deal of style [was] displayed. The brass band is now serenading the General and the newly married couple. A marriage in the garrison is of infrequent appearance."[60] Will Young wrote in his journal that "Connor has three columns readying to march against all Indians north and east of Denver and Camp Collins. Waiting for supplies from [the] Missouri [River] to start."[61] After a few days, Connor sent officers down the road to "hurry up" the government freight trains.[62]

Connor had brought with him Companies L and M of the 2nd California Cavalry, a detachment of the 11th Ohio under Capt. Jacob H. Humphreville, and Capt. Nicholas O'Brien's company of 7th Iowa Cavalry with two mountain howitzers. Other units assembled at Fort Laramie, the expedition then moving to Camp Dodge and then on to Garden Creek, four and a half miles southwest of present-day Casper, Wyoming. As delays continued, however, they were sent back to Fort Laramie. In June they moved southwest of Fort Laramie, some twenty miles to the mouth of the Chugwater, because of the need for grass.[63]

The troops celebrated July fourth by artillery and rifle practice. The target of the artillery was a sandstone ledge on the west side of the river opposite the camp. One observer recalled that Nicholas O'Brien made a remarkable shot at a prominent monument that stood on top of the ledge. Several shots had been fired, but all had missed. O'Brien knocked it down with his first shot. Will Young wrote in his journal that Captain O'Brien fired a salute at noon, and the sutler's store was closed for the rest of the day.[64]

On the fifth, Finn Burnett remembered that "every teamster, citizen as well as government employees, were ordered to load all the grain that they could possibly haul on their wagons. Leighton's train was the last one to leave camp, and as we pulled up to the great pile of forage, loading all that we could get on the wagons, there must have been at least two thousand sacks left for lack of transportation."[65]

On July 2, the raiders returned to the Platte Bridge vicinity, cutting telegraph wire. Wounded in the fighting that followed was Sergeant Holding; a min'e ball entered the lower part of his ear. The shooter, believed to be a white man, was himself shot through the breast by Private Hammond.[66] The same day, Maj. Martin Anderson ordered more troops to Platte Bridge Station. This increased the number of enlisted men to 120.[67] About this time, a large party of Sioux and Cheyennes attacked a group of Washakie's Shoshonis on the Sweetwater River. After killing the chief's favorite son, Snow Bird, they mutilated the boy's body within his father's sight and then left with about 400 of their enemies' horses. The Shoshonis followed, recovering their horses and driving off the Sioux.[68]

On July 3, Capt. James Greer received orders to send ten men to Sweetwater Station to repair the telegraph line. The men of the 11th Kansas refused to go in such small numbers. A detail of ten additional men brought the same response, but when ten more men, two teamsters, and one citizen volunteered to make the trip, they assented. The party returned on July 3, and during the next week other detachments worked on the lines between Platte Bridge and Sweetwater Station. On July 4 a strong escort left from Fort Laramie to repair the telegraph line between that post and South Pass.[69]

Repeated raids on soldier stock caused the men at La Prelle Creek to develop a novel way of dealing with the problem. Josiah Hubbard remembered how they gave their horses special training:

> And we were never free from anxiety in regard to our horses and mules, which it was necessary to herd for grazing from one to three miles distant from camp, thus offering a tempting bait to the Indians to attempt their capture by their favorite method of a stampede. We borrowed their tactics to the extent of using the stampede as a protective measure. Twice a day the herd went out to graze, and twice a day it was stampeded back to camp. That is, it was always brought in by a sudden start and on the run, so that the animals were quite effectually trained to stampede for camp.
>
> Sentries were posted to command all approaches to the grazing ground with instruction to fire the moment any suspicious movement was observed, while those in charge of the herd had orders to stampede the animals to camp promptly upon hearing the alarm shot. Twice during our stay at these posts the alarm was given, but on both occasions prompt action combined with previous training, brought the animals safely to camp.[70]

On July 12, 1st Lieutenant Bretney and a detachment of Company G of the 11th Ohio arrived at Platte Bridge Station, and a dispute arose between Bretney and Captain Greer concerning who was in command. Bretney finally terminated the argument, ensconcing himself in the office of the telegraph operator, whom he drove out with cocked pistols. That evening, the men of his company drank copious amounts of whiskey, upsetting some travelers camping nearby. The next day, telegraphic orders confirmed Greer as the post's commander and named Major Anderson of the 11th Kansas as the new commander of the district, with headquarters at Platte Bridge. This meant that Anderson had charge of all troops from Fort Laramie to South Pass.[71] This sequence of events did nothing to improve the strained relations between the 11th Ohio and the 11th Kansas.

Back in Denver, tempers remained hot. The *Rocky Mountain News* in a July 15 article noted that at present, Indians were rampaging in California, Nevada, Arizona, New Mexico, Colorado, Nebraska, Minnesota, Montana, Oregon, and Utah, and that sentiment for extermination grew stronger and stronger. The *Rocky Mountain News* reported that on July 20, or shortly thereafter, a party of the joint committee of Congress, appointed to investigate the civil and military management of Indian affairs, would arrive. The *News* declared, "The people of Denver, being anti-Indian, are not happy to have them come to town."[72] The Doolittle committee was soon to see some of the problem firsthand. On July 30, a party of about thirty Indians attacked a train of emigrants forty miles west of Julesburg, killing and scalping two men and capturing one wagon and team. The rest escaped. Senators Doolittle and Foster passed the spot a short time after, narrowly escaping a fight or capture.[73]

In the west, raiding continued. On July 16, on Rock Creek in Wyoming, a man named West lost his life while out hunting stock. On July 27, Indians attacked an ox train carrying commissary supplies to Salt Lake and killed two men. On July 28, again on Rock Creek, Cheyennes attacked a wagon train, killing Mary Fletcher, wounding her husband Jasper, and kidnapping her daughters, young Mary, age fourteen, and Lizzie, age two. Two other men also lost their lives.[74]

In the middle of July, Connor decided to make an inspection of the southern mail route. On his return to Fort Laramie, he reported that the Indians had possession of the road between Virginia Dale and Sulphur Springs and that he was sending mails over the interrupted part of the line in wagons with large escorts. On July 15, Connor reported that his commissary stores ordered from Fort Kearny and Cottonwood Station for the campaign would arrive in ten days and that the contractor's train in about fifteen. He planned to start the left column in six days with what supplies he had. He noted that he had five companies of the 11th Kansas on the road, but they were "insubordinate and disobedient," due in large part to Colonel Moonlight telling them that they were entitled to be mustered out.[75] He ended his letter by stating that he had heard nothing of the Indians in the north. "They have the best of it at present," he wrote, and added "I wish they had Contractor Buckley under their scalping knives."[76]

On July 21, Connor reported that part of the 1st Nebraska Cavalry stationed at Fort Kearny had mutinied, declaring that the war was over and that they were entitled to discharge. He ordered Colonel Heath to suppress the disturbance with grape and canister and ordered the leaders brought to trial. Again he complained about the delay in supplies, noting that there was only one contractor's train this side of Julesburg, loaded only with bacon. Originally headed for Denver, Connor had the train diverted for his use on the forthcoming campaign. He also reported that he had heard nothing about the mowing machines ordered for Powder River, bemoaning the loss of precious time due to the dalliance of contractors.

The interminable delays finally prompted Connor on July 27 to ask Asst. Adj. Gen. J. W. Barnes to see if he could do something to hurry delivery, declaring that he was starting on his expedition with scant supplies of stores and many barefooted horses.[77] To remedy the situation, Connor had been obtaining some supplies from Denver and other places, acting without regard to the quartermaster for the District of the Plains, Parmenas T. Turnley. In a letter to the chief quartermaster of the Department of the Missouri, Turnley noted that he was as ignorant as an "Afghanistan" concerning the need for the supplies and requested a different assignment.[78]

On July 9, Connor named Henry Palmer as acting assistant quartermaster for the expedition, giving him the responsibility of getting the transportation together. Palmer found that there were only about seventy government wagons at Fort Laramie, and needing nearly three times that amount, he queried Connor. The general ordered him to contract with citizen outfits. Palmer hired forty from Ed Creighton, under charge of Thomas Alsop, thirty from Tom Pollock, and lesser numbers from other entrepreneurs, so that by the end of July, 185 wagons stood ready to roll.[79]

To some, Connor's actions appeared highly irregular, and to others, a violation of regulations. Having received complaints from Lt. Col. Fred Meyers, his chief quartermaster, who had received Turnley's letter, Pope wrote Dodge on August 11, telling him that Connor was ignoring quartermaster and commissary staff and violating law and regulations in making the contracts by himself and forcing officers to pay public money for them. "Stop all this business at once," Pope ordered, "and if necessary relieve Connor from duty and order him to his home." The next day, however, Pope reconsidered and told Dodge that he did not wish to relieve Connor until completion of the Indian expedition and not even then, unless necessary. "It is evident, however," Pope wrote, "that he has been acting with a high hand, and in violation of law and regulations."[80]

Connor issued detailed orders to his two other columns before leaving. To Cole he gave the following instructions:

> You will proceed with your column to the best and most practicable route to the East base of the Black Hills. . . . Move thence along the east base of the Black Hills to Bear's Peak [Butte], situated at the northeast point of the hills and where large forces of hostile Indians are supposed to be camped. From Bear's Peak you will move around the North base of the Black Hills to the Three Peaks, from thence you will strike across the country in a northwesterly direction to the north base of Panther Mountains, where

you will find a supply depot and probably part of my command. You will see by the lines marked out on the map, I enclose herewith, the route to be taken by you and the other columns of the Expedition. If after you turn to the northeast point of the Black Hills, I should desire to change our course or ascertain your whereabouts I will make the fire signals communicated to you by Gen. Heath. You will not make fire signals unless it is to answer mine, or in case you require assistance.

Connor added a controversial dictum: "You will not receive overtures of peace, or submission from the Indians, but will attack and kill every male Indian over twelve (12) years of age." He further reminded Cole that it was reported that a large band of Indians had congregated at the base of Bear Butte and instructed him to endeavor to surprise them.[81] Cole's column consisted of 311 officers and men of the 12th Missouri Cavalry and 797 officers and men of the 2nd Missouri Light Artillery—in all 1,108 men.

Connor's instructions to kill all male Indians over the age of twelve brought a swift rejection from General Pope. On August 15, the assistant adjutant general of the District of the Plains sent a message in which he reported that Pope had disapproved the order.[82]

Lt. Col. Samuel Walker received orders to march directly north from Fort Laramie with six companies of 16th Kansas Cavalry and a detachment of the 15th, comprising a light battery, a total of about 600 officers and men. His instructions were to join Cole's force somewhere beyond the headwaters of the Cheyenne and then rendezvous with Connor's force on about September 1 in the vicinity of the Rosebud River.[83] Walker's command required resupplying, the men being "almost naked" when they reached Fort Laramie.[84] Connor wrote Dodge that he planned to direct the movements of the columns by fire signals.[85]

On July 25, Connor issued orders to his subordinates, in some instances repeating previous instructions:

During the absence of the General commanding, on the Powder river Indian expedition, he places the utmost confidence in the ability of his sub-district commanders to protect the overland mail, telegraph, freighters, emigrants, and settlers within their respective sub-districts.

Troops should always have on hand twenty days' rations of ground coffee, hard bread (with plentiful supply of salt), to be carried on their horses, so that they can be moved out promptly upon receiving any information of hostile Indians. Care should also be taken to have on hand a supply of ammunition.

Officers commanding expeditions thus ordered out will not leave a trail after once striking it, until they have overtaken and punished the Indians. To accomplish this object, the command will be supplied with an extra issue of salt in order that when rations are exhausted the men may kill what game the country affords and subsist upon it. Any officer who abandons a trail without first exhausting every means to overtake and punish the Indians (even if it becomes necessary to subsist on horse-flesh) will be court-martialed and dismissed from the service.

Hostile Indians will be pursued and punished without reference to sub-district lines. The war must be prosecuted with the utmost vigor and energy. By this means only can we expect a lasting and beneficial peace. Parleys will not be held with the Indians. They must first be severely chastised and to understand that punishments, and not presents as heretofore, will in future be meted them for their crimes. By such a course alone can we hope for a peace of any duration. They have massacred our men, women and children; burned, stolen and otherwise destroyed our property, and committed outrages upon innocent women which sicken the soul and crush the pleadings of mercy. They are now to be made to feel that by good conduct only can they be saved from annihilation, before we can listen to any terms with them.

No outrages will be permitted upon their women and children, neither will they be killed. They will be taken prisoners and held by the military authority, subject to further orders from these or superior headquarters.

The General commanding relies upon the active, prompt and cheerful co-operation of every officer and soldier in this district during the coming campaign. All available troops must be continually moving, either in pursuit or in search of hostile Indians.

The mail escorts will be never less than four men—more, if necessary. The escort will always remain within 300 yards of the coach.

Troops, when passing along the telegraph line, will promptly repair the wire whenever required without waiting for orders to do so. Commanding officers will furnish prompt assistance to telegraph operators to repair the lines when down, and they will report to these headquarters any operator who fails promptly to report breaks on the line and to call for necessary assistance to repair them.

It is possible that the hostile Indians now north of these head-quarters may, in small numbers attempt to gain the rear of the advancing columns of the Powder river Indian expedition and commit depredations upon the mail and telegraph roads. While it is thought that these roads are now, or soon will be, sufficiently protected against all efforts they may make, it is deemed advisable, and sub-district commanders are instructed accordingly, to be always prepared to concentrate a sufficient force and immediately pursue and chastise any band of Indians who may exhibit enough temerity to venture upon such a proceeding.[86]

Just as Connor was completing his arrangements, word came of disaster at Platte Bridge Station. The Sioux and Cheyennes had struck again, but this time their numbers were much larger because the avengers had united with their northern tribesman. Such fabled fighting men and leaders as Red Cloud, young Crazy Horse, Little Wolf, and Dull Knife were now joined with their relatives and kinsman. Two units of 11th Kansas and 11th Ohio Volunteers had been trapped outside of Platte Bridge Station and at the nearby Red Buttes. Twenty-eight lay dead, and the survivors feared the worst. Quickly Connor mobilized the nine companies of the newly arrived 6th Michigan Cavalry and sent them hurrying northwest along the Oregon Trail. It was about 100 miles to the little outpost, and time was running out.

CHAPTER SIX

The Battles of Platte Bridge and Red Buttes

By MIDSUMMER, THOUSANDS OF OGLALAS, MINNICONJOUS, BRULES, SANS Arcs, Arapahos, and Northern and Southern Cheyennes were in camp on the Tongue and Powder Rivers.[1] About July 20, they held a war council, agreeing that their next target would be Platte Bridge Station. This was the place where travelers crossed the Upper Platte River to the north side, there to continue on west along the Oregon Trail or swing north to the Montana goldfields. Destroy the bridge, they reasoned, and the hated whites would have difficulty in entering the game lands of the Sioux, Cheyenne, and Arapaho.

After war dances and military preparations, the tribesmen began the journey. George Bent guessed that 3,000 were in the line that stretched for two miles across the plains. Old Man Afraid of His Horses, Young Man Afraid of His Horses, and Red Cloud led the Sioux. Prominent among the Cheyennes were Dull Knife, White Bull, and Roman Nose. To guard against premature raiding, the Foolish Dogs military society policed the caravan in front and rear. On the evening of July 24, the avengers had reached a point about six miles from their destination.

The plan agreed to was simple: ten warriors acting as decoys would lead soldiers toward a big hill to the north, where the rest lay concealed.[2] At about 1:00 P.M., July 25, soldiers at Platte Bridge Station noticed about twenty warriors on the bluffs. A detachment of the 11th Kansas went out to drive them off.[3] Lt. William Drew of Company I, 11th Kansas, remembered the scene:

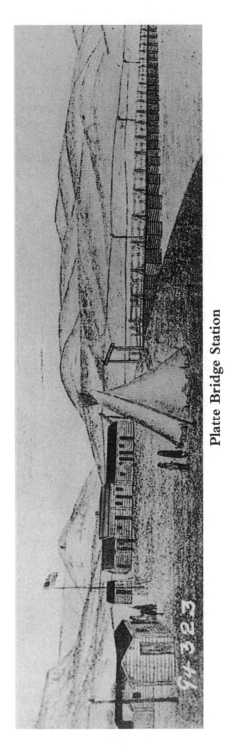

Platte Bridge Station

Located near present-day Casper, Wyoming, Platte Bridge Station guarded the upper crossing of the North Platte River. From a drawing made by Bugler C. Moellman, Co. G, 11th Ohio, in 1863. NATIONAL ARCHIVES

Just after dinner . . . someone called out "Indians." . . . On the north side of the river about 15 or 20 Indians on horseback were moving leisurely along. In a few minutes about a dozen men[4] were mounted, and crossing the bridge, they commenced skirmishing with the enemy. As fast as our men moved on, the Indians fell back, until our men had gone about three miles from the bridge. All this time the Indians were increasing in numbers, until there were about forty in plain sight. . . . At the time an order was received from the station for the men to come back, as the Indians were showing themselves on the south side of the river, east of the station. As our men fell back toward the bridge, Indians kept coming out of the ravine, until there were about fifty in sight, showing that their maneuvering had been for the purpose of leading our men as far away from all support as possible, and to then wipe them out by superior numbers. Our men reached the station without any loss.[5]

About 4:00 P.M., the mail ambulance driver arrived from Fort Laramie and reported that raiders were attempting to run off the cattle herd, located about two miles east. With the mail party was Caspar Collins, having been at the post to secure remounts for his men.[6] Quickly dispatched to the scene were Captain Greer and sixteen men of Company I, accompanied by Corporal Grimm's squad, numbering about 30 men in all.[7] Under the charge of the troops, the warriors began to fall back. A Cheyenne chief, High-Backed Wolf, was shot through the bowels but managed to stay on his pony until he reached a thicket, where he tumbled off. Privates Lord and James discovered the chief lying still. He appeared dead, but when the soldiers began to scalp him, the Cheyenne suddenly sat up and began to plead for his life. They shot him through the brain.[8]

That evening Major Anderson inspected arms. Seventy or eighty of the men had rifles, while the remainder had revolvers.[9] The men of the 11th Kansas had Smith single-shot, breech-loading carbines, while the 11th Ohio troops had seven-shot repeating Spencers, and the 3rd Infantry had Springfield muskets. Anderson found that less than twenty rounds per man remained for the Smith carbines, and not much more for other weapons. Some of the men began running bullets and making Smith cartridges. Spencer cartridges could not be reloaded. The little garrison also had a 12-pounder howitzer that served it well. On June 17, an inspection report noted that the cannon and its forty-eight shells were in good condition.[10]

The avengers spent the night in camp behind the big hill, two miles north of the bridge. The chiefs decided that there were too many soldiers

1st Lt. Henry C. Bretney
*Commanding Co. G of the 11th
Ohio Cavalry, Bretney guarded
the Pacific Telegraph all the
way from Platte Bridge Station
to South Pass.*

FORT CASPAR MUSEUM

in the stockade to risk a direct attack, so they again decided to use the decoy ploy. If this worked, then they planned to storm the stockade.[11]

In the first hours of the morning of July 26, a small detachment reached Platte Bridge Station from the west. Leading the group of ten men of Company G, 11th Ohio, was 1st Lt. Henry Clay Bretney. Capt. A. Smyth Lybe of the 3rd U.S. Volunteer Infantry accompanied the party. Both Bretney and Lybe had been ordered to Fort Laramie to receive pay for their men, the money having just arrived.

Upon arrival, Bretney awakened Major Anderson to tell him that he had passed Sgt. Amos Custard of the 11th Kansas and his wagon train on their way back from Sweetwater Station. Bretney reported that he had encouraged the sergeant to join him, fearing that Indians were in the area and that Custard might have trouble getting in. Custard refused the offer and made his camp at a point about halfway to Platte Bridge, about three miles east of Willow Creek.[12] Bretney offered to take a detachment and go get Custard, but Anderson did not think it necessary.

As dawn broke on the morning of July 26, the garrison consisted of the following: 87 men of the 11th Kansas (70 from Company I, 3 from

Company H, and 14 from Company K), 14 men of Company K of the 3rd U.S. Infantry, and 14 men of Company G of the 11th Ohio. Officers for the 11th Kansas were Major Anderson, commanding; Capt. James A. Greer; and Lieutenants Clancy, Drew, and Walker. Bretney and Collins led the 11th Ohio detachment, and Lybe the 3rd U.S. Volunteer Infantry. In all, there were 7 officers and 113 men.

When Bretney met Anderson in the morning, he again offered to bring in Custard, requesting 75 to 100 men and the howitzer, but the major said no. Anderson did agree, however, to send twenty men, but no Kansas line officer would volunteer to lead the party. August 25 was the mustering out date for the regiment, and none were going to risk their lives unless ordered to do so. Impetuously, Caspar Collins declared he would go if given more men.

The rising sun revealed Indians in vastly increasing numbers upon the hilltop north of the road. The warriors paraded, making warlike gestures and sounding their war cries.[13] Anderson requested to see Collins at 7:00 A.M., telling him that he must take twenty men and rescue Custard. When the young lieutenant objected to the size of the force, the major asked him

Maj. Martin Anderson
Commanding Platte Bridge Station on July 26, 1865, Anderson sent young Caspar Collins to his death.
KANSAS HISTORICAL SOCIETY

if he was refusing to obey his command. Collins answered that he always obeyed orders and left the office.

Anderson instructed Collins not to take the road running west along the river bottom. He was to proceed straight north to the top of the bluff and then turn west, keeping close to the brow of the hill that paralleled the road. He was to join the old road where it ascended to the main ridge. This would take him directly to the wagon train. By taking this route, he would remain in full sight of the fort and have an open view to the north.

Collins's detachment consisted of twenty-five men from Companies I and K of the 11th Kansas, under Sgt. Adolph Hankammer, Sgt. Isaac B. Pennock, and Cpl. Henry Grimm. The men carried single-shot breech-loading .50-caliber Smith carbines. Collins gave his cap to Pvt. James B. Williamson, telling him to keep it to remember him by.[14] At 7:30 A.M., the detachment moved out in high spirits. Wearing a new uniform, Collins had Bretney's pistols in his boots. With a cigar clenched in his teeth, the young lieutenant ordered his troops forward across the bridge.[15]

Lieutenant Drew later described the road and its surroundings:

> Nearly one-half mile west of the bridge, on the north side of the river, there was a growth of willow, forming quite a screen. Nearly the same distance east, on the north side of the river, a deep gulch came down from the north to the river. After crossing the bridge, the road takes a northwest course over the bottom and up on to the bluff, along the edge of which it runs for a mile or two in plain sight of the river and station. The telegraph line runs along on the side of the road. The country north of the road is covered with sand hills and deep ravines.[16]

After the troops left Platte Bridge Station, observers noted two bands of Indians west of the river but south of the road. Major Anderson ordered Bretney and Lybe to take twenty men and follow Collins's detachment on foot to protect his rear. Bretney and his men moved toward the bluffs, while Lybe and his Galvanized Yankees formed a skirmish line to the west. Lybe intended to keep the Indians from cutting off a retreat to the bridge. Some traders, trappers, and citizens, who had been staying at the bridge, soon joined the group, making a total of about thirty men.[17]

When Collins's little command reached the bluff about a quarter mile distant, they saw two Indians atop telegraph poles cutting the wires. The lieutenant ordered an attack, and the charge caused the troops to leave the road and the sight of the river. Immediately, about 400 Cheyenne Dog

Commissary Sgt. Amos Custard

Sergeant Custard stubbornly refused offers of assistance and led a small detachment into a fatal confrontation at Red Buttes. KANSAS HISTORICAL SOCIETY

Soldiers led by Big Horse emerged from the screen of willows near the stream west of the bridge. With war whoops filling the air, the warriors raced north over the bottom land and up the bluff in pursuit of the disappearing column.[18]

Seeing the approach of the Dog Soldiers, Collins wheeled his men by fours left into line, facing south. The rough ground hid other Indians coming from the other directions. Soon they encircled the little command. Seeing that their only hope was to return to the bridge, the soldiers rode forward into the mass of swirling avengers.[19]

The great numbers of warriors crowded together may have saved most of the little force. Many Sioux and Cheyennes did not use firearms for fear of hitting their own tribesmen, but chose lances, tomahawks, and sabers to do their killing. The Shoshonis later told of hearing the chiefs yell, "Stop firing. You are killing our own men."[20] Soldiers also benefitted from the fact that their retreat was downhill, and those warriors who used firearms tended to fire high. Being so close, the warriors grabbed the soldiers' coat collars and tried to pull them from their horses.[21]

During the dash to the bridge, one soldier's horse fell, shot through the body, its rider calling for help. Collins heard the cry, and though he had been shot through the hip, he turned his horse about and came rushing back. For some reason, however, the horse became unmanageable and broke away.[22] Suddenly, an arrow found its mark, lodging itself in Collins's forehead. George Bent remembered seeing Collins through a dense cloud of dust and gun smoke, with "an arrow sticking in his forehead and his face . . . streaming with blood."[23] Collins reached the top of the bluff before falling off his horse; his lifeless body tumbled down the hill before coming to rest.[24]

All but four of the detachment made it to Platte Bridge. Cover fire by Bretney and his followers and a defensive foray by Captain Greer and twenty men of the 11th Kansas were key factors in the escape.[25] A blast from the howitzer helped to scatter the nearest Indians.[26] While the battle of Platte Bridge was over in a half hour—sixty minutes at most—for another hour the Cheyennes and Sioux tried to decoy the soldiers away from the bridge. The defenders had become wary of this tactic, however, and did not leave their secure position.[27]

Killed on the battlefield were Pvts. George W. McDonald and Sebastian Nehring of Company I and Pvts. George Camp and Moses Brown of Company H. Wounded were Sgt. Adolph Hankammer, Cpl. Henry Grimm, and Pvts. Henry W. Hill, Jesse J. Playford, Benjamin P. Goddard, George D. May, Harley L. Stoddard, Harvey Craven, and Andrew Baker.

All were from Company I, except Hankammer, who served in Company K, and Baker, who served in Company L.[28]

After attacking Collins's command, the raiders cut the telegraph wires both east and west. At 9:00 A.M., Anderson sent a detachment of seventeen men under Lt. George Walker to make repairs east of the post, a distance of about two miles. This would allow him to wire Fort Laramie for help. Accompanying the repair party was Captain Lybe and about ten infantrymen. Their job was to protect the men from sudden attack while they worked.[29] Finding that about 1,000 feet of wire had been destroyed, Walker divided his force in half and started the men working at either end. Sergeant McDougal and Privates James A. Porter, Joseph Hilty, and Chappel took a position about a quarter mile east to watch for Indians.

With the working party to the east, Walker was just dismounting when he heard the boom of the howitzer, a prearranged signal to retreat as Indians were coming. Waiting for the men from the west, he headed back to the bridge. In looking back, Walker saw Private Chappel, now afoot, and Privates Porter and Hilty riding close by him. Rushing back, Walker found that Porter and Hilty had both been speared in the back. Walker was able to rescue the two riders, who clutched their horses' necks and stayed in the saddle. The mortally wounded Porter fell into the arms of his comrades, who carried him to the post. He was dead upon arrival at 11:30 A.M. Some men of Company I came out from the stockade to cover the retreat.[30]

In the meantime, tempers flared among the officers of the 11th Kansas and the 11th Ohio—emotions fostered by Colonel Moonlight erupting under the tensions of war. At 9:30 A.M., Anderson had assembled the remaining officers for a conference. There Bretney confronted him, calling Anderson a murderer and unfit to command. When Greer became involved in the argument, Bretney struck him.[31] As a consequence, Anderson ordered Bretney's arrest and detention; however, Anderson later thought better of it and released him that afternoon at 3:00 P.M. While in confinement, Bretney offered to take 100 men and the howitzer to rescue Custard.

Custard had left Willow Springs early that morning with three men of Company D in the lead. The advance party came within sight of Platte Bridge Station around 11:00 A.M., at a point about five miles west of the post. At once, a howitzer sounded, indicating Indians in the area, and soon large numbers of warriors came into view. Putting Cpl. James Shrader in charge of the wagons, Custard began to assemble a force to meet the Indians' attack on the left.

In riding forward, Shrader suddenly found himself cut off from the wagons behind him and also from Custard's skirmishers. Pvts. Henry Smith,

Byron Swain, Edwin Summers, and James Ballau had also been separated, so Shrader joined them, directing the men to the river on the right, about a half mile away. Reaching the banks, the men plunged into the stream. When he reached the other side, Summers veered to the southwest, where he was overtaken by Indians and killed. At the same time, Private Ballau had his horse shot from under him, and another bullet ended his life.[32]

Crossing the river, Shrader, Smith, and Swain stopped in a deep ravine thick with brush. They reloaded their cartridges with dry powder and moved down the ravine for about a half mile. Reaching another ravine about a half mile away, they were able to follow it to the river and on to the post. Twenty men went out to meet them, three of them giving up their mounts to the weary fugitives. About twenty warriors gave chase, but the soldiers were able to make it back to Platte Bridge Station.[33]

In the meantime, Sergeant Pennock observed Custard's wagon train.

[Three and a half miles from the post] H and D detachments corralled or tried to corral their wagons but did not succeed very well. We could see the Indians in swarms charge down upon our boys, when they would roll volley after volley into them. It seemed to us as though the boys were in a strong position, twenty in all being the number.[34]

Custard's men had arranged their two wagons to cover themselves from the north, south, and east. This left the west side unprotected.[35] In their haste, the men stopped the wagons in a hollow rather than up on a knoll, thus increasing their vulnerability.[36] The defenders piled bedding, boxes, and sacks of corn under the wagons. Most fought from behind these barriers, but four men chose to fight from within, firing through holes cut in canvas covers. Custard's men had Smith .50 breech-loading percussion carbines, which under ideal conditions could be fired fourteen times a minute, and the attackers soon gave up headlong charges to shoot from fixed positions.[37]

The best account that survives from the victors is that penned by George Bent in May 1906, in a letter to George Hyde:

The soldiers got under the wagons and used their bedding sacks of corn and miscellaneous boxes for breastworks. . . . 22 soldiers were killed in this part, one driver swam across and got away. . . . Indians were killed in this battle, 4 soldier were in the wagons that done [sic] good shooting. . . . The Indians were shooting at those under the wagons. Someone spoke of smoke coming from the wagons. . . . Then the Indians shot at this wagon several times, [a] lot of them together. Wolf Tongue, Roman Nose in fact several brave warriors said all to get ready that they were going to ride around the wagons and empty soldiers' guns. Those on foot to charge up against the wagons. . . . They rode around the wagons at first good many shots came from under the wagons and once three or four shots from the wagon. Then all the Indians made war whoop and charged from all sides. . . . They were shooting the soldiers under the wagons and those in the wagon three of them had been one soldier they threw out of the wagon and killed him on the ground. . . .

The Cheyennes killed here [on July 25–26] were Young Wolf, High Wolf [High-Backed Wolf], Young Bear, Old Bull Hair, Stray Horse, Spit, and Roman Nose's brother [Horse Black].[38]

After the fight was over, a Cheyenne named The Youngest Old Man walked among the dead. He suddenly cried out. "Someone is biting me!" It was a soldier not yet but soon to be dead, who had bitten him in the heel.[39]

Firing ceased about 4:00 P.M., and defenders at Platte Bridge Station could see a large cloud of smoke, indicating burning wagons. About 5:00 P.M., Lieutenant Bretney and three enlisted men of Company G crossed the bridge to look for the dead. They found the body of Pvt. Moses Brown near the bluff. Just as they sighted another corpse, a party of warriors came into view, and the four men quickly returned to the post.[40] In late afternoon, warriors moved off by twos and threes, until at sundown not a living soul was to be seen. At their camp behind the big hill, they celebrated the deaths of twenty-eight soldiers well into the wee hours. One Cheyenne danced clothed in Caspar Collins's blue coat.[41]

The survivors speculated on the Indian dead and wounded. Veterans noted that the avengers had thrown away their scalps. To one schooled in Indian ways, this meant that more had been lost than killed.[42] The men also found that the Sioux and their allies had split a great many telegraph poles to make travois in which to transport their dead and wounded.[43] Lieutenant Drew later heard from Indian sources that 60 had been killed and 130 wounded. Another Indian source set the total lost at 210. George Bent wrote that only eight warriors died.[44]

Riders began appearing on the bluffs south of the river shortly after daybreak on July 27, and soon there were hundreds in sight.[45] After destroying five miles of telegraph line, they began drifting away until by 8:00 A.M. only a few remained.[46] A detachment repaired the line in the afternoon. Expected reinforcements from Deer Creek arrived about 3:00 P.M.: they were fifty men of the 11th Kansas under Lt. Josiah Hubbard, carrying 5,000 rounds of ammunition. Hubbard later remembered, "We were cheered lustily as we came in."[47]

Another search party left the post on the afternoon of July 27, the men spreading out fan-shaped. After an hour, they found the body of Caspar Collins on the banks of Dry Creek. It was hardly recognizable.[48] Collins had been stripped naked, the back part of his head caved in, the brains, heart, and bowels taken out, and the feet and hands cut off. According to one observer, warriors had driven twenty-four arrows into his body, which had been wrapped in telegraph wire.[49] The remains were placed in a specially crafted box lined with blankets. Burial was on the south side of the river, east of the station.[50] Also found were the bodies of Sebastian Nehring and George McDonald. The former had his severed legs bound to his body with telegraph wire. His hands had been cut off and his tongue and heart cut out. McDonald's body had been stripped and mutilated. Several arrows protruded from the corpse.[51] Another party brought in three dead bodies near the river, one pincushioned with fifty-eight arrows.[52]

Near one of the bodies, the searchers found a piece of paper that contained this message:

> I was taken prisoner about seven months ago at La Bonte Station. You must be careful or you will be killed. There are between three and four thousand Indians here, and about another thousand expected here in a day or two. They belong to the Cheyenne, Sioux, and Arapahoe, with a few Comanches and Blackfeet. You killed one of their principal chiefs belonging to the Cheyennes yesterday, and they swear they will have a terrible revenge upon you for it. The intentions are to clean out all the stations on this road and then go onto the Ft. Collins road and clean that out. I shall escape from them if I can.[53]

On July 28 twenty-five men left the post to search for the Custard dead.[54] After they had traveled about five miles, they found twenty bodies. Seventeen of the men lay on their faces, their naked, mutilated bodies held to the ground with long spears. All but one had been scalped. A wagoner was strapped to his feed box, where hot irons from the hubs of the wagon wheels had been seared into his back. The charred remains of one man were among the coals of a burned wagon.[55] Some of the men had the bands from wagon wheels around their necks, and others heavy chains wrapped around their bodies, all apparently heated before being applied.[56] Pvt. John B. Buchanan found Adam Culp, the only member of the 11th Ohio with the group, tied to a wagon wheel. A hot skillet had been put upon his back. The carnage included skulls cut open and brains taken out, hearts and livers removed, sinews taken from the legs, and arms, hands, and feet cut off. One man was headless.[57]

Burial took place on the battleground the next day.[58] By that time the bodies had been long in the sun, and they were in bad condition. The men put seven in one grave, thirteen in another, and one in a solitary grave by the river. Those interred in two graves were Pvt. Rice B. Hamilton of Company I, 11th Kansas, and Pvt. Adam Culp of Company I, 11th Ohio, who were serving as teamsters; eleven men of Company H, 11th Kansas—Commissary Sgt. Amos J. Custard and Pvts. Jesse E. Antram, William Brown, George Heil, August Hoppe, John Horton, William B. Long, Ferdinand Schafer, Samuel Sproul, Thomas W. Young, and William West; and seven men of Company D, 11th Kansas—teamster Martin Green and Pvts. William D. Gray, William H. Miller, Thomas Powell, Samuel Tull, Jacob Zinn, and John R. Zinn. The men named the little prominence Custard Hill.[59]

Search parties did not find the body of Pvt. James Ballau, which apparently washed away. Including the deaths of Private Porter in Walker's command and the four enlisted men of the 11th Kansas with Collins, the total casualties on July 26 were one officer and one enlisted man of the 11th Ohio and twenty-six men of the 11th Kansas killed, and nine or ten men wounded,[60] including Joseph Hilty, who lost two ribs from a spear thrust.[61] Warriors engaged in the fighting numbered perhaps as many as 1,500.[62] Fairfield and Wilson estimated 2,000. Shoshoni scouts said that there were at least 3,000 Indians in the camp, as did the traders at Platte Bridge. Cheyenne and Arapaho oral history records the same number.[63]

On July 30, Company K, 11th Kansas, left for Deer Creek. At the same time, a detachment from the garrison made an attempt to repair the telegraph line, but the damage was too extensive.[64] The troops at Platte Bridge Station began to run out of food on July 31. As the days passed, the garrison worried over the nonappearance of the 6th Michigan, which was supposed to have arrived on July 29.[65] On August 2, however, the troops finally appeared. Traveling with them was Sergeant Todd of the 11th Kansas, bringing rations for fifteen days. On August 3 at 5:30 A.M., Company K, the last of the 11th Kansas troops, left Platte Bridge to be mustered out at Fort Kearny on September 19.[66]

The engagement at Platte Bridge brought no honor to the 11th Kansas, and there would be repercussions and eventually an investigation. But at the moment, the focus was on the Powder River expedition, a chance to even the score and take the war to the homeland of the Sioux and their allies. A total of 2,266 officers and men and 179 Indian auxiliaries had already started north from three locations, and hopes were high in the settlements. The Indian War of 1865 was about to reach its climax.

CHAPTER SEVEN

Connor Strikes Back

CONNOR LED HIS COLUMN OUT OF FORT LARAMIE ON JULY 30. SINCE THE command left just a few days after the Battles of Platte Bridge and Red Buttes, the men may have expected to engage some of the Sioux and Cheyennes almost immediately. The raiders, however, had already begun their journey back to the villages on Powder River to hold their traditional summer ceremonies.[1]

When Connor departed, his force consisted of 558 soldiers, 179 Indians, and 195 teamsters and wagon masters. Indian units were 95 Pawnee led by Frank North, and 84 Winnebago and Omaha led by Capt. Edwin Nash and Little Priest. Robert Wheeling was the chief train master. With Connor's column were 185 wagons and 226 heads of beef cattle. Connor organized his staff as follows: Capt. C. J. Laurant, acting assistant adjutant; Capt. Samuel Robbins, 1st Colorado Cavalry, chief engineer; Capt. Henry E. Palmer, acting assistant quartermaster; Capt. W. H. Tubbs, acting commissary of subsistence; and Lt. Oscar Jewett, aide-de-camp. A special unit of fifteen men of the Signal Corps of United States Volunteers joined the command, serving under 1st Lt. J. Willard Brown and 2nd Lt. Alonzo V. Richards. The sutler for the expedition was A. C. Leighton, and the scouts were Jim Bridger, Jack Stead, Nick and Antoine Janis, Jim Daugherty, Mitch Bouyer, John Richard, Jr., Antoine Le Due, J. J. Brannan, and a Bordeaux.[2]

Col. J. H. Kidd led Connor's left wing, with six companies of the 6th Michigan, about 200 men. Activated at Grand Rapids on October 13, 1862, the 6th Michigan had guarded the defenses at Washington before participating in the battle of Gettysburg, the battle of the Wilderness, and many other engagements. While in Virginia, it had been under the divisional command of Maj. Gen. George Armstrong Custer. After the Grand Review of troops in Washington, the regiment received orders to head for

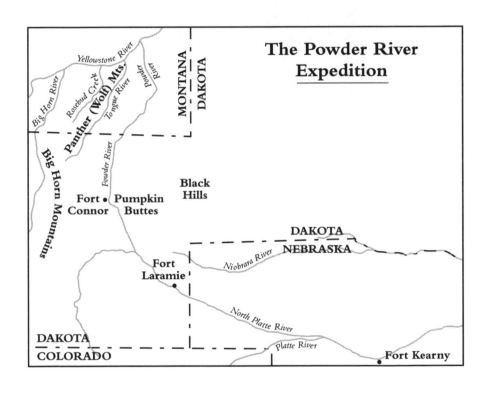

James Bridger

Jim Bridger, who was the premier scout of his era, led Connor's division of the Powder River Expedition. KANSAS HISTORICAL SOCIETY

Fort Laramie. They reached the post on July 25, poorly armed and demanding discharge. The Michigan troops were destined to garrison the military post that Connor planned to establish on Powder River. James Kidd, when a major in the field, had designed his regiment's flag. He had been wounded in combat at Falling Waters, Maryland, and Winchester, Virginia, and six weeks earlier had received the brevet of major general of volunteers for gallant and meritorious service in the Civil War.[3] The rest of the troops were sixty-eight men of Company F of the 7th Iowa Cavalry under command of Capt. Nicholas J. O'Brien, 1st Lt. John S. Brewer, and 2nd Lt. Eugene F. Ware; sixty men of Company E of the 11th Ohio Cavalry under command of Capt. J. L. Humphreville; and fifteen men on detached service from Company G of the 11th Ohio commanded by Lt. John B. Furnay.

Also a part of the left wing were the ninety-five Pawnee Indians under Capt. Frank North and his lieutenants, Charles Small and Jimmy Murie. Gen. Samuel R. Curtis, commander of the Department of the Missouri, while on his way to Fort Kearny in the summer of 1864, had stopped in Columbus to persuade McFayden and Frank North to engage the services of seventy Pawnee Indians to accompany an Indian expedition as guides and scouts. The Indians furnished their own horses and equipments and were paid $25 per month. Curtis later suggested to North that he form a company to be called the Pawnee Scouts. In January 1865, the Pawnee Scouts were officially created, mustered in, and sent to Fort Kearny to receive horses and equipment. From there they went to Julesburg and then to Fort Laramie to join the Powder River expedition.[4]

Capt. Albert Brown commanded Connor's right wing, which consisted of sixty men of Company M of the 2nd California Cavalry under Brown; forty-nine men of Company L of the 2nd California Cavalry under Capt. George Conrad; a fourteen-man detachment of the 2nd Missouri Artillery; and eighty-four Winnebago and Omaha Indians under command of Capt. E. W. Nash, with their leader Little Priest.

Connor outlined his plans to General Dodge:

> I will proceed down Tongue River to the general rendezvous of the columns on Rosebud River; expect to direct movements of the different columns by fire signals. If I don't succeed in finding and punishing Indians before arriving at general rendezvous and can there ascertain their whereabouts, I intend to go after them, even if it is to Heart River. Should Indians show no disposition to take risk of a general engagement I will again distribute the columns, carrying rations on horses, and scour the country thoroughly. Circumstances may, however, arise when I arrive on the ground which will cause me to change my plans somewhat.[5]

In his absence, Connor intended to keep the roads open and to run the mail through with government teams and soldier drivers. Optimism was high for success. The *Rocky Mountain News* affirmed that Connor would engage in a "little wholesome blood letting," and the *Miner's Register* declared, "Those acquainted with General Connor's past reputation certainly need no reassurance of his determination to pursue them to the bitter end, and with his fast accumulating strength there is little doubt but that he will sweep down upon them on every hand, with an impetuosity that shall make corpses of the greater part before investigating committees, or peace experimenters can arrest his course."[6]

At the same time that Connor was preparing to march north to engage the Sioux and their allies, however, President Johnson had instructed Commissioner of Indian Affairs William P. Dole to undertake an effort to convince the warring tribes to make peace. His mission was to make treaties with tribes in the West that would put roving Indians on "suitable" reservations where by agriculture and "industrious pursuits" they could sustain themselves. Commanders of military districts were instructed to cooperate fully.[7] Thus, as the Red Chief started on the warpath, the Great White Father offered the olive branch, and the problem of bifurcated authority became evident once again. Anyone who had been dealing with Indian matters knew that these actions were not mutually supportive. The president did not cancel the expedition, however, and Connor still had the chance to strike a critical blow.

Connor and his left wing under Captain Kidd blazed a new trail into the north country.[8] This new route, which would be taken by all future travelers, crossed the North Platte at Bridger's Ferry and followed the Mormon Trail along the north bank. A mile or two west of, but across from, the site of the future Fort Fetterman, Connor turned north and went up Sage Creek Valley. The path that he pioneered from here to the future site of Fort Phil Kearny in July 1866 was a new road that would be incorporated into the Bozeman Trail.[9] According to teamster Finn Burnett, Jim Bridger never failed to inform the command of the approximate distance from one camp to the other, the lay of the country over which they traveled, the availability of grass on which they depended for subsistence of the horses and mules, and the source of water and whether it was plentiful, good, or bad.[10]

On July 31, they reached Horseshoe Station, and on August 1, they went into camp at La Bonte's Ford. There they were joined by Captain Frank North and his Pawnees, who apparently arrived the midnight previous. From that point on the Pawnee scouted far and wide in every direction, returning every once in a while to get their orders from Frank North and then disappearing in a rush.[11]

After the troops were in camp on August 1, a portion of the 6th Michigan Cavalry arrived and also a large train of wagons loaded with supplies. Connor then turned north, following Sage Creek, pioneers keeping in advance to smooth the way.[12] The command then marched to Brown's Springs and then followed the Dry Powder.[13]

To many of the volunteer troops, this adventure was a novel one. Charles Adams experienced the silence of the new route when on guard duty:

> After a few days out I was detailed on picket, and well do I remember it. I was posted a quarter of a mile from camp (alone) at dark in the sage brush, with instructions to move some 50 yards

after dark, so that if Indians should be watching, they would not know just where to pounce upon me. In case I should see or hear Indians moving toward camp I was to fire and then do the best I could. Well, I did not see any Indians, but I imagined I could hear everything. I was relieved at midnight and it appeared to me I had been there 24 hours.

There is no fun in sitting alone in the brush half the night with wolves howling all around and not knowing when a grizzly or some other wild animal may be on one, to say nothing of the rattlesnakes.[14]

After leaving the North Platte River, Capt. George Conrad and Capt. Albert Brown's companies of the 2nd California, being the best mounted, were used for scouting to complement North's Pawnees. In effect, they functioned as a fourth column in Connor's command. Brown took a westerly route. He was to skirt the western edge of the Big Horn Mountains and reunite with Kidd on a designated fork on the Powder River. Conrad and Brown skirmished with Indians on July 26 and August 1. The Pawnee Scouts brought in scalps and horses that they captured day by day. On August 11, the expedition reached the Powder River, 175 miles north of Fort Laramie.[15] Here the Pawnee found vestiges of an Indian camp of some 150 lodges. Found on the ground were scraps of telegrams taken by them at Julesburg in February and the scalp of a white man.[16]

While the Powder River Expedition played out its drama in the shadows of the Big Horns, raiders continued to make life difficult for those who guarded the Oregon Trail west of Fort Laramie. On August 13, 150 Indians attacked a detachment at Willow Springs, stampeding the stock. The 6th Michigan troops charged them on foot and recovered some of the animals. In the meantime, the large number of Sioux and Cheyennes that had gone north were holding their medicine ceremonies, the Sioux their Sun Dance and the Cheyennes their four-day Sacred Arrow ceremony. Afterwards, they broke up into groups, the Sioux and the Cheyennes moving north to hunt buffalo, and the Arapahos west to Tongue River.[17]

The troops eventually went down the Dry Fork of Powder River to the main stream. There they forded to the west side and traveled southward up the valley approximately three miles to a low tableland. This was on a plain exactly fifty-six feet above the river level. On August 14, Connor selected this site upon which to erect a fort.[18]

Capt. J. W. Kidd was in charge of the post, which was laid out according to a plan prepared by Capt. Robbins, engineer for the District of the

Plains. Kidd designated a military reserve of twenty square miles, the initial point beginning ten miles due north from the flagstaff.[19]

Henry Palmer described the scene:

> The first timber was cut today for building a stockade. . . . Our stockade timber was cut twelve feet long and was from eight to ten inches in thickness. These poles were set four deep in the ground in a trench. Every soldier and all the teamsters who could be urged to work were supplied with axes, and the men seemed to enjoy the exercise, chopping trees and cutting stockade timber.[20]

When they were finished, Connor's men had built a small stockade about 120 feet square with two bastions at the outer and opposing angles. Inside were two buildings for quartermaster stores, each thirty by ninety-six feet. The fort stood about 100 yards from the face of the bluffs on the northwest side of the river and commanded a clear view in nearly every direction. To the east loomed Pumpkin Buttes, which could be seen for many miles by random travelers. In September, the men built two barracks of unhewn cottonwood logs, chinked and mud-plastered. Each measured twenty-five by ninety feet. These were followed by two officers' quarters, twenty by thirty feet, of hewn cottonwood. The men also constructed a post hospital, twenty-four by thirty feet, and some shops and teamsters' quarters. This completed the work accomplished by the volunteer troops in 1865.[21]

While the fort was being built, Indian auxiliaries scouted the area, encountering several small raiding parties returning from the Platte. Traveling with one of these was Yellow Woman, George Bent's stepmother. Discovering the party, Pawnee scouts disguised themselves as Cheyennes or Sioux and were able to get close enough to charge the group, killing Yellow Woman and four others who had ridden ahead of the main body. At the same time, some of the cavalry attacked the rest of the Cheyennes, who abandoned their plunder and escaped.[22]

There were several other incidents while at Fort Connor. While the stockade was being constructed, Winnebagos scouting a few miles northwest ran into a large war party. Little Priest, becoming separated, found himself surrounded, fighting on foot hand to hand. His warriors charged and rescued him, the chief coming away with two scalps "of which he was very proud." A short time after this while scouting near Crazy Woman's Fork of the Powder, Frank North ran into another group and became separated, his horse being killed. Bob White, a Pawnee sergeant, came back to help him. North told him to get some more men. Instead of obeying, White jumped off his horse and lay down beside Frank saying: "Me heap brave, me no run, you and me killed plenty Sioux, that better." Together they held off the enemy until help arrived.[23]

Teamster Finn Burnett remembered that after the garrison had moved inside the completed stockade, two companies of the 11th Ohio regiment came into camp at night. Thinking the fort was under attack, the sentinel fired his gun and every man turned out. The men did not take time to put on their boots, and cactus-covered ground took its toll, the men filling the air with imaginative complaints.[24]

On August 16 at 2:00 P.M., a few Indians made their appearance on some of the bluffs a short distance from the fort. The bugler sounded the call for "Boots and Saddles," but Connor, learning that there were but one or two lodges, ordered revelle and sent Captain North with his company of scouts in pursuit. Robbins, Jewett, and several other officers went with them but returned by dark. North and forty Pawnees traveled sixty miles, crossing the Powder River seven times that night. One of the scouts went on foot the whole distance and never lost the trail once. They overtook the Cheyennes at daybreak, attacking and killing all of them, and returned to the camp that afternoon.[25]

When North returned to camp, he reported that after traveling about sixty miles he saw campfires. A little later he discovered mounted Indians, with one Indian woman and one wounded Indian on a travois. The encumbrance made the trail easy to follow during the night. According to North, the Cheyennes, when pursued, were more interested in escaping than fighting, making it easier to dispatch them.[26] North had in tow sixteen horses and ponies and twelve mules with government brands, and the scouts brought back quantities of coffee, sugar, dried apples, tobacco, calico dresses, and several Indian trophies, including scalps.[27] The Pawnees had also found a quantity of white women's and children's clothing, two infantry coats issued by the government to Indians at Fort Laramie in the spring, and a number of letters and papers of the 7th Michigan, then on duty on the Overland Trail.[28]

Quartermaster Palmer described the ensuing victory dance as the most savage that he had ever witnessed. Warriors formed a circle and danced around the fire, holding up their bloody scalps, brandishing their hatchets, and exhibiting the spoils of the fight. Although at first some of the officers found the dance interesting, they soon tired of the singing. Finally, General Connor had had enough, and in the wee hours of the morning, he ordered the officer of the day to stop the noise. After considerable discussion, North succeeded in quieting the group. The war dance continued every night thereafter but ended at 10:00 P.M.[29]

On August 18, Connor moved the camp two miles farther up the river for better grazing. While this was in process, one of the Pawnee scouts accidentaly discharged his revolver while examining it; the ball entered the forehead of one of his companions and killed him instantly. The Indians viewed the incident as a portent of evil to come.[30]

On August 20 at 2:00 P.M., North and some of his Pawnees left the camp in pursuit of newly discovered Sioux. The scouts' horses, however, were weak, having been used to hunt buffalo and black tail deer earlier in the day. North and a few of the Pawnee did engage about 100 of the enemy. The Pawnees succeeded in killing one, believed to be a Cheyenne chief, took his scalp, and returned to camp. They also captured six mules. Not satisfied with the skirmish, Connor sent Captain Marshall with a detachment of Company E, 11th Ohio, and Captain O'Brien with a detachment of Company F, 7th Iowa, in pursuit.[31]

On August 21, Marshall returned, reporting that he had found three Indians that morning, two of whom he killed. He recovered ten mules.[32] At this time, the anxiously awaited wagon train and troops from Fort Laramie arrived. The command broke camp on Powder River at 6:30 A.M. Passing through Fort Connor, they traveled in a northwesterly direction, headed for Tongue River. After eight miles, the column passed the bodies of the two Indians killed by Marshall's party. One of the men took a silver ring from the finger of one. On it was the inscription "S. L. Matthews Company A 1 Michigan, Cav." The party camped on Crazy Woman Creek for the night.[33]

On August 23, the Pawnees killed three Grizzly bears, a mother and two cubs. They camped on Clear Fork of the Powder River, where some of the men prospected, finding traces of gold.[34] Palmer described the foothills of the Big Horns:

> From this point on to Montana—in fact, along the whole base of the Rocky mountains to the British Possessions—the country is perfectly charming, the hills are covered with a fine growth of grass, and in every valley there is either a rushing stream or babbling brook of pure, clear snow water filled with trout, the banks lined with trees, wild cherries, quaking asp, some birch, willow and cottonwood. No country in America is more picaresque than the eastern slope of the Big Horn mountains.

Later he commented on the quantity of game:

> We found it an easy matter to ride up within fifteen or twenty rods of a band of buffalo before they would scamper off, and the strange sight of a moving train, signal flags and the large column of cavalry

so excited the antelope and deer that they were to be seen at almost any hour of the day on neighboring hill, sometimes in close proximity to the train. It was an easy matter to ride up to within good revolver range of an antelope. Members of the Signal Corps enjoyed themselves hugely by hiding behind some little hillock or clump of sage brush and signaling to the incautious, confiding antelope to come up and smell of their pistols.[35]

From August 10 to September 25, the whole command of 747 souls depended entirely on wild game for meat. Out of 226 heads of beef cattle, only 3 were slaughtered, those because they were lame.

While Connor and his men enjoyed a brief respite in the Big Horns, trouble in Montana continued. About daylight on August 24 near the Gallatin River, between thirty and forty Sioux attacked Messrs. Davis and Hyde's party in bed, wounding a man named Buchanan in the arm. The whites retreated to hills about two miles distant, taking cover in a point of rocks, where they fought until about 9:00 A.M. The Indians killed one man named Smith, when he rose to fire. The raiders then attacked Colonel Kimball and his party, camped about eight miles on the Gallatin side of the first group. In this case, the Indians feigned peace and shook hands with some of the men before firing and killing Colonel Kimball and riding off. The *Montana Post* reported other men found dead and scalped and demanded that the governor call out the militia, invoking the rallying cry of the highlanders of Cawnpore: "Think of the ladies. Think of the babies."[36]

After killing Kimball, the Sioux traveled about three miles farther toward the Gallatin and surrounded three wagons loaded with lumber belonging to Knox & Company. The teamsters unhitched on a little rise of ground, instructing a Sioux-speaking Mexican of their party to parley. While the talk proceeded, some half-bloods arrived from Bozeman, led by John Richard, Jr., and Mitch Bouyer. Seeing what was happening, they fired upon the Indians, killing one. The rest fled, their only plunder being Cyrus A. Bradbury's bedding and provisions.

The men returned to Bozeman, gathering a party of thirty-four, including ten Crow Indians. The pursuers followed the trail at a gallop and sighted the Sioux about five miles away. Seeing that they were followed, the raiders turned and rode at full speed. The chase continued until near dark, but after crossing the river, the Indians disappeared. The party buried Colonel Kimball and Mr. Smith, who was scalped. Buchanan, of Hyde's party, when making his escape, headed for Emigrant Gulch. Within a half mile of the Yellowstone, he discovered a dead white man, scalped, stripped, and mutilated. Fearing that there were other Indians in the area, he decided to go back. He was hiding in the brush when the scouting party passed by and was able to join them.[37]

The Indians continued to raid in the south. On August 25, Indians attacked along the Overland Trail between Big Laramie and Rock Creek, killing the driver of a wagon, wounding its owner, and dispatching his wife and a daughter. They left another daughter with seven arrows in her body. Passersby found the little girl and took her to Laramie, where she eventually recovered. She reported that a white man had shot the first arrow.[38]

In the raid near Little Laramie, the Indians killed Sergeant Cooley of the 1st Colorado Cavalry. They shot him through the head and captured two government teams of six mules each. Attacking Perry Abbott's train three miles east of Rock Creek, they had a moving fight for five miles before withdrawing. At the Rock Creek Ranch, no one died, but the Indians plundered the store of whiskey and other goods. At John Richard, Sr.'s, ranch on Rock Creek, they took all he had. Once the king of the North Platte, Richard was left destitute and never recovered from the loss.[39]

At Little Laramie, the Indians ran off eighty heads of stock belonging to Phillip Mantel and captured all the soldiers' horses. The soldiers retreated from their station to the Mantel Ranch, where they made a stand from morning to dark. One discharged soldier, John Owens, formerly of the 2nd California Cavalry, went out fishing and was killed. Many Indians were believed to have been killed and wounded during the fight. The Indians burned the Cooper's Creek Station. The 7th Michigan Cavalry killed at least eight in the fight, but since the raiders lashed themselves to their horses, it was impossible to tell how many others were killed or wounded.[40]

On August 24, Connor's hunters succeeded in driving fifteen buffalo into the wagon corral in the camp on Clear Fork of Powder River, and the men feasted that evening.[41] That day most of the 2nd California under Capt. Albert Brown rejoined the command after completing their scouting duty. They brought with them some rocks containing silver and declared that the region through which they had passed abounded in such ore.

The column that arrived was in poor shape. Connor's right wing had had a difficult time traveling through the rocky southern part of the Big Horn Mountains. The force ran out of rations, and horses began dying—the Winnebagos lost more than half their mounts. The desperate situation prompted Brown to head directly for Connor's command on the Powder River. Coming out of the mountains at the headwaters of Crazy Woman Creek, the bedraggled party reached the Powder River near present-day Kaycee, Wyoming, and then followed it down to Fort Connor. They arrived on August 23, only to find that Connor had left that morning. Moving quickly to catch up, they found the general on Clear Creek the next day.[42]

On August 25, the troops passed Lake DeSmet. There they found herds of buffalo. The soldiers dispatched a number of them, even General Connor joining in the sport. On August 26, the command left the Piney Fork at 6:00 A.M. When the troops reached the top of Lodgepole Ridge, the divide between the waters of the Powder and the Tongue and just beyond the future site of Fort Phil Kearny, Jim Bridger reported smoke from an Indian village about fifty miles away. Although Connor could not see the smoke, he sent North with some Pawnees to check it out.[43] The column began moving down Prairie Dog Creek (then called Peno Creek), eventually coming to the Tongue. On August 28, just after sunset, one of the Pawnees who been out with Captain North came into camp to report discovery of an Indian village about thirty-five miles west. Connor immediately began to assemble his attack force of about 310 men. The command consisted of Lieutenant Evans and 40 Omaha scouts; Lieutenant Small and 30 Pawnee scouts; Captain O'Brien and 100 artillerymen, with two cannons; Captain Brown with 38 California volunteers; and Captain Marshall with 60 men of the 11th Ohio. Connor selected those with the best horses, leaving about 200 men in camp under the command of Edwin R. Nash of the Omaha scouts. The men hurriedly ate supper and then hit the trail, hoping to surprise the village at daybreak.[44]

The village discovered by Jim Bridger was an Arapaho one, and its inhabitants had been on the warpath. The principal chiefs were Black Bear and Medicine Man, who had recently left the Fort Collins, Colorado, area. In April 1865, Black Bear and his 400 followers had been assigned land in that region on which to hunt in return for a pledge of peace. In the same place were Friday and Wolf Moccasin's group, which had been there since July 1864. Wolf Moccasin eventually allied himself with Black Bear and Medicine Man, quit drawing rations from the fort, and joined the chiefs in hunting for subsistence. A majority of the Arapahos soon became restless, probably due in part to the success that the Sioux and Cheyennes were having in the raiding along the Overland and Oregon Trails. They told Black Bear, Medicine Man, and Friday that they were planning to return to the warpath, stating that the chiefs could stay where they were or continue to lead them. Black Bear and Medicine Man opted for war, departing at night with most of Friday's stock.[45] The Arapahos began raiding in June, Fort Laramie blaming them for "most of the outrages committed on the overland mail route west of Denver."[46] Black Bear and Medicine Man's group returned to the Powder River region in August. This was the village that lay along the banks of Tongue River on the morning of August 29. Black Bear had gone with some of the warriors to fight the Crows on the Big Horn River, however, leaving Medicine Man and many of the older men and the women and children in camp.[47]

When Connor's troops were ready to move out on the evening of August 28, the general issued an order that no man should speak above a whisper and that when horses attempted to whinny, they should be jerked up with a tight rein. The line of march was up the valley of Tongue River. They found the main road, but it was clogged with underbrush and fallen timber. Because the night was quite dark, they made slow progress. Some marveled at the skill of Jim Bridger, who led them forward through rough rocky defiles and over stretches of darkened plains.[48] At daylight, they topped a rise and saw before them a large mesa of 500 or 600 acres covered with Indian ponies.[49] About a half mile to the left was the Indian camp, dotted with tipis.[50]

Before the attack, Connor made a short speech. Pvt. P. W. Brown of Company K, 11th Ohio Cavalry, remembered that Connor spoke these words:

> Over the hill is the Indian village, and there are supposed to be about 2,500 warriors. When we arrive at the top of the hill I will give the command "Charge!" I want every man to get to the village as soon as possible. I want every man to make as much noise and yell as loud as he can. I want him to kill as many Indians as he can, but do not want any women or children killed and any scalping done.[51]

As they approached the village about 8:00 A.M., they saw an Indian on a high point riding in a circle—the sign of danger.[52] Officers passed the word for the men to close up and follow the general and not to fire a shot until he did. Connor took the lead, and at the top of the hill gave the command to the bugler to sound the charge. Private Brown remembered that "the noise commenced and away we went, helter-skelter, every man for himself. The men certainly obeyed orders when it came to making noise."[53]

At the first sight of the attackers, the ponies set up a tremendous whinnying and galloped toward the Indian village. More than a thousand dogs began barking, and hundreds of Arapahos made the hills ring with their yells. As they neared the village, the command divided, some turning to the right, others to the left, forming a large crescent. The Indians had some of their tipis down and ponies packed. Some of the animals were so heavily laden that when they tried to run, the packs pulled them over, and they lay on their backs with their feet in the air. By the time the soldiers reached the village, most warriors had secured their war ponies. Probably half of the women and children were mounted, and some had already taken up the line of march up the stream to a new camp. Connor ordered a volley into the village, and the troops rode on.[54]

Capt. J. Humphreville of the 11th Ohio recalled that "the fight was something terrific."[55] For the first half hour or so, the howitzers pounded the village, firing so rapidly that one of them became heated and temporarily useless. Disregarding orders, the Indian scouts killed Arapaho Indians indiscriminately—men, women, and children falling under their scalping knives.

Riding far in advance, Connor, his staff, and Sutler A. C. Leighton suddenly found themselves caught in a cross fire between troops and warriors. The general ordered his companions to lie down on their horses, and just as they did this, a shot struck the bugler just below his cartridge belt. The ball was afterwards found under the skin between his shoulders.[56]

There was pandemonium in the village, with men, women, and children, horses and dogs, all running hither and yon. The soldiers entered the village, and engaged in hand-to-hand fighting with the warriors. Many Indian women remained to fight bravely beside their husbands and tribesmen. Henry Palmer remembered that "unfortunately for the women and children, our men had no time to direct their aim; bullets from both sides and murderous arrows filled the air; squaws and children, as well as warriors, fell among the dead and wounded."[57] Captain Humphreville and the Indian scouts killed several Arapahos hiding behind a pile of buffalo robes stacked along the riverbanks.[58] Many of the tribesmen were able to reach a high point near the village where they rallied, but they could not stand long before the soldiers' Spencers.[59]

Connor charged straight through the village and kept on after the Indians for twelve miles up Wolf Creek. Including about fifteen Pawnee scouts, there were about thirty in the party, most of them officers.[60] Eventually, the pursuers' horses began to tire and give out. Finally, Connor halted his small squad. The Arapahos, noticing the paucity of numbers, immediately turned upon the little party, making a desperate effort to surround them. The men fell back as rapidly as possible, reinforced every few moments by some stragglers, who had endeavored to keep up. With this help they managed to return to camp.[61]

One incident occurred during the ride. Henry Palmer remembered that they had encountered a little Indian boy:

During the chase up Wolf creek with the General, one of North's braves picked up a little Indian boy that had been dropped by the wayside. The little fellow was crying, but, when picked up by the soldier Indian, fought like a wildcat. One of our men asked the Indian what he was going to do with the papoose. He said; "Don't know; kill him, mebby." He was told to put him down and not to injure the bright little fellow. The Indian obeyed, and at least one papoose owed his life to the kind-hearted soldier.[62]

Back near the village, the fighting was desperate. A number of Indians in the brush along the creek fired at soldiers who were at work destroying the village. Capt. Nicholas O'Brien received an order to drive them out. When he and his men skirmished along the creek, driving the warriors ahead of them, two women came out of the brush. The older woman extended her left hand, saying "How! How!" A. C. Leighton came up behind the two women and called to O'Brien to look out as the older woman had a hatchet in her right hand behind her back. The warning came just in time to save O'Brien's life. The woman threw the hatchet just as Leighton called, and it grazed the officer's head. He had a pistol in his hand and shot reflexively, killing the woman. When he realized what he had done, he was appalled and said, "Great God, boys, don't ever tell that I killed a squaw." In a reminiscence, one of his men remembered, "We never did tell on him until he had passed away to the far land beyond, where he could apologize to the lady for his discourtesy."[63]

Private Johnson of Company K, 11th Ohio, received a bizarre wound in the fighting. An arrow passed through his cheek and tongue and lodged itself in his jawbone, making extraction difficult.[64] Lt. Oscar Jewett, Connor's aide-de-camp, was wounded, shot through the left thigh. At six feet three inches, twenty-seven-year-old Jewett was a conspicuous target. His bugler also had a flesh wound between the shoulders.[65] Asst. Surg. Julius Wenz, 6th U.S. Volunteers, reported that he treated four men for injuries. The first had two bullet wounds in his back and/or hips. Wenz operated to remove one of the projectiles. A second man had two bullet wounds in the thigh; Wenz again operated to extract a musket ball. A third soldier had a flesh wound in the arm, which did not require surgery. As might be expected, the most complicated case was that of Private Johnson. Wenz used chloroform in his operation to extract the arrow "with difficulty" because it was embedded in the man's facial bones. Wenz examined a fifth man, an Omaha scout, whom he noted had died from a ball passing directly through the heart, causing instantaneous death.[66] Sgt. Charles M.

Latham of the Signal Corps received a wound in the heel. He had been through the entire war in the Army of the Potomac without injury and wore a medal for his bravery. The wound led to lockjaw, and he died a few days later.[67]

In the Arapaho village, the men found all the jerked buffalo meat they could eat and carry, and to many a ravished soldier, such as Charles Adams, "it tasted good."[68] The command rendezvoused in the village about 12:30, and the men were set to work destroying Indian property. Scores of buffalo robes, blankets, and furs were heaped up on lodgepoles, with tipi covers and dried buffalo meat piled on top, and burned. Connor ordered that the two dead be placed on one of these piles, burning the bodies to keep Indians from mutilating them. During the halt, the Arapahos came close to the camp and made several attempts to recover their stock. The mountain howitzer, under the skillful management of Captain O'Brien, prevented them from completing their objective. One of the artillery pieces had become disabled during the battle, the axletree of the gun carriage being broken. They left the wheels and broken axle near the river and saved the cannon.

The troops remained in the village until about 2:30. Driving about 500 to 600 head of ponies, Frank North and his Pawnees were soon far ahead. The Arapahos pressed them on every side, sometimes charging up to within fifty feet of the rear guard. They seemed to have plenty of ammunition but did most of their fighting with arrows, although some had muskets. Before dark, the troops were nearly out of ammunition, only about forty having a few rounds apiece.

The Arapahos showed no signs of stopping the fight, but kept on pressing the troops, charging upon them, then dashing away. About 11:45, they made the last of their forays, and the troops were alone. The men reached their base camp about 3:00 A.M. the next day after marching 110 miles without rest or refreshments, except for the jerked buffalo taken from the Indian village.

Connor took eight women, including one of Black Bear's wives, and thirteen Indian children back to camp with him.[69] After a rest, Connor ordered that the Arapaho women be mounted on ponies and brought before him. Through an interpreter, he gave them a long talk. He said he wanted them to tell their men that he had lots of soldiers, and there were lots more of them coming, and that unless they went to Fort Laramie and made peace, he would kill them all, capture all their women and children, and destroy all of their property. He gave them a paper stating what he had said and told them they could go.[70] Connor provided an escort of 11th Ohio troopers, because the Pawnees and Winnebagos wanted to kill them and take their scalps.[71]

The Indian casualties were sixty-three Arapahos killed, including the son of Black Bear. The troops burned 250 lodges and captured 500 ponies. They also destroyed tons of jerked buffalo meat, buffalo robes, and other camp equipment.[72]

The next day, Connor had the whole command bring everything they had taken from the village and put it in a pile. The Pawnees, thinking that he intended to divide among them what they had taken, brought everything, including fifty or sixty scalps.[73] But Connor had been enraged by the plundering that took place in the Indian village during the fighting and ordered the pile burned. He then made a speech in which he told the assembled group that in forthcoming battles he would detail white troops with instructions to shoot any soldier red, white, or black, who was found plundering during battle. After the battle, they might help themselves. Connor singled out the Winnebago chief, Little Priest, and three others of his tribe for their bravery and conduct, and did the same for Frank North and fifteen of his Pawnees.[74]

When the story of the defeat of the Arapahos on Tongue River reached the settlements, the press rejoiced. "Glorious News!" headlined the *Rocky Mountain News.* In a later column, the newspaper sarcastically declared,

> Oh! Gen, Connor is a horrible man, and it seems to us he ought to be "investigated." Can't there be something done to stop him in his mad career. Head him off for Heaven's sake! Why Sand Creek is no where! every beat of the lightning wires tells of horrible slaughter of "innocent" Indians, and if we can believe the damming tale he even destroys their villages and burns their winter stores. Oh! for an investigating committee to head him off.[75]

First to benefit from the ecstatic citizenry in Denver was Gen. Grenville Dodge. On September 21, he was the honored guest at a supper at the Planter's House. Among those attending were twenty-five ladies and their escorts and General Dodge's staff, numbering 110 persons in all. Decorated with flags and evergreens, the tables were arranged across one end and in two lines down the entire length of the spacious dining room. The menu attested to the festivity of the occasion.

SOUP

Oyster . . . . .Oyster

MEATS

Roast Pig . . . . .Roast Turkey
Roast Beef . . . . .Roast Chicken
Baked Goose, with . . . . Apple Jelly

SIDE DISHES

Pressed Corn Beef . . . . .Cold Boiled Ham
Cold Roast Beef . . . . .Buffalo Tongue
Braised Mutton Chops, with . . . . .Currant Jelly
Villevons of Chicken . . . . .Villevons of Chicken

ENTRIES

Oyster Salad . . . . .Cold Sardines
Lobster Salad . . . . .Cold Oysters
Tomato Catsup . . . . .Walnut Catsup
Worchestershire Sauce . . . . .Pickled Beets
Pickled Beets . . . . .Cucumber Pickles

VEGETABLES

Potatoes . . . . .Tomatoes
Baked Squash . . . . .Radishes

FRUIT

Watermelons . . . . .Strawberries
Pine Apples . . . . .Peaches

PASTRY

Pound Cake . . . . .Fruit Cake
Jelly Cake . . . . .Fancy Cake
Brandy Jelly . . . . .Madeira Jelly

DESSERT

Almonds . . . . .English Walnuts
Filberts . . . . .Figs
Raisins . . . . .Candies
Tea . . . . .Coffee

WINE LIST

Mumm's Vrisenay .Sparkling Ohio Catawba
Heidstick . . . . .Sparkling Hock
Sauterno . . . . .Sherry
St. Julien . . . . .Madeira
Port, Claret . . . . .Deidzelman Hock

Following the feast were many toasts and responses. Among those honored were General Dodge; General Connor, whose name brought a perfect storm of cheers; the states of Iowa and Colorado, soon to be bound by a continental railroad; the Army of the United States; D. A. Butterfield and the newly opened Smoky Hill route; the city of Denver; the Ladies of Denver; the Press of Colorado; and, finally, James McNasser and his ability to get up a good supper. The guests retired at 1:00 A.M., conspicuous in their consumption and confident in their ability to meet all challenges and solve all problems.[76]

In the meantime, Connor was on the march. The day after his battle with the Arapahos, Connor began moving down Tongue River, looking for Cole and Walker.[77] The column did not make good time, the grazing being very poor because of great herds of buffalo and elk. The animals provided excellent meat, but it was difficult to find sufficient grass for the horses and mules. Consequently, the animals soon became thin and weak. Particularly affected were the horses of the 11th Ohio Cavalry. Bred in the East, they had great difficulty in adjusting to the plains environment, a life without grain. By September 3, the troops had lost 225 horses, and the men had to destroy a number of wagons.[78]

On September 1, the troops heard what they thought was a cannon shot, and Connor sent Frank North and about twenty Indian scouts and Captain Marshall and thirty of the 11th Ohio to see if Cole was near. The detachment found nothing, however.[79] On the night of September 2, three of the civilian scouts—Bridger, Rulo, and Nick Janis—declared that they heard "medicine wolves" among the many that had serenaded the troops every evening. The medicine wolf, they explained, was a kind of supernatural animal whose howling foretold trouble in camp. Acting on their beliefs, the three gathered their gear and went downriver about a half mile to spend the night.[80] In general, Connor and his men did not think much of their guides, except for Bridger. As Henry Palmer put it, "There are several guides with Genl. Connor, receiving large pay but; nearly all of them are ignorant and unreliable and as useless as an old watch without a dial."[81]

September 3 was a cold, dreary day, with rain most of the time and some snow. According to Burnett, a number of the men had discarded their boots for moccasins, which they had captured in the village. But now the footwear was precious, and the accompanying sutler sold all of the boots and shoes he had in stock that day.[82] On September 5, the men remained in camp, waiting to hear of the whereabouts of Cole. Captain Marshall returned at dark from the Rosebud with no news. North also returned from his scout at the mouth of Tongue River with a terse message: no grass, no news. In order to find better grass, Connor did an about-face and marched fifteen miles.[83]

On September 8, Connor sent small scouting parties in every direction. Captain Humphreville and part of his company left for Rosebud, while North and the Pawnee Scouts headed for Powder River in search of Cole. On September 9, it was still raining and snowing, with roads muddy and almost impossible to use. The next day, the rain stopped, but the three days' drenching made Tongue River rise two feet, making it impassable. On September 11, Connor moved the camp a mile up the river to await the return of scouting parties. Previous to leaving camp, the men hoisted a signal flag by the side of a large cottonwood tree from which the bark had been removed and instructions placed upon it for the guidance of Cole and Walker. Humphreville returned with no news.[84]

Connor could ignore the situation no longer; he had a real problem. Two-thirds of his command under Nelson Cole and Samuel Walker had not appeared. If he did not find them soon, his whole expedition would be in jeopardy. Where were Cole and Walker?

CHAPTER EIGHT

The Sawyers Expedition

WHILE GENERAL CONNOR AND HIS TROOPS MOVED NORTH TO SEARCH for the Sioux, Cheyennes, and Arapahos, a civilian expedition entered the Powder River country from the east. It posed a much greater threat to the united tribes than military operations, for its purpose was road building, the forerunner of emigration and settlement.

The Sawyers expedition was formed in response to citizens in Sioux City, Iowa, who wanted the Missouri River city to become the primary supply depot for trips to the Montana gold fields. Sioux City felt it could offer the most direct overland route, at the expense of Council Bluffs and Omaha.[1] District Congressman Asahel Wheeler Hubbard was able to obtain legislation, approved March 3, 1865, to finance the so-called Niobrara-Virginia City Wagon Road.[2]

On March 14, James Sawyers, a former lieutenant colonel of the Northern Border Brigade, Iowa State Militia, was given responsibility by the War Department for carrying out this project. Then forty years old, Sawyers had been a successful merchant in Sioux City before the war and had recently become involved with Charles and Daniel Hedges in the cattle and freighting business. A long business and political association with Representative Hubbard helped to explain his appointment as superintendent of the wagon road expedition.[3]

The proposed route was to follow the Niobrara River westward, turning north to the Powder River country of Wyoming to join the Bozeman Trail to Virginia City. On a map, this route looked advantageous: it was hundreds of miles shorter than the Platte Valley route to Fort Laramie. Possible resistance by the Sioux, Cheyennes, and Arapahos, and the lack of support facilities in the form of road ranches, forts, and communications lines, did not deter Congress from appropriating $50,000 to outfit the Sawyers wagon road expedition in 1865.

On March 31, Sawyers received detailed instructions on how he was to proceed. The expedition proper consisted of fifty-three men, including the engineer, clerk, physician, guides, scouts, pioneers, herders, and drivers. There were 45 yokes of oxen, 5 saddle horses, 5 mules, and 15 wagons loaded with chains, tools, tents, camp equipage, and subsistence for six months. The military escort brought twenty-five wagons, each drawn by six mules. In addition, there were five emigrant teams and a private freight train of thirty-six wagons, the latter so coupled as to be drawn by eighteen teams of oxen of six yokes each.[4]

Congressman Hubbard persuaded Maj. Gen. John Pope to provide an escort of 200 cavalry. In the end, the command consisted of Companies C and D of the 5th U.S. Volunteer Infantry (Galvanized Yankees), 118 men commanded by Capt. George W. Williford. The escort joined the expedition at the mouth of the Niobrara River. The troops were later augmented by a detachment of twenty-five men from Company B of the 1st Battalion, Dakota Cavalry, commanded by Lt. John R. Wood. Assistant Surgeon Smith accompanied the troops, and Dr. D. W. Tingley was the physician for the expedition. The engineer was Lewis H. Smith of Fort Dodge, Iowa, who had served with Sawyers in defense of Iowa's northern border in 1862–63. Also a lawyer and former judge, the thirty-year-old served as Sawyers's principal assistant.[5] Thus, there were 143 men in all. Gen. Alfred Sully of the sub-district furnished forty Springfield rifles, which Sawyers distributed among the civilians in the party.[6]

The expedition left the mouth of the Niobrara on June 13, 1865. Guides and scouts moved out first. The chief guide was Ben F. Estes, a former sergeant in Company A of the Dakota Cavalry who had been with Lt. Gouverneur K. Warren's exploring party in 1856. Paul Dorien was the other guide, but he deserted soon after leaving the Niobrara. Sawyers hired Baptiste Defond, a Yankton half-breed, to replace him. Defond served faithfully until his discharge at Bighorn Crossing.[7] The scouts were John F. Godfrey, originally from Bangor, Maine, and recently a lieutenant colonel in the Civil War, and Charles W. Sears of Onawa, Iowa.

The cavalry served as an advance scouting arm as well. The guides, scouts, cavalry, and pioneers moved well in advance of the main body, finding the best route, looking for Indians, and improving the road where necessary. Following in the order of march were a platoon of infantry with a howitzer. Then came Sawyers's wagons, another platoon of infantry, the emigrants and the private freight train, and, finally, the last platoon of infantry with the other howitzer.[8]

The expedition encountered no resistance until it reached the badlands around Pumpkin Buttes in present-day Wright, Wyoming. At noon on

August 13, the party corralled near some small springs to water the stock. Nathaniel D. Hedges, the brother of Charles and Daniel Hedges who was in charge of the private freight train and referred to as sutler for the expedition, decided to scout ahead. About one and a half miles from camp, he was surprised and killed by a party of Cheyennes. The raiders also drove off seven cavalry horses. Soldiers retrieved the scalped and mutilated body of the nineteen-year-old, whom Sawyers described as "a genial and pleasant companion . . . of very correct habits." The next day, at 5:00 P.M., they buried Hedges in a rude coffin made from boards of an abandoned government wagon. The site was in the center of the corral, so that livestock might trample the ground, concealing the burial.[9]

On August 14, the caravan traveled two and a half miles, corralled on a knoll near Bone Pile Creek, and turned out cattle for water and grass. The men dug rifle pits for defense. Guarded by twenty men, the cattle and oxen grazed peacefully nearby. Picketed on a high peak of the hills surrounding the camp was Private Jarvis of the Dakota Cavalry. He had reached an ascent from where there was a gradual slope of perhaps one mile back to camp. Leaving his horse to graze nearby, he sat there contentedly smoking his pipe, when, suddenly he heard a noise. Looking behind, he saw Indians crawling toward him from the other side of the peak. One glance was enough, and he was mounted and on his way. Fortunately, he possessed a fast horse, the animal carrying him swiftly down the slope, a dozen mounted Indians in pursuit. Commotion reigned in camp. Men hurriedly drove stock into the corral, while others grabbed rifles and ran to meet Jarvis to cover his retreat. Dodging the many arrows aimed at him, the private reached safety, losing only his hat. The Indians retreated, and nothing more was seen of them that evening.[10]

At sunrise on August 15, about 600 Dog Soldiers and Crooked Lances of the Southern Cheyennes, Dull Knife's Northern Cheyennes, and Red Cloud's Oglalas appeared on the surrounding bluffs.[11] Fighting began when they charged down over the plain, shooting into the corral. The soldiers and citizens repulsed each charge, however, and at about noon, the Indians called for a truce. Sawyers and Captain Williford left the corral to talk. George and Charlie Bent went with Dull Knife, Bull Bear, and Red Cloud to meet them. George Bent, acting as interpreter, wore the staff officer's uniform that he had appropriated at Julesburg. It was during this talk that the Indians learned about the new fort on the Powder River, and Sawyers and Williford learned about the death of Caspar Collins and the others at Platte Bridge and Red Buttes.[12]

Bent said that there was one condition that must be met if the Cheyennes were to make peace: the hanging of Colonel Chivington. He also said that the Indians believed that they were strong enough to fight U.S. troops, that they preferred to do it, that they knew the government would withdraw troops in the fall, and that they would then have it their own way again.[13]

After some parleying, over the objections of Captain Williford, Sawyers agreed to give them some bacon, sugar, coffee, flour, and tobacco in return for safe passage. Peace ended when two of the troops ventured out among the warriors. Suddenly, the Indians fired their weapons at the two, killing them both. They were Pvts. Anthony Nelson[14] and John Rouse[15] of Company B, Dakota Cavalry. Williford opened up with his artillery, and the Indians left immediately. A reconnaissance party discovered Nelson's body and brought it to camp. The men buried him at dark in a rifle pit on the north side of the corral.[16] Rouse's body was never found. Whites reported the deaths of eleven to forty warriors, but Indian sources state that none died.[17] The party continued without further incident.

On August 17, Captain Williford sent out a scouting party composed of Godfrey, Sears, Estes, and Defond. They reported back on August 19 that a good road could be made to the Powder River, and that from appearances, General Connor had passed down the Dry Fork about two days since with a large train.[18] On August 23, Captain Williford having refused to escort the train further, Sawyers sent Godfrey and Defond to discover, if possible, the whereabouts of Connor. They found Fort Connor about thirteen miles below, but learned that the general had gone on an expedition to Tongue River. On August 24, the whole party camped on the east side of Dry Fork about one mile from Fort Connor.

On August 25, they remained in camp. A party of Indians harassed the herders in the forenoon and stole one horse and killed two oxen. Godfrey returned with an order from Connor to Williford and his Galvanized Yankees to remain at Fort Connor and for Kidd to furnish Sawyers with a thirty-five-man escort of Company L, 6th Michigan Cavalry, to the Bighorn River. When the march resumed, the train consisted of fifty-seven wagons with 350 head of cattle. Besides tools and gear, the wagons carried sugar, coffee, apples, canned fruits, candles, soap, and kerosene.[19]

Because it was twenty-six miles to the next water on Crazy Woman Creek, and because of the oppressive heat, Sawyers determined to make a night march. The expedition started for Crazy Woman Fork at 4:00 P.M., arriving at 10:00 A.M. on August 27, when the wagons were corralled. The journey continued on August 27. Starting at 3:00 P.M., they arrived at 9:00 A.M. on August 28 at the Clear Fork of the Powder. The next day, despite heavy rain, the expedition made a sixteen-mile march, camping on Big Piney. At noon the expedition passed a half mile west of Lake DeSmet.[20]

Sawyers and his men had no idea that at the same time they were passing Lake DeSmet, Connor and his men were laying waste to the village of Black Bear and Medicine Bear.

The party continued to make good progress, fording the Big Piney on August 30 and, after crossing several divides, camping on Beaver Creek. The next day, the wagon train covered twenty-two miles, fording Goose and Wolf Creeks and the Little Tongue River. That night, one-armed Capt. Osmer F. Cole of Galesburg, Illinois, Company L, 6th Michigan, was surrounded and killed by Indians while scouting in advance of the train.[21]

On September 1, the party traveled two and half miles and crossed the north branch of Tongue River. There Indians attacked the rear guard and drove off loose livestock. The train attempted to proceed after crossing, but the surrounding bluffs soon became alive with Indians. These were the warriors from the Arapaho village seeking revenge.[22]

Albert M. Holman, a nineteen-year-old oxen driver at the time, described the scene in a reminiscence:

> In a double column our train forded Tongue river, but this task was so arduous that by the time the last wagon was over, the leading wagons were half a mile in the lead. Forty head of loose oxen were bringing up the rear and were still in the water when the Indians, about 100 in number, and of the Arapaho nation, swooped down on them and succeeded in cutting several off from the train. The wagon drivers couldn't use their guns as their oxen required their entire attention. We formed an irregular corral with our wagons and took the defensive against the Indians who by this time had been increased to about 600. They would ride in circles around our corral and shoot at us from under their horses necks. All were bareback and the way they yelled would shame the most ardent football rooters of our big colleges.[23]

More were not killed because the Arapahos reloaded with insufficient powder, so that bullets did not have enough force to inflict many dangerous wounds. Warriors began to invade dense timber along the river, but a few shells from the howitzer forced them back. The Indians did not immediately attack again, but started building great fires and barbecuing some of the captured livestock. Thinking the Arapahos were appeased, the expedition broke corral and, in two columns, entered the low hills beyond Tongue River. Seeing the movement, warriors rode ahead and fired upon the caravan from the hills. Not knowing what lay ahead, Sawyers and his men decided to return to Tongue River, where they would still have a good supply of water.

Attacking from all sides and especially the rear, the warriors poured volleys into the wagon train, but again, the bullets lacked force, and many of them hit the sides of oxen with a thud, but failed to break skin. Approaching the river farther down than the first fording, the wagons experienced heavy fire. Twenty-five Indians circumvented the train and rode ahead to a vantage point along a high bank. James Dilleland, driving an oxen team in the lead, was struck in the back by a bullet, the musket ball entering about two inches to the left of the last lumbar vertebrae and coming out about two inches below the navel. In a few minutes, E. G. Merrill, a driver of one of the emigrant teams from Cedar Falls, Iowa, took a ball in the left side. The missile entered near the anterior extremity of the eighth rib, where it lodged beneath the skin at a point nearly opposite on the right side. The ball passed sufficiently deep to damage both the stomach and liver, and the man died in a few hours from internal hemorrhaging. Comrades placed both men in one of the wagons, and as no reserve drivers were in the train, Dilleland's wagon followed along without a guiding hand.

For the fifth time since reaching Tongue River, the men formed a corral—sixty canvas wagons arranged in a large circle with all the loose oxen and cattle on the inside. Now, they were momentarily safe, being out of rifle range. The Indians went into camp about a quarter mile up river. Firing continued throughout the day.

On the second night, both forces held the same positions. That evening, Sawyers offered a substantial reward to anyone who would volunteer to find Connor and bring reinforcements. That night, three men with rations stealthily stole away on the perilous undertaking.

On September 2, some rain fell during the night, but the morning was cool and fine. From 250 to 300 Indians milled about, keeping well out of range. In the forenoon, the chiefs signified their wish for a talk, advancing under a white flag. They said they were Arapahos and that four days before, Connor had surprised them in camp, killing many of them, taking large numbers of ponies, and burning their village. They agreed to send three of their number with three of Sawyers's men to Connor, "they wishing for their ponies and we for more men." A dozen Indians agreed to stay with the whites as hostages, and Sawyers turned the stock out to graze.[24]

On September 3, Dilleland died. Toward night on the next day, the three Arapaho Indians returned, stating that many whites were coming. The truce was terminated and the hostages released. They declined to stay at camp, seeming suspicious of more trouble. At sunrise on September 5,

Capt. James Kellog of the 6th Michigan Cavalry with twenty-seven men rode into camp. They had mail for Connor's command but had been attacked and sought refuge. They reported that Sawyers's three messengers had gone on down Tongue River to find General Connor. On September 6, after dark, the men interred Captain Cole on the north side of the corral in a rifle pit and buried Dilleland and Merrill on the southeast side. To distract some Indian visitors who had come to trade, one of the men took out his violin and regaled the bunch with music. A number of the men danced cotillions, jigs, and reels, while shovels opened and closed graves in the darkened corral.[25]

The train remained *in situ* for the next week. On September 12, a large majority of the men refused to proceed without an escort, the 6th Michigan having orders not to go beyond the Bighorn River. Consequently, Sawyers regretfully announced that the next day they would return to Fort Connor. The men, however, wanted a change in leadership. In his account of the affair, Holman states:

> We were wrought up to a high pitch of excitement for this was a critical time and we felt that we must do something to prevent total annihilation. Some suggested a change of leader. It was quickly put to a vote and a new leaders was chosen. . . . Since we had acted so impulsively in electing a new commander, it was suggested by Col. Sawyers that another vote be taken, and so the men were told to step on either side of an imaginary line, but the verdict was the same as before.

When the party learned that the military escort had orders prohibiting them from crossing the Bighorn, the mutineers proposed to burn all but thirteen wagons and employ the teamsters thus freed as an escort. Sawyers refused to listen to this, and it was determined to retreat to Fort Connor.[26]

Sawyers tells the story a little differently:

> My teamsters through fear had mutinied and had taken my whole outfit one day's travel back toward home. As soon as I made known the same to Capt Brown he said to quell all such mutinies on the plains was to kill the leaders but as I had few enough men to handle our teams I rather begged not to kill them.[27]

On September 13, just after the train had turned back for Fort Connor, Capt. Albert Brown with Company L of the 2nd California Cavalry and a company of Omaha and Winnebago scouts under Capt. Edwin Nash reached the scene. Brown had been delayed because of cloudbursts that had caused streams and dry washes to run full. Brown restored harmony in the train, and on September 15, they renewed their journey. On the sixteenth, they reached the Little Bighorn River. That night, Little Priest came in with six Arapaho prisoners. Brown ordered Captain Nash to feed them from his company stores, which Nash declined to do. Brown then decided to send them back to their camp, the Indians promising to meet the party with their whole band the next day a few miles down the road. Brown provided an escort of thirty of his men, as the Winnebagos wanted to kill them.[28]

On September 19, the train moved six miles up the Bighorn Valley to the Bozeman Trail ferry, where the river was about 400 feet across. Because of recent rains, the men experienced considerable difficulty in finding a ford with a depth of three and a half feet. The pioneers improved the approaches to the crossing, while the rest of the men worked to get the wagons across. All the teams were on the west bank and the wagons corralled by 11:00 A.M. Captain Brown's orders from General Connor did not permit him to proceed any farther, the west bank of the Bighorn being Crow country and outside of the war zone. He prepared to report back to Fort Connor. Before leaving, he detailed Sgt. James Youcham and seven men of the 2nd California to accompany the party to Virginia City.[29]

Sawyers and his party continued on to the Yellowstone, following Bozeman's 1864 route. They had no difficulty in fording the river, and reached Bozeman on October 5. By October 12, Sawyers was in Virginia City, having traveled 1,039 miles after leaving the Niobrara. There he gave an interview to the *Montana Post,* in which he praised his route, noting that the only interference on the trip came from the Indians, who had detained him twenty-five to thirty days. In Virginia City, he paid off his men, sold the outfit, and left for home on the overland stage by way of Denver, arriving in Sioux City on December 3. He then headed for Washington to report in person to Secretary of Interior James Harlan.[30]

General Dodge, however, did not think much of Sawyers's effort. In a letter to his superiors, he called the journey a failure, declaring that while it was ostensibly a survey to make a road through a comparatively unknown country, it was, in his opinion, a ruse to escort eighty private wagons to Virginia City, and that Sawyers and his men had done practically nothing to develop a road, such as building bridges and making other improvements.[31]

However, the Sawyers expedition's effect was to contribute at least one important change to the route of the Bozeman Trail. When Sawyers reached Clark's Fork, after the difficult and circuitous route via the Yellowstone, he wrote in his journal that a cutoff could be made more directly west to Pryor's Fork and thence across country to Clark's Fork, thereby saving more than twenty miles. Several diaries and accounts of the 1865 expedition contribute much to our knowledge of the actual measurements and distances involved.[32]

The effort by Sawyers and the government's $50,000 went for naught. Although the entrepreneur successfully retraced his route in 1866 and brought another train to Virginia City, his road was already obsolete because of the construction of the Union Pacific Railroad, then in progress.[33] The Sawyers expedition had another more immediate consequence. It drew away from Connor's command forces that could have otherwise been utilized in his efforts to punish the Sioux and their allies. At the time that Sawyers and his men were under fire from Arapahos on Tongue River, Connor was searching desperately for the rest of his command, and the companies that he gave Sawyers for rescue and escort deprived him of more scouting efforts and may have delayed his liaison with his subordinates, causing him to miss opportunities to engage his enemies in what might have been the concluding battle of the Sioux and Cheyenne war.

CHAPTER NINE

Cole and Walker

When they began their marches toward Powder River in the early summer of 1865, little did Nelson Cole and Samuel Walker know that they would become involved in one of the great adventures of the nineteenth-century Indian wars.

Col. Nelson Cole had been through Columbus, Nebraska, about the first of June. He had no guide, and finding that Luther North had done some scouting for a company of soldiers there, he sent for him and asked him to provide that service. North told him that he had never been farther than the head of the North Loup and did not feel like taking the responsibility. The next day, Cole passed through Pawnee Agency and hired a man named George Sandas as guide. Sandas was from Chicago and had never been west of the Missouri River until he came to Pawnee Agency. Not being able to find knowledgeable guides would cause Cole serious problems. Several Pawnees accompanied the column for several weeks.[1]

It took Cole ten days to get his wagon train in shape. Most of the mules provided had been not been broken, and he described the teamsters as "in the main worthless." In the absence of contractors' goods that had not yet arrived, he had to purchase supplies from vendors in Omaha, which cost $15,000. Connor ordered him to leave no grain behind, and to comply, he had to hire some civilian transportation. Finally, on July 1, Cole began his march with the 12th Missouri Cavalry and the 2nd Missouri Light Artillery. The 12th Missouri carried Spencer carbines, repeaters that held seven shells in the magazine. Having a range of 900 yards, the Spencer was a very effective weapon in the hands of a trained man.[2] Maj. Lyman G. Bennett joined the command en route on July 4 to serve as the column's engineer. The Pawnee guides dubbed him "Pohote the Willa," meaning Hill Climber, since he was often heading for high ground to make observations for his maps.[3]

On July 22, the first trouble occurred in Cole's command. When ready to start, several enlisted men of the 2nd Missouri refused to move. When informed, the colonel instructed the lieutenant in command to shoot the first man who disobeyed the order. Mounting his horse, the lieutenant told his charges that he would shoot "the first son of a b——" who refused to comply with the order, and the men relented, later to face a court-martial.[4] The next day, a stampede resulted in the loss of a number of horses. First Lt. Charles Springer of Company B, 12th Missouri, blamed the men of the 2nd Missouri for the incident, calling their actions malicious and willful and designed to end the expedition.[5]

Cole employed two more guides, but they were no better than Sandas. It was rumored that Sandas and his companions lost Cole's command before they got to the Niobrara River, and that the colonel threatened to hang the former. When the column reached Bear Butte on August 14 at the northern end of the Black Hills, the threesome informed the colonel that they did not know the country west of that point. By this time, the troops had traveled some 560 miles in forty-three days since leaving Omaha; the mules and horses were beginning to give out, and several wagons had been abandoned and burned.[6]

In the meantime, Lt. Col. Samuel Walker's column prepared to leave Fort Laramie to effect a rendezvous with Cole's troops.[7] Walker was supposed to leave Fort Laramie on July 20, but his troops refused to go, claiming that they had enlisted to fight rebels, not Indians; that the war for which they enlisted was over; and that they should be mustered out. In response to Walker's request for assistance, Captain Price, acting for General Connor, hurried two companies of California Cavalry and a detachment of the 11th Ohio to the scene with two howitzers, double-shot with grape and canister. The dissidents succumbed, and Walker had seven ringleaders arrested and placed in irons. The command left on August 5.[8] He took forty days' supplies packed on mules.[9]

Walker's column marched in a northwesterly direction up Rawhide Creek, across the Cheyenne to the Bell Fourche, and along the west base of the Black Hills to the right of Devil's Tower toward the Little Missouri, until it intercepted Cole's command on August 19.[10] Cole's column had been delayed in reaching the area for a number of reasons besides the incompetence of its guides. Along the way, scurvy became prevalent among Cole's men. Two men died of the disease, but surgeons were able to find a species of onion, which the soldiers ate avidly, and which in most cases had the desired result.[11] Cole got poison ivy so bad that one of his eyes swelled shut. In the valley of O'Fallon's Creek, the troops were reduced to drinking water recently contaminated with buffalo excrement. On July 19, Pvt. Nicholas Thomason disappeared while on flanking duty, believed to have been captured by Indians.[12]

Walker's column had fared better because it was out of Fort Laramie for only a little over two weeks, and it had pack mules, so it could move faster. Walker suffered from the same lack of intelligence as Cole, however: his guides "knew nothing of the country before them."[13]

Cole and Walker met about forty miles north of Devil's Tower, near Pine Creek in what is now the northeastern corner of Wyoming. The two columns did not camp together but marched several miles apart, mostly to assure enough grass for their horses. From there, the troops marched together a short distance north into Montana and then west to Powder River, reaching that river about August 30 at a point about fifty miles from the Yellowstone. On the march to Powder River, Walker likened the earth to a heap of burnt ashes, in which he declared that his horses sank to their knees at every step. The men noticed warriors watching them in small parties, and Walker had ten worn-out horses killed to keep them from falling into Indian hands.[14]

The Sioux and Cheyenne camp was within a few miles of where the troops struck the Powder, but the men were not aware of the large Indian force until they encountered it in early September. This camp may have contained as many as 1,000 lodges and 6,000 people, consisting of the coalition of Oglalas, Brules, Minniconjous, Northern Cheyennes and 2,000 Southern Cheyennes. The gathering was unprecedented to that time.[15]

On August 29, running out of rations, Cole sent Lt. A. S. Hoagland and twenty men with Raymond, his most reliable guide, on a scout to find Connor's whereabouts. They returned on September 1 about 3:00 P.M. without news, having visited Tongue River, the Panther Mountains, and Rosebud Creek. Cole immediately ordered rations cut to half and prepared to march to the Panther Mountains where Connor had said that supplies would be waiting.

As he was writing his intentions to Walker, Cole learned that Sioux had attacked a small guard of Company K of the 2nd Missouri Light Artillery that had been herding some company horses a mile distant from camp. The Indians succeeded in driving off nineteen or twenty of the animals. Cole ordered the command to pursue the raiders, leaving only a few to guard the camp. An advance party of seven men under Capt. Edward S. Rowland was the first to engage the Sioux, killing several and recovering the stock. But another band of about forty-five warriors appeared suddenly from a gully, killing Sergeant Holt and three others and mortally wounding the remaining two enlisted men.[16] One of the wounded men came wandering into camp. He wore only a shirt and was taken for an Indian before his true identity was discovered. He had been shot several times with arrows. His head and hair were a mass of blood, with deep gashes on his face and head. A little farther on, they found the other man, his body pierced with arrows and a bullet hole through his stomach. He had been stripped and scalped, his skull completely bare. One of the wounded had been shot with a poisoned arrow, sealing his fate.[17]

The main body of the command arrived shortly thereafter and the battle continued, with the warriors falling back, but Cole's men could not pursue rapidly enough because of their worn-out horses. On the other hand, Indians had few firearms, and the troops carried Spencer carbines, which gave them an advantage. Finally, darkness intervened, and the troops returned to camp. Cole estimated that the Indians numbered between 400 and 500 and that his troops had killed 25 and wounded many more.[18]

Later that evening, two soldiers of the 2nd Artillery brought in two dead comrades, their bodies tomahawked and horribly mutilated. The men had been out hunting when they encountered a war party. The two men who escaped fought bravely, killing at least two of the Indians. They brought in the corpse of one, whom a Sioux guide for the 16th Kansas identified as a noted Cheyenne. The warrior had one bullet through his forehead, one through the heart, and one through the throat.[19]

That night the officers held a meeting. Cole left the decision as to what to do next to his officers, and they decided to head for the Yellowstone in hopes of locating General Connor or finding abundant game to replace depleted rations. Walker took the lead. The terrain soon turned to sagebrush, prickly pear cactus, and greasewood, showing nothing edible for the starved mules and horses. The animals supped on cottonwood bark. During the night the temperature plummeted, and a cold storm engulfed the exhausted commands.[20] The commanders decided to turn back and head for Fort Laramie, the closest military post known to them. Cheers from the troops approved the decision.[21]

On September 3, the journey back began. During the march downriver and back to grass, 225 horses and mules perished from excessive heat, exhaustion, and starvation. Consequently, a number of wagons had to be destroyed, as well as a large amount of now unnecessary quartermaster stores, such as saddles, brushes, curry combs, and harnesses.[22]

On September 4, the second day up Powder River, Walker's column took the lead. Cole traveled only two miles before stopping to feed his animals after finding some good grass. At about dusk, the Indians again made their appearance, attacking a small party of fifteen men of the 12th Missouri Cavalry sent back to the last camp to complete the burning of abandoned wagons. About seventy-five warriors skirmished for a while and then withdrew, the troops pursuing them for a number of miles. The men slept with their arms that night, expecting an attack in the morning. During the night Pvt. H. Grote died of scurvy.[23]

At daybreak, just after breakfast, the fighting was renewed. Company M, 2nd Missouri Artillery, occupied the woods along the west bank of Powder River and protected the rear of the camp. Stationed on the right was the 12th Missouri Cavalry. The line of the 2nd Missouri Artillery extended to the corral of the commissary train on the left, with parts of three companies deployed from the train to the woods. The men held their places for three hours as Sioux and Cheyenne warriors dashed forward and backward, trying to draw them out. Cheyenne sources reported that the lack of firearms kept them from breaking the soldiers' line that day. The fabled warrior Roman Nose distinguished himself by riding three times parallel to the army line within range of the volunteers' carbines, and three times returning unscathed.[24] At one point, about twenty warriors made a dash for the wagon train, but the teamsters had been armed the night before and held them back.[25]

Near disaster occurred when ten men from Company B, 12th Missouri, under Lieutenant Springer, crossed the river without orders and soon found themselves outnumbered. It looked to the young officer as if the attackers "appeared to grow out of the ground."[26] Springer and his detachment barely escaped, losing two men in the process, Pvts. James D. Morris and George McCully. An enlisted man of the 2nd Missouri Artillery also died in the same charge, shot by an Indian who in turn was shot by Lieutenant Smiley.[27]

About 8:00 A.M., the Sioux and Cheyennes attempted a grand coup de mars by attempting to cross a party of about 1,000 to the west bank of the river. The Indians came dashing down from the bluff in a confused mass, "yelling like a set of fiends let loose from the infernal regions," and as the advance entered the river, which was less than fifty yards wide, the Missourians opened up. Warriors in the rear were continually rushing up, pushing the advance directly into the army fire. This disastrous situation completely demoralized the Indians, who fled in every direction.[28]

Colonel Cole guessed that the Sioux and Cheyennes in this attack numbered at least 1,000, and he noted that all the hilltops, divides, and margins of the nearest bluffs held hundreds more. The 3-inch guns that the Missourians had served them well, scattering groups of warriors and preventing mass attacks. The fighting continued until 10:00 A.M., when the Indians withdrew. Cole estimated between and 200 and 600 Indians had been killed or wounded.[29]

Cole immediately moved his column twelve miles upriver, where he found grass. The volunteers kept moving, making eight to twelve miles the next few days. On September 7, a party of five men of the 12th Missouri left the main column to search for game on the opposite side of the river. Two of the men were about a quarter mile ahead when eighteen warriors rushed out of a ravine. The men, mounted on mules, tried to flee, but were soon overtaken by the fresh ponies. The attackers shot Pvt. William Bradshaw, Company D, 12th Missouri, through the body with two arrows, killing him instantly, but Pvt. Josephus Rich, an experienced frontiersman, was able to seek cover in a hollow where he killed three and wounded three others before being rescued. The soldiers recovered Bradshaw's body, his friend removing one of the arrow heads, which he took home with him. They buried Bradshaw where they found him.[30]

On September 8, they once again encountered the Sioux and Cheyennes in force. Walker was again in the lead, with Cole's company of pioneers smoothing the way when the attack began. Lyman Bennett described the scene:

> We had a long stretch of beautiful road along a wide level valley and then came to a bend in the river which skirted high precipitous bluffs for a mile. To move the command over these bluffs was impossible and we prepared a road across the river which was forded without any difficulty. While Captain Bordman with his pioneers was preparing the road, the 16th moved on in advance and were perhaps two miles ahead. We had just completed the road and the head of Col. Cole's column had crossed the river when a firing was heard with the 16th and looking that way we saw Indians swarming out from the woods and ravines and blackening the hills and valley.[31]

The advance guard of twenty-five men of the 16th Kansas was nearly a mile ahead of the column. Soon surrounded by hundreds of warriors, they fell back rapidly to the riverbank, which was high and afforded good protection. However one of the men, who was poorly mounted, did not make it. After killing him, the warriors took the skin from his head and face and cut off his ears and one arm.

Lieutenant Colonel Walker arrived to form a skirmish line, every fourth man becoming a horse holder. As the line moved forward, the Sioux and Cheyenne warriors retreated, crossing back and forth in front, keeping just out of range. Suddenly, the soldiers saw a group of about a dozen dis-mounted men, fighting in the midst of circling warriors. The men were hunters who had left camp that morning. Captain Bordman's men soon rescued them.[32]

In the meantime, Cole ordered his trains corralled and his troops moved without delay to support the Kansans. The battle may have involved as many as 3,000 to 4,000 Sioux and Cheyennes, perhaps the largest engagement ever fought by the army on the Northern Plains.[33] Lieutenant Springer simply reported, "they were thicker than fiddlers in hell."[34] But after "a spirited and lively use" of the Spencer carbines and the two moun-tain howitzers of Company M, 16th Kansas, the Indians dispersed, Cole noting that they did not fight with the same energy of a few days before.[35]

The troops crossed the river, fighting chilling north winds, and traveled fifteen miles before making camp. Cole tripled the guard, and three com-panies kept their horses saddled.[36] That night the beleaguered command experienced a winter storm that killed 414 horses and mules in the two commands.[37] P. C. Stepps remembered the event:

> A great storm broke upon us, the rain commencing as night came on and pouring in torrents all night, turning cold towards morn-ing. Over 300 dead mules and horses were counted the next morning I stayed with my horse all night and moved him around to keep him alive. When morning broke he could stand up but could move his feet but a few inches at a time. It was several days before it was safe to ride him.[38]

Cole recalled that first it rained, then hailed, then rained again, then snowed and sleeted. The openness of the camp and the severity of the storm made fires impossible, and picket officers marched their men in cir-cles to prevent freezing. Walker remembered that about dark it turned freezing cold, the rain penetrating to the bone. By midnight horses began to drop. "God forbid," Walker wrote in his report, "I shall ever have to pass such another night." The officer later counted his losses as 250 mules and horses dead and 150 unfit for service.[39]

When the storm had not abated in the morning, Cole moved his men and remaining animals two and a half miles into a sheltering woods, where fires could be lit and the horses and mules fed cottonwood bark and the lit-tle grass that was there. The surviving animals had been without grain for sixty days. The loss of so many more horses meant the discard of more sup-plies and accouterments. Tents, men's clothing, officers' trunks, and ord-nance stores were among the equipage left behind.[40]

On September 10, Cole ordered Companies A, B, C, and D of the 12th Missouri to turn their horses over to the 2nd battalion. This order met with great displeasure. Lieutenant Springer noted that the men who still had horses were those who had taken the best care of them, and to turn them over to others who had lost theirs was an outrage.[41] That day the column moved again, with Indians harassing the rear but soon tiring of the sport after the artillery began throwing shells among them. Crossing the mouth of the Little Powder, the troops came upon the site of what had been a large Indian village, estimated to have held 1,500 to 2,000 lodges.[42]

The next several days the columns crossed and recrossed the Powder, the gullies, ravine, and steep hills on either side dictating this form of travel. The men encountered quicksand along the route, and some of the animals that bogged down had to be left to die.[43] The command was now in desperate straights. Where was Connor?

CHAPTER TEN

Rescue and Reversal

ON SEPTEMBER 15, ONE OF CONNOR'S SOLDIERS AND TWO PAWNEE scouts found the lost command. About 6:00 P.M., September 11, North arrived in Connor's camp, having come from Powder River about fifty miles away. He reported discovering about 250 dead cavalry horses, undoubtedly belonging to Cole's command.[1] Most of them had been shot through the head at the picket line. North surmised that Cole and Walker had been hard-pressed by the Indians and had been forced to dismount their men and shoot their horses. The emaciated condition of the horses showed that the Indians had denied them the chance to forage. The trail was well marked, moving off three wagons abreast, and showed that Cole had pushed on up the river in the opposite direction from the course that he had been ordered to take.[2]

The news led Connor to redouble his efforts to open communication; otherwise, continuing in his present direction, Cole might have to travel 400 miles before he could find any food for his men.[3] North also reported that he had discovered a large village a short distance up the bottoms. In order to give this intelligence to Connor, North had returned to the camp on Tongue River in less than twenty-four hours, having travelled during the night.[4]

On September 12, at 7:00 A.M., Connor dispatched volunteer Sgt. Charles L. Thomas[5] and two Pawnees to carry the following message to Cole:

> Fearing that for some unforeseen cause you may be deterred from reaching the Rendezvous, as I ordered & having waited on this River several days & Scouted the Country for you, I have given up all hopes of your coming. Follow my track up this River and thence South to Ft. Connor on Powder River 160 miles south of here. P. E. Connor, Brig. Genl. Com'd'y.[6]

137

Thomas later wrote an account of his ride:

So I rode out of Conners [sic] camp at 7 o'clock in the morning & the next morning at sunrise I rode into powder river, on the oft bank I found the trail of Cole command; after riding a few miles I saw where they had camp. I was now & had been for miles closely followed by scores of Indians; my old Spencer rifle was getting so hot I could not hold the barrel with my necked hand; not cannons, but Indians to the right, Indians to the left, it seamed that at ever turn I should rush into the jaws of death.

I could not turn back for thair were hundreds behind me; twelve oclock & no Cole, but indians thicker, fidlers in hell; three oclock my horse getting verry tired, aminition getting low & Coles command not in sight yet, the horse keeps the trail & I keep hooting at the nearest man.

Now I see a body of men acrost the trail to far yet to tell who they are, but great hope rise within that it is Coles men, but no it is Indians. I keep steady on untill with in one hundred yards, stop & fire. Indians brake & run two empty sadles, not mine, one horse followes the other; one has a dead Indian fastend to the halter strap. I get the horse for I dont know when my noble one will drop; the Sun is getting low & so is my Sperit, but all at wonst I see some thing that makes my heart leap; by the side of the trail lays a man it is one of Coles men [J. G. Hutson, Company L, 2nd Missouri Light Artillery].

He has been dismounted for severl days, is bearfooted, has walked for miles through prickley pears & cactus untill he cold walk no more; he had throwen away his gun & accuterments & layed down resigned to await his fate whitch in a short time would have been death & he would have been numbered with the unnowen dead.

I got him on my Indian horse & when the sun sank to rest that night I rode into Coles camp & gave him Conners dispatch I did not get the mans name or co at the time & did not think so mutch About that ride then as I do now So some 8 or 10 years ago.[7]

After giving the message to Cole on the evening of September 15,[8] Thomas left the next morning with Lieutenant Jones and fifteen men to make the return trip. On September 17, he delivered a dispatch to Connor, having ridden about 250 miles in five days.[9]

Help came none too soon for Cole and Walker and their men. Pvt. Ansel Steck, Company D, 12th Missouri Cavalry, later wrote about the severe test of the soldiers' stamina and will:

> We were surrounded by thousands of Indians, with whom we had been fighting for several days. At least one half of our troops were already dismounted; the horses had been shot because they were too weak to go any more. Our wagons & extra camp equipage had been burnt & the command was without rations or clothing & hundreds of the dismounted men were barefooted. The entire command was disheartened & discouraged, for our guides do not know where to lead us to find food.[10]

After the disastrous loss of horses, Cole ordered any excess personal items burned, each man contributing something—an old hat, an old shirt, a pair of pants, a looking glass, a box of medicine. Tents, saddles, harnesses, and 100 wagons fed the fires, until the baggage had been reduced by half.[11]

In response to Connor's orders, Cole's troops began the march toward Fort Connor. At the same time, the men began eating dead horses and killing mules for food.[12] High water made travel difficult, as the column had to cross and recross the Powder on its way south.[13]

In the meantime, Connor and his troops had been moving up Tongue River. With all his scouting parties out, Connor now had only about 150 men to guard a large train of 500 head of captured stock, with the Arapahos on his left, the Sioux and Cheyenne on his right, and he knew not what in front.[14] Some in the command were becoming disillusioned. Lyman Bennett wrote in his diary, "So far Genl. Connor cannot boast of having done much but kill horses." He also was tired of hearing about the prowess of North and the Pawnee Scouts: "To say that Capt. North and his scouts killed all, or anything like half of the Indians they attacked, is sheer nonsense. July 2 scalps were exhibited and it is well known that had they killed all of the Indians, the Pawnee, would have brought along the scalps as grand trophies."[15]

When the general had learned of the whereabouts of Cole's command, he rushed a few boxes of hardtack forward. It had been three weeks since the men had had any food except mule meat and a few berries and wild rosebuds.[16] One of Cole's men had been so hungry that when a mule got stuck in quicksand, he laid out a pole cut from the bank of the stream, crawled out on it, and cut a piece of living flesh from the animal's back, which he cooked and devoured. Walker reported that if one of his horses died and it happened to be in good flesh, within two minutes twenty men would pounce on it, strip its bones, and eat the meat raw.[17]

On the evening of September 15, Captain Marshall and fifty men from Fort Connor rode into camp. The troopers generously gave the ravenous men their rations, refusing offers of payment. On September 17, a small advance party went forward to Fort Connor. On September 19 and 20, the main body of troops staggered in, where they received as much food as they could eat.[18] According to Henry Palmer, Cole's men were half starved, very ragged and dirty, resembling tramps more than they did soldiers. Walker remembered that one-third of his men were barefoot, their feet bleeding at every step.[19]

That night the Winnebagos and Pawnees held a victory dance. Bedecked in the spoils of war and brandishing their tomahawks, they swirled to the beat of four drums. Cherry brandy and cigars from the sutler ended the day for Lieutenant Springer and his friends.[20] In the meantime, the Sioux had left the immediate region, heading for the Little Missouri.[21]

On September 20, the columns made permanent camp within five miles of Fort Connor. The men washed in the river, changed their wardrobes, and feasted, army fare never tasting better. Laughter and singing filled the air, sounds not heard for many days.[22]

Walker reported his losses for the campaign as one man killed and four wounded, but he could not estimate the Indian dead; in fact, he could not positively say that he had killed even one. He had seen a number fall, but they were always carried away by their comrades. Cole's final tally was twelve killed, two missing, and one wounded, and 600 horses dead.[23] In the campaign, Cole's men had traveled 1,700 miles, forded rivers, built bridges, cut miles of road along the sides of mountains and rivers, and engaged the great fighters of the plains in mortal combat.[24] It was something to tell the grandchildren.

At the same time that North and his scouts had found Cole's trail, they had discovered signs of the Indian village for which they had looked so long. Immediately, Connor prepared to form Cole and Walker's troops into an attack force. He planned to hit the village hard, but the 11th Ohio regiment's horses were in such poor condition that he thought it best to let them rest for two or three days on good grass. The next morning about dawn, two companies of the 6th Michigan regiment came into camp with orders for General Connor to cease the campaign. Captain Marshall and a detachment followed with a dispatch ordering Connor to a new job in Salt Lake City. Thus, he had no choice but to disband the force and head west. Maj. Gen. John Pope, commander of the Division of the Missouri, had issued the order on August 22, abolishing the District of Plains and ordering Connor to take over the newly created District of Utah.[25]

General Dodge himself had journeyed to Fort Connor, which he had reached on September 1. His purpose was to personally convey orders, "under direction of the authorities at Washington," to General Connor to return all troops to Fort Laramie, stop all operations against the Plains tribes, and attempt a meeting with them to agree on ceasing hostilities. Dodge thought the peace movement was a mistake, and on his return to Fort Laramie, he wrote Pope the following letter:

> I consider the Indian matters here of so much importance, and no one can judge of them so well as when he is on the ground, that I desire to make a proposition to the Government. If the Government will allow me to keep General Connor in the field with not to exceed 2,000 men of his present force, leaving the forces you have designated to garrison posts on the plains, I will settle these Indian difficulties before spring satisfactorily to the Government and bring about a peace that will be lasting. I may do it in a month or two; or it may be longer. The additional expense to the Government will be the pay of that number of troops for the time detained. All the stores, forage, etc., to support them are here and en route. As soon as we settle with them we can send the troops in and take 2,000 more from our post in addition and muster them out. General Connor left Powder River with sixty days' supplies, and I am satisfied if we will allow him he will settle the matter before he returns. Should he come back by our orders without settling the matter, the entire tribes will be down on our lines, and we will have our hands full, and more too. The forces for Utah I will soon have on the road and when Connor gets back he can go right there.[26]

Dodge's proposition gained no support.

The conclusion of the Powder River campaign was due to a number of factors. First was the increasing influence of the Indian Commission fostered by Governor Edmunds of Dakota Territory and appointed by the president. The work of the body was about to begin, with Owen Guernsey, member; Captain Ruth, commission secretary; and R. B. Hill, its reporter, arriving in St. Louis on September 3. The commission's first meeting was in Council Bluffs on September 10.[27]

The creation of the commission caused some observers to note the inconsistency in the approach to the Indian problem. The *Army and Navy*

Journal declared, "We are now approaching the red men with the olive-branch in one hand and a carbine in the other. To the descendants of UNCAS we leave the choice."[28] Confusion concerning appropriate action was no more evident than on September 15, when Northern Superintendent Taylor, who was a member of the commission, noted in his annual report that the Indians had continued to raid, pillage, and destroy life and property in the region and recommended a winter campaign against them.[29]

Too, a Congressional Committee on Indian Affairs was visiting in the West that summer, investigating the situation and advocating a peace policy. The army was slow in responding to these pressures, but when the operations of these groups began, the army hierarchy reacted. The final blow came from the secretary of war, who found that requisitions for supplies for the projected military operations against Indians far exceeded the appropriations for such purposes.[30]

Connor was very angry when he read the order to cease hostilities and vowed that he would discover and attack the village the next morning, destroy it, and suffer the consequences. His officers pleaded with him not to disobey the order, warning him that he would be cashiered and dishonored, and he relented.[31] Connor returned to Fort Connor on September 24, and on September 26, he left for Fort Laramie with three ambulances, Frank North and the Indians driving the stock. Following the group were Cole and Walker and their men. As they passed some of the Missourians on foot, Connor threw out an old pair of boots for a barefoot soldier, who praised him loudly.[32] The volunteers reached Fort Laramie on October 4. On October 7, Cole received orders to proceed with his regiment to Fort Leavenworth, Kansas, there to be mustered out.[33]

Another unit being mustered out was Company G of the 11th Ohio. Withdrawing from the little outposts of South Pass Station, St. Mary's Station, Three Crossings Station, and Sweetwater Station, Company G took its time coming in. Pvt. Perrin Finch remembered that the men had persuaded Lieutenant Bretney to go down the north side of the Platte River to avoid places where they could be reached by telegraph. Taking somewhat longer than expected by the commanding officer of Fort Laramie, Bretney received a dressing down upon arrival.[34]

Connor arrived at Fort Laramie on September 29 with 610 horses—the number remaining from those captured during the campaign.[35] The post's officers heartily welcomed the arrivals. After a serenade by the band and a fine dinner, the men had time to become presentable again in clean blue broadcloth and gilded buttons.[36]

In the meantime, raiding had continued in the region. Indians had attacked Horseshoe Station on September 18 and stole six mules. The same days, they took eighty-three horses from a group of mountaineers two miles from Fort Laramie. On September 19, they appropriated fifteen mules and three horses from the post herd and absconded with another thirty-five animals seven miles away. About forty Indians attacked Cold Springs twenty-nine miles east of Fort Laramie and drove off the entire herd of twenty-four animals. In late September, Indians attacked a small group of quartermaster employees, camped on the right bank of the North Platte River seven miles west of the station at O'Fallon's Bluff. They killed J. H. Temple and wounded three others.[37]

Connor remained at Fort Laramie until October 4, when he left for Denver. On October 1, General Dodge wrote him a nice letter: "I congratulate you and thank you for the success you have met with. Please also extend my thanks to your command for their success and for the fortitude they have shown under such trying circumstances and hardships."[38] This was all the thanks that he would get from his superiors. When Connor returned to Fort Laramie, he found that in effect he had been replaced by Brig. Gen. Frank Wheaton, who now commanded the newly revived District of Nebraska. This now included the territories of Nebraska and Montana and that portion of Dakota Territory lying west of the western boundary of Nebraska. Connor also learned that he had received severe criticism from the War Department for the killing of several women in the Tongue River Fight.[39]

Connor was also being investigated for his personal contracting for the expedition. Dodge defended him to the end. In a communication to the assistant adjutant general, Department of the Missouri, he stated that he was astonished at the work accomplished by Connor in view of all the obstacles that had to be overcome, not the least of them being the lack of men and supplies as planned. As it was, Dodge wrote, Connor had to strip his posts to get troops for his expedition and incur necessary and unavoidable expenses in employing citizens to construct shelter for stores and other necessary purposes. In conclusion, Dodge declared, in his view, General Connor had done what was best for the service.[40]

Smarting under multiple criticisms, Connor boxed up all of his reports and sent them to Salt Lake with the excuse that he wished to examine them before making a formal report to the War Department. A few weeks after reaching Salt Lake, the documents were consumed in a fire.[41]

In many respects, the Powder River expedition had been a disappointment. Instead of delivering a devastating blow to the victors at Platte

Bridge and Red Buttes, Connor's grand plan had been disrupted by incompetence, bungling, weather, and terrain, as well as vacillating government policy. The expedition did, however, publicize the Bozeman Trail. Furthermore, the presence of newly built Fort Connor on the Powder River encouraged emigrant travel along the road in 1866. This in turn would bring the army into the field again, expecting to complete the task that Connor had begun.

CHAPTER ELEVEN

Prospects

NEWS OF THE RESULTS OF THE CAMPAIGN BEGAN TO HIT THE EASTERN newspapers early in October, after Connor and his men reached Fort Laramie. A letter originating from the post was published in the *Washington Evening Star* on October 3. It reported that Indian losses were from 400 to 500, while Captain Cole of the 6th Michigan and twenty-four men were killed and two wounded. According to the letter, the Arapahos acknowledged a loss of sixty-eight braves in the Tongue River battle.[1] A few days later, the *Army and Navy Journal* touched on an important weakness that impaired operations:

> The expedition was carried out under the most embarrassing circumstances. Not a pound of stores intended for the expedition arrived in time for use; the troops were mutinous, and claimed their discharge because the Rebellion had ceased, and regiments were ordered to be mustered out as soon as they arrived on the plains.[2]

When queried, Connor stated that he did not feel "sore" over the treatment accorded him personally. He believed, however, that government Indian policy was mistaken and very unjust and injurious to the western people. He also stated that he was sorry that he was not better supported during the season.[3] On October 7, Connor left Fort Laramie for Denver.[4]

In the meantime, government officials expressed great optimism about the possibilities for peace. The secretary of the interior reported that Governor Newton Edmunds and others appointed to treat with the Sioux of the Upper Missouri had met in council with the Minniconjous, who claimed to represent the views not only of the Sioux west of the Missouri, but also of the Northern Cheyennes and Arapahos. The principals agreed that they could not get everyone together until next spring, but, wrote the secretary, "There is little room for doubt that the Cheyennes and Arapahos and other tribes heretofore hostile will yield to the prevailing anxiety for an early restoration of friendly relations with the Government and embrace the first opportunity that may be presented them of signing a treaty."[5] The commissioners, however, were successful in concluding a treaty with the Minniconjous on October 10 at Fort Sully. A correspondent reported that all parties expressed cordial feelings of friendship and goodwill at the conclusion of the ceremony, when government representatives distributed presents, an event followed by the "liveliest demonstrations of satisfactions" by participants.[6]

On October 12 to 14 at the Little Arkansas, John B. Sandborn and other commissioners met with Little Raven's Southern Arapahos and Black Kettle's Southern Cheyennes and concluded a treaty. The commissioners repudiated Chivington's actions at Sand Creek, promising to make restitution for the property lost or its value.[7] While Little Raven and Black Kettle said they could only sign for themselves, the treaty stated that the chiefs were fully authorized by their respective tribes to act in their behalf.[8] But even the Indian Bureau admitted that the agreement had been accepted only by Indians who were not fighting along the Oregon Trail. Another treaty promulgated at Fort Sully established peace in Dakota Territory, but the main fighting of the year had been in Wyoming. Only a few of the Western Sioux signed the document. Most Brules and Oglalas did not participate in treaty negotiations, and only three men from the latter group signed the paper, and they did hold prominent positions in the tribe.[9]

To deal with these nontreaty Sioux, General Dodge used Indian emissaries to carry the word that the government wanted to meet with them. Principal among them was Big Ribs, who arrived at Fort Laramie on October 17.[10] His mission was to tell the Lakota that the Great White Father took pity on them and did not wish to fight them. Rather, he wished to make peace and give them presents as he did before the war. They were to know that the Great Father had whipped his enemies, the bad white men in the states, and if the Sioux and Cheyennes did not make peace, he would send thousands of soldiers during the winter and next spring to destroy them.[11]

Big Ribs was instructed to carry the message to certain chiefs and headmen. The list given to him identifies the leaders of many of the bands that had been fighting the army in Nebraska, Wyoming, and Montana in 1865. Big Ribs was to speak with the following:

Oglala: Man Afraid [of His Horses], Back Wound or Mischief Maker, Hair Plait, Corn Band, Swift Bear, Big Partisan, Bear That Looks Back, and Tall Indian.

Brules: Spotted Tail, Red Leaf, Standing Elk, and Song Face.

Bad Faces: Black Bear, Red Cloud, Long Soldier, The Man That Steals the White Man's Horse, Sitting Bear, and Trunk.

O Yoki ha pas: Standing Bear, Single Crow, Red, and Black Foxes (Bissonette's brother-in-law).

Minniconjous: Roman Nose, Low Horse, Little Bull, and White Bull.

Cheyennes: Gray Head, Bull Bear, Dull Knife, Tall Bull, Flake Foot, Double Head, White Clay, Spotted Elk, Man That Stands in the Water, Little Wolf, Big Head, Old Bear, Little Bear Wolf, Spotted Wolf, and White Man.[12]

After receiving his instructions, Big Ribs left the post on October 19 and headed for the Lakota camps. According to one observer, he was gorgeously arrayed in fine clothes and brass buttons.[13]

On October 15, Connor and his staff arrived in Denver. There they received "all honors that could be bestowed" and were guests at a grand feast at the Planter's Hotel. According to one newspaper, the affair was replete "with military salutes, music, toasts and responses, a dining hall hastily fitted up, tables well loaded, fair women, brave men, and sparkling wine. It was a spontaneous expression of the feeling of the town and of Colorado for one of the first of gentlemen and of soldiers."[14] The *Rocky Mountain News* called the banquet, with its rare viands and choice wines, the "ne plus ultra" of feasts. The toasts and responses were as follows:

1. Gen. P. E. Connor, Our Distinguished Guest. Response by General Connor.

2. The Army of the Frontier. Response by General Upton.

3. California and Her Soldiers. Response by Capt. Geo. F. Price.

4. Colorado and Her Resources. Response by Hon. Wm. Gilpin.

5. The Short Route to the Pacific. Response by Gen. B. H. Hughes.

6. The First Regiment Colorado Volunteers, the Heroes of Apache Canon, Pigeon's Ranch, Peralto, and Valverde. Response by Capt. I. S. M. Robbins.

7. The Ladies. Response by Henry C. Leach.

8. The Press. Response by Maj. S. Whiteley.

9. The Irish Soldiers in the Army of the Union. Response by James M. Cavanaugh.

The reportage ended with the declaration, "Our citizens had assembled to do honor to one of who, above many others, has proven himself entitled to our best considerations, and we feel confident, as the press, the mouth piece of the people, should be, when we assert that wheresoever General Connor's lot in the life may be cast he will carry with him the best wishes and highest esteem of every true citizen of this Territory."[15] The next day Connor and his staff, escorted by more than thirty carriages filled with prominent citizens, traveled forty miles to the mountain town of Central City, where they were again feted and shown the greatest hospitality.[16] To the editor of the *Blackhawk Mining Journal*, O. J. Hollister, Connor appeared to be "a man of superior good sense, of uncommon sagacity and persistence, scrupulously honorable and more tender of the honor of the Service, if possible, than of his own—an upright incorruptible, patriotic man, precisely the one to carry on a Indian war." Later the Colorado legislature passed a resolution calling for Connor to command a new department or district that included Colorado.[17]

This was Connor's final tribute. He went on to Salt Lake City, but he had little to do. On February 16, 1866, he received approval for a leave of absence with permission to visit Washington, D.C. By War Department General Order No. 23 dated April 10, he was mustered out effective April 20, along with a number of other volunteer generals.[18]

In the meantime, many of the Cheyennes and Arapahos, despite all the discussions, treaties, and pledges of peace, were back on the warpath. Late in October, groups of Cheyennes and Arapahos crossed the Platte, leaving a trail of death and destruction in their wake. On October 21, they killed a man on the trail near Harlow's Ranch, between Julesburg and Valley City, and wounded another. The next morning, about 100 warriors attacked a train of sixty wagons but were repulsed. The timely arrival of Lieutenant Thorton and forty men of the 13th Missouri Cavalry, and a bit later of some men of the 6th West Virginia Cavalry stationed at a post not too far away, saved the day. One teamster died and four suffered severe wounds. The Indians left three dead on the field.[19]

The plains raiders soon controlled most of the Platte route, and stage lines threatened to stop their regular runs unless the Indians were cleared from the area. Emigrant trains had to be well armed and maintain a constant guard against surprise attacks. Some newspapers believed that an indecisive military policy was responsible for the renewal of the Indian raids and called for immediate changes.[20]

The worst incidents of the fall occurred in southern Nebraska. One the evening of October 23, Indians attacked a small wagon train ten miles west of Alkali Station, killing several whites and burning some of the wagons. Three solders died in a rescue attempt.[21] First into the field was Bvt. Brig. Gen. H. H. Heath. On October 28, a portion of the command, about seventy-six men of Companies A and B, 7th Iowa Cavalry, and Companies E and K, 1st Nebraska Volunteer Cavalry, arrived at Alkali Station. That night, about 300 Sioux attacked a train six miles west, killing four of the ten drivers: Albert Gaskill, George W. Selby, H. G. Gorton, and his sixteen-year-old son, Elijah, all from Wayne County, Iowa. General Heath learned of the attack about 11:00 P.M. "Boots and Saddles" were sounded at once, and in a few moments the men were on the trail. When the rescue party arrived, they found that the men had been stripped, except Gaskill, and filled with arrows. Selby had been burned to a crisp, only a foot remaining in the ashes to mark his passing. The attackers ran off sixteen mules, mutilated twenty oxen so badly that they had to be killed, and burned six wagons.[22]

In early morning, Heath sent an advance party of thirty-six men, consisting of detachments of Companies A, E, and K, 1st Nebraska Volunteer Cavalry, and of Company B, 7th Iowa, commanded by Captain Krumme and Lieutenant Cutler. Striking southwest for the headwaters of White Man's Fork of the Republican, their job was to overtake the raiders and find their camp. Later in the morning, the remainder of the command, consisting of detachments of Companies A and E, 7th Iowa, and the 6th West Virginia Cavalry, numbering about 100 men, under General Heath, moved out. Owing to the fact that there were but little or no supplies at Alkali and the need for rapid movement, they took the trail with only hard bread and coffee in their saddle bags. That day they traveled fifty miles over barren sand hills before camping, suffering from hunger and thirst.

At daylight, the troops took the trail southwest, 124 men in all, and found the Indians on White Man's Fork. In a pitched battle, the soldiers killed twenty-one of the enemy. Among the Indians was a bugler, who gave numerous calls, but all different from any that the soldiers knew. The troops were gone five days, three days on half rations and two days without water or food. Casualties were several wounded and eleven horses killed. Heath claimed fifty Indians killed and wounded.[23]

Depredations continued, however. A few days later, Indians made another attack near Alkali Station and were repulsed. Near Julesburg, raiders attacked the wagon train of the Clark Bros. of Bellevue, Nebraska, stealing eighty-seven head of cattle and many oxen, prompting the Omaha *Nebraska Republican* to declare, "In spite of all claims and wishes to the contrary, we are forced to the conclusion that Indian troubles on the Plains are serious and increasing."[24]

Farther east, life went on. Nicholas O'Brien married Emily Boynton of New York on November 7, 1865, at McGregor, Iowa. The couple left for Omaha, where they were met by General Wheaton and officers of his staff. At the Herndon Hotel, the leading hotel of the city, they were given a reception. The hosts served elaborate refreshments and drank many toasts to the prosperity and happiness of the newlyweds. The main talk in the city concerned construction of the Union Pacific Railroad, and optimism for the future prevailed. Everything was gay and festive, the citizens of Omaha giving many parties in honor of railroad officials.[25]

In early November, commissioners completed other treaties with the Minniconjous, Blackfeet Sioux, and Two Kettle Sioux, numbering about 6,200, and with portions of the Yanktons, Sans Arcs, and Hunkpapas, about 6,400 persons.[26]

In late November, the attacks continued on the Overland dispatch route, with stations burned and abandoned and the stock stampeded for about 100 miles. Near Buthton Station, a fight ensued between occupants of the adobe ranch, one of whom was Thomas R. Davis, writer and artist for *Harper's Weekly*, and a band of Cheyenne Indians. The firing continued for a short time. Then a voice addressed the occupants in excellent English, asking if the treaty had been signed. The occupants replied in the affirmative and asked what person with the Indians spoke such good English. From behind a pile of boards near the adobe, a man made his appearance, announcing himself to be the son of William Bent. It was George Bent on his way home from a summer of warring. He told them that the Cheyennes had thought that the stock was the property of the Pawnees and Pottawattomies, which were supposed to be hunting in the vicinity. Bent said that he was traveling with Fast Bear, who wanted peace. After much talk, the occupants of the "Dobe" came out, and a general handshaking took place.

The Indians said that they could go at once, and began to drive up the stock so the station men could hitch them up. While thus engaged, some parties on the little bluff or bank nearby opened fire on the whites with their bows and revolvers. At this moment, Fast Bear and a number of his warriors were about the coach and seemed surprised at the renewal of hostilities, but ran immediately off to the shelter of the bank, turning and looking at the party of whites, as if they thought they were going to run upon them. Merwin, who was in the coach at the time, was killed instantly, as was one of the stock tenders. Both were shot in many places with arrows and revolver balls. The other stock tender was taken prisoner.

At the first shot, the carpenters and others started for the bluff nearby, the warriors in hot pursuit, firing at the fugitives with the rifles, pistols, and arrows. None received injury. Seeing that the idea of running away from mounted Indians was not likely to prove successful, the party took refuge in buffalo wallows—four of the party in one and two in another. The Indians began riding in a circle about the small group of men. Night coming in, the Indians withdrew.

Later on, they discovered the body of Van Kechten, one of the carpenters. The wolves had eaten him with the exception of his hands, feet, and face. The men buried him as well as they could. The next day, they reached Chalk Bluffs, where they found a number of stock tenders, drivers, and others who had fled from the stations. They found that Merwin had been shot full of arrows and that some of the fugitives from Buthton had from a distance seen the Indians, roasting the stock tender taken at Downer over a slow fire. He cried so piteously that they cut his tongue out.[27]

On the evening of November 24, they reached Monument Station, where Captain Stroud had a camp. There Dr. Monument dressed the wounds of a soldier who had been scalped alive. They had just reached this station when they were attacked by a large band of Indians, who did not fight, but ran as soon as they opened up on them from the coach windows. General Brewster fired twice at a white man.[28]

On November 25 near Fort Connor, about twenty Sioux attacked Little Priest, the leader of the Winnebago Scouts, and three of his men. The warriors separated Little Priest from the rest and chased him for ten miles before he decided to abandon his horse in order to defend himself. Wounded four times, once through the abdomen, he held his attackers at bay, killing four of them and three of their horses before they withdrew.[29]

In late December, two cavalrymen who had been stationed at St. Mary's moved to Fort Caspar. They had run out of wood, and because there was no telegrapher in residence, the men had no reason to remain. On January 11, 1866, Col. Henry Maynadier, the new commander of Fort Laramie, informed A. J. Squires that troops would be returned to St. Mary's when transportation could be obtained to supply wood. Sometime during the winter, Indians burned South Pass Station, giving it the name of "Burnt Ranch." Nothing is known of the details of the incident.[30]

Nevertheless, 1865 ended on a hopeful note. Colonel Maynadier reported to his superiors on December 29 that Red Cloud had sent him word professing friendship and stating that he wished to make peace. The chief estimated that he would reach Fort Laramie in two or three weeks.[31] In anticipation of the meeting, Wheaton told Maynadier to give the Oglala Indians presents upon arrival and determine immediately their relationship with the Cheyennes and the Arapahos. Wheaton wanted the Lakotas to break with these allied tribes and either persuade them to come in or help the army fight them.[32]

Colonel Maynadier was a good choice as the army's representative. Born in 1830, he had graduated from West Point in 1851. He served initially with the 1st Artillery, then switched to the 10th Infantry, where he fought at Vicksburg and Fredericksburg. Becoming a major in the 12th Infantry on November 4, 1863, he received a number of special assignments for the next sixteen months, including a stint in the office of the adjutant general in Washington. He became the colonel of the 5th U.S. Volunteers on March 27, 1865. His varied experience and tact would be important in the negotiations to come.[33]

CHAPTER TWELVE

Spotted Tail's Daughter

IN THE DEAD OF WINTER, RAIDING CEASED, AND BOTH FRIEND AND FOE sought shelter, as surviving the cold on the plains pushed all other concerns aside. Feelings of frustration and resentment, however, continued among the population in frontier settlements. Most vociferous was the *Rocky Mountain News,* which called for a change in governmental policy from pampering to punishment:

> When shall be there an end to the present imbecile policy that government is pursuing towards these Indians? There is an end of human endurance and patience, and if something is not done soon to quiet these savages, the people of Colorado will rise in defiance of efforts to prevent them, the fabled stones of malicious slanders concerning Sand Creek, shall be more than realized in the dark, bloody and relentless vengeance they will wreak upon their treacherous enemies.[1]

There were some things that were happening during this period of respite that held promise. As spring drew near, soldiers at Fort Laramie had a surprise. On March 1, they saw what appeared to be a flag of truce, anchored on the summit of a nearby hill. Surrounding it were dozens of Indians of both sexes. As experienced frontiersmen knew, women present in the party indicated a peaceful mission. An investigating cavalry detachment was soon on its way and in a short time returned with the Indians. They were members of Standing Elk's band of Brule Sioux. Hungry, freezing, and humble, they had come to give themselves up.

Colonel Maynadier sent word to the rest of the Brules, inviting them to come in for food and talk. Cooks prepared great amounts of meat and beans and served gallons of coffee. The post quartermaster provided some Indians with blankets and extra items of clothing.

After feasting, Standing Elk made a speech, detailing his plight:

> I come many miles to make peace with my white brother. We have suffered much. The white man has dogged my tracks for many moons. The white man has slain my young men and out-raged my squaws, my ponies are the white soldier's war horses. He rides them to battle with my warriors. The white men fight well, they are brave, but the red men can't live without meat. The white soldier has killed all his buffalo, antelope, and deer. None are left for us to kill. To show the white brother we want peace, I have brought all my people with me, and many of my old women and little papooses have frozen to death on the way.[2]

In the end, the Brules camped a few miles up the Laramie, Standing Elk surrounded by his personal guard of 500 warriors. The soldiers confiscated the Brules' firearms but let them retain their bows and arrows.

Contact with Starving Elk was not the only Indian diplomacy being conducted at Fort Laramie. Chief Spotted Tail of the Brules had sent Colonel Maynadier a message, informing him that he wanted to bring the body of his deceased daughter to Fort Laramie for burial.[3] She had spent some time around the post and became enamored of white ways. Some said that she had fallen in love with an Ohio officer, at least from a distance.[4] Her final wish was that she find her last resting place in the post cemetery, near the burial of Old Smoke, a relative and chief who had lived near Fort Laramie for many years as a friend of the whites.[5] Maynadier remembered the girl, whom he had met some five years before, when she was about twelve years old, and he welcomed the chief's' coming. In fact, on March 8, he and several officers rode out to meet Spotted Tail and escort him and his entourage to the post. The Brules had been camping 260 miles north on Powder River, following the Fouts affair, and there she became ill. Some believed that the young woman had contracted consumption. Maynadier said that her death was the cause of exposure and the Indian's hard life.[6] The Brules had had a bad winter, with unusual depth of snow and very cold days and nights, and they had lost many women and children. To survive, they had killed and eaten most of their ponies. Spotted Tail summed it up by saying, "Our hearts were on the ground, my brother." "If we had to swim through the snow," he said, "we would have come."[7]

The body lay in state in a room in "Old Bedlam," the commanding officer's office and residence. Flags, muskets, and sabers decorated the walls. Maynadier had a coffin made, and post trader Col. William G. Bullock donated a fine red cloth to cover it. Maynadier suggested a sunset burial, telling Spotted Tail that "as the sun went down it might remind him of the darkness left in his lodge when his beloved daughter was taken away, but as the sun would surely rise again, so she would rise, and some day we would all meet in the land of the Great Spirit."[8] Tears appeared on the chief's cheeks as Maynadier spoke.

The officer also told Spotted Tail that in two or three months, peace commissioners would come to Fort Laramie to meet with him and other tribal leaders. According to Maynadier, the chief responded as follows:

> This must be a dream for me to be in such a fine room, and surrounded by such as you. Have I been asleep during the last four years of hardship and trail, and am dreaming that all is to be well again, or is this real? Yes. I see that it is, and the beautiful day, the sky blue and without a cloud, the wind calm and still, suit the errand I come on, and remind me that you have offered me peace.

Spotted Tail
Chief of the Brules, Spotted Tail led his tribe in war following the Chivington Debacle and then a few months later made peace with the United States Government.
LIBRARY OF CONGRESS

We think we have been much wronged and are entitled to compensation for the damage and distress caused by making so many roads through our country and driving off and destroying buffalo and game. My heart is very sad, and I cannot talk on business. I will wait and see the counsellors the Great White Father will send.[9]

Maynadier had a platform to hold the coffin constructed about 200 yards north of the post. Many other Indian burials had been placed in the vicinity on scaffolds about eight feet above the ground.[10]

Soldiers placed the coffin on the wheels of an artillery caisson to draw it to the place of burial. Then came a 12-pounder mountain howitzer. Following were the 300 Indians in Spotted Tail's train and many of the 600 officers and men of the garrison, all marching to the solemn music of the post band.[11] The Brules killed two white ponies, nailing the heads by their ears to the posts, facing toward the rising sun. Tribesmen attached the tails to the posts facing toward the sunset. Underneath the heads were barrels of water for the animals to drink as they conveyed the girl to the spirit land.[12]

Parents, relatives, and friends placed jewelry and wearing apparel in the coffin. Officers added such items as gauntlet gloves, moccasins, looking glasses, and red flannel, these all intended to keep the maiden comfortable on her journey. Nicholas O'Brien put in a greenback so that she could buy what she wanted on her way to the spirit world. Finally, Spotted Tail gave a little red book to the post chaplain, the Reverand A. Wright. It was an episcopal prayer book that Maj. Gen. William Harney had given the girl many years before. The chaplain dropped it in.

Many hands raised the pine box to the platform, placing its head to the east. Chaplain Wright preached an improvised sermon, translated by Sefroy Iott, the post interpreter. Wright told the assemblage that the girl would look after her father, mother, and friends. Soon they would meet in the land of abundant game, where there were no more snowstorms, tears, or dying. The mother of the dead girl wept openly during the ceremony, and the father-chief often dabbed at his eyes.

The result of the burial at Fort Laramie was the beginning of trust between Maynadier and Spotted Tail, and the chief agreed to meet with commissioners in the spring. In concluding a letter to the commissioner of Indian affairs in Washington, written the day after the burial, Maynadier declared, "The occurrences of such an incident is regarded by the oldest settlers, men of most experience in Indian character, as unprecedented, and as calculated to secure a certain and lasting peace." In fact, Spotted Tail never went to war against the whites again. Perhaps it was as Col. Henry Carrington later surmised: "As his daughter was adopted by the white man's Great Spirit, he had no heart to fight the white man any more."[13]

On March 12, Spotted Tail and Red Cloud approached Fort Laramie for a council. Maynadier and his officers went out to meet them near the crossing of North Platte River two miles east of the post. There were about 200 warriors in the party, the Sioux drawn up in a line, singing and shouting. Besides the two chiefs were other prominent leaders, among them Standing Elk, Brave Bear, and Trunk.[14] Maynadier rode into Fort Laramie with Spotted Tail on one side and Red Cloud on the other, presenting, as he put it, "a gay and novel appearance."[15] In all, there were about 700 Brules and Oglalas that camped nearby, the people described as being destitute of everything.

After hearing their complaints, mostly about whites coming into their hunting grounds, their difficult winter, and their poverty, Maynadier gave them the expected feast and some hard bread and a little coffee and sugar. During their discussion, Red Cloud indicated that he wanted to meet the Great White Father, and Maynadier promised to look into the possibility. On the same day that Maynadier met with Spotted Tail and Red Cloud, Swift Bear and forty lodges arrived in the area, camping near the trading house of the chief's brother-in-law, James Bordeaux. This was nine miles east of Fort Laramie on the North Platte River.[16]

With these events, prospects for peace on the plains looked promising. The surrender, capture, and discussions with these bands of Sioux were good beginnings for treaty negotiations, which were planned to begin at Fort Laramie on May 20.[17] Red Cloud, the fabled Oglala chief, a man who had counted eighty coups against his Indian enemies in war, was the key. Just emerging as a leader of the resistant Sioux in the southern half of the Northern Plains, he commanded respect. Blessed with a beautiful oratorical voice, his words complemented his deeds. While the Indian War of 1865 was over, Red Cloud would determine whether there would be an Indian War of 1866.

CHAPTER THIRTEEN

Conclusions

"IT SEEMS THAT GOVERNMENT DOES NOT APPRECIATE THE MAGNITUDE OF the difficulties on the plains," wrote Grenville Dodge to John Pope on August 25, 1865.[1] The grand plans of these two men never were implemented in ways imagined. From the perspective of nearly a century and a half, obstacles to success seemed insurmountable, but what made them especially difficult were inefficiency, incompetence, disloyalty, graft, corruption, partisan politics, competing national interests, false economy, and, worst of all, indifference. In many respects, the Indian War of 1865 was a forgotten war. The nation looked elsewhere—to Reconstruction, to troubles with Mexico, and to railroad development.

The specifics of the situation have already been detailed. The problem of supply was a limiting factor in the war of 1865. Units in the West suffered from lack of equipment. Troops were often poorly armed. The *Miner's Register* noted that one regiment arrived only with sabers and a few revolvers.[2]

Lack of good horseflesh may have been the army's Achilles' heel. Not only were the animals slow in coming, but also many of them were unserviceable or soon would be. Apparently army inspectors were not too particular in accepting remounts. In February 1865, the Omaha *Nebraska Republican* reported that the army had recently purchased 100 heads of horses, but after arriving, the stock turned out to be unfit for service and had to be condemned.[3] General Dodge reported that in the spring of 1865, he did not have a single serviceable horse on the plains and that every man there had to be remounted.[4] Furthermore, volunteer troops sent for in June came dismounted.[5] General Connor attributed his late start on the Powder River expedition to lack of horses. "The stock I had was very inferior," he wrote, "and there was not enough transportation for the absolute wants of the expedition."[6]

More important than the difficulty of always providing enough animals to meet demand was the fact that the cavalry's big American horses needed grain to remain fit. This meant that the army had to transport feed in wagons on expeditions, which reduced its ability to move rapidly and strike swiftly. Moreover, the animals needed grass to supplement their diet, and this was often difficult to obtain. Horses were often picketed at night to keep them safe from Indian raiders; consequently, they did not always get to graze.[7]

Another problem was the quality of the goods provided to troops. The furnishing of substandard equipment and munitions was common in the Civil War, with graft, corruption, and fraud rampant.[8] As might be expected, fighters on the frontier were not exempt from this pernicious plundering. Officers of the 7th Iowa complained bitterly when issued Gallager carbines that were of inferior quality. Following the battle at Rush Creek, Colonel Collins wrote his superiors that the howitzer under command of Lieutenant Brown did not prove as useful as expected, owing to the defective character of the ammunition. Many of the shells failed to burst at all, and some exploded at the muzzle of the gun.[9]

The timely delivery of military supplies was a critical factor in the Powder River campaign. As has been pointed out, the inability of army procurement to provide these supplies was a near fatal handicap to General Connor. Part of the problem was an organizational one: The Quartermaster Department in Washington advertised and awarded contracts, and staff officers who conducted business had no comprehension of conditions in the West. They did not understand the difficulties in securing transportation in an unsettled land, the time needed to cover the huge distances involved, and the severe climatic conditions to be encountered, including extremes in temperature from 120 degrees in summer to 50 below in winter and snow at almost any time. Coupled with flooding from mountain runoffs in June, drought in July and August, hail sometimes the size of hen's eggs, and grasshoppers devouring what grass was left, the Northern Plains freighter lived an exciting life.[10]

In the end, the government did not let contracts until May 1, and unbelievably, contractors had until December 1 to deliver goods for a campaign meant to begin in June! When supplies finally arrived in Nebraska, they had to be hauled by government trains from Fort Kearny and Cottonwood to Fort Laramie.[11] In the meantime, as we have seen, Connor had hired his own transportation and stripped the posts in his district of supplies, while his expeditionary force twiddled their thumbs around Fort Laramie for six weeks.[12] In Omaha, Nelson Cole had to buy several thousand dollars worth of supplies and break his mules before he could begin his march.[13] As the *Army and Navy Journal* reported, "Not a pound of stores intended for the expedition arrived in time for use."[14] On the other hand, while soldiers waited upon the bureaucracy, whites were selling ammunition to Indians. The *Rocky Mountain News* called it "a foolish practice that was widespread."[15]

General Dodge named delay, caused by the fiasco in contracting, as the principal factor in limiting Connor's success on the Powder River expedition. "Could General Connor have moved in June, or even by July 1st," Dodge wrote, "I have no doubt he would have succeeded in inflicting thorough and effectual chastisement upon all the tribes in hostility on the north and carried out my instructions in the matter fully and completely."[16]

What even seems more incredible was that Connor came under severe censure for getting his own transportation and supplies so that he could carry out his orders. On August 29, the day of the battle on Tongue River, Dodge sent the first of a series of reports responding to criticism of Connor's actions. He noted that citizens teams were transporting stores to Powder River because the contractors had refused to take them beyond Fort Laramie. Furthermore, none of the Powder River stores had yet reached that post, the wagons having passed Fort Kearny on August 16.[17] In the last of these letters, dated November 1, Dodge stated that in his view, Connor had acted in the very best interests of the service and recommended him for promotion. At that point, the matter was dropped, since Connor had been transferred and interest focused on peace efforts.[18]

Generals Dodge and Connor suffered from another basic deficiency—manpower. One underlying cause was the vastness of the landscape. An editorial in the Omaha *Nebraska Republican* explained the problem:

> We admit we had had quite a number of troops, yet they have been inadequate to the task. The thoroughfare from here to Denver is six hundred miles in length, and for the protection of that alone we have not had troops sufficient, yet a line equal in length and more difficult to protect from Julesburg to Laramie and from thence west, has been entrusted to these same troops, and they have been expected to protect it. That they have succeeded well considering their numbers and the task allotted them no one will doubt. Yet we claim that they have always been inadequate to the work, and that our Indian war will never terminate until we either whip or persuade them (the Indians) into submission.[19]

Dodge made the same points in his correspondence with superiors, noting that "never before have we had one-half or one-third of the country that we now have to protect." He mentioned that among his difficult tasks was to guard 3,500 miles of overland trail each day.[20]

Not only was it difficult to guard such a vast expanse, but the numbers of troops originally requisitioned did not serve. When Dodge planned his grand strategy, he expected to have 12,000 troops in his department; however, he received only 6,000. In investigating the situation, he learned that as many as 4,740 men had been ordered to his department. They had been transported from the previous theater of war, equipped, and marched to the various posits on the plains. Then suddenly they received orders to be mustered out, leaving the region "without any benefit whatever being received from them."[21]

It was bad luck that Dodge and Connor entered the fray just as many volunteer units had completed their Civil War service and headed for home. On May 1, 1865, there were 1,034,064 volunteer troops under arms, but by November 15, 800,963 of them had been paid, mustered out, and transported to their respective states by the Quartermaster Corps.[22] As spring became summer, many of these troops still in the West became mutinous. They had no heart for their duty, chiefly because they considered themselves entitled to their discharge since the war was over.[23]

Some historians have blamed the poor showing in 1865 on volunteer troops. Richard Ellis has stated that the attitude of the volunteer troops and their officers seriously affected military operations.[24] Dodge blamed state authorities and the press throughout the West for encouraging volunteer troops to resist going on the plains.[25] Dodge attributed a 25 percent desertion rate to this foment.[26]

Four volunteer regiments under Dodge's command engaged in mutinous conduct. One hundred ninety men of the 6th West Virginia refused to cross the plains from Fort Leavenworth to Fort Kearny. On July 21, Connor reported that part of the 1st Nebraska Cavalry stationed at Fort Kearny had mutinied. He ordered Colonel Heath to suppress the disturbance with grape and canister and ordered the leaders brought to trial. In July, both Cole and Walker had to use force to get their men to move toward Powder River.[27] When horses stampeded in Cole's column, one officer attributed it to the men of the 2nd Missouri, calling their actions malicious and willful and designed to end the expedition.[28] Too, some officers and men of the 11th Kansas were vocal in their views about service in Wyoming, and Caspar Collins obviously became a victim of these feelings. Although causing some delays, there is no evidence to show that these circumstances played a major role in the overall performance of troops engaged in the war. When attacked, they fought; when tested, they endured.

Critics of the campaign of 1865 have concentrated on motivation and the lack of discipline on the part of volunteer troops. The reverse of the coin was just as important: the Sioux, Cheyennes, and Arapahos were highly motivated. They were out to even the score, but more than that, they were products of a warring society. It was through war and the taking of horses that men gained respect, prestige, power, and honors, as well as secured mates and a place at meetings and councils.[29] As native populations contracted at mid-nineteenth century, the fighting men of these cultures adapted in a number of ways. They took multiple wives, and they renewed the warrior's code of courage.

The Cheyennes were a perfect example. A small tribe, numbering perhaps 4,000 in 1865, they compensated for their numbers by their ferocity in war. In his classic study, George Bird Grinnell called them the "Fighting Cheyennes" and described their mind-set:

> The fighting spirit was encouraged. In no way could a young man gain so much credit as by the exhibition of courage. Boys and youths were trained to feel that the most important thing in life was to be brave; that death was not a thing to be avoided; that in fact, it was better for a man to be killed while in his full vigor rather than to wait until his prime was past, his powers were failing and he could no longer achieve those feats which to all seemed so desirable.[30]

The Cheyenne Dog Soldiers emerged during this period. The elite of the elite, they were a military society that evolved into a separate tribal unit. They took orders from their own military chiefs, not band leaders, and often lived apart. Many of them were half Sioux, causing some to refer to them as the Cheyenne Sioux. Among these men were the bravest of the brave; to be a chief among them was to expect to die.[31]

Sudden changes in plans also affected the Powder River expedition. The original plan had been for Alfred Sully and his troops from Dakota Territory to march from the Black Hills and meet Connor on Powder River, but owing to difficulties in Minnesota, his force had been diverted to Devil's Lake.[32] Thus, Dodge had to find new troops to take his place, those commanded by Cole and Walker, who proved less than enthusiastic about their new assignment.

Important in the lack of success were poor communications and lack of knowledge of the habits of the enemy, plains weather, and often difficult terrain. Faulty intelligence became apparent early in the conflict. During his campaign in southern Nebraska and northern Kansas, January 15 to 27, General Mitchell was dismayed that he had not been able to learn where the Indians had gone or what they intended to do. The only result of the expedition was the crippling of fifty men from freezing and accidents, the ruin of 100 horses and six wagons, and a loss of morale.[33]

Incompetent guides greatly complicated the Powder River expedition. In general, Connor and his officers depreciated their scouts, except for Jim Bridger. According to Henry Palmer, nearly all of them were uninformed, unreliable, and therefore useless.[34] Connor, however, also had Captain North and the Pawnee Scouts, who were always forging ahead and looking for targets.

Cole and Walker suffered the most from incompetence. Their guides repeatedly misled them, being entirely ignorant of the country. According to Dodge, apparently Walker made no effort whatsoever to communicate with Connor or ascertain his position. The inability of Cole and Walker to rendezvous with Connor prevented him from carrying out his plans fully and successfully.[35]

There was also a lack of communication between Connor and General Sully, who had the other large expedition in the field against the Sioux in 1865. On August 8, General Sully reported that he was on the east side of the Missouri River about fifty or sixty miles from an Indian village of over 2,000 Sioux, Cheyenne, and Arapaho lodges. While he was debating what to do, he mentioned that he had read in the papers that Connor was moving to Powder River in pursuit of the Indians who had fled the Platte, but he did not know where the troops intended to look for them.[36]

These were some of the specifics that limited the U.S. Army in carrying out its mission in 1865. There were also some general causes that affected performance on both sides, stemming from differences in culture, methods of warfare, training, and technology.

One of these was the ability to move quickly over the plains, and in this case, the Indians had the advantage. William Devine, who served at Fort Laramie in 1865, succinctly explained the situation when he wrote, "It was conceded that summer was not the best time [to go on campaign], because the Indian was more mobile with his travois, than the white man with his wagons."[37] Numbers of infantry and cavalry, dependent upon slow-moving supply trains, traveled about the western vastness, looking for Indians who could disperse and vanish almost instantly. Not only was the Indian hard to locate and engage in battle, but his way of warfare was strikingly different. Eleventh Kansas veteran Josiah Hubbard remembered the Indian's methods and skills in war:

Without any misuse of language it might be said, either that he hunted his human enemy, or that he made war on the game animals marked for capture or slaughter. In both cases there was the same careful and patient study of the habits of his antagonist, and of surrounding conditions; the same large use of the elements of surprise, ambuscade, and stealthy approach, and when the time for action came, the same, swift, strong stroke, into which was put all the force and energy at his command.[38]

Henry Carrington, who was to fight Red Cloud and his warriors in 1866, described their skills in much the same way. "In ambush and decoy," he wrote, [the Indian] "is splendid, in horsemanship, perfect; in . . . battle, wary and careful; in victory, jubilant; in vengeance, terrible and fiendish."[39]

The men who served in the army in 1865 had no training for this new kind of war. They did not have a manual for fighting Indians, nor was one developed during the rest of the nineteenth century. Articles in military magazines concerning strategy or tactics covered episodes in the Civil War or European wars. The irony of the Indian war was that the army learned little from it. Its obsession with conventional warfare unfitted it for its mission in the unsettled West, and it lost the opportunity to develop techniques that could have been applied in the many campaigns to follow in the nineteenth century. Furthermore, the army's frontier experience did not prepare it for orthodox war.[40]

When one counts the casualties among the soldiers who fought in the Indian War of 1865, the numbers are not great. While they possessed vastly superior equestrian skills, many Indians did not possess firearms, and those that did were handicapped in their use. Several commanders, including Col. William Collins, noted their adversaries tended to fire too high.[41] In a speech delivered in Omaha in June 1886, Brig. Gen. George Crook further explained the problem. During the Civil War years, he stated, the possession of the muzzle-loading gun gave the Indian but little advantage over the bow and arrow, because reloading was so difficult on horseback. Too, when fighting on foot, the length of time it took to reload often enabled the soldier to charge and dispatch him with the bayonet. In those days, Crook likened twenty soldiers to 100 Indians.[42] Because many of the cavalry had Spencer repeaters, they definitely had the edge.

The most effective weapons of all during the fighting in 1865 were the portable cannons. Troops used them with spectacular results during the two battles of Julesburg, the engagement at Rush Creek, the defense of Platte Bridge Station, and the attack on the Arapaho village. Cole and Walker probably owed their survival to the guns they had with them.[43]

Artillery seemed to be the ideal weapon in fighting guerilla warfare. One of the Indian's purposes in war was to win honors, and cannons denied them face-to-face confrontations. Shells looped over hills made hiding more difficult. Cannonading also tended to even the numbers, permitting outmanned troops to hold their own. In 1866–67 the army continued to use artillery, such as in protecting Fort Kearny and in rescuing troops from the Wagon Box Fight. A decade later, however, in the Great Sioux War of 1876–77, few commanders used artillery, forgetting lessons learned, as if what had come before meant nothing.

Finally, lack of a well-defined Indian policy undermined the army's efforts to subdue the Plains Indians. Bifurcation of authority for control over the tribes between the Department of the Interior and the War Department complicated matters. The former often fed, clothed, and supplied the Indians with weapons, while the latter chased them over the plains.[44]

One characteristic of the war was its barbarism. The mutilation of females as well as males by Chivington's men at Sand Creek was an atrocity, only matched by the cutting and burning of white soldiers and civilians by warring Sioux, Cheyennes, and Arapahos. Few whites understood, however, that Indians were not torturing their victims, but rather, preparing them for a degraded future. Responding to the white accusations that soldiers killed at the battle of Red Buttes had been tortured by the Sioux and Cheyenne prior to dying, George Bent replied: "This is all nonsense. The Plains Indians never tortured prisoners, but shot them at once, during the fighting."[45]

Mutilation was done for a different purpose. These tribes believed that a man's spirit was capable of sustaining life after death. The essence of the man, including his ethereal body, sought an eternal home, where spirits lived in tipis, hunted game, and did all those things that gave them pleasure when they were on earth.[46] The spirit remained with the body a short time after human life ended. During this period, if the body was compromised, that condition would prevail when the spirit left with its bodily essence. Thus, warriors cut their enemies' hamstrings so they could not walk in eternity. They cut out their eyes, so they could not see. They cut off their hands so they could not hold things, and so on. Thus, the motive was for an enemy's eternal suffering and unrest.[47]

Emotions ran high as fighting continued in the West, and some leaders advocated extermination. While Chivington apparently was the first to publicly proclaim that "nits make lice," others followed suit, including Colonel Moonlight in his speech in Denver on February 9. On July 4, Connor issued orders to Cole and Walker that included the injunction to attack and kill every male Indian over twelve years of age.[48] General Pope's quick rescinding of this order did not appease eastern humanitarians, and many continued to look upon the frontier army as led by sadists and butchers. Such feelings led to a stronger peace movement than might have been.

Plains Indian warriors, on the other hand, did not often spare life when on the warpath. Adult enemy males were killed. So were women and children, depending on the circumstances. If conditions were right, raiders captured women to become slaves or members of the tribe. Children also were often spared, to be raised as the Indians' own. But sometimes whole families were slaughtered. Violence begat violence, and both sides paid the price.

Just as war can bring out the worst in mankind, it can also birth the best. Who can forget the courage of Roman Nose as he rode down the line, the sacrifice of Lieutenant Bretney in carrying out his duties, the power of Spotted Tail's daughter to mend the wounds of decades, or the bravado of young Caspar Collins, with cigar in teeth, riding to his death. From such things are traditions formed and legends made.

There is no doubt that the Indian War of 1865 was a drain on the U.S. Treasury. The War Department expended over $20 million for suppression of Indian hostilities during 1865, double what it spent in 1864.[49] Part of the expense was due to the practice of discounting. When a disbursing officer was without funds for eight or ten months, government vouchers were forced in the market at the discounted, ruinous rate of 20 percent.[50]

From the army's perspective, the efforts of its soldiers did have some positive results. In 1865 the frontier army's mission was to protect emigrants, miners, and settlers from Indian hostility and guard lines of transportation and communication binding East to West. Except for several weeks in January and early February, and several weeks grouped here and there, the army did its job in keeping the overland trails open and the transcontinental telegraph up and running.

Connor's effort to carry the war to the Sioux and their allies had striking consequences in this regard. In parley with James Sawyers and Captain Williford on August 15, George Bent expressed great fear concerning Connor and said they were concentrating their forces to meet him. The threat to the homeland sent many pillaging warriors northward to protect their families, and while Connor and his troops tarried in Powder River country, the overland roads became relatively safe. Not until Connor returned to Fort Laramie upon the order of his superiors did extensive raiding begin again on emigrant highways.[51]

The war also resulted in the final routing of the Bozeman Trail. Heading north from a point near the present town of Douglas, Wyoming, Connor had blazed a trail to the future site of Fort Phil Kearny, constructed the following year. Following in his wake, Sawyers improved the trail for travelers.[52]

When he reached Virginia City, Montana, Sawyers promoted the trail in a press interview. On October 12, he boasted that the Indians caused the only delays, their attacks lengthening his travel time by twenty-five to thirty days. He reported that his 600 heads of stock had good grass, except at Pumpkin Buttes, and that game and timber were plentiful. He noted that only one breakdown had occurred, and that was when a spindle snapped when a wagon wheel was carelessly cramped. Sawyers stated that once the Indians had been subdued, the only disadvantage to the route was the soil. When wet, it turned into black gumbo, but, he explained, in dry weather, soil of this type was very easy on oxen's cloven hooves.[53] In his final report, Sawyers indicated that the road could be shortened and improved by making cutoffs at different locations and recommended an appropriation of $20,000 to undertake the work. He concluded:

> The importance of having this route more fully developed, and kept open for travel by protection against Indians, can hardly be overestimated. It is at least six hundred miles nearer than the route which has hitherto been travelled by many—of Salt Lake—with wood, water, and grass in abundance, and no mountain ranges of importance to cross, and upon the whole a first-rate route to travel over. . . . By this route a stage may be run from the Missouri river to Virginia City in eight (8) days, whereas it now takes sixteen (16) days by the present stage route, when they run upon time.[54]

In the end, the summer's activity increased public awareness of the Bozeman Trail and what is today north-central Wyoming. Establishment of Fort Connor at the Dry Fork crossing encouraged more emigrants to follow the Bozeman cutoff in 1866, thus applying pressure to the Sioux and their allies to fight for their last best hunting grounds in the foothills of the Big Horn Mountains.

In their fights with the Plains Indians, troops suffered two major setbacks: the loss of fifteen men outside of Fort Rankin in the near ambush at Devil's Dive on January 6, and the loss on July 26 of Caspar Collins, Sergeant Custard, and twenty-six men in the battles of Platte Bridge and Red Buttes. On the other hand, the avengers had some bad moments: the Pawnee Scouts killed twenty-seven Cheyennes on August 17, and Connor and his force laid waste to the village of Black Bear and Medicine Man and killed sixty-three Arapahos on August 29. Indian and white sources vary widely on casualties in Cole and Walker's fight with the Sioux and Cheyennes on September 3, 4, and 8.[55] Military estimates ranged from 200 to 600 Indians killed, while the avengers reported only one dead, an elderly Sioux named Black Whetstone, dispatched by an exploding howitzer shell.[56] In another sense, the September fights were especially rewarding to the avengers. The Sioux and their allies gained honors from the encounters. They counted coups, captured horses, and generally showed their bravery in the face of fire.[57]

To the army, the most disappointing aspect of the Powder River expedition was that it did not run its course. Connor was ready to reorganize, retool, and return to the field when he received orders disbanding the expedition and sending him to Utah. In writing his reminiscences, Finn Burnett speculated on a different outcome:

> What a pity, what a misfortune that he [Connor] did not disobey it. If he had he would have ended the Sioux war, there would have been no Fetterman massacre, no Custer battle, no eleven years of Indian atrocities, thousands of lives would have been saved, and the settlement of the West would not have been retarded for years. Whoever, or whatever power it was who opposed him continuing their nefarious work until they broke his heart. . . . . They ruined the life of a fine, brave officer, and defeated the finest organization of veteran Indian fighters that had ever been organized in the West, and caused our government to expend millions of dollars, and was the cause of the death of many brave pioneer men and women and children.[58]

From the viewpoint of white frontiersmen, Burnett was probably right in speculating that Connor might have struck a fatal blow. Like William Harney before him and George Crook after him, Connor knew that persistence in pursuit was the key to defeating the Plains Indian. Keep the pressure on, especially in the fall and winter, when ponies were weak and supplies ran low, and the unrelenting had a chance to destroy the will to resist.[59] Looking back in 1887, General Crook called Connor "the best Indian fighter in service at that time."[60] Given a chance, he might have proved it.

Finally, the war of 1865 marked the end of an era. This was the last time that Brules, the northern and southern branches of the Cheyennes, and the Arapahos came together in large numbers to form an effective alliance that could disrupt travel along the Oregon-California and Overland roads and effectively engage thousands of U.S. troops in Powder River country. When the year ended, the Southern Cheyennes and Arapahos who had come north were back on the Central and Southern Plains,[61] and Spotted Tail and his segment of the Brules had become friends of the whites, the renowned warrior never to ride the war trail again. There would be new alliances, fashioned by the Oglala Sioux warrior-chief Red Cloud in the shadows of the Big Horn Mountains in Wyoming and Montana, and by the Hunkpapa warrior and spiritual leader Sitting Bull in Montana and the Dakotas, but never again would the Sioux and their allies take the offensive as they did at Julesburg, Mud Springs, Rush Creek, Platte Bridge, Red Buttes, Pumpkin Buttes, and Powder River. What John Chivington wrought, the avengers avenged. As the circle of fire drew tighter, the last battles on the Northern Plains became more reactive rather than active, meant to defend a homeland rather than to punish a perpetrator. Although Red Cloud's War of 1866–68 was successful in closing the Bozeman Trail and destroying the forts that protected it, and the Great Sioux War of 1876–77 had within it the Sioux's greatest military victory, in retrospect, these seem to be reflexive actions of a people doomed to defeat and repression. In many ways, the Indian War of 1865 was the last real Indian war on the Northern Plains.

EPILOGUE

At the request of William O. Collins, the 11th Ohio held an investigation concerning the death of his son. The court of inquiry convened at Fort Laramie on April 7, 1866, with Maj. John Evans as its president. Limited to officers of the 11th Ohio, it did not hear testimony from any of those participating in the battle. The findings of the court were as follows:

1st. That Major Anderson was unaware of the position of the train on the evening of the 25th, for when the Indians were seen that evening the probability of the destruction of the train was discussed by the officers and men of the garrison. In view of which fact it would appear that Major Anderson should have sent relief to them under cover of the night, or if unable to relieve them, to have at least sent a messenger to apprise them of the danger by which they were threatened and have thus diverted the fate that befell them the next day.

2nd. It is not clearly understood that Major Anderson had authority or could at least with propriety send lieutenant Collins (an officer not directly under his command, but causally at the post en route to join his company at Sweetwater Bridge) on this perilous duty, whom he had never seen before that day, when he had a captain, first and second lieutenants belonging to the company from which the men sent out under Lieutenant Collins were selected and also another line officer of his own regiment, all present at the post for duty.

3rd. No good reason is evident why Major Anderson did not recall Lieutenant Collins and his party when in plain view of the post he was being surrounded by so vastly superior a force of Indians who he could not see, but who were plainly visible from the garrison before he had gone half a mile, when it was perfectly evident that it would be impossible for him to go through with so small a force.[1]

No further action was taken.

At 10:00 A.M. on March 21, 1866, Caspar Collins's remains were reinterred in the Fort Laramie cemetery. The army exhumed the burial on July 14, transporting it by rail to Hillsboro, Ohio. There an honor guard carried the remains to their resting place in Greenfield Cemetery. Collins's comrades in arms formed the escort. A large stone monument marks the grave. Its inscription reads: "Lt. Caspar Wever Collins, Born Hillsboro, Ohio, September 30, 1844. Killed in battle leading a forlorn hope against the Indians at Platte Bridge, July 26, 1865."[2]

William Oliver Collins continued his law practice in Hillsboro, Ohio. He was one of the leaders in commemorating the nation's centennial on July 4, 1876. A hemorrhage of the stomach caused his death at 11:00 A.M., October 26, 1880. Located at 130 Collins Avenue, the home of William O. Collins still stands, its southern-style architecture distinctive in this Midwestern town.[3]

Some did not let setbacks on the plains hamper their future endeavors. Thomas Moonlight had a successful political career. The people of Kansas elected him their secretary of state in 1868. In 1884, President Cleveland appointed him governor of Wyoming, and eight years later made him minister to Bogota, Colombia. Moonlight died at Leavenworth on February 7, 1899.[4] After military service, Martin Anderson returned to a farm near Circleville, Kansas. In 1866 he became state treasurer, serving one term, and then won election as mayor of Holton, serving for two terms. He moved to Topeka in 1892, where he died July 9, 1897.[5]

Mustered out effective April 20, 1866, Patrick Connor became a leader in developing the Gentile community in Utah. He started the *Union Vedette,* the first daily newspaper printed in the territory, discovered Nevada's first silver mine, and wrote the state's first mining law. Introducing navigation on the Great Salt Lake, he built the first silver-lead smelting works and founded the town of Stockton. Connor died on December 17, 1891, in Salt Lake City and was buried with military honors at Fort Douglas.[6] Nelson Cole went back to business in St. Louis. He became state commander of the Military Order of the Loyal Legion, and then national commander for two years. He died on July 31, 1899, while in charge of a home unit in the Spanish American War, holding the rank of brigadier general of volunteers.[7]

Grenville Dodge resigned from the army on May 30, 1866, to become the chief engineer of the Union Pacific Railroad, where he gained national prominence. He was a delegate to Republican National Conventions in 1868, 1872, and 1876. He later served as president of the Commission to Inquire into the Management of the War with Spain. He died in Council Bluffs, Iowa, on January 3, 1916. General Dodge is buried in Walnut Hill Cemetery.[8]

Nicholas J. O'Brien left the army on February 1, 1866. He served as sheriff of Laramie County, Wyoming, in the 1870s. During the Spanish American War, he accompanied Wyoming troops to the Philippines. Elected commander of the Wyoming chapter of the Grand Army of the Republic, the Civil War veterans association, he moved to Lander and then to Denver in 1904. He also commanded the GAR in Colorado before his death on July 29, 1916.[9]

Mustered out in the summer of 1866, Eugene Ware eventually settled in Kansas, becoming prominent in politics, serving in the state senate, and holding other important positions. In 1872 he became editor of the *Fort Scott Monitor*. Two years later, he began publishing poems under the nom de plume Ironquill, which brought him national recognition. He became a member of the Kansas bar and began practicing law in Topeka. In 1902, Theodore Roosevelt appointed him commissioner of pensions, a job he held for two years. In the spring of 1911, he moved back to the family farm in Cherokee County. He died at Cascade, Colorado, on July 1, 1911, and is buried in Fort Scott National Cemetery.[10]

Henry Bretney apparently never lost his anger over the death of his friend Caspar Collins. Shortly after reaching Fort Laramie, on September 28, he achieved the rank of the captain, but on the same day, he appeared before a general court-martial. The first charges were that Bretney had been so intoxicated on September 11, 15, and 25 that he was unable to properly perform his duties. The first time was when he arrived with his company, the second when he failed to have his company appear at post headquarters as ordered, and the third when he was functioning as officer of the day. Prosecutors added an additional charge of conduct unbecoming an officer and a gentleman for being so intoxicated on September 25 that he was unable to stand erect in the presence of his superior. The court found Bretney guilty and ordered him dismissed from the service, which occurred on November 1. He eventually returned to Ohio. Although evidence is not conclusive, it is probable that he reentered the service under the name of H. C. Brett on September 11, 1867. Private Brett served in Company B, 2nd Cavalry, until July 20, 1868, when he deserted with a number of others at or near Salt Lake City. Henry Clay Bretney married

Mary Elizabeth Jackman on June 27, 1871. Moving to Lebanon, Kentucky, Bretney died from rheumatic heart disease on June 8, 1875.[11]

After service in Washington, D.C., and Charleston, South Carolina, Henry Maynadier died in the post hospital at Savannah, Georgia, at 2:45 P.M. on December 3, 1868. He was thirty-eight years old.[12]

After the burial of his daughter at Fort Laramie, Spotted Tail never fought the whites again. His tribe eventually settled on the Rosebud Reservation, where he lived as the leader of his people until his death by the hand of his enemy, Crow Dog, on August 5, 1881.[13]

Roman Nose had a special war bonnet made for him, its power depending upon his adherence to two taboos, one of which was not to eat food taken from a dish with a metal utensil. Several days before the battle of Beecher Island on September 17, 1868, Roman Nose ate a piece of fry bread that had been removed from the fire with a metal fork. Learning this, he knew that he would die in his next encounter. Late in the afternoon of the seventeenth, after repeated urging by his comrades, Roman Nose led a charge in which he was mortally wounded, dying the next day, a warrior's death for a great warrior.[14]

George Bent lived in Colony, Oklahoma, in the later years of his life, where he carried on a lengthy correspondence with George Hyde. The collected letters made a book, the best record of the Indian side of the war of 1865. George Bent died on May 19, 1918.[15]

On February 3, 1865, John Chivington left the service to avoid prosecution for his actions at Sand Creek.[16] After his son, Thomas, drowned in the North Platte River, Chivington journeyed to Nebraska City, Nebraska, to administer the estate. There he seduced his daughter-in-law, later marrying her on May 13, 1868, at the strong urging of the bishop of the Methodist Church in Chicago. The bride's parents published the following notice in the *Nebraska City News*:

> We, the undersigned, take this method to inform the public that the criminal act of John M. Chivington, in the marrying our daughter, Mrs. Sarah M. Chivington, the widow of Thomas M. Chivington, was unknown to us, and a thing we very much regret. Had the facts been made known to us of the intentions, some measures would have been taken to prevent the consummation of so vile an outrage, even if violent measures were necessary.
>
> Hoping that this may be of sufficient explanation, we remain, etc.
>
> John B. Lull
> Almira Lull[17]

George Bent and Wife
*One of the Indian leaders in the War 1865, George Bent left an important
written record of the fighting.* FORT CASPAR MUSEUM

Chivington lived in Nebraska City until July 1868, when he went to
Washington, D.C., to pursue a $37,000 Indian depredation claim. He lived
in Omaha from late summer 1868 until February 1869, when he went to
Washington, D.C. again. He was in Troy, New York, during the winter of
1869. He then returned to Washington and stayed until the fall of 1870,
when Sarah left him and went back to Nebraska City.

She described their marriage during this time in a letter to Pension
Examiner Sherman Williams:

Part of that summer & winter we spent in N.Y. with my relatives
from who he borrowed money & did not return it. The spring of
'70 we returned to Washington & he spent his time trying to get
money without labor. Nov '70 I came home to visit—as I supposed. He urged me to leave my baggage, & he would send it; I
never saw it again, not a change of clothing did I have. I never saw
him again until two years last Nov. he passed up the street. . . .

The early spring of '71 he skipped as I heard afterward to Canada, numerous letters came inquiring of me his whereabouts, but I knew nothing of him. Then I had several communications of his base actions of which I had been in ignorance of. Left me without means of support. I had no desire to live with a criminal. Then I applied for a divorce on the grounds of non-support.[18]

She obtained a divorce from him in October, 1871.

Chivington married Isabella Arenzer on November 25, 1873, in Cincinnati, Ohio. He was fifty-one, she forty. During their first four years of marriage, they lived on a nearby farm. He also preached some. Chivington returned to Denver in 1882, eventually residing at 1235 Stout Street. He served as a market master for one year, an undersheriff for two years, and a city sanitary inspector for eight months. Then he was sick for a year with the grip. Finally, he became coroner for the city of Denver, once being accused of taking money from the pockets of the dead.[19] During this period, he repeatedly spoke to pioneer groups in the region on the battle of Sand Creek, his remarks always being well received. In his speech, Chivington made no apologies, made a point of approving the killing of armed Indian women, and always ended with the ringing declaration, "I stand by Sand Creek."[20]

Chivington's later life mirrored his earlier one, his misanthropic deeds including, as one historian put it, "forgery, lying, deceit, thievery, wife battering, bullying and probably arson and insurance fraud."[21] In 1867, the editor of the *Omaha Daily Herald* labeled him a "rotten, clerical hypocrite," which seems kind.[22]

Chivington had palsy in later life. His hands shook, so that he could not write legibly. During his last months, his wife had to help him dress. Isabella noted that "he had a succession of spells . . . him being out of his head, he would ask insane questions about where we lived." He died on October 4, 1894, the examining physician listing the cause of death as diarrhea, injury to the rectum, and indigestion.[23] John Milton Chivington was buried in Fairmount Cemetery in the city where he gained fame.[24]

CHAPTER 1: CONTEXT

1. Cornelius Conway, *The Utah Expedition* (Cincinnati, 1858), 8.
2. Eugene F. Ware, *The Indian War of 1864,* introduction by John D. McDermott (Lincoln: University of Nebraska Press, 1994), 225.
3. Richard Burton, *Look of the Old West, 1860: Across the Plains to California* (Lincoln: University of Nebraska Press, 1963), 22.
4. James Reagan, "Military Landmarks," *The United Service* (August 1880), 160.
5. Quoted in Brian Doyle, "A Head Full of Swirling Dreams," *Atlantic Monthly* (November 2001), 148.
6. Letter from Caspar Collins, Sweetwater Bridge, April 18, 1865, to his aunt, William O. Collins Family Papers, Denver Public Library, Denver, Colorado. See also letter from Henry Clay Bretney, Jr., Jacksonville, Florida, January 27, 1936, to Alfred J. Mokler, Casper, Wyoming, Item 7, Miscellaneous Papers, Ellison Collection, Denver Public Library.
7. Letter from Randolph B. Marcy, Fort Laramie, September 2, 1857, to his daughter in W. Eugene Hollon, *Beyond the Cross Timbers: The Travels of Randolph B. Marcy, 1812–1887* (Norman: University of Oklahoma, 1955), 210.
8. Michael Tate, "From Cooperation to Conflict: Sioux Relations with the Overland Emigrants, 1845–1865," *Overland Journal* 18 (Winter 2000–2001), 18–31.
9. Charles E. Young, *Dangers of the Trail in 1865: A Narrative of Actual Events* (Geneva, NY: n.p., 1912), 52.
10. C. B. Hadley, "The Plains War in 1865," *Publications of the Nebraska Historical Society,* vol. 5 (Lincoln: Jacob North & Company, 1902), 278.
11. Young, *Dangers of the Trail,* 44, 54.

12. Mr. Bowles, Letter from Denver, *Springfield* (Massachusetts) *Republican,* May 29, 1865; Young, *Dangers of the Trail,* 45

13. Bowles, *Springfield* (Massachusetts) *Republican,* May 29, 1865.

14. James C. Olson, "From Nebraska to Montana, 1866: Diary of Thomas Alfred Creigh," *Nebraska History* 29 (September, 1948), 209; Charles S. Warren, "The Territory of Montana," *Contributions to the Historical Society of Montana,* vol. 2 (Helena: Montana Historical Society, 1896), 63–64; Robert G. Athearn, ed., "From Illinois to Montana in 1866: The Diary of Perry A. Burgess, *Pacific Northwest Quarterly* 41 (January 1950), 43; "Montana—Its Mining Resources," Omaha *Nebraska Republican,* November 10, 1865, 1.

15. John S. Gray, "Blazing the Bridger and Bozeman Trails," *Annals of Wyoming* 49 (Spring 1977), 39–40, 50. The definitive work on the Bridger Trail is James Lowe, *The Bridger Trail* (Seattle, WA: Arthur H. Clark, 2000).

16. Sherry L. Smith, *The Bozeman Trail* (Cheyenne: Wyoming Recreation Commission, 1981), 6, citing Dan Cushman, *The Great Northern Trail: America's Route of the Ages* (New York: McGraw-Hill Book Co., 1966), 135; *Reports of the Special Indian Commissioners 1867* (Washington, D.C., 1868), 61.

17. Sherry Smith, *The Bozeman Trail,* 6.

18. Gray, "Blazing the Bridger and Bozeman Trails," 30–35, 39–40, 47.

19. *Montana Post,* April 15, 1865, in "The Bent Road to Montana," *Omaha Republican,* April 19, 1865, 1. For a hyped discussion of the abundant resources along the trail, see John Bozeman, Letter of September 10, 1864, the *Montana Post,* September 17, 1864.

20. Yankton *Dakotaian,* March 1 and February 18, 1864; Gray, "Blazing the Bridger and Bozeman Trails," 39.

21. The Senate ratified the treaty on May 24, 1852, reducing the annual payments from fifty years to ten years. Although the Cheyennes, Sioux, and Arapahos ratified this amendment, the other tribes did not. See Fitzpatrick to A. Cumming, November 19, 1853, Senate Executive Document 1, 33rd Congress, 1st session, Vol. 1, serial 690, p, 367, cited in Alban W. Hoopes, *Indian Affairs and Their Administration, with Special Reference to the Far West, 1849–1860* (Philadelphia, 1932), 205.

22. *Army Navy Journal,* September 9, 1865, 1.

23. "The Red Men: Indian Population," *New York Times,* August 3, 1865, 2.

24. *Report of the Secretary of Interior,* 1865 (Washington, D.C., 1865), 191, 373, 582; *Defendant's Brief on Their Motion for New Trial, Abraham T.*

Litchfield v. the United States and the Sioux, Cheyenne, and Arapahoe Indians, Filed September 14, 1891, Indian Depredations Claim of Samuel R. Darland 366, Records of the United States Court of Claims, Record Group 123, National Archives, 10. Hereafter cited as RG 123.

25. Agent Valentine McGillycuddy, in response to an Indian depredations claim, investigated the 1865 war and reported his findings to the Indian claims commissioner. Speaking of the tribes doing the raiding in Colorado, Nebraska, and Wyoming in 1865, he stated that there were "ranging through his latter region the following bands of Indians, viz: the 'Kiyaksas' or 'Cut Offs,' now of Pine Ridge Agency, the Upper Brules, now at Rosebud Agency, the Northern Arapahos, now at Shoshone Agency, and the Northern Cheyennes, now of Pine Ridge Agency at Fort Keogh, M.T. In addition there was a small mixed band of predatory Sioux under a chief named 'Two Face'; the latter band has since became absorbed into the different Sioux Agencies." See Statement of Valentine T. McGillycuddy, U.S. Agency at Pine Ridge, March 28, 1885, Claim of William H. Harlow 2990, RG 123.

26. House Executive Document 1, 38th Congress, 2nd session, "Report of the Commissioner of Indian Affairs," 167.

27. P. W. Brown, "The 11th Ohio Cav.," *National Tribune,* March 31, 1910, 7.

28. Collins's original command, the 1st Battalion, 6th Ohio Volunteer Cavalry, became the 1st Independent Battalion, Ohio Volunteer Cavalry, in the summer of 1862. With the addition of a second battalion on July 31, 1863, it took the name most commonly associated with it—the 11th Ohio Volunteer Cavalry. Two new companies were added from recruits shortly thereafter, Companies K and L. See *Official Roster of the Soldiers of the State of Ohio in the War of the Rebellion, 1861–1866* (Akron, OH: Werner PTG & Litho. Co., 1891), 547; Brown, "The 11th Ohio Cav.," 7.

29. Robert Luther Thompson, *Wiring a Continent, The History of the Telegraph Industry in the United States, 1832–1866* (Princeton, NJ: Princeton University Press, 1947), chapter 25; James D. Reid, *The Telegraph in America* (New York: Derby Brothers, 1879), 490–97; J. Ross Browne, *Resources of the Pacific Slope* (New York: D. Appleton and Company, 1869), 434–37.

30. John D. McDermott, *Frontier Crossroads: The History of Fort Caspar and the Upper Platte Crossing* (Casper, WY: City of Casper, 1997), 27

31. Josiah M. Hubbard, "A Little Taste of Indian Warfare," *The Army and Navy Club of Connecticut, Report of Twenty-Ninth Annual Meeting, Pequot*

House, June 21, 1907 (Case, Lockwood & Brainard Company, 1907), 37.

32. The pioneering study is LeRoy R. Hafen, *The Overland Mail, 1849–1869* (Cleveland: Arthur H. Clark, 1926). The scholarly definitive work is Roscoe P. Conkling and Margaret B. Conkling, *The Butterfield Overland Mail* (Glendale, CA: Arthur H. Clark, 1955). Louise Erb et. al., *The Overland Trail in Wyoming* (1990) and Edward R. McAuslan's work of the same name, *The Overland Trail in Wyoming* (Wyoming Geological Association, 1961) are also useful.

33. Newton Edmunds, "Governor's Message," December 7, 1864, *Council Journal of the Fourth Session of the Legislative Assembly of the Territory of Dakota* (Yankton, SD: G. W. Kinsbury, Printer, 1865), 33.

34. Maurice Matloff, ed., *American Military History* (Washington, D.C.: Office of the Chief of Military History, 1969), 282.

35. Raphael P. Thain, comp., *Notes Illustrating the Military Geography of the United States* (Washington, D.C.: Government Printing Office, 1881), 67, 75, 82.

36. Stephen Fairfield, "The Eleventh Kansas Regiment at Platte Bridge," *Transactions of the Kansas State Historical Society, 1903–1904,* vol. 3 (Topeka, KS: Geo. A. Clark State Printer, 1904), 352–53.

37. George Bird Grinnell, *The Fighting Cheyennes* (Norman: University of Oklahoma Press, 1955), 132–37.

38. J. W. Vaughn, *Indian Fights: News Facts on Seven Encounters* (Norman: University of Oklahoma Press, 1966), 8–9.

39. Henry E. Palmer, "Powder River Indian Expedition of 1865, With a Few Incidents Preceding the Same," in *Civil War Sketches and Incidents, Papers Read by Companions of the Commander of the State of Nebraska, Military Order of the Loyal Legion of the United States,* vol. 1 (Omaha, NE: The Commandery, 1902), 59–60. Henry Palmer originally presented his account on February 2, 1887, before the Order of the Loyal Legion.

40. For a thorough discussion of the 1864 raid, see Ronald Becher, *Massacre along the Medicine Road: A Social History of the Indian War of 1864 in Nebraska Territory* (Caldwell, ID: Caxton Press, 1999), 148–210.

41. The most recent study of the Sand Creek Massacre is National Park Service, *Sand Creek Massacre Project,* 2 vols. (Denver: National Park Service, Intermountain Region, 2000). This is in response to Public Law 105–243 of October 6, 1998, which authorized establishment of the Sand Creek Massacre National Historic Site. Land acquisition is now under way. See also Stan Hoig, *The Sand Creek Massacre* (Norman:

University of Oklahoma Press, 1961), 31, 145–62; Jean Afton, David Fridtjof Halaas, and Andrew E. Masich, with Richard Ellis, *Cheyenne Dog Soldiers: A Ledgerbook History of Coups and Combat* (Denver: Colorado Historical Society and the University Press of Colorado, 1997), xviii; David J. Berthrong, *The Southern Cheyennes* (Norman: University of Oklahoma Press, 1963), 68–69; Grinnell, *The Fighting Cheyennes,* 14; James T. King, *War Eagle: Life of General Eugene A. Carr* (Lincoln: University of Nebraska Press, 1963), 94–95. There were many contemporaries, however, who lauded Chivington's actions. One of these was Eugene F. Ware, who wrote: "But there was never anything more deserved than that massacre. The only difficulty was that there were about fifteen hundred Indian warriors that didn't get killed. . . . While he [Chivington] was getting ready, the refugee Indians who were being fed at Fort Lyons went out and plundered some trains and killed some women and children, and carried their scalps to the Cheyenne villages up on Sand Creek." See Ware, *Indian War of 1864,* 309.

42. "Census of Indians in Upper Arkansas Agency, 1860," Letters Received, District of Colorado, Entry 3259, Part II, Records of United States Army Commands, Record Group 393. Hereafter cited as RG 393.

43. George Bent is the principal source for the Indian side of the 1865 war. The third child of William Bent and Owl Woman, a Cheyenne, he was born on July 7, 1843. After public education in Westport and St. Louis, Missouri, at age seventeen he enlisted in the Confederate Army. Captured during the siege of Corinth, Mississippi, he received parole and went to Bent's Fort, where he lived among his mother's people. Wounded in the hip at Sand Creek, he recovered sufficiently to join his kinsman on the warpath. In later life, he lived at Colony, Oklahoma, and conducted a long correspondence with George Hyde, resulting in the book *Life of George Bent, Written from His Letters,* ed. Savoie Lottinville (Norman: University of Oklahoma Press, 1968). See H. L. Lubers, "William Bent Family and the Indians of the Plains," *Colorado Magazine* 12 (January 1936), 19–22; Dan L. Thrapp, *Encyclopedia of Frontier Biography,* vol. 1 (Lincoln: University of Nebraska Press, 1988), 97–99.

44. *Report of the Secretary of Interior,* 1865 (Washington, D.C., 1865), 191.

45. Robert M. Utley, *Frontiersmen in Blue: The United States Army and the Indian, 1848–1865* (New York: Macmillan Company, 1967), 294–97, 300–301; John Stands In Timber and Margot Liberty, *Cheyenne Memories,* 2nd ed. (New Haven, CT: Yale University Press, 1998), 170.

CHAPTER 2: JULESBURG

1. The purported death of Beni at the hands of Jack Slade in 1861 has been the subject of many stories and much myth. The latter is said to have cut off the ears of the former before ending his life. For an example of a lengthy, jocular recounting of the killing of Beni, see Eli Perkins, "Wild Humor of the Plains," *Chicago Tribune*, May 31, 1877, 6. See also Byron G., Hooper Jr., "A Capsule History of the Julesburg Area," *The Denver Westerners Monthly Roundup* 19 (November 1961), 6–7.

2. Being a home station meant that the stage company provided eating and sleeping accommodations for employees and passengers. See Hooper, "A Capsule History of the Julesburg Area," 6.

3. Some passengers, however, found Holladay's promises unkept. T. W. Lavin was one who learned that the Concords were often "rickety hacks, lumber wagons, drays, &," meals sometimes went for $2.50 to $3, and passengers often had to walk part of the way due to breakdowns. See T. W. Lavin, "From Montana," *Rocky Mountain News*, May 26, 1865, 2. See also "The Overland Stage Line," *New York Times*, January 31, 1865, 4; "Speaker Colfax on Indians," January 11, 1865, 2, "The Overland Mail Line," January 27, 1865, 4, "Overland Treasure Express," February 7, 1865, 3 and "The Overland Stage Line," October 16, 1865, 3, *Rocky Mountain News*.

4. The Lodgepole Creek road had replaced the first northwest connector to Ash Hollow in 1860. Although the Lodgepole Creek route was twenty-five miles longer, it avoided the difficulties in dealing with California Hill, Windlass Hill, and the sandy drag up the North Platte River from Ash Hollow to Court House Rock. See Merrill J. Mattes, *The Great Platte River Road: The Covered Wagon Mainline via Fort Kearny to Fort Laramie* (Lincoln: Nebraska Historical Society, 1969), 333–338; William S. Greever, *The Bonanza West: The Story of the Western Mining Rushes, 1848–1900* (Norman: University of Oklahoma Press, 1961, 173–174; Andrew F. Rolle, *The Road to Virginia City: The Diary of James Knox Polk Miller* (Norman: University of Oklahoma Press, 1960), 25.

5. Hooper, "A Capsule History of the Julesburg Area," 6; C. F. Parker, "Old Julesburg and Fort Sedgwick," *Colorado Magazine* 7 (July 1930), 139–41; Ruth Dunn, *Indian Vengeance at Julesburg* (North Platte, NE: Ruth Dunn, 1972), 2; Ware, *Indian War of 1864*, 245; Hyde, *Life of George Bent*, 169–70.

6. Nicholas J. O'Brien, Military Service Record, Records of the Office of the Adjutant General, Record Group 94, National Archives, Washington, D.C. Hereafter cited as RG 94; "Demise of a Veteran," unidentified newspaper clipping, Nicholas J. O'Brien File B-Ob6-nj, American Heritage Center, Laramie, Wyoming; Ware, *Indian War of 1864*, 95.

7. Ware, *Indian War of 1864*, 95.

8. For biographical sketches of Ware's life and career see John D. McDermott, "Introduction," in Ware, *Indian War of 1864*, xi–xix; James C. Malin, "Eugene F. Ware's Literary Chronology," *Kansas Historical Quarterly* 37 (Autumn 1971), 314; Grace Lowry, "Life of Eugene Ware" (M.S. thesis, Kansas State Teachers College, Pittsburg, Kansas, July 1936); Charles S. Gleed, "Eugene Fitch Ware," 19–41; J. S. West, "Eugene Ware," 65–71, in *Kansas Historical Collections*, vol. 13 (Topeka: Kansas Historical Society, 1913–1914); and "Eugene F. Ware," in *The National Cyclopedia of American Biography*, vol. 9 (New York: James T. White & Company, 1899), 202. See also Military Service Record of Eugene F. Ware, Records of the Office of the Adjutant General, RG 94, Eugene F. Ware Biographical File, Kansas State Historical Society, Topeka.

9. Ware, *Indian War of 1864*, 239–40; Letter from James W. Peabody, Omaha, Nebraska, January 3, 1865, to Joel F. Wisely, Letters Sent, Office of Medical Director, Records of the Department of Kansas, Entry 3215, Records of United States Continental Commands, RG 393.

10. The army changed the name to Fort Sedgwick in honor of Maj. Gen. John Sedgwick, who died in the battle of Spottsylvania. See Daniel S. Day, "Fort Sedgwick," *Colorado History* 42 (Fall 1965), 19–20; Parker, "Old Julesburg and Fort Sedgwick," 144.

11. Statement of Nicholas J. O'Brien, March 4, 1888, Claim of William H. Harlow 2990, Records of the United States Court of Claims, RG 123. See also Ware, *Indian War of 1864*, 228, 236–37, 272; Hooper, "A Capsule History of the Julesburg Area," 10.

12. Grinnell, *The Fighting Cheyennes* 183.

13. George Bent says there were ten, but he names only Big Crow. See Hyde, *Life of George Bent*, 171.

14. Hyde, *Life of George Bent*, 170–71; Grinnell, *The Fighting Cheyennes*, 183; Jean Afton et. al., *Cheyenne Dog Soldiers*, 238; Fred H. Werner, *Heroic Fort Sedgwick and Julesburg: A Study in Courage* (Greeley, CO: Werner Publications, 1987), 20.

15. Nicholas J. O'Brien, "Captain O'Brien's Dash thru Indians and Fire at Julesburg," *Rocky Mountain News,* December 26, 1915. This is quoted at length in Dunn, *Indian Vengeance at Julesburg,* 5; Day, "Fort Sedgwick," 28; Afton et. al., *Cheyenne Dog Soldiers,* 268; Account of J. A. Towers (Julesburg, Colorado), *Grit Advocate* 21 (October 1910).

16. Those killed were Sgt. Alanson Hanchett; Cpls. William H. Gray, Anthony Koons, and Walter B. Talcott; and Pvts. George Barnett, Hiram W. Brundage, Henry H. Hall, David Ishman, James Jordan, Davis Lippincott, Edson D. Moore, Amos C. McArthur, Thomas Scott, and Joel Stebbins. John Murphy, a nineteen-year-old Irishman, died a few months later in the post hospital. Bodies buried in the cemetery were transferred in 1871 to Fort McPherson, where they remain today. See Ware, *Indian War of 1864,* 325–29; "The Battle at Julesburg—More Particulars," *Rocky Mountain News,* January 10, 1865, 2; Dunn, *Indian Vengeance at Julesburg,* 10, 16.

17. "The Battle at Julesburg," *Rocky Mountain News,* January 10, 1865, 2; Letter from Valley Station," *(Central City, Colorado) Miner's Register,* January 8, 1865, 2; Hyde, *Life of George Bent,* 172.

18. O'Brien, "Captain O'Brien's Dash," *Oskaloosa (Kansas) Independent,* January 14, 1865.

19. "From Down the Platte," *Rocky Mountain News,* June 9, 1865, 2; "From Colorado," *Chicago Tribune,* January 11, 1865, 2; O'Brien, "Captain O'Brien's Dash"; Hyde, *Life of George Bent,* 172; Grinnell, *The Fighting Cheyennes,* 186–87.

20. The uniform was worn by George Bent during the fight with General Connor's troops on Powder River. See Hyde, *Life of George Bent,* 172; Dunn, *Indian Vengeance at Julesburg,* 15; "Give the Address," *Rocky Mountain News,* January 30, 1865, 3.

21. Hyde, *Life of George Bent,* 173; Grinnell, *The Fighting Cheyennes,* 187.

22. "From Colorado," *Chicago Tribune,* January 11, 1865, 2; Palmer, "Powder River Indian Expedition of 1865," 61–62; Ware, *Indian War of 1864,* 325–27; Hyde, *Life of George Bent,* 174.

23. "From Down the Platte," *Rocky Mountain News,* June 9, 1865, 2; Hyde, *Life of George Bent,* 175; Dunn, *Indian Vengeance at Julesburg,* 16.

24. From Down the Platte," *Rocky Mountain News,* January 9, 1865, 2. See also "Indian Matters," *Miner's Register,* January 10, 1865, 2.

25. Letter from Mitchell, Omaha, Nebraska, January 8, 1865, to Major General Curtis, Letters Received, Records of the Department of Kansas Entry 3215, RG 393.

26. See *Testimony in the Claim of Ben Holladay for Losses and Damages,* 46th Congress, 2nd session, 1880, Servate Miscellaneous Document 19, 29; Berthrong, *The Southern Cheyennes,* 225. Berthrong cites Moonlight to Curtis, January 7, 1865; William Mooney, "Report of the 11th Ohio for the Year 1865," Records of the 11th Ohio Volunteer Cavalry, Records of the Office of the Adjutant General, RG 94; *Rocky Mountain News,* January 11, 1865; "Mr. McCollough's Letter," *Rocky Mountain News,* February 3, 1865, 2.

27. Hyde, *Life of George Bent,* 181–82; *Testimony in the Claim of Ben Holladay for Losses and Damages,* 29; "McCullough's Letter," 2.

28. "From Down the Platte," 2; "Indian Cruelty," *Rocky Mountain News,* January 14, 1865, 3; "Indian Matters," 2.

29. Thomas Moonlight, January 11, 1865, District of Colorado, Letters Sent, Department of the Plains, Entry 3254, RG 393.

30. *New York Times,* January 14, 1865.

31. *Rocky Mountain News,* January, 27, 1865.

32. "Letter from Valley Station," *Miner's Register,* January 8, 1865, 2.

33. "The Julesburg Affair," *Rocky Mountain News,* January 11, 1865, 2.

34. The *Nebraska Republican* stated that there were only six left by General Curtis to protect Julesburg. See (Omaha) *Nebraska Republican,* February 3, 1865, 2. Born in Richland County, Ohio, on April 4, 1823, Robert R. Mitchell served during the Mexican War, ending up as a captain in the 15th U.S. Infantry. Moving to Kansas in 1856, he became a member of the territorial legislature and served as state treasurer from 1858 to 1861. Beginning his Civil War career as colonel of the 2nd Kansas, he later led the 13th division of Gen. Don Carlos Buell's army in the battle of Perryville. He commanded the District of Nebraska of the Department of Kansas at Omaha from February 28, 1864, to March 28, 1865, and the Department of Kansas to August 22, 1865. See Robert B. Mitchell Pension File 196683, Records of the Veterans Administration, Record Group 15, National Archives, Washington, D.C. Hereafter cited as RG 15. See also James Grant Wilson and John Fiske, eds., *Appletons' Cyclopedia of American Biography,* vol. 4 (New York: D. Appleton and Company, 1898), 346.

35. Ware, *Indian War of 1864,* 329, 332.

36. Grinnell speculates that this was the village site that the Indians called the Cherry Creek camp. See Grinnell, *The Fighting Cheyennes,* 188–89, fn. 6.

37. "New America," *Chambers Journal* 4 (April 13, 1867), 23.

38. Young, *Dangers of the Trail in 1865,* 78.

39. "Indians and Things," *Rocky Mountain News,* January 19, 1865, 2.

40. "Special Notices," *Rocky Mountain News,* January 30, 1865, 3.

41. "Proclamation," January 17, 1865, 2; and "For the War," January 18, 1865, 2, *Mountain News.*

42. "The Indians," *Rocky Mountain News,* January 17, 1865, 2.

43. "Indians on the Smoky Hill," *Rocky Mountain News,* January 27, 1865, 2.

44. Ware, *Indian War of 1864,* 332–51; *Nebraska Republican,* February 3, 1865, 2.

45. Telegram from General Mitchell, Fort Kearny, January 29, 1865, to Major General Curtis, Telegrams Received, Department of Kansas, RG 393; Ware, *Indian War of 1864,* 346.

46. Ware, *Indian War of 1864,* 353–54; Telegram from General Mitchell, Fort Kearny, January 29, 1865, to Major General Curtis, Telegrams Received, District of Nebraska, Entry 3198, Part II, RG 393.

47. Telegram from General Mitchell, Fort Kearny, January 29, 1865, to Major General Curtis, Telegrams Received, Department of Kansas, RG 393; Telegram from J. J. Kennedy, Valley Station, January 16, 1865, to Colonel Moonlight, Letters Received, District of Colorado, Entry 3259, Part II, RG 393; Ware, *Indian War of 1864,* 354.

48. Claim of Holan Godfrey 2559, RG 123; A. K. McClure, *Three Thousand Miles through the Rocky Mountains* (Philadelphia: J. P. Lippincott & Company, n.d.), 69–71.

49. On April 15, Frank C. Young passed by the Morrison Ranch and recorded the scene in his journal. There in the middle of the road was an Indian killed in the January 15 raid, left by his dispatchers "to be driven over, and kicked, and cut up, and made the object of execrations by every passing pilgrim." The man lay on his back, "with lusterless eyes staring at the sky, his right arm cut off at the elbow, both legs off and lying by his side, his body gashed and mutilated—a ghastly testimony to the ferocious hatred engendered in the Plainsman against him and his kind." See Frank C. Young, *Across the Plains in '65* (Denver: Frank C. Young, 1905), 198. The army arranged for Mrs. Morrison's freedom at Fort Rice on June 21. Her child died along the way. See "The 'Friendly' Indians," *Rocky Mountain News,* July 7, 1865, 1.

50. Letter from J. W. Ford, Valley Station, *Rocky Mountain News,* January 17, 1865; "Further News from Down the Road," *Rocky Mountain News,* January 17, 1865, 2.

51. Letter from Commander of Detachment, Valley Station, January 16, 1865, to Assistant Adjutant General, District of Colorado, Letters

Received, District of Colorado, Entry 3259, Part II, RG 393; "From Down the Road," *Rocky Mountain News,* January 18, 1865, 2; "From the West," (Omaha) *Nebraska Weekly Republican,* January 27, 1865, 1.

52. O'Brien, "Captain O'Brien's Dash."

53. Ware, *Indian War of 1864,* 355–57; C. B. Hadley, "The Plains War in 1865," *Publications of the Nebraska Historical Society,* vol. 5 (Lincoln: Jacob North & Company, 1902), 274–75.

54. Telegram from General Mitchell, Fort Kearny, January 29, 1865, to Major General Curtis, Telegrams Received, Department of Kansas, RG 393.

55. See *The War of the Rebellion: A Compilation of the Official Records of the Union and Confederate Armies,* Series I, vol. 48, pt. 1 (Washington, D.C.: Government Printing Office, 1898), 40, 41. Hereafter cited as *OR.* Colonel Livingston's report of February 5 gives a partial list of depredations committed by the Indians during these raids along the Platte.

56. According to Berthrong, James Beckworth found them there between January 9 and 12. See *Southern Cheyennes,* 227.

57. Grinnell speculates that this is the creek now know as White Man's Fork. The *Nebraska Republican* of February 10 mentions the river as the previous campsite. See Grinnell, *The Fighting Cheyennes,* 188, fn. 5; *Nebraska Republican,* February 10, 1865, 2.

58. There in the spring of 1865 they signed a peace treaty. See Hyde, *Life of George Bent,* 177; Grinnell, *The Fighting Cheyennes,* 188.

59. Grinnell, *The Fighting Cheyennes,* 189.

60. "More Indian Fighting," *Rocky Mountain News,* January 30, 1865, 2; "From Valley Station," *Rocky Mountain News,* January 31, 1865, 2; Statements of William H. Harlow, January 8, 1886, and July 10, 1891, Claim of William H. Harlow 2990, RG 123; "Graphic Account of Western Troubles," *Omaha Nebraska Weekly Republican,* February 17, 1865, 2.

61. Hyde, *Life of George Bent,* 175, 177–79; *Nebraska Republican,* February 2, 1865, 2, and February 3, 1865, 2; *Rocky Mountain News,* January 30 and 31, 1865; Day, "Fort Sedgwick," 30; Statements of James H. Southerland (Central City, 1874), Oliver P. Wiggins (October 7, 1886), Nicholas J. O'Brien (Cheyenne, April 30, 1886), and Agent J. P. McGillycuddy (Pine Ridge, July 30, 1885) in Claim of James H. Southerland 3367, Indian Depredation Claims, Entry 700, Records of the Indian Bureau, Record Group 75; C. B. Hadley, "The Plains War in 1865," 274–75; Statements of William H. Harlow, January 8, 1886, and July 10, 1891, Claim of William H. Harlow 2990, RG 123;

"Graphic Account of Western Troubles," (Omaha) *Nebraska Weekly Republican* February 17, 1865, 2.

62. Hyde, *Life of George Bent,* 179.

63. *Nebraska Republican,* February 3, 1865, 2; *Testimony in the Claim of Ben Holladay for Losses and Damages,* 29; Hyde, *Life of George Bent,* 83.

64. *Rocky Mountain News,* February 1, 1865, 3.

65. Hyde, *Life of George Bent,* 181–82.

66. Claim of John A. Morrow 888, RG 123.

67. Letter from H. H. Heath, Headquarters, East Sub-District of Nebraska, Fort Kearny, N.T., October 31, 1865, to Lt. John Lewis, Acting Assistant Adjutant General, District of Nebraska, Letters Received, District of Nebraska, Entry 3198, Part II, RG 393.

68. Hyde, *Life of George Bent,* 181; *Testimony in the Claim of Ben Holladay for Losses and Damages,* 29.

69. Ware, *Indian War of 1864,* 362.

70. O'Brien, "Captain O'Brien's Dash."

71. "Graphic Account of Western Troubles," 2, 65; O'Brien, "Captain O'Brien's Dash."

72. Claim of G. D. Connelly and E. D. Bulen 2849 and Statement of E. D. Bulen, August 22, 1865, Claim of William E. Dillon and John H. Maxon 2850, RG 123. C. B. Hadley claimed that the force had been augmented by a group of about sixty-five newly arrived freighters who had corralled their wagons about 100 yards northwest of Fort Rankin, but no others mention the party. See Hadley, "The Plains War in 1865," 274–76.

73. Hyde, *Life of George Bent,* 182; O'Brien, "Captain O'Brien's Dash."

74. See sketch of "The Burning of Julesburg" by 7th Iowa cavalryman T. H. Williams in Dunn, *The Burning of Julesburg* (North Platte, NE: Ruth Dunn, 1973), 5. After the burning of the town, residents rebuilt on a new site four miles east. Situated outside of the military reservation so that businesses might sell liquor, the second Julesburg lasted until June 23, 1867, when the Union Pacific tracks reached the north bank of the South Platte, causing a mass exodus to the more profitable location. The building of a branch line to Denver in 1881 precipitated a move to the city's present location.

75. Statement of Nicholas O'Brien, *Defendant's Brief on Their Motion for New Trial, Abraham T. Litchfield v. the United States and the Sioux, Cheyenne, and Arapahoe Indians,* 6.

76. Grinnell, *The Fighting Cheyennes,* 193.

77. Ware, *Indian War of 1864,* 372–73; O'Brien in Dunn, *The Burning of Julesburg,* 5.

78. Dunn, *The Burning of Julesburg,* 10.

79. Ware, *Indian War of 1864,* 377; O'Brien in Dunn, *The Burning of Julesburg,* 10–11, 14–15. Grinnell refers to the ranch as Gittrell's Ranch. See Grinnell, *The Fighting Cheyennes,* 193.

80. Statement of William H. Harlow, July 10, 1891, Claim of William H. Harlow 2990, RG 123.

81. Letter from R. M. Mitchell, District of Nebraska, Omaha, February 8, 1865, Special Orders, District of Nebraska, Entry 3204, and Letter from H. H. Heath, Headquarters, East Sub-District of Nebraska, Fort Kearny, N.T., October 31, 1865, to Lt. John Lewis, Acting Assistant Adjutant General, District of Nebraska, Entry 3198, Part II, RG 393; Frank A. Root and William Elsey Connelley, *The Overland Stage to California* (Topeka, 1901), 360–61.

82. Telegram from Livingston, Alkali Station, February 2, 1865, Letters Received, District of Nebraska, Entry 3198, Part II, RG 393. See also Maj. Gen. Samuel Curtis, Headquarters, Department of Kansas, Fort Leavenworth, January 31, 1865, to Colonel Moonlight, Letters Received, District to Colorado, Entry 3259, Part II, RG 393; "Indian Matters," 2; "Letter from Fort Kearny," *Nebraska Republican,* February 10, 1865; O'Brien in Dunn, *The Burning of Julesburg,* 15; "More Indian Depredation," (Omaha) *Nebraska Weekly Republican,* February 10, 1865, 4.

83. Letter from H. H. Heath, Headquarters, East Sub-District of Nebraska, Fort Kearny, N.T., October 31, 1865, to Lt. John Lewis, Acting Assistant Adjutant General, District of Nebraska, Entry 3198, Part II, RG 393.

84. "Martial Law," and "To the People of Colorado," *Rocky Mountain News,* February 6, 1865, 2; "Indian Matters," 2.

85. Letter from Robert Mitchell, Omaha, February 3, 1865, to Col. R. R. Livingston, Alkali Station, Special Orders, Headquarters, District of Nebraska, Entry 3204, Part II, RG 393.

86. "The Indian War in the West," *Nebraska Republican,* February 3, 1865, 2; "Indian Wars on the Plains," *Oskaloosa Independent,* February 18, 1865, 2.

87. "Death to Indians," *Miner's Register,* February 11, 1865, 2. For similar sentiments, see "Indian Affairs," *Miner's Register,* July 28, 1865, 2.

88. Claim of Jules Ecoffey and Joseph Bissonette 2208, RG 123. For the life of Bissonette, see John D. McDermott, "Joseph Bissonette," in *The Mountain Men and the Fur Trade of the Far West,* ed. LeRoy Hafen, vol. 4 (Glendale, CA: Arthur H. Clark Company, 1967), 49–60.

CHAPTER 3: MUD SPRINGS AND RUSH CREEK

1. About twenty miles north of Sidney and about eight miles northwest of Dalton is one of the state of Nebraska's least-known and least-visited historic properties, the site of Mud Springs Station. A plot 150 by 150 feet preserves the ground once occupied by the Mud Springs Pony Express Station, which later became the army's telegraph outpost. Archaeological evidence indicates periodic occupation of the site from 8000 B.C. Apparently, the stopping place earned its name because buffalo liked to wallow in its waters, churning up sediment and creating a mud flat. See "Mud Springs Pony Express Station National Register of Historic Places Inventory-Nomination Form," mss. 1971, State Historic Preservation Office Files, Nebraska Historical Society, Lincoln, Nebraska.

2. One of the boys of Company K, 11th Ohio, "The Battle of Mud Springs," *Rocky Mountain News,* February 21, 1865, 2. Dated February 15, Fort Halleck, D.T., this article represents the composite story of three men of the 11th Ohio who fought at Mud Springs, having just arrived from Fort Laramie.

3. (Omaha) *Nebraska Republican,* February 10, 1865; Root and Connelley, *The Overland Stage to California,* 360–61; Grinnell, *The Fighting Cheyennes,* 193–94; Berthrong, *Southern Cheyennes,* 229; Hyde, *Life of George Bent,* 187.

4. The state monument and the surrounding battlefield have been listed in the National Register of Historic Places. For a legal description of the parcel, a site drawing, and a history of the property, see "Mud Springs Pony Express Station National Register of Historic Places Inventory-Nomination Form." See also Federal Writers' Project, *Nebraska: A Guide to the Cornhusker State* (New York: Hastings House, 1939), 305; Paul Henderson, "The Story of Mud Springs," *Nebraska History* 32 (June 1951), 108–19; "Mud Springs, Historic Spot in West Nebraska Is Again Placed on Map," *Lincoln Star,* June 12, 1939; Merrill J. Mattes, *The Great Platte River Road: The Covered Wagon Mainline via Fort Kearny to Fort Laramie* (Lincoln: Nebraska Historical Society, 1969), 337–38; William S. Greever, *The Bonanza West: The Story of the Western Mining Rushes, 1848–1900* (Norman: University of Oklahoma Press, 1961), 173–74; Herman R. Lyon, "Freighting in the 60's," in *Nebraska Historical Society Publications,* vol. 5 (Lincoln: Nebraska State Historical Society, 1907), 265; Raymond W. Settle and Mary Lund Settle, *Saddles and Spurs: The Pony Express Saga* (Harrisburg, PA: The Stackpole Company, 1955), 132; Merrill J. Mattes and Paul Hender-

son, *The Pony Express from St. Joseph to Fort Laramie* (St. Louis, MO: The Patrice Press, 1989), 57–61; Ted Stutheit, *The Pony Express on the Oregon Trail* (Lincoln: Nebraska Game and State Parks Commission, 1987), 14; "Graphic Account of Western Troubles," 2; Letter from H. H. Heath, Headquarters, East Sub-District of Nebraska, Fort Kearny, N.T., October 31, 1865, to Lt. John Lewis, Acting Assistant Adjutant General, District of Nebraska, Entry 3198, Part II, RG 393.

5. For accounts of the organization of the transcontinental telegraph company and the construction of its line through what was then Nebraska and Wyoming Territory, see Thompson, *Wiring a Continent,* chapter 25; Reid, *The Telegraph in America,* 490–97; Phil Ault, *Wires West: The Story of the Talking Wires* (New York: Dodd, Mead & Company, 1974), 44–47, 77; and William E. Unrau, *Tending the Talking Wire: A Buck Soldier's View of Indian Country, 1863–1866* (Salt Lake City: University of Utah Press, 1979), 10–12.

6. Richard Burton, *The City of the Saints and across the Rocky Mountains to California* (Niwot, CO: University Press of Colorado, 1990), 70.

7. Mattes, *The Great Platte River Road,* 474; "Historical Sketch of Cheyenne County," in *Nebraska Historical Society Publications,* ed. Albert Watkins, vol. 18 (Lincoln: Nebraska State Historical Society, 1920), 36.

8. Caspar Collins, Map of Mud Springs, William O. Collins Collection, Special Collections, Colorado State University Library, Fort Collins, Colorado.

9. Letter from Winfield S. Davis, Company H, 11th Ohio, to his sister, Mud Springs, March 7, 1865, Winfield S. Davis Pension File, Records of the Veterans Administration, RG 15. From New Alexandra, Ohio, Winfield S. Davis entered the service on June 22, 1863, at the age of eighteen. He died of disease at Mud Springs on May 31, 1865. See *Official Roster of the Soldiers of the State of Ohio,* 571.

10. William O. Collins's report of the February campaign took the form of a letter from Collins, February 15, 1865, Fort Laramie, to John Pratt, Acting Assistant Adjutant General, District of Nebraska. A handwritten copy of the letter is found in the William O. Collins Papers, FF5 Letters 51–59, Denver Public Library, Denver, Colorado. The report is available in printed form in William Mooney, "Report of the 11th Ohio for the Year 1865," Records of the 11th Ohio Volunteer Cavalry, Records of the Office of the Adjutant General, Record Group 94. Hereafter cited as Collins Report. File FF7 in the Denver Public Library contains an early draft of Collins's annual regimental report, which covers his February activities in summary form.

11. One of the boys of Company K, 11th Ohio, "The Battle of Mud Springs," 2. According to this source, there were 500 cattle in the herd.

12. William Oliver Collins was born in Sommers, Connecticut, on August 23, 1809. After graduating from Amherst College in 1833, he migrated to Hillsborough, Ohio, where he practiced law. In 1843 he married Catherine Weaver, who bore him three children. When the Civil War began, Collins raised the regiment that was to become the 11th Ohio Volunteer Cavalry and became its colonel. Collins led his regiment to Wyoming in 1862, where the troops performed exemplary service in guarding the Overland and Oregon Trails and the Pacific Telegraph. See "Death of Colonel Wm. O. Collins," unidentified newspaper clipping, c. October 27, 1880, William O. Collins Papers, FF13, Denver Public Library; Agnes Wright Spring, *Caspar Collins: The Life and Exploits of an Indian Fighter of the Sixties* (Lincoln: University of Nebraska Press, Bison Book Edition, 1969), 35–36, 68–69.

13. Collins Report, 92–93, 97. For accounts of the Mud Springs campaign based solely on the Collins Report, see David P. Robrock, "The Eleventh Ohio Volunteer Cavalry on the Central Plains, 1862–1866," *Arizona and the West* 25 (Spring, 1983), 39–41 and Spring, *Caspar Collins,* 61–69. Built during the fall of 1864, Fort Mitchell stood a few miles west of Scotts Bluff. See John Warning, *War of the Plains: Fort Mitchell on the Oregon-California Trail* (Minatare, NE: Fort Mitchell Historical Association, 1988), 14–18; Merrill J. Mattes, "Old Fort Mitchell, Nebraska, Revisited," *Overland Journal* 7, no. 2 (1989), 2–11; Dean Knudsen, "Fort Mitchell: Forgotten Outpost of the Plains," *True West* 39 (December, 1992), 20–23.

14. Enrolled on August 3, 1863, at the age of twenty-seven, Ellsworth became a first lieutenant on September 16. On May 1, 1865, he became captain of Company E. See *Official Roster of the Soldiers of the State of Ohio,* 570; Military Service Record of William Ellsworth, Records of the Office of the Adjutant General, RG 94.

15. David C. Peck, "In Indian Country," *National Tribune,* March 10, 1898, 8. William H. Idlet entered the service in February 1861, at the age of thirty-two, and reenlisted on February 3, 1864. He died on March 19, 1865. See Whitelaw Reid, *Ohio in the War: Her Statesmen, Her Generals, and Soldiers,* 2 vols. (New York: Moore, Wilstach & Baldwin, 1868), 571.

16. Grinnell, *The Fighting Cheyennes,* 195.

17. Letter from Winfield S. Davis, Company H, 11th Ohio, to his sister, Mud Springs, March 7, 1865, Winfield S. Davis Pension File, RG 15.

18. Peck, "In Indian Country," *National Tribune,* 8.
19. Sgt. William Hall had enlisted on June 22, 1863. He was about twenty-six years old at the time of the Mud Springs fight. Standing 5 feet 11½ inches, he had fair complexion, light hair, and blue eyes. He died on January 7, 1866, at Cold Springs Station, Dakota Territory. The certificate of death states that he died of "disease unknown, fell from his horse dead while in the discharge of his duty." See Military Service Record, RG 94; *Official Roster of the Soldiers of the State of Ohio,* 570.
20. Peck, "In Indian Country," 8.
21. Collins Report, 93.
22. David Peck estimated 1,500 to 2,000, as did G. W. Nelson. Colonel Livingston reported nearly 2,000 Indians, while W. S. Davis fantasized 5,000. See Peck, "In Indian Country," March 10, 1898, 8; G. W. Nelson, "Out on the Plains," *National Tribune,* May 1, 1890, 3; *New York Times,* February 21, 1865, 1; and Letter from Davis to his sister, Mud Springs, March 7, 1865, Winfield S. Davis, Pension File, RG 15.
23. Collins Report, 94.
24. One of the Boys of Company K, 11th Ohio, "The Battle of Mud Springs," 2. See also "Indian Fight," (Central City, Colorado) *Miners' Register,* February 24, 1855, 2.
25. Collins Report, 93.
26. Grinnell, *The Fighting Cheyennes,* 196.
27. Hyde, *Life of George Bent,* 190.
28. One of the casualties at Mud Springs was twenty-two-year-old John Biehn. The private never recovered, dying of his wounds at Fort Laramie on February 24, 1865. Another was Imry Loucerback, about twenty-eight years old, whose wounds caused his discharge from the army on April 4, 1865. See *Official Roster of the Soldiers of the State of Ohio,* 553–54.
29. Born in Miami, Ohio, William Brown enlisted on October 10, 1861, at the age of twenty-seven. He was 5 feet 10 ½ inches tall, with a dark complexion, gray eyes, and brown hair. He became a second lieutenant of Company B on November 21 and a first lieutenant of Company A on March 3, 1863. He was mustered out on April 1, 1865. See Military Service Record, RG 94.
30. Nelson, "Out on the Plains," 3. From Easton, Ohio, George W. Nelson enlisted on March 7, 1864, in Company I, 11th Ohio. Mustered out July 14, 1866, he wrote about his part in Mud Springs and Rush Creek in the *National Tribune* on May 1, 1890, and August 15, 1901.

Nelson based his writings on a diary, in the form of a small passbook, which he kept from March 7, 1864, to March 7, 1865.

31. Special Order No. 3, Headquarters in the Field, Mud Springs, February 8, 1865; "Consolidated Morning Report of Expedition to Open Communications between Fort Laramie and Julesburg," William Collins Family Papers, Denver Public Library.

32. Rush Creek is now known as Cedar Creek. The stream that now bears the name of Rush Creek discharges into the North Platte about forty miles father east. In the 1920s, the Cheyennes knew the stream as Deep Holes Creek. See *History of Cheyenne County, Nebraska, 1986* (Dalton, TX: Curtis Media Corporation, 1987), 23; Grinnell, *The Fighting Cheyennes,* fn. 11, 196.

33. Collins Report, 94.

34. Geo. W. Rowan, "Fighting the Sioux," *National Tribune,* January 30, 1890, 3.

35. Hyde, *Life of George Bent,* 191–92.

36. Rowan, "Fighting the Sioux," 3.

37. Collins Report, 94.

38. Born in Logan, Ohio, in 1835, Robert F. Patton enlisted on October 20, 1861, as a private in Company A, 6th Ohio Volunteer Cavalry. Appointed to the officer ranks in October 1864, he stood five feet seven inches, and had a light complexion, black hair, and blue eyes. He had been a gunsmith prior to enlistment. See Military Service Record, RG 94.

39. Hyde, *Life of George Bent,* 192. Yellow Nose was a Ute who had been captured with his mother on the Rio Grande in about 1854. Brought up by Spotted Wolf, he became a renowned warrior, living to fight in the battle of the Little Bighorn, eleven years later. See Grinnell, *The Fighting Cheyennes,* fn. 12, 201; Thomas B. Marquis, "Red Ripe's Squaw," *Century Magazine* 118 (June 1929), 203–4.

40. Nelson, "Out on the Plains," 3.

41. Born in Ross County, Ohio, in 1832, William H. Hartshorn entered the service on October 19, 1861. He reenlisted in Company H, 11th Ohio Volunteer Cavalry, on December 1, 1863. Standing five feet ten inches, with blue eyes, dark hair, and a fair complexion, he had been a farmer before enlisting. Serving first at Fort Halleck, he moved to Fort Laramie in the first days of February 1865. See Military Service Record, RG 94; *Official Roster of the Soldiers of the State of Ohio,* 571. Born in 1842 in Randolph County, Indiana, John A. Harris enlisted in Company D, 7th Iowa, in April 1864. Unmarried and a farmer by

occupation, he stood five feet eleven inches and had blue eyes, brown hair, and a ruddy complexion. See Military Service Record, RG 94; Pension File WC-817-102, RG 15.

42. Indian sources confuse Hartshorn's runaway as an attempt to carry a message to Fort Mitchell or Fort Laramie. See Hyde, *Life of George Bent,* 193; Grinnell, *The Fighting Cheyennes,* 201.

43. Peck, "In Indian Country," 8; One of the boys of Comapny K, 11th Ohio, "The Battle of Mud Springs," 2.

44. Collins Report, 95–96.

45. Peck, "In Indian Country," 8.

46. Collins Report, 97–98.

47. *Nebraska Republican,* March 10, 1865, 2. The official miltary estimate of Indians involved in the battle of Rush Creek was 2,000. See Grenville M. Dodge, *The Indian Campaign of Winter of 1864–1865* (Denver: Colorado Commandery of the Loyal Legion of the United States, 1907), 13.

48. Letter from Col. R. R. Livingston, February 11, 1865, Fort Rankin, to Maj. Gen. G. M. Dodge, *OR,* Series I, vol. 48, pt. 1, 815–16.

49. Collins Report, 96. Collins was undoubtedly aware of the initial strategy employed by telegraphers to keep marauders away from the line. Crediting Mud Springs telegraph operator Thomas J. Montgomery with the information, the *Dalton* (Nebraska) *Delegate* described the method as follows: "The Indians had been taught the dangers of interfering with the wires by a few demonstrations made to them by operators. Shocks from the wires had taught them it was bad medicine to try to interfere with them." See "Pioneer Mud Springs Telegraph Operator Dies," *Dalton* (Nebraska) *Delegate,* November 9, 1932.

50. Hyde, *Life of George Bent,* 193. Some of the men in Collins's regiment estimated as many as 200 killed in the February fighting. See One of the boys in Company K, 11th Ohio, "The Battle of Mud Springs," 2.

51. On July 26, 1865, Collins's only son would lose his life in the battle at Platte Bridge Station.

52. Collins Report, 98.

53. Letter from Caspar Collins, April 15, 1865, Sweetwater Station, in *The High Land Weekly News,* July 6, 1865, 1.

54. Collins did not believe that the howitzer had been that important. In his report, he noted, "The howitzer under command of Lt. Brown was admirably served but did not prove as useful as was expected, owing to the defective character of the ammunition, many of the shells failing to burst at all, and some bursting at the muzzle of the gun. I . . . ask that

proper steps be taken, to condemn such ammunition as is worthless or doubtful and that better be furnished to the troops stationed here. All supplies for this service should be of the best quality, as they are forwarded but once in the year, and mistakes cannot be seasonably remedied." See Collins Report, 97.

55. Rowan, "Fighting the Sioux," 3. Born on May 22, 1845, near Benton, Tennessee, George W. Rowan enlisted as a trumpeter in Company D, 7th Iowa Volunteer Cavalry, on December 23, 1862. He was five feet four inches tall and had blue eyes, light hair, and a light complexion. When enlisting, he gave his occupation as farmer. After completing his service on December 23, 1865, he became a lawyer. He married Catherine P. Berger on December 30, 1875, and fathered a son, George, in 1886. Rowan died in Chohalis, Washington, on May 28, 1919, at the age of seventy-two years and six months. See Military Service Record, RG 94; Pension 1047284, RG 15.

56. Nelson, "Out on the Plains," 3.

57. Francis M. Drake, "Fighting the Sioux, *National Tribune,* November 28, 1898, 6.

58. One of the boys of Company K, 11th Ohio, "The Battle of Mud Springs," 2.

59. Ibid.

60. Nelson, "Out on the Plains," 3.

CHAPTER 4: HANGING OF THE CHIEFS

1. For biographical treatments, see John T. Granger, *A Brief Biographical Sketch of Major-General Grenville M. Dodge* (Ayer Company, 1981); Jacob R. Perkins, *Trails, Rails, and War: The Life of General G. M. Dodge* (Ayer Company, 1981); George F. Ashby, *Major General M. Dodge (1831–1916): Maker of History in the Great West* (New York: The Newcomen Society of New England, 1947); Wilson and Fiske, *Appletons' Cyclopedia of American Biography,* 2: 192–93.

2. (Central City, Colorado) *Miner's Register,* February 11, 1865, 2.

3. Richard N. Ellis, *General Pope and Indian Policy* (Albuquerque: University of New Mexico Press, 1970), 74; Grenville M. Dodge, *Battle of Atlanta and Other Campaigns* (Council Bluffs, Iowa, 1910), 84–85.

4. *Nebraska Republican* 10, 1865, 2; Peter Cozzens, *General John Pope: A Life for the Nation* (Urbana and Chicago: University of Illinois Press, 2000), 246.

5. Letter from Secretary of Interior J. P. Usher to Secretary of War E. M. Stanton, January 12, *OR,* Series I, vol. 48, pt. 1, 490–92; H. D. Hamp-

ton, "The Powder River Expedition, 1865," *Montana* 14 (Autumn 1964), 4; Henry E. Palmer, "Powder River Indian Expedition of 1865," 95; Robert A. Murray, *Military Posts of Wyoming* (Ft. Collins, CO: The Old Army Press, 1974), 68.

6. Fred B. Rogers, *Soldiers of the Overland* (San Francisco: The Grabhorn Press, 1938), 147.

7. Ibid., 148–49.

8. Telegram from Connor, Cottonwood, March 29, 1865, to Colonel Moonlight, Letters Received, District of Colorado, Entry 3259, Part II, RG 393; Robert Bruce, ed., "The Powder River Expedition of 1865," *The United States Army Recruiting News* 10 (August 1928), 7; General Orders No. 12, Headquarters, District of Colorado, February 15, 1865, in *Rocky Mountain News,* February 24, 1865, 2.

9. Charles C. Goodwin, "General P. E. Connor," in *As I Remember Them* (Salt Lake City: Salt Lake Commercial Club, 1913), 265; O. J. Hollister, "Gen. P. Edward Connor," *Salt Lake Daily Tribune,* December 21, 1891; C. G. Coutant, *History of Wyoming* (Laramie, WY: Chaplin, Spafford & Mathison, Printers, 1899), 533; Palmer, "Powder River Indian Expedition of 1865," 95, "Gen. Connor to Command," *Miner's Register,* February 18, 1865, 2; "General Connor," *Rocky Mountain News,* April 26, 1865, 2; "Gen. Connor," (Omaha) *Nebraska Republican,* March 30, 1866, 1.

10. Rogers, *Soldiers of the Overland,* 149.

11. Cozzens, *General John Pope,* 243; *OR,* vol. 48, pt. 2, 237–38.

12. Samuel Bowles, who traveled with Senator Colfax's party on an inspection of the plains during the summer of 1865 and who had an opportunity to observe them, commented that these former Rebel troops had proved to be excellent soldiers. See "The Indians on the Plains," *Rocky Mountain News,"* June 26, 1865, 2; *OR,* vol. 48, pt. 1, 760–61; Bruce, "The Powder River Expedition of 1865," 7; "FRONTIER," "The Indian Campaign," *New York Times,* March 31, 1865, 1.

13. "In the Field," *Rocky Mountain News,* February 24, 1865, 2.

14. "Fort Kearny News," *Rocky Mountain News,* March 17, 1865, 2; Palmer, "Powder River Indian Expedition of 1865," 8, 64.

15. Charles R. Tuttle, *A New Centennial History of the State of Kansas* (Madison, WI, and Lawrence, KS: The Interstate Book Company, 1876), 507-8; William E. Connelley, *History of Kansas* (Chicago: The American Historical Society, 1928), 843–44; J. W. Vaughn, *The Battle of Platte Bridge* (Norman: University of Oklahoma Press, 1963), 3–5; "Military History of the Eleventh Kansas Volunteer Cavalry," in *Report*

of the Adjutant General of the State of Kansas, 1861–1865 (Topeka, KS: n.p., 1896), 198, 200, 205–6, 214–15; Albert Castel, *A Frontier State at War* (Ithaca, New York: Cornell University Press, 1958), 99, 140–44.

16. Robert M. Utely, *Frontiersmen in Blue* (New York: Macmillian, 1967), 303.

17. Letter from "M," February 26, 1865, in (Omaha) *Nebraska Republican,* March 3, 1865, 2.

18. "From the Plains," *Rocky Mountain News,* March 1, 1865, 2, in "Enterprise," *Rocky Mountain News,* March 30, 1865, 2.

19. "The Grand Illumination," *Rocky Mountain News,* March 1, 1865, 3.

20. Letter from "M," 2; "All about Friendly Indians," *Rocky Mountain News,* February 24, 1865, 2.

21. Useful general histories of Fort Laramie include LeRoy R. Hafen and Francis M. Young, *Fort Laramie and the Pageant of the West* (Glendale, CA: Arthur H. Clark Company, 1938), and Remi Nadeau, *Fort Laramie and the Sioux Indians* (Englewood Cliffs, NJ: Prentice Hall, 1967).

22. *A Manual of Military Telegraphy for the Signal Service, United States Army, Embracing Permanent and Field Lines* (Washington, D.C.: Government Printing Office, 1872), 27; Hubbard, "A Little Taste of Indian Warfare," 37. For the full story of these little posts, see John D. McDermott, *Dangerous Duty: A History of Frontier Forts in Fremont County, Wyoming* (Lander, WY: Fremont County Historic Preservation Commission, 1993), and *Frontier Crossroads.*

23. Letter from Henry Bretney, Jr., January 27, 1936, to Alfred J. Mokler, Item 7, Miscellaneous Papers, Robert S. Ellison Collection, Denver Public Library, Denver, Colorado.

24. John Lafferty, Statement of September 25, 1905, Henry Bretney Pension File, Records of the Veterans Administration, RG 15. According to Lafferty, "Capt. Bretney was afraid of nothing and was a fighter and liked to get in all the scraps with Indians and he had a hand in every one possible we had up and down the road. He always did his duty and was the best officer we had." See Statement of John Lafferty, n.d., Folder 11, no. 4; Bretney Papers, Wyoming State Archives, Cheyenne, Wyoming.

25. Bretney owned two horses that he had purchased from emigrants, a black and a sorrel, the latter of which was very fast. See Notes by Henry Clay Bretney, Jr., written on a letter from Finn Burnett, San Diego, California, October 25, 1933, to Henry Clay Bretney, Jr., Bretney Papers.

26. Letter from Cotton Mather to Agnes Wright Spring, May 1, 1916, Fort Collins, Colorado, William O. Collins Family Papers, FF11, Denver Public Library.

27. Letter from Caspar Collins, Fort Laramie, September 20, 1862, to his mother; letter from Sweetwater Bridge, April 18, 1865, to his aunt; "Hot Bath Use by the Indians"; and letter from Julius A. Meyers, Denver, Colorado, June 11, 1915, to Agnes R. Wright Meyers, FF11, William O. Collins Family Papers; Violet Morgan, *Folklore of Highland County* (Greenfield, OH: The Greenfield Printing and Publishing Company, 1947), 94; Letter from Caspar Collins, Fort Laramie, February 23, 1863, to his cousin, Fort Caspar Collections, Fort Caspar, Wyoming; Caspar Collins Military Service Record, Records of the Office of the Adjutant General, RG 94.

28. No adult photograph of Caspar Collins has survived. For many years, historians believed that U.S. Signal Corps Photo 102,953 included Collins. However, careful examination of the officers' insignia showed the men to be members of the 4th U.S. Infantry. This unit served at Fort Laramie from 1867 to 1871. See McDermott, *Dangerous Duty,* 127, fn. 66.

29. John Lafferty, Statement of September 25, 1905, Henry Bretney Pension File, RG 15.

30. W. T. Kame, Medford, Oregon, c. 1905, to Bretney, C-1654, Folder 4, Bretney Papers.

31. John B. Furay, "Record of Current Events in the Military History of 'G' Company 11th Ohio Cavalry Vols. for the Eight Months Ending Oct. 1, 1865," C-1645, Folder 10, and Statement of C. B. Cook, Worthington, Ohio, January 13, 1905, Folder 11, no. 4, Bretney Papers. See also Descriptive Book, 11th Ohio, RG 94; *Official Roster of the Soldiers of the State of Ohio,* 548. James Patton remembered that "Capt Bretney was so lame and crippled from rheumatism that he could not attend the burial of . . . Rhodes." See James F. Patton, Columbus, Ohio, November 15, 1904, to H. C. Bretney, C-1654, Folder 4, Bretney Papers.

32. "Indians Whipped," *Miner's Register,* April 14, 1865, 2; *Official Roster of the Soldiers of the State of Ohio,* 548. See also "Large Capture of Indians," *New York Times,* March 31, 1865, 1.

33. George E. Hyde, *Spotted Tail's Folk* (Norman: University of Oklahoma Press, 1961), 118.

34. Letter from Ira Taber, August 5, 1870, to Moonlight, Thomas Moonlight Papers, WA MSS 351, Beincke Rare Book and Manuscript Library, Yale University, New Haven, Connecticut.

35. Stephen H. Fairfield, "The Eleventh Kansas Regiment at Platte Bridge," in *Transactions of the Kansas State Historical Society, 1903–1904,* vol. 7 (Topeka, KS: Geo. A Clark, Printer, 1904), fn., 352–53.

36. Thomas Moonlight, "The Kansas Soldiery," *Leavenworth Daily Conservative,* December 27, 1865, 1.

37. Charles Waring, *Riley County* (Manhattan, Kansas) *Democrat,* August 26, 1909.

38. Camp Dodge stood to the west of Casper Mountain Road on the east bank of the west fork of Garden Creek. On September 28, 1926, F. G. Burnett of Fort Washakie, Wyoming, who had served there, his son, Doctor W. G. Burnett, Ambrose Donko, and R. S. Ellison visited the site, which was then located on the Carpenter Ranch. Burnett remembered a commissary and kitchen and a well near the creek. According to Burnett, the troops camped up the valley to the south about a half mile. In his letters home from Camp Dodge, Private Fred Marvin wrote of his life in a tent, noting that in early May a biweekly singing school had been established and that many of his comrades were good singers. See "Camp Dodge Site, Wyoming," R. S. Ellison Papers, Brigham Young University, Provo, Utah; Waring, *Riley County Democrat,* August 26, 1909; William Elsey Connelley, *The Life of Preston B. Plumb, 1837–1891* (Chicago: Brown & Howell Company, 1913), 36; E. C., "Recitals and Reminiscences," *National Tribune,* June 13, 1905; Letter from Marvin, Camp Dodge, May 5, 1865, to his father, original owned by Joshua Landish, Las Vegas, Nevada, Maxon Collection, Fort Caspar.

39. General Orders No. 4, District of the Plains, Denver, Colorado, April 8, 1865, Records of the District of the Plains, RG 393.

40. The Galvanized Yankees generally performed well on the Oregon Trail. When inspected at South Pass Station in July, Company I of the 3rd U.S. received favorable mention. In his report, Captain Stephen E. Jocelyn wrote: "At South Pass here is a detachment of fourteen infantry[men] of the 3rd U.S. Volunteers. . . . Generally they are a fine looking lot of men, hailing from nearly every state in the South, generally however from Georgia and Alabama—quite a few belonging unmistakably to the class called 'poor whites' and very few can write their names, as we saw by an examination of their muster rolls. Yet they are intelligent and obedient, standing in the latter respect, as in efficiency, much above the 'jayhawkers.'" See Dee Brown, *The Galvanized Yankees* (Lincoln: University of Nebraska Press, 1963), 18, 35.

41. *Official Roster of the Soldiers of the State of Ohio,* 547; Connelley, *The Life of Preston B. Plumb,* 196.

42. *Denver News,* April 25, 1865; "Another Indian Fight," *Nebraska Republican,* May 5, 1865, 2; William Mooney, "Report of the 11th Ohio for the Year 1865," Records of the 11th Ohio Volunteer Cavalry, Records of the Office of the Adjutant General, RG 94; *Official Roster of the Soldiers of the State of Ohio,* 548; "From Fort Kearney [sic]," *Nebraska Republican,* September 1, 1865, 2; Letter to the Editor from A. L. R., Fort Laramie, May 1, 1865, in "From the Plains," *Oskaloosa* (Kansas) *Independent,* May 20, 1865, 1; Bill Bryans, *Deer Creek: Frontiers* [sic] *Crossroad in Pre-Territorial Wyoming* (Glenrock, WY: Glenrock Historical Commission, n.d.), 135–36.

43. The Fort Laramie guard book has an entry showing that Big Crow, Cheyenne Indian, was confined February 9, 1865, by order of Provost Marshall. See Letter 1, W. M. Camp Papers, Robert Ellison Collection, Denver Public Library. See also Letter to the Editor from A. L. R., in "From the Plains," 1; "William Baumer—1826–1869," *Omaha Weekly Herald,* October 27, 1869, 4; Ronald Becher, *Massacre along the Medicine Road: A Social History of the Indian War of 1864 in Nebraska Territory* (Caldwell, ID: Caxton Press, 1999), 363.

44. J. J. Hollingsworth, "The End of Old [sic] Crow," *National Tribune,* January 12, 1911, 8.

45. Telegram from Connor, Denver, Headquarters, District of the Plains, April 22, 1865, to Lt. Col. William Baumer, Fort Laramie, Records of the District of the Plains, RG 393.

46. This may have been Big Crow's attempt to die from rifle fire rather than hanging, which the Plains Indians feared among all deaths. According to Col. Henry Carrington, the Sioux and Cheyennes believed that "as the spirit departs, the feet being raised from the earth, so shall that spirit hover over delightsome scene, only to be tortured by endless cravings and impossible attainment." See Henry B. Carrington, *The Indian Question* (Boston: De Wolfe & Fiske Company, 1909), 9.

47. Robert Bayles, "Hanging of Two Face," *National Tribune,* January 26, 1911, 8. Bayles confuses Big Crow with Two Face. See also Robert Bayles, "Soldiering on the Plains," *National Tribune,* March 3, 1910, 7.

48. Susan Bordeaux Bettelyoun and Josephine Waggoner, *With My Own Eyes: A Lakota Woman Tells Her People's History,* ed. and introduction by Emily Levine (Lincoln: University of Nebraska Press, 1999), 84–85.

49. See also *Miner's Register,* April 27, 1865, and *Nebraska Republican,* May 5, 1865, 2; Rogers, *Soldiers of the Overland,* 151.

50. General Orders No. 4, District of the Plains, Denver, Colorado, April 8, 1865, Records of the District of the Plains, RG 393; Fairfield, "The Eleventh Kansas Regiment at Platte Bridge," 353; Connelley, *The Life of Preston B. Plumb,* 196.

51. "From Fort Kearney," *Nebraska Republican,* September 1, 1865, 2; Mooney, "Report of the 11th Ohio for the Year 1865," 2–3; "Indian Fight," *Miner's Register,* May 14, 1865, 2; "Indian Trouble," *Rocky Mountain News,* May 13, 1865, 2.

52. Letter from H. H. Heath, Headquarters, East Sub-District of Nebraska, Fort Kearny, N.T., October 31, 1865, to Lt. John Lewis, Acting Assistant Adjutant General, District of Nebraska, Entry 3198, Part II, RG 393.

53. Letter from Moonlight, Fort Laramie, June 6, 1865, to Assistant Adjutant General Price, Letters Sent, District of the Platte, RG 393.

54. Acting Assistant Adjutant General Price, May 5, 1865, to Col. Moonlight, Letters Sent, District of the Plains, RG 393.

55. Letter from Capt. Lee P. Gillette, Fort Kearny, June 2, 1865, to Acting Assistant Adjutant General, District of the Plains, and Statements of Washington Fulton (May 31, 1865), Jefferson Fields (May 31, 1865), Peter J. Flynn (June 5, 1865), and John Twyman, (June 5, 1865), Letters Received, District of Colorado, Entry 3258, Part II, RG 393; "More of the Indian Trouble," *Rocky Mountain News,* May 26, 1865, 2; "Indian News," *Rocky Mountain News,* June 2, 1865, 2.

56. "Indian Fight on the Little Blue," *Rocky Mountain News,* May 31, 1865, 2; "B," "From the Border," *Chicago Tribune,* May 26, 1865, 2.

57. Furay, "Record of Current Events in the Military History of 'G' Co."; Letter from James A. Green, Headquarters Station, Sweetwater Bridge, D.T., May 23, 1865, to Acting Assistant Adjutant General, Letters Received Relating to the Sioux Indians, 1863–1866, Entry 1187, Records of the Department of the Dakota, RG 393.

58. Letter from B. Godfrey, Camp on Deer Creek, May 21, 1865, to Major Adams, Letters Received, District of the Plains, Entry 618, RG 393; Bryans, *Deer Creek,* 136; Letter from M. H. Sydenham, Fort Kearny, May 24, 1865, in "From the West," *Nebraska Republican,* June 2, 1865.

59. Telegram from Price, Acting Assistant Adjutant General, Julesburg, May 22, 1865, to Connor at Fort Kearny, Letters Sent, District of the Plains, RG 393; *Official Roster of the Soldiers of the State of Ohio,* 548; Mooney, "Report of the 11th Ohio for the Year 1865"; Furay, "Record of Current Events in the Military History of 'G' Co."

60. When he reached Salt Lake City, Colfax had a new view of the Plains Indian. In a newspaper story, he was quoted as follows: "If I ever had any particular love for the 'noble red man,' it is pretty much evaporated during this triI do not think as much of him as I did. They were looking down the hills at us, as we have since learned, and had it not been that Mr. Otis and I had our hair cut so short at Atchison that it would not have paid expenses to be taken even by Indians, they might have scalped us." See *Miner's Register,* July 27, 1865, 2.

61. "Indians Captured," *Rocky Mountain News,* May 19, 1865, 2.

62. Palmer, "Powder River Indian Expedition of 1865," 64; Leroy W. Hagerty, "Indian Raids along the Platte and Little Blue Rivers," *Nebraska History* 28 (October–December 1947), 251.

63. Moonlight, Fort Laramie, May 26, 1865, to Acting Assistant Adjutant General Price, Julesburg, Telegrams Received, and Moonlight, Fort Laramie, May 27, 1865, to Acting Assistant Adjutant General Price, Julesburg, Letters Sent, Records of the District of the Plains, Entry 614, RG 393. See also Dorothy Johnson, "The Hanging of the Chiefs," *Montana* (Summer 1970), 60–69.

64. The statement, which appeared in Senate Report, 39th Congress, 2nd session, 1866–1867, 90–91, is reproduced in Johnson, "The Hanging of the Chiefs," 67–68. In an interview with A. E. Sheldon on July 31, 1903, the Oglala Bawling Bull, a member of Two Face's band, stated that his chief had "assaulted" her. See "Interviews with Red Cloud and Sioux Indians," Box 59, A. E. Sheldon Collection, Nebraska Historical Society, Lincoln, Nebraska.

65. Miss Roper lived and married in Beatrice, Nebraska. Mrs. Eubank went back to her friends in Laclede, Missouri, dying on April 4, 1913, in McCune, Kansas. See Palmer, "Powder River Indian Expedition of 1865," 64; Hagerty, "Indian Raids along the Platte and Little Blue Rivers," 251.

66. B. M, A., "Execution of Two-Face and Black-Foot," *Rocky Mountain News,* June 27, 1865, 2. Written at Fort Laramie on May 26, the account appeared first in the *Cincinnati Commercial.*

67. Moonlight, Special Order No. 11, Headquarters, District of the Plains, Fort Laramie, May 25, 1865, Records of the District of the Plains, RG 393.

68. Coutant, *History of Wyoming,* 441–42.

69. B. M. A., "Execution of Two-Face and Black-Foot," 2. See also account of eyewitness Charles Bolton, "The Hanging of the Sioux," *National Tribune,* June 9, 1910, 3, and letter from Ira Taber, August 5,

1870, to Moonlight, Thomas Moonlight Papers, WA MSS 351, Beincke Rare Book and Manuscript Library, Yale University. The envelope also contains a rebuttal written by Taber at Moonlight's request in response to a critical letter published in the Topeka, Kansas, newspaper concerning the hanging of the chiefs.

70. Moonlight, Fort Laramie, May 27, 1865, to Acting Assistant Adjutant General Price, Julesburg, Letters Sent, Records of the District of the Plains. See also Henry P. Rice, "Young Henry P. Rice Marches away to the Indian Wars," *San Bruno* (California) *Herald,* March 2, 1934.

71. Will H. Young, "Journals of Will H. Young, 1865," *Annals of Wyoming* 7 (October 1930), 381.

CHAPTER 5: FOUTS'S FIASCO AND MOONLIGHT'S MISTAKE

1. Fred B. Rogers, *Soldiers of the Overland,* 153.

2. Ibid., 154–56.

3. Ibid., 156.

4. *Rocky Mountain News,* August 1, 1865, 2.

5. Letter from Pvt. Bruce Vandoren, South Pass, June 1, 1865, to his father, John Vandoren, in "Soldier's Letter," *Easton* (Ohio) *Register,* July 29, 1865, 2; John B. Furay, "Record of Current Events in the Military History of 'G' Co."; Telegram from Col. Thomas Moonlight, Fort Laramie, May 27, to George Price, Telegrams Sent, Fort Laramie Post Records, Records of United States Army Commands, RG 393; Letter from P. B. Plumb, Headquarters, 11th Kansas, Near Platte Bridge, Dakota, June 1, 1865, to Acting Assistant Adjutant General, Letters Received, District of Colorado, Entry 3258, Part II, RG 393.

6. Letter from Mary A. R. Jenkinson, Los Angeles, July 26, 1940, to Henry Clay Bretney, Jr., Bretney Papers.

7. Moonlight, June 3, 1865, Acting Assistant Adjutant General Price, Headquarters, District of the Plains, Telegram Book, Records of the District of the Plains, RG 393; William Mooney, "Report of the 11th Ohio for the Year 1865," 1.

8. Statement of James F. Patton of Company G, C-1654, Folder 11, no. 4, Bretney Papers; "Rocky Ridge Attacked and Burned," *Wind River Mountaineer* 4 (October–November 1989), 9–11; Letter from Col. Preston B. Plumb, Camp Dodge, June 1, 1865, to Lt. Ira Taber, *OR,* Series I, vol. 48, pt. 1, 724–25; Letter from Lieutenant Bretney, Platte Bridge, June 1, 1865, to Colonel Moonlight, Letters Sent, Records of

the 11th Ohio, Entry 3546, Records of the Office of the Adjutant General, RG 94.

9. William Unrau, *Tending the Talking Wire: A Buck Soldier's View of Indian Country, 1863–1866* (Salt Lake City: University of Utah Press, 1979), 252; Coutant, *History of Wyoming,* 448–49; William L. Marion, "St. Mary's Stage Station," *Annals of Wyoming* 30 (April 1958), 40–41; Paul and Helen Henderson, "Our 40," Henderson Collection, American Heritage Center, Laramie, Wyoming, 3.

10. Telegram from D. L. Haywood, Horse Shoe Station, May 28, 1865, to Colonel Moonlight, Letters Received, District of Colorado, Entry 3258, Part II, RG 393; Moonlight to Acting Assistant Adjutant General Price, May 28 and May 29, 1865, Headquarters, District of the Plains, Telegram Book, Records of the District of the Plains, RG 393; *Annual Report of the Adjutant General of the State of Missouri* (Jefferson City: S. P. Simpson, 1865), 380–382.

11. Letter from Moonlight, Fort Laramie, May 29, 1865, to Acting Assistant Adjutant General Price, Letters Sent, District of the Plains, RG 393.

12. Letter from Acting Assistant Adjutant General Price, District of the Plains, Julesburg, May 30, 1865, to Col. C. W. McNally, Commanding Officer, Camp Rankin, Letters Sent, District of the Plains, RG 393.

13. "Diary of . . . [Isaac] Pennock," *Annals of Wyoming* 33 (July 1951), entry for June 3, 1865, 8.

14. Ibid.

15. First Sgt. S. B. White, Platte Bridge, June 5, 1865, to Col. T. Moonlight, Fort Laramie, Letters Sent, Records of the 11th Ohio Volunteer Cavalry, RG 94.

16. E. C. Tonganoxie, "Recitals and Reminiscences," *National Tribune,* June 13, 1905.

17. Letter from Plumb, Headquarters, 11th Kansas Cavalry, Camp Dodge, near Platte Bridge, Dakota, June 4, 1865, to Acting Assistant Adjutant General Ira I. Taber, Fort Laramie, District of Platte, Entry 618, RG 393. This letter is duplicated in Records of the District of the Plains, Entry 3258, RG 393. Lt. Henry C. Bretney, "Statement of Ordnance Lost June 3, 1865," August 1865, Mokler Collection, Casper Community College, Casper, Wyoming; Waring, *Riley County* (Manhattan, Kansas) *Democrat,* August 26, 1909; "A Old Landmark Destroyed," (Casper, Wyoming) *Natrona County Tribune,* September 28, 1899.

18. Alfred James Mokler, *Fort Caspar (Platte Bridge Station)* (Casper, WY: The Prairie Publishing Company, 1939), 18; Letter from Plumb, Head-

quarters, 11th Kansas Cavalry, Camp Dodge, near Platte Bridge, Dakota, June 4, 1865, to Acting Assistant Adjutant General Ira I. Taber, Fort Laramie, District of Platte, Entry 618, RG 393; Pennock Diary, entry for June 3, 1865, 8; *OR,* vol. 48, pt. 1, 548; Furay, "Record of Current Events in the Military History of 'G' Co." 2; Unrau, *Tending the Talking Wire,* 253.

19. Mokler, *Fort Caspar,* 11.

20. "Indian Trouble, on the North Platte," *Rocky Mountain News,* June 8, 1865, 2.

21. House Executive Document 369, pt. 1 (1865), Serial 3436, 295; *OR,* vol. 48, pt. 2, 762; "Indian Troubles Again," *Miner's Register,* June 15, 1865, 2.

22. "Indian News," *Rocky Mountain News,* June 26, 1865, 2; *Miner's Register,* June 30, 1865, 2.

23. Statement of M. Courtright, "Indian Troubles on the Yellowstone," *Montana Post,* June 24, 1865.

24. "Reported Murder by Indians," (Omaha) *Nebraska Republican,* August 811, 1865, 1.

25. See John D. McDermott, "James Bordeaux," in *French Fur Traders and Voyageurs in the American West,* ed. LeRoy R. Hafen, introduction by Janet LeCompte (Glendale, CA: Arthur H. Clark Company, 1995), 42–57.

26. Statement of U.S. Indian Agent Vital Jarrot, July 19, 1866, Claim of Clement Lamoureaux and James Bordeaux 732, RG 123.

27. Young, "Journals of Will H. Young, 1865," 381.

28. Statements of G. P. Beauvais (June 26, 1866), Sefroy Iott (July 7, 1866), and Louis Rubideaux, (February 17, 1888); Claim of Clement Lamoureaux and James Bordeaux 732; Claim of Leon F. Pallady 8266, Record of the United States Court of Claims, Indian Depredation Claims, RG 123.

29. William D. Fouts Military Service Record, RG 94.

30. "William D. Fouts," *Pfantz-Fouts Newsletter* 9 (March 1986); Arlene Fouts McCan, "Captain William D. Fouts," (Plymouth, Indiana, 1982), typescript, Item MP-58, Fort Laramie Collections, Fort Laramie National Historic Site, Wyoming. A copy is also found in the Nebraska Historical Society Library 921 F762c, Lincoln, Nebraska; Death of Mrs. Fouts," *South Bend* (Indiana) *Tribune,* May 22, 1886; "Mrs. Morrison, Pioneer Dead," and "Pioneer Resident Takes to Grave Memories of Indian Warfare Days," *South Bend Tribune,* January 18, 1935, 3.

31. Telegram from Connor, Julesburg, June 15, 1865, to General Dodge, Letters Sent, Records of the District of the Plains, Entry 3254, Part II, RG 393.

32. Statement of White Bird, Pine Ridge, October 14, 1921, Claim of Leon F. Pallady 8266, RG 123.

33. McCan, "Captain William D. Fouts."

34. Statements of Louis Rubideaux, February 17, 1888, and October 27, 1888, Claim of Clement Lamoureaux and James Bordeaux 732, RG 123; Report of Capt. John Wilcox, *The Roster and Record of Iowa Soldiers in the War of the Rebellion,* vol. 4 (Des Moines: State Printer of Iowa, 1910), 1254–56; *OR,* vol. 48, pt. 2, 322–24.

35. George E. Hyde, *A Sioux Chronicle* (Norman: University of Oklahoma Press, 1956), 168; Telegram from Connor, Julesburg, June 15, 1865, to General Dodge, Letters Sent, Records of the District of the Plains, Entry 3254, Part II, RG 393; A. L. R., Camp Horse Shoe, D.T., June 23, 1865, in "From the Plains," *Oskaloosa* (Kansas) *Independent,* July 8, 1865, 1.

36. Telegram from Wilcox, Fort Mitchell, June 15, 1865, to Colonel Moonlight, Letters Received, District of Colorado, Entry 3258, Part II, RG 393; "Indian Fight," *Miner's Register,* June 16, 1865, 2; "More of 'Friendly Indians,'" *Rocky Mountain News,* June 15, 1865, 2; and "Col. Moonlight's Eclipse," *Rocky Mountain News;* August 3, 1865, 2; "More Indian Troubles," *Nebraska Republican,* June 23, 1865, 1; "Sioux Indian Murders," *New York Times,* June 16, 1865, 2; Dean Knudsen, "Death at Horse Creek," *True West* 36 (March 1989), 14–21; Robert M. Utley, *Frontiersmen in Blue,* 318.

37. L. W. Emmons quoted in Fairfield, "The Eleventh Kansas Regiment at Platte Bridge," fn., 360. See also letter from Ira I. Tabor, to Acting Assistant Adjutant General Price, Fort Laramie, June 19, 1865, Records of the District of the Plains, RG 393; "'Friendly Indians' Again," *Rocky Mountain News,* June 21, 1865, 2; "Col. Moonlight's Eclipse," 2; A. L. R., in "From the Plains," 1.

38. Anonymous, California Volunteer, Letter from Fort Laramie, June 24, 1865, *Rocky Mountain News,* August 24, 1865, 1.

39. Letters from Henry E. Palmer, Omaha, Nebraska, June 20 and July 30, 1904, to Stephen H. Fairfield, Military History of the 11th Kansas, MS 617, Folder 12, Kansas Historical Society, Topeka, Kansas.

40. Letter from Connor, Julesburg, June 15, 1865, to General Dodge, Division of the Missouri, Letters Sent, Records of the District of the Plains, RG 393.

41. Letter from Connor, Julesburg, June 20, 1865, to Dodge, Letters Sent, Records of the District of the Plains, RG 393; "Items from Julesburg," *Rocky Mountain News,* July 7, 1865, 1.

42. Moonlight fought being mustered out. On July 15, Connor informed Dodge that "Moonlight is at Kearney [*sic*] and refuses to give the Commissary of Muster the proper data to muster him out. I have ordered Commissary to muster him out without it." In his history of the 11th Kansas, Moonlight explained that his mustering out came about because of the early retirement of Company G. According to Moonlight, this left the regiment with one company less than the requisite number, resulting in an immediate reduction in command staff. See Connor, July 15, 1865, to Dodge, and Connor, July 17, 1865, to Dodge, Letters Sent, Records of the District of the Plains, RG 393; Thomas Moonlight, "The Kansas Soldiery," *Leavenworth Daily Conservative,* December 27, 1865, 1; Letter from Henry E. Palmer, Omaha, Nebraska, June 20, 1904, to Stephen H. Fairfield, Military History of the 11th Kansas, MS 617, Folder 12, Kansas Historical Society.

43. Letter from Henry E. Palmer, Omaha, Nebraska, July 30, 1904, to Stephen H. Fairfield, Military History of the 11th Kansas, MS 617, Folder 12, Kansas Historical Society.

44. General Order No. 12, Julesburg, Colorado, June 21, 1865, General Orders, District of the Plains, RG 393.

45. Letter from Dodge, St. Louis, July 28, 1865, to Acting Assistant Adjutant General Joseph Bell, Division of the Missouri; *OR,* vol. 48, pt. 2, 329; Dodge to Assistant Adjutant General Bell, Division of Missouri, Fort Leavenworth, November 1, 1865; *OR,* vol. 48, pt. 2, 335–48. The report is also found in Letters Sent, Department of the Missouri, RG 393, and Miscellaneous File, Entry 287, RG 94.

46. Circular to Superintendent of Indian Affairs and Indian Agents, July 22, 1865, in "Treatment of Hostile Indians," *New York Times,* August 3, 1865, 2; "How Indians Are to Be Dealt with," *Eaton* (Ohio) *Register,* July 29, 1865, 1; "Military History of the Eleventh Kansas Volunteer Cavalry," in *Report of the Adjutant General of the State of Kansas, 1861–1865* (Topeka, 1896), 210; J. W. Vaughn, *The Battle of Platte Bridge* (Norman: University of Oklahoma Press, 1963), 17; George Morton Walker, "Eleventh Kansas Cavalry, 1865, and Battle of Platte Bridge," *Kansas Historical Collections, 1915–1918,* vol. 14 (Topeka: Kansas Historical Society, 1918), 335.

47. Peter Cozzens, *General John Pope,* 259.

48. Utley, *Frontiersmen in Blue,* 309–13.

49. "Indian Commission," *Nebraska Republican,* August 4, 1865, 1; *Army and Navy Journal,* September 9, 1865, 1; Utley, *Frontiersmen,* 309.

50. *OR,* vol. 48, pt. 2, 849, 951.

51. Nelson Cole Military Service Record, RG 94; Anna Cole Pension File 4396, Records of the Veterans Administration, RG 15; Walter B. Stevens, *History of St. Louis, The Fourth City,* vol. 2 (St. Louis. MO: The S. J. Clarke Publishing Company, 1909), 230–31; *In Memoriam, Nelson Cole* (Military Order of the Loyal Legion of the United States, Commandery of the State of Missouri, 1899).

52. *Defendant's Brief on Their Motion for New Trial, Abraham T. Litchfield v. the United States and the Sioux, Cheyenne, and Arapahoe Indians,* 10; "General Connor's Indian Expedition," *Rocky Mountain News,* June 21, 1865, 2.

53. Palmer says that the rendezvous point was the mouth of the Rosebud, but diarist O. J. Hollister wrote that Connor stated that they were "to rendezvous at Panther mountains on Rosebud creek, not far beyond Tongue river." See Palmer, "Powder River Indian Expedition of 1865," 66; O. J. Hollister, *Blackhawk Mining Journal,* October 20, 1865. See also William Devine, "The Connor Expedition," typescript, Item In2-bat-pre, American Heritage Center, Laramie, Wyoming.

54. Samuel Walker, Military Service Record, RG 94; C. G. Coutant, *The History of Wyoming,* 539.

55. Will C. Ferrill, "The Sixteenth Kansas Cavalry in the Black Hills," *The Rocky Mountain Herald,* July 2, 1928, 4.

56. Pennock Diary, entry for June 24, 1865, in Mary Hurlbut Scott, *The Oregon Trail through Wyoming: A Century of History 1812–1912* (Aurora, CO: Powder River Publishers, 1959), 90–91; Unrau, *Tending the Talking Wire,* 262; *OR,* vol. 48, pt. 2, 548; Furay, "Record of Current Events in the Military History of 'G' Co.," 2; Letter from Sgt. Albert L. Rivers, Camp Horse Shoe, June 22, 1865, to Friend Roberts, *Oskaloosa* (Kansas) *Independent,* July 8, 1865; Bill Bryans, *Deer Creek,* 136; Fairfield, "The Eleventh Kansas Regiment at Platte Bridge," 356; Pennock Diary, 11; A. L. R., in "From the Plains," 1.

57. Telegram from Major Mackey, c. June 30, 1865, Telegrams Received, District of the Plains, RG 393.

58. Cozzens, *General John Pope,* 262.

59. Connor responded to the sixth toast, "Our Army and Navy," by stating that he was not a speech maker, and like General Sheridan, he had put this part of his education off until he had more time to attend to it. He finished by declaring that he would devote his best energies to protect-

ing citizens' interests and saving their scalps. See "The Parting Banquet," *Rocky Mountain News,* June 3, 1865, 2.

60. Young, "Journals of Will H. Young, 1865," 381.

61. Ibid.

62. "From the West—Indian News," *Nebraska Republican,* July 7, 1865, 2; *Rocky Mountain News,* July 12, 1865, 2; "How Indians Are to Be Dealt with," 1; "Gen. Connor's Indian Expedition," *Chicago Tribune,* June 21, 1856, 1.

63. Letter from Connor, Julesburg, July 20, 1868, Letters Sent, District of the Plains, RG 393.

64. Young, "Journals of Will H. Young, 1865," 381.

65. F. G. Burnett, "History of the Western Division of the Powder River Expedition," *Annals of Wyoming,* 8 (January, 1932), 570. This was reprinted in the *Sheridan* (Wyoming) *Post,* February 23, 1936.

66. Letter from Fort Laramie, July 3, 1856, in *Nebraska Republican,* July 7, 1865, 2; Pennock Diary, 12; Furay, "Record of Current Events in the Military History of 'G,' Co." 2.

67. Fairfield, "The Eleventh Kansas Regiment at Platte Bridge," 356.

68. Virginia Cole Trenholm and Maurine Carley, *The Shoshonis* (Norman: University of Oklahoma Press, 1964), 215.

69. Letter from Fort Laramie, July 4, 1865, in *Nebraska Republican,* July 7, 1865, 2.

70. Josiah M. Hubbard, "A Little Taste of Indian Warfare," 42.

71. Pennock Diary, 13–14, 16.

72. "Indian Outrages in Utah," *Rocky Mountain News,* July 15, 1865, 2; "Indian Commission," *Nebraska Republican,* August 4, 1865, 1.

73. Telegram from Julesburg, July 31, 10:00 A.M., in "More Indian News," *Nebraska Republican,* August 4, 1865; "Latest by Telegraph," *Rocky Mountain News,* July 31, 1865, 1.

74. Letter from Col. C. H. Potter, Headquarters, South Sub-District of the Plains, Denver, Colorado, August 7, 1865, to Acting Assistant Adjutant General Price, Letters Received, District of the Plains, Entry 3218, Part II, RG 393; *Rocky Mountain News,* July 20, 1865, 2; Mrs. A. M. F. Cook, "Captured by Indians," in *Second Biennial Report of the State Historian of the State of Wyoming for the Period Ending September 30, 1922* (Sheridan, WY: The Mills Company, 1923), 101–2.

75. Connor was correct in his assessment of the disposition of many of the men serving in the 11th Kansas. The *Oskaloosa Independent* reported on July 1 that "the boys are indignant that they must be kept from their homes merely to aid an aspiring officer to gain a name on their bravery

and suffering. They think they should be treated as all other soldiers under the orders of the Sec. of War for mustering out. At one time their indignation almost reached the point of insubordination, but they took the best course, and resolved to wait as patiently as possible for the hour of deliverance." See "The Eleventh Regiment," *Oskaloosa Independent,* July 1, 1865, 2.

76. Salt Lake *Union Vedette,* July 15, 1865; *OR,* vol. 48, pt. 2, 1059, 1084.

77. Letter from Connor, Fort Laramie, July 27, 1865, to Barnes, copy in Collection 617, Military History of the 11th Kansas, Kansas Historical Society.

78. Letter from Asst. Q.M. Parmenas T. Turnley, Denver, Colorado, July 28, 1865, Grenville Dodge Papers, Iowa Historical Society, Des Moines, Iowa.

79. Palmer, "Powder River Indian Expedition of 1865," 64–67.

80. Letter from Gen. John Pope, Commander, Department of the Missouri, St. Louis, August 11, 1865, to Dodge, Entry 287, Miscellaneous Files, Records of the Office of the Adjutant General RG 94.

81. Letter from Connor, Fort Laramie, July 4, 1865, Letters Sent, District of the Plains. Palmer later described Cole's route: "He marched from Omaha, Nebraska, to Columbus, thence up the Loup, north fork, to its head, thence north across the Niobrara, Cheyenne river, to the east base of the Black Hills, around the north side, through the present site of Fort Meade, near the present city of Spearfish, on to the Little Missouri and to Powder river, intercepting Walker's command on the Belle Fourche. He was ordered to meet Conner [*sic*] at the mouth of the Rosebud." See Palmer, "Powder River Indian Expedition of 1865," 69.

82. Letter from Acting Assistant Adjutant General Price, Fort Laramie, August 15, to Connor, Letter Sent, District of Plains, Entry 3254, 393.

83. Letter from Connor, Fort Laramie, July 28, 1865, to Walker, Letters Sent, District of the Plains, RG 393; O. J. Hollister, *Blackhawk Mining Journal,* October 20, 1865. Palmer described Walker's route, stating that the column left Fort Laramie marching in a northwesterly direction up Rawhide Creek. It crossed the Cheyenne and proceeded to the Bell Fourche. It then moved along the west base of the Black Hills to the right of Devil's Tower toward the Little Missouri until intercepting Cole's command. See Palmer, "Powder River Indian Expedition of 1865," 66.

84. Luther H. North, "The Pawnee Battalion," *National Tribune,* April 27, 1922, 3; Letter from Luther North, Columbus, Nebraska, December 17, 1928, to Robert Ellison, Item 47, C1-C50, Robert S. Ellison Papers, Denver Public Library, Denver, Colorado.

85. Letter from Connor, Julesburg, July 20, 1865, Letters Sent, District of the Plains, RG 393.
86. D. Hampton, "The Powder River Expedition, 1865," *Montana* 14 (Autumn 1964), 4.

CHAPTER 6: THE BATTLES OF PLATTE BRIDGE AND RED BUTTES

1. For more detailed accounts of the battles, see McDermott, *Frontier Crossroads,* 61–74. Two useful earlier works are J. W. Vaughn, *The Battle of Platte Bridge* (Norman: University of Oklahoma Press, 1963), and Mokler, *Fort Caspar.* See also Jerome A. Greene, *Reconnaissance Survey of Indian–U.S. Army Battlefields of the Northern Plains* (Denver: National Park Service, 1997).
2. The decoys followed the little stream known as Dry Creek, which is now called Casper Creek. It flows southeasterly into the North Platte River about a half mile northeast of Platte Bridge. See Vaughn, *Platte Bridge,* 42.
3. "Statement Regarding Fight at Platte Bridge . . . by John H. Crumb in company with John B. Buchanan, in the Office of R. S. Ellison at Casper, Wyoming, September 12, 1927," and letter from John H. Crumb to Robert S. Ellison, c. 1926, Maxon Collection, Fort Caspar Collections, Fort Caspar, Wyoming.
4. Pennock, who was with the party, states that there were ten men. See Pennock Diary, 18.
5. William Y. Drew, "The Platte Bridge Fight by One Who Was There," (Burlington, Kansas) *Osage County Chronicle,* April 20, 1882. This is the first of five articles that gives Drew's account. The others were published on April 27, May 11, May 18, and May 25, 1882. These were reprinted in the *Casper Star-Tribune,* September 10, 11, 12, and 13, 1918.
6. J. W. Vaughn places the site in the vicinity of Tenth Avenue and Cedar Street in downtown Casper. See Vaughn, *Platte Bridge,* 50.
7. George Morton Walker, "Eleventh Kansas Cavalry, 1865, and Battle of Platte Bridge," in *Kansas Historical Collections, 1915–1918,* vol. 14 (Topeka: Kansas Historical Society, 1918), 336; Pennock Diary, 18; Statement of White Bull, September 8, 1908, and Statement of Crazy Head, September 10, 1908, George Grinnell Notebook 348 (1908), MS 5, Grinnell Collection, Southwest Museum, Los Angeles, California, 60, 121–22.

8. Drew, "The Platte Bridge Fight by One Who Was There," April 20, 1882; Mokler, *Fort Caspar,* 19; Paul Wellman, "Kansas Troops Fight in Fierce Platte Bridge Battle," *Wichita Eagle,* November 11, 1931.

9. Vaughn says that of the remainder who did not have rifles, half had no arms at all. See Vaughn, *Platte Bridge,* 54; "Military History of the Eleventh Kansas Volunteer Cavalry," 210.

10. Drew, "The Platte Bridge Fight by One Who Was There," April 20, 1882; Letter from Drew, Washington, Iowa, June 1, 1901, to William E. Connelley, William E. Connelley Papers, Kansas Historical Society; "Military History of the Eleventh Kansas Volunteer Cavalry," 212; Letter from Captain Price, Platte Bridge, June 17, 1865, to Inspector General, Department of the Missouri, Letters Sent to the Inspector General, District of the Plains, Entry 3268, RG 393.

11. Vaughn, *Platte Bridge,* 42–43; Letter from George Bent to George Hyde, May 22, 1906, Coe Collection, Beinecke Library, Yale University, New Haven, Connecticut.

12. Statement (author unknown), Fort Laramie, November 22, 1868, Caspar Collins Military Service Record, RG 94; Letter from Henry C. Bretney, Jr., Jacksonville, Florida, January 26, 1936, to Alfred J. Mokler, Casper, Wyoming, Item 7, Miscellaneous Papers, Ellison Collection, Denver Public Library; I. C. C. Isely, "Lord Unhurt in Three Battles in One Day," *Wichita Beacon,* November 11, 1928.

13. Jean Wilson, "Indian Fights and Atrocities," *Leavenworth Daily Times,* August 30, 1865; Maj. W. H. Evans, Fort Laramie, April 7, 1866, to Adjutant General, Washington, D.C., Records of the 11th Ohio, Records of the Office of the Adjutant General, RG 94; Frances Seely Webb, "The Indian Version of the Platte Bridge Fight," *Annals of Wyoming* 32 (October 1960), 235.

14. Walker, "Eleventh Kansas Cavalry," 337; Fairfield, "The Eleventh Kansas Regiment at Platte Bridge," 357; Ferdinand Erhardt, "At Platte Bridge," *Topeka Capital,* reprinted in the *National Tribune,* July 11, 1918; Vaughn, *Platte Bridge,* 56–58; Violet Morgan, *Folklore of Highland County* (Greenfield, OH: The Greenfield Printing and Publishing Company, 1947), 95.

15. F. H. Wright, "The Last Stand of Casper [*sic*] Collins, *Chicago Tribune,* c. August 3, 1925, Fred Baum Collection, American Heritage Center, Laramie; Mari Sandoz, *Crazy Horse: Strange Man of the Oglalas* (New York: Hastings House, Inc., 1942), 163, 166–67.

16. Drew, "The Platte Bridge Fight by One Who Was There," April 20, 1882.

17. Walker, "Eleventh Kansas Cavalry," 336–37; Drew, "The Platte Bridge Fight by One Who Was There."

18. Drew, "The Platte Bridge Fight by One Who Was There," April 27, 1882; Henry Lord, "Henry Lord of Dodge City Tells of the Battle of Platte Bridge," *Emporia* (Kansas) *Gazette,* August 9, 1934, 173–75; Letters from Bent to George Hyde, May 10, 1905, and May 22, 1906, Coe Collection, Yale University; Jean Wilson, "Indian Fights and Atrocities"; Webb, "The Indian Version of the Platte Bridge Fight," 235; Waring, *Riley County Democrat,* August 26, 1909; Letter from Pvt. Fred Marvin, Fort Laramie, August 7, 1865, to his father, and "Statement Regarding Fight at Platte Bridge . . . by John H. Crumb," Maxon Collection, Fort Caspar Collections.

19. In his study, Vaughn states, "The place where the fight occurred was about half a mile west and half a mile north of the bridge, or several hundred yards north of the present cemetery marker." See Vaughn, *Platte Bridge,* 95–96. A sketch map showing the site of the burials appears in Alfred James Mokler, *Transitions of the West: Portrayal of the Indian Problem in the West and the Trials of the Pioneers Who Reclaimed This Country from Savagery to Civilization* (Chicago: R. R. Donnelly & Sons Company, 1927), 137. For descriptions of this part of the battle, see Statement of White Bull, September 8, 1908, George Grinnell Notebook 348, 123, and Statement of Big Rascal, August 26, 1911, Notebook 350, 143–44, MS 5, Grinnell Collection, Southwest Museum, Los Angeles, California; W. H. Evans, Fort Laramie, April 7, 1866, to Adjutant General, Washington D.C., Records of the 11th Ohio, Records of the Office of the Adjutant General, RG 94; Vaughn, *Platte Bridge,* 59; Waring, *Riley County Democrat,* August 26, 1909; Pennock Diary, entry for July 26, 1865, 19.

20. Fairfield, "The Eleventh Kansas Regiment at Platte Bridge," 352-62. See also Wilson, "Indian Fights and Atrocities"; Drew, "The Platte Bridge Fight by One Who Was There," April 27, 1882.

21. Drew, "The Platte Bridge Fight by One Who Was There," April 27, 1882; "Statement Regarding Fight at Platte Bridge . . . by John H. Crumb." John Lafferty tells his story in "Owners of Collins' Boyhood Home Visitors to Fort Casper [*sic*]," *Casper Tribune,* n.d., Fort Caspar Vertical File, Natrona County Public Library, Casper, Wyoming.

22. William Haywood, who was with Collins, remembered that he and the young officer had gone back to rescue a dismounted, wounded soldier who had shouted "Don't leave me." After helping the man, Collins lost control of his horse, which carried him back into the midst of the

attacking warriors. See letter from W. H. Haywood, Owensmouth, California, n.d., FF14, William O. Collins Family Papers; Bill Judge, "I Am No Coward," *Old West* (Summer 1979), 24; Susan Badger Doyle, "Indian Perspectives of the Bozeman Trail," *Montana* 40 (Winter 1990), 61; "Statement Regarding Fight at Platte Bridge . . . by John H. Crumb"; Letter from John H. Crumb to Robert Ellison, c. 1926, Maxon Collection; and Ferdinand Erhardt, "11th Kansas at Platte Bridge, Wyoming," mss., c. 1904, Military History of the 11th Kansas, Collection 617, Kansas Historical Society.

23. George Hyde, *Life of George Bent,* 222; Bent to Hyde, May 22, 1906, Coe Collection, Yale University.

24. Waring, *Riley County Democrat,* August 26, 1909; W. H. Evans, Fort Laramie, April 7, 1886, to Adjutant General, Washington, D.C., Records of the 11th Ohio, RG 94.

25. Statement of Henry Clay Bretney, Jr., "Florida Man on Pioneer Trails," *The Laramie Republican Boomerang,* June 28, 1933; "Statement Regarding Fight at Platte Bridge . . . by John H. Crumb."

26. Wilson, "Indian Fights and Atrocites." Pennock Diary entry of July 26, 1865.

27. The Cheyenne Indians kept Collins's horse for many years. It had a reputation for being hard-headed, flighty, and often uncontrollable. Letter from George Bird Grinnell, New York, February 2, 1916, to Agnes R. Wright, FF11, William O. Collins Family Papers; Waring, *Riley County Democrat,* August 26, 1909; Friend in Mokler, 33–34; Drew, "The Platte Bridge Fight by One Who Was There," May 11, 1882.

28. "Roster of the Eleventh Cavalry Regiment," in J. W. Vaughn, *The Battle of Platte Bridge* (Norman, OK: University of Oklahoma Press, 1963), 69, 70; Ferdinand Erhardt, "At Platte Bridge," *National Tribune;* Fairfield, "The Eleventh Kansas Regiment at Platte Bridge," 35–59; Hubbard, "A Little Taste of Indian Warfare," 45.

29. Walker, "Eleventh Kansas Cavalry," 337.

30. "Charles Waring," in *Portrait and Biographical Album of Washington, Clay, and Riley Counties, Kansas* (Chicago: Chapman Bros., 1890), 701–2; Waring, *Riley County Democrat,* August 26, 1909; Walker, "Eleventh Kansas Cavalry," 337–38; Wilson, "Indian Fights and Atrocities"; Isley, "Lord Unhurt in Three Battles"; Pennock Diary, 19; Spring, *Caspar Collins,* 89.

In recalling the action many years after, Lieutenant Drew accused Captain Lybe of cowardice. He stated that when other men of Company I went out to cover the retreat, they had cursed the officer for leaving his post before their comrades in the 11th Kansas had reached it. He also noted that Captain Walker's horse had "got under such headway that it did not stop until it had carried him safely into the station, without his having fired a shot." See Drew, "The Platte Bridge Fight by One Who Was There," May 18, 1882.

31. Henry Bretney, Jr., reported that he had found a scrap of paper written by his father that read: "thrashed Captain G., who had applied an insulting term to me, in presence of Major Anderson; then the Major and I engaged in a heated argument." See Letter from Bretney to Mokler, January 27, 1936, 1.

32. Letter from Pvt. Fred Marvin, Fort Laramie, August 7, 1865, to his father, Maxon Collection; James W. Shrader, "Red Buttes Fight,"mss., July 24, 1904, Collection 617, Kansas Historical Society; Letter from George W. Drew to William K. Connelley, June 1, 1910, Box 31, William E. Connelley Collection, Kansas Historical Society; Shrader's account in "Three Jim's Fight Battles Over Again at Oskaloosa," *Leavenworth Times,* May 11, 1928.

33. "The Platte Bridge Fight," *Topeka Daily Capital,* July 3, 1882.

34. Pennock Diary, entry for July 26, 1865, 19. Disagreement exists concerning the location of the Custard fight. Those who saw the action from Platte Bridge identify initial contact at a point about five miles west of the post. These include Shrader, Pennock, Erhardt, George Walker, and George Bent. William Drew reported that the end occurred two and a half miles from Platte Bridge, while Charles Waring believed the distance was two miles. See James W. Shrader, "Red Buttes Fight"; Pennock Diary, entry for July 28, 1865; Ferdinand Erhardt, "11th Kansas at Platte Bridge, Wyoming"; Letter from George M. Walker, Washington, Iowa, June 1, 1901, to William E. Connelley, William E. Connelley Papers, Kansas Historical Society; Drew, "The Platte Bridge Fight by One Who Was There," May 18, 1882; Waring, *Riley County Democrat,* August 26, 1909.

35. Drew, "The Platte Bridge Fight by One Who Was There," May 18, 1882.

36. "Statement Regarding Fight at Platte Bridge . . . by John H. Crumb"; Jean Wilson, "The Indian Butcheries," *Leavenworth Daily Conservative,* August 31, 1865; Letter from George W. Drew to William K. Connelley, June 1, 1910, Box 31, William E. Connelley Collection; Walker, "Eleventh Kansas Cavalry," 339.

37. Vaughn, *Platte Bridge,* 30.

38. Bent to Hyde, May 3, 1906, Coe Collection. For an expanded account, see Hyde, *Life of George Bent,* 220–21. George Grinnell recorded an account of the Custard fight by the Cheyenne Crazy Head on September 10, 1908. His version reads: "They tried to corral the wagons but there was not time, and they halted the wagons in line. C[razy] H[ead] reached the fight just as the last two mules were being cut loose and he happened to get one of the mules. They killed all the soldiers. The I[ndian]s all dismounted and rushed to the wagons. Some the I[ndian]s were killed close to the wagons. When they got to the wagons and tore off the covers there were still soldiers alive in the wagons." See George Grinnell, Notebook 348 (1908), MS 5, Grinnell Collection, Southwest Museum, Los Angeles, 64.

39. Statement of Crazy Head, September 10, 1908, Grinnell, Notebook 348, Grinnell Collection, 64.

40. Drew, "The Platte Bridge Fight by One Who Was There," May 18, 1882; *Rawlins* (Wyoming) *Republican,* January 26, 1922; Coutant, *History of Wyoming,* 473; Wilson, "Indian Fights and Atrocities."

41. Drew, "The Platte Bridge Fight by One Who Was There," May 25, 1882; Pennock Diary, 20; Sandoz, *Crazy Horse,* 169.

42. Drew, "The Platte Bridge Fight by One Who Was There," May 25, 1882. See also Isley, "Lord Unhurt in Three Battles," November 11, 1928.

43. Pennock reported in his diary on July 28: "We counted about forty lodge pole trails on which they had fixed stretchers to carry off their wounded." See Pennock Diary, 21. See also Drew, "The Platte Bridge Fight by One Who Was There," May 25, 1882; Letter from George W. Drew to William K. Connelley, June 1, 1910, Box 31, William E. Connelley Collection.

44. Drew, "The Platte Bridge Fight by One Who Was There," May 25, 1882; "Lord Unhurt."

45. Pennock Diary, 19–20; Wilson, "Indian Fights and Atrocities"; Walker, "Eleventh Kansas Cavalry," 339. Letter from Drew to Connelley, June 1, 1910, Connelley Collection.

46. Pennock Diary, 19.

47. Hubbard, "A Little Taste of Indian Warfare," 43–44, 74–75.

48. John Crumb located the body as follows: "We found the body about one-half mile from the rise, from the lowland right north of the ridge up on the tableland, which was about half a mile from Casper [Dry] Creek, and about a quarter of a mile from the line of retreat followed

by the detachment or detail." See "Statement Regarding Fight at Platte Bridge . . . by John H. Crumb."

49. Friend in Mokler, *Fort Caspar*, 34; Waring, *Riley County Democrat*, August 26, 1909.

50. Friend in Mokler, *Fort Caspar*, 70.

51. Pennock Diary, 20; Waring, *Riley County Democrat*, August 26, 1909; Fairfield, "The Eleventh Kansas Regiment at Platte Bridge," 359; Erhardt, "11th Kansas at Platte Bridge."

52. Pennock Diary, p, 20; Mokler, *Fort Caspar*, 50.

53. Telegram from Anderson to General Connor, July 27, 1865, Platte Bridge, Telegrams Received, District of the Plains, RG 393.

54. Both Drew and Fairfield in their accounts stated that troops went out to look for Custard and his men on July 27, but Pennock's diary fixes the date as July 28. See Pennock Diary, 21.

55. Pennock Diary, 21; Drew, "The Platte Bridge Fight by One Who Was There," May 21, 1882; "Statement Regarding Fight at Platte Bridge . . . by John H. Crumb"; Robert S. Ellison, "Memorandum Concerning the Number of Soldiers Killed in the Platte Bridge and Red Buttes Indian Fights, July 26, 1865," mss., Maxon Collection, Fort Caspar Collections; Fairfield, "The Eleventh Kansas Regiment at Platte Bridge," 359; Hubbard, "A Little Taste of Indian Warfare," 45.

56. John Friend, "Notes on Battle," William O. Collins Family Papers; John Friend, "Platte Bridge Fight," *Carbon County* (Rawlins, Wyoming) *Journal*, March 7, 1885.

57. Drew, "The Platte Bridge Fight by One Who Was There," May 21, 1882; Fairfield, "The Eleventh Kansas Regiment at Platte Bridge," 359–60.

58. Wilson, "Indian Fights and Atrocities" and "The Indian Butcheries"; Samuel J. Crawford, *Kansas in the Sixties* (Chicago, A. C. McClurg & Company, 1911), 266.

59. Vaughn, *Platte Bridge*, 99.

60. Pennock Diary, 21. Others reported a single trench, lined with blankets. S. H. Fairfield, "Some Fake History," unidentified newspaper clipping, c. June 1911, Maxon Collection, Fort Caspar Collections; Letter from S. H. Fairfield, Alma, Kansas, June 2, 1911, to George W. Martin, Collection 617, Military History of the 11th Kansas, Kansas Historical Society; "Special to the Tribune," *Lawrence Daily Tribune*, July 29, 1865, 2; Mokler, *Fort Caspar*, 50.

61. "Statement Regarding Fight at Platte Bridge . . . by John H. Crumb."

62. Pennock Diary, 19.

63. Fairfield, "The Eleventh Kansas Regiment at Platte Bridge," 360; Wilson, "Indian Fights and Atrocities"; Telegram from Major Martin Anderson, Platte Bridge, July 27, 1865, to General Connor, Telegrams Received, Records of the District of the Plains, RG 393; Pennock Diary, 20–21; Hyde, *Life of George Bent,* 223; "Great Battle with 1000 Indians at Platte Bridge," *Yankton Union and Dakotaian,* August 5, 1865, 2; "Indian Battle at Platte Bridge," Central City, (Colorado) *Daily Miner's Register,* July 29, 1865, 2; "Fight at Platte Bridge Station," *Rocky Mountain News,* July 29, 1865, 1; Letter from George W. Drew to William K. Connelley, June 1, 1910, Box 31, Collection; Webb, "The Indian Version of the Platte Bridge Fight," 235; Letter from Bretney to Mokler, January 27, 1936; Mokler, *Fort Caspar,* 12; George Bird Grinnell, "Sioux, Cheyenne, Arapaho War Customs," Folder 246, George Bird Grinnell Collection, MS 5, Southwest Museum.

64. Pennock Diary, 21.

65. The 6th Michigan had arrived at Fort Laramie on July 25. Half armed, the troops voiced their dissatisfaction with their extended service and demanded their discharge. See Rogers, *Soldiers of the Overland,* 165.

66. "From Kansas and the Plains," *Chicago Tribune,* August 10, 1865, 2.

CHAPTER 7: CONNOR STRIKES BACK

1. F. G. Burnett, "History of the Western Division of the Powder River Expedition," *Annals of Wyoming* 8 (January 1932), 571; Account of Captain B. F. Rockafellow in LeRoy Hafen, *The Powder River Campaigns and Sawyers' Expedition* (Glendale, CA: Arthur H. Clark Company, 1961), 171; Susan Badger Doyle, "The Evolution of the Bozeman Trail," mss, Sheridan County Fulmer Library, Sheridan, Wyoming, 5.

2. Henry E. Palmer, "The Powder River Expedition," *National Tribune,* April 12, 1908, 7; Louis Vasmer Caziarc, Memorandum, September 29, 1883, Alonzo P. Richards Pension File 381298, Records of the Veterans Administration, RG 15.

3. The Central City, Colorado, *Miner's Register* lauded the coming of the Michigan veterans, noting that the 6th came fresh from the experience of sixty-three hard-fought battles, beginning with Gettysburg and ending at Appomattox Court House. See "Connor and the Indians," *Miner's Register,* June 21, 1865, 2; Rogers, *Soldiers of the Overland,* 165; Pennock Diary, entry for June 3, 1865, 21–22; Spring, *Caspar Collins,* 93; John Robertson, *Michigan in the War* (Lansing: W. S. George & Company, State Printers and Binders, 1880), 395–96, 596–70, 865;

Record of Service of Michigan Volunteers in the Civil War, 1861–1865 (Lansing: Senate and the House of Representatives of the Michigan Legislature, n.d.), 1–12; Frederick H. Dyer, *A Compendium of the War of the Rebellion,* vol. 2 (New York: Thomas Yoselhoff, 1919), 1272–73.

4. Palmer, "The Powder River Expedition," 7; Caziarc, Memorandum, September 29, 1883, Alonzo P. Richards Pension File 381298, Records of the Veterans Administration, RG 15.

5. Letter from Connor, July 28, 1865, to Dodge, *OR,* Series I, vol. 48, pt. 2, 1129–30.

6. "Gen. Connor," *Rocky Mountain News,* July 10, 1865, 1; "Connor and the Indians," *Miner's Register,* June 21, 1865, 2.

7. "Indian Affairs," *Chicago Tribune,* June 24, 1865, 1.

8. For nice summaries of the Powder River expedition, see H. D. Hampton, "The Powder River Expedition, 1865," *Montana* 14 (Autumn 1964), 2–15, and Robert Bruce, ed., "The Powder River Expedition of 1865," *The United States Army Recruiting News* 10 (August 1928), 6–8, 15.

9. *OR,* vol. 48, pt. 2, 1130; Coutant, *History of Wyoming,* 506-7. For a discussion of Connor's route in relation to earlier trips along the east side of the Big Horn Mountains, see Susan Badger Doyle, "The Bozeman Trail, 1863–1868: The Evolution of Routes to Montana," *Overland Journal* 20 (Spring 2002), 10–11, and "The Evolution of the Bozeman Trail," 6. See also Susan Badger Doyle, ed., *Journeys to the Land of Gold: Emigrant Diaries from the Bozeman Trail, 1863–1866,* vol. 1 (Helena: Montana Historical Society, 2000), 341–42.

10. "The Powder River Indian Expedition: A Diary Kept by One of the Staff of General Connor," American Heritage Center, Laramie, Wyoming, 4.

11. P. W. Brown, "Fighting in the Indian Country in the 60's," *National Tribune,* June 6, 1910, 3.

12. Rockafellow in Hafen, *The Powder River Campaigns,* 172; Doyle, "The Evolution of the Bozeman Trail," 5.

13. Doyle, "The Evolution of the Bozeman Trail," 5–6; "A Diary Kept by One of the Staff of General Connor," 4.

14. Charles W. Adams, "Indian Campaign," *National Tribune,* February 17, 1898, 6.

15. Caziarc, Memorandum, September 29, 1883, Alonzo P. Richards Pension File; Bruce, ed., "The Powder River Expedition of 1865," 15; Burnett, "History of the Western Division of the Powder River Expedition," 570–72.

16. "A Diary Kept by One of the Staff of General Connor," 7.

17. Doyle, "Indian Perspectives of the Bozeman Trail," 61.

18. "A Diary Kept by One of the Staff of General Connor," 8. The post became Fort Reno on November 11, 1866, to honor Gen. Jesse L. Reno, one of the fallen heroes of the Army of the Potomac. Finn Burnett visited the site in 1928 and "found that the channel of the river had changed, and that the valley where the expedition had camped had been eroded away, and that the river was flowing along the edge of the table land on which fort was erected." See Burnett, "History of the Western Division of the Powder River Expedition," 570-71.

19. Letter from Acting Assistant Adjutant General C. G. Laurant, In the Field, Powder River, D.T., August 15, 1865, to Captain Kidd, Letters Sent, District of the Plains, Entry 3254, Records of U.S. Army Commands, RG 393. See also Robert Murray, *Military Posts in the Powder River Country of Wyoming, 1865–1894* (Lincoln: University of Nebraska Press, 1968), 13–27.

20. Palmer, "Powder River Indian Expedition of 1865," 73.

21. Letter from Acting Assistant Adjutant General C. G. Laurant, In the Field, Powder River, D.T., August 8, 1865, Letters Sent, District of the Plains; "A Diary Kept by One of the Staff of General Connor," 8; Murray, *Military Posts,* 13–27.

22. Hyde, *Life of George Bent,* 227; Doyle, "Indian Perspectives of the Bozeman Trail," 61.

23. Burnett, "History of the Western Division of the Powder River Expedition," 572.

24. Letter from Burnett to Albert W. Johnson, Harding Court, Rock Springs, Wyoming, June 17, 1931, in Burnett, "History of the Western Division of the Powder River Expedition," 579.

25. "A Diary Kept by One of the Staff of General Connor," 8–9.

26. "NEBRASKA," Fort Connor, D.T., Powder River, August 19, 1865 in "From the West: Successful Fight with the Indians," (Omaha) *Nebraska Republican,* September 15, 1865, 1. This took place where the town of Sussex is now located, about thirty miles east of Kaycee. See C. C. Rawlings, "Conner [sic] Battle One of Many Blood Engagements along Bozeman Trail," *Sheridan Press,* July 17, 1963. One diarist reported that twenty-four were killed instead of twenty-seven. See "A Diary Kept by One of the Staff of General Connor," 8.

27. "A Diary Kept by One of the Staff of General Connor," 8–9; Luther H. North, "The Pawnee Battalion," *National Tribune,* April 27, 1922, 3. Finn Burnett described the incident in his reminiscence: "A few days

later, saw a large war party, thought to be those who had killed Collins a few days before. Connor told North to go after them. Leighton and Burnett went with them. Left Connor about 3 p.m. Followed them through the night, surrounded the camp, and at dawn attacked, killing all 42 [sic] of them—two of them women [sic]. Had a number of white scalps, including that of a light curly-haired girl, white clothing, a number of Ben Holiday's [sic] horses, branded B.H." See Burnett, "History of the Western Division of the Powder River Expedition," 573.

28. Letter from Grenville Dodge, Camp Mitchell, August 28, 1865, Letters Sent, Department of the Missouri, Entry 2127, RG 393; "NEBRASKA," in "From the West: Successful Fight with the Indians," 1; "The Indian Expedition," *Eaton* (Ohio) *Register,* August 31, 1865, 2; "The Indian War," *Chicago Tribune,* September 29, 1865, 1; George Bird Grinnell, *Two Great Scouts and Their Pawnee Battalion: The Experience of Frank J. North and Luther H. North* (Lincoln: University of Nebraska Press, 1973), 91–92. Among the letters found were some belonging to Pvt. G. W. Barker, who had been killed by Indians on the Little Laramie on August 5. His body had been in a wagon and piles of bacon piled around him and the whole ignited. See "Indian Difficulties," *Rocky Mountain News,* October 6, 1865, 3.

29. Palmer, "Powder River Indian Expedition of 1865," 73–74.

30. "A Diary Kept by One of the Staff of General Connor," 9; "The Indian Expedition," 2.

31. "A Diary Kept by One of the Staff of General Connor," 10; Palmer, "Powder River Indian Expedition of 1865," 74.

32. *Army and Navy Journal,* September 2, 1865, 17, stated that Marshall had captured twenty horses and several packages of plunder, which had evidently but recently come into their possession.

33. "A Diary Kept by One of the Staff of General Connor," 10.

34. Ibid., 10–11.

35. Palmer, "Powder River Indian Expedition of 1865," 76, 96. Another member of the expedition wrote on August 24, "Vegetation is luxuriant, game abundant, weather delightful, and everything appears to conspire, so far as to make the trip interesting and agreeable." See "From Connor's Expedition, *Miner's Register,* September 25, 1865, 2.

36. "Indian Murders on the Yellowstone," *Montana Post,* September 2, 1865; reprinted as "Indian Murders on the Yellowstone," *Nebraska Republican,* September 29, 1865, 2.

37. "Indian Murders on the Yellowstone."

38. W. L. Kuykendall, *Frontier Days: A True Narrative of Striking Events on the Western Frontier* (Rawlins, WY: J. M. and H. L. Kuykendall, 1917), 92–93; "More Indian Atrocities," *Nebraska Republican,* August 25, 1865, 1; "Indian Atrocities," *Yankton Union and Dakotaian,* September 2, 1865, 2.

39. John Baptiste Richard was born in St. Charles, Missouri, on December 14, 1810. He came to the Fort Laramie area in the early 1830s, where he worked for the American Fur Company's competition, finally acting independently. Richard married Mary Gardiner, a half-blood living with the Northern Oglalas or Smoke People, and cemented an alliance with that tribe that was to last until his death. His many ventures included ownership of Richard's Bridge over the North Platte near present-day Casper, Wyoming, from 1853 to 1865. For a biography of Richard, see John D. McDermott, "John Baptiste Richard," in *The Mountain Men and the Fur Trade of the Far West,* ed. LeRoy Hafen, vol. 2 (Glendale, CA: Arthur H. Clark Company, 1965), 289–303. For a detailed account of his life at Richard's Bridge, see McDermott, *Frontier Crossroads,* 1–21.

40. "More Indian Atrocities," 1; "Indian Atrocities," 2.

41. Palmer, "Powder River Indian Expedition of 1865," 96.

42. "A Diary Kept by One of the Staff of General Connor," 11.

43. Palmer, "Powder River Indian Expedition of 1865," 77–78; Burnett, "History of the Western Division of the Powder River Expedition," 574; William Devine, "The Connor Expedition," typescript, Item In2-bat-pre, American Heritage Center, Laramie, Wyoming.

44. Edwin R. Nash, "Diary, August 28, 1865," Manuscript Division, Library of Congress, Washington, D.C.; Palmer, "Powder River Indian Expedition of 1865," 79; "A Diary Kept by One of the Staff of General Connor," 13; Burnett, "History of the Western Division of the Powder River Expedition," 574; P. W. Brown (Company K, 11th Ohio), "Fighting in the Indian Country in the 60's," *National Tribune,* June 9, 1910.

45. "The Arapahoes at Ft. Collins," *Rocky Mountain News,* July 8, 1865.

46. Letter from Fort Laramie, July 3, 1856, in *Nebraska Republican,* July 7, 1865, 2; "Indian Outrages," *New York Times,* July 4, 1865, 5.

47. See interview with Medicine Man's wife in Nash, "Diary, August 29, 1865." In a letter to Pope, Dodge repeats Connor's statement that he attacked Medicine Man's band. See General Dodge, Central City, Colorado, September 27, 1865, to General Pope, Letters Sent and Received, Department of the Missouri, Entry 2127, RG 393.

48. Palmer, "Powder River Indian Expedition of 1865," 79–80; Account of A. J. Shotwell in Rogers, *Soldiers of the Overland,* 203.

49. There have been a number of popular accounts of the battle on Tongue River written over the years. Most rely on Henry Palmer's work, some on remembrance of stories told by participants in the fight many years later, and others on speculation. These include Mrs. J. E. Chappell, "Military Occupation and Forts in Johnson Company 1865 to 1868," *Buffalo* (Wyoming) *Voice,* December 9, 1921, 1, 4, and Burton Hill, "Powder River Expedition of Major Patrick E. Connor, 1865, Johnson County Historical Society Meeting, May, 1964," typescript, Johnson County Library, Buffalo, Wyoming.

50. Palmer, "Powder River Indian Expedition of 1865," 80; Burnett, "History of the Western Division of the Powder River Expedition," 575; Shotwell in Rogers, *Soldiers of the Overland,* 203.

51. Brown, "Fighting in the Indian Country in the 60's." Charles Adams of the same company remembered the speech slightly differently but recalled that they were enjoined to avoid killing women and children "as much as possible." Connor also told them to save the last bullet for themselves. See Adams, "Indian Campaign."

52. Adams, "Indian Campaign."

53. Brown, "Fighting in the Indian Country in the 60's."

54. Adams, "Indian Campaign"; Brown, "Fighting in the Indian Country in the 60's."

55. Account of J. L. Humphreville in Rogers, *Soldiers of the Overland,* 201.

56. Adams, "Indian Campaign"; Palmer, "Powder River Indian Expedition of 1865," 80–81.

57. According to Burnett, "This boy was between seventeen and eighteen years old. He was a member of the Second California Volunteers. I do not remember his name. He was known as Little Dick by his comrades. He was a brave little soldier, and refused to go to the ambulance under the doctor's care, making light of his wound. I remember that he was riding a small nervous cream-colored horse which caused him a great deal of trouble and pain. He carried dispatches back and forth over the field during the day, and at night during our return to camp, thirteen miles down Tongue river, and refused to ride in the ambulance with others who were wounded." See Burnett, "History of the Western Division of the Powder River Expedition," 575.

58. Humphreville in Rogers, *Soldiers of the Overland,* 202.

59. Palmer, "Powder River Indian Expedition of 1865," 81.

60. O. J. Hollister stated that when Connor halted, he had with him only thirteen officers and ten men. See Hollister, *Blackhawk Mining Journal,* October 20, 1865. See also Adams "Indian Campaign"; Palmer, "Powder River Indian Expedition of 1865," 82; Caziarc, Memorandum, September 29, 1883, Alonzo P. Richards Pension File; Rawlings, "Conner Battle One of Many."

61. Luther North recalled that Frank North and fifteen Pawnee scouts, who were with Connor in the pursuit, were responsible for saving the party. Other eyewitness accounts, however, do not mention this. See letter from Luther North to Ellison, December 17, 1928, Columbus, Nebraska, Item 47, Luther North Papers, C1-C50, Ellison Collection, Denver Public Library, Denver, Colorado.

62. Palmer, "Powder River Indian Expedition of 1865," 84.

63. Burnett, "History of the Western Division of the Powder River Expedition," 575.

64. Brown, "Fighting in the Indian Country in the 60's"; Burnett, "History of the Western Division of the Powder River Expedition," 575; Asst. Surg. Julius Wenz, 6th U.S. Volunteers, "Classified Return of Wounded and Injuries Received in Action on 29th Day of August 1865, Battle of Tongue River, D.T.," Entry 6240, Records of the Surgeon General, RG 94.

65. Palmer, "Powder River Indian Expedition of 1865," 85.

66. Wenz, "Classified Return of Wounded and Injuries Received in Action on 29th Day of August 1865"; Oscar Jewett Pension File 227.164, Records of the Veterans Administration, RG 15.

67. Palmer "Powder River Indian Expedition of 1865," 81–82.

68. Adams, "Indian Campaign"; Letter from Franklin Tubbs, Fort Laramie, October 6, 1865, to his father, Tubbs Collection, MSS. 2877, American Heritage Center, Laramie, Wyoming.

69. Palmer, "Powder River Indian Expedition of 1865," 82–85.

70. Letter from Fort Laramie, October 1, 1865, in *Washington Evening Star,* October 3, 1865, 1; "W.," Camp Near Ft. Laramie, October 6, 1865, "The Indian Campaign," *Nebraska City News,* October 28, 1865, 1; Palmer, "Powder River Indian Expedition of 1865," 82; Brown, "Fighting in the Indian Country in the 60's"; "A Diary Kept by One of the Staff of General Connor," 13.

71. Burnett speaks of the Pawnee scouts stopping to loot the village. This was true of the part of the company under the command of North's lieutenants Charles Small and Jimmy Murie. See Letter 2 from Luther

North to Robert Ellison, December 17, 1928, Columbus, Nebraska, Item 47, C1–C50, Ellison Collection, Denver Public Library.

72. Loretta Fowler states, "Black Bear's band of about 500 persons was surprised and attacked. Thirty-five warriors were killed and several women and children were taken prisoner (and later released) and five hundred horses and mules were captured." See Fowler, *Arapahoe Politics, 1851–1978: Symbols in Crises of Authority* (Lincoln: University of Nebraska Press, 1982), 44.

73. "A Diary Kept by One of the Staff of General Connor," 13, 27.

74. Letter 2 from North to Ellison, December 17, 1928, Columbus, Nebraska, Item 47, Luther North Papers.

75. "Glorious News!", *Rocky Mountain News,* September 20, 1865, 1; "The Powder River 'Murderers,'" *Rocky Mountain News,* September 21, 1865, 2.

76. "Complimentary Supper to Major General Dodge and Staff at the Planter's House," *Rocky Mountain News,* September 22, 1865, 4.

77. Palmer, "Powder River Indian Expedition of 1865," 82; Adams, "Indian Campaign"; P. W. Brown, "The 11th Ohio Cav.," 7; Elsa Spear Edwards, "A Fifteen Day Fight on Tongue River, 1865," *Winners of the West* (December 1939), 10–12; Diary kept by one of Connor's staff from July 29 to September 14, Lyman Gibson Bennett Papers, Wyoming State Archives, Cheyenne; Charles Rawlings, "General Conner's [*sic*] Tongue River Battle," *Annals of Wyoming* 36 (April 1964), 69–73.

78. Burnett, "History of the Western Division of the Powder River Expedition," 576.

79. Palmer, "Powder River Indian Expedition of 1865," 85.

80. "A Diary Kept by One of the Staff of General Connor," 17.

81. Palmer, "Powder River Indian Expedition of 1865," 85.

82. Letter from Burnett to Albert W. Johnson, Harding Court, Rock Springs, Wyoming, June 17, 1931; Burnett, "History of the Western Division of the Powder River Expedition," 579.

83. "A Diary Kept by One of the Staff of General Connor,"15; Palmer, "Powder River Indian Expedition of 1865," 86.

84. Palmer, "Powder River Indian Expedition of 1865," 86–87; Statement of Henry E. Palmer in "Application for a Medal of Honor: Case of Charles L. Thomas," August 1894, Record and Pension Office, File 392759, RG 92, National Archives; "Diary Kept by One of the Staff of General Connor," 15–16.

CHAPTER 8: THE SAWYERS EXPEDITION

1. Sawyers's report was printed as "Wagon Road from Niobrara to Virginia City," House Executive Document 58, 39th Congress, 1st session, 1865–1866, 10–36, Serial 1256, and has been reprinted many times, including in "Report of Col. James A. Sawyers," *South Dakota Historical Review* 2 (October 1936), 3–46. I have chosen, when possible, to use the most recent reprinting in Susan Badger Doyle, ed., *Journeys to the Land of Gold: Emigrant Diaries from the Bozeman Trail, 1863–1866,* vol. 1 (Helena: Montana Historical Society, 2000), 357–70, because of its revealing annotations. The diary reproduced here, however, is only from August 9 on. Hereafter cited as Sawyers Report. For a good secondary account of the expedition, see W. Turrentine Jackson, *Wagon Roads West: A Study of Federal Road Surveys and Construction in the Trans-Mississippi West, 1846–1869* (Berkeley and Los Angeles: University of California Press, 1964), chapter 17. Another useful collection is LeRoy and Ann W. Hafen, *Powder River Campaigns and Sawyers' Expedition of 1865,* Far West and Rockies Series, vol. 12 (Glendale, CA: Arthur H. Clark Company, 1961). Accounts of the expedition include those of James A. Sawyers, Dr. D. W. Tingley, Capt. George W. Williford, and Albert M. Holman.

2. Serving in Congress from 1863 to 1869, Hubbard was from Sioux City. See "Sawyers," *South Dakota Historical Review,* fn. 1, 3; "The Wagon Road Bill Approved March 3, 1865," *Yankton and Dakotaian,* May 13, 1865, 2.

3. James Sawyers Military Service Record, Records of the Office of the Adjutant General, RG 94; Report of Col. James A. Sawyers, *South Dakota Historical Review* 2 (October 1936), 48. For biographical details, see Doyle, *Journeys,* 355–66; Harvey Inghman, *The Northern Border Brigade: A Story of Military Beginnings* (n.p., 1926), 83; Marshall McKusick, *The Iowa Northern Border Brigade* (Iowa City: Office of State Archaeologist, The University of Iowa, 1975), 155–61.

4. *Yankton and Dakotaian,* June 10, 1865, 2; "Sawyers," fn. 6, 13; Albert H. Holman and Constant R. Marks, *Pioneering the Northwest* (Sioux City, IA: Deitch & Lamar Company, 1924), 9; Doyle, *Journeys,* 371–72.

5. "Sawyers," 4–5.

6. Ibid., 4.

7. A. M. English, "Dakota's First Soldiers: History of the First Dakota Cavalry, 1862–1865," *South Dakota Historical Collection,* vol. 9 (Pierre,

SD: South Dakota Historical Society 1918), 309–10; Doyle, *Journeys,* 345.

8. "Sawyers," 6.

9. The body was later reinterred in Cincinnati, Ohio, in a grave next to his mother's. See Doyle, *Journeys,* 358, fn. 13; Letter from Capt. George Williford, Fort Connor, D.T., October 9, 1865, to Acting Assistant Adjutant General William Burn, Grenville Dodge Papers, Iowa Historical Society, Des Moines, Iowa; Report of Capt. George W. Williford, 5th U.S. Volunteer Cavalry, Fort Connor, August 29, 1865, *OR,* Series I, vol. 48, pt. 1, 388; Sawyers Report, 358; Diary of John Colby Griggs in Eli R. Paul, ed., "A Galvanized Yankee along the Niobrara River," *Nebraska History* 70 (Summer 1989), 154; Lewis H. Smith, "Lewis H. Smith Diary," in Doyle, *Journeys,* 373. Smith wrote a more detailed account of his experiences in diary form that appeared in the *Sioux City Journal,* December 23, 1865; January 6, 13, and 27, 1866; February 10 and 17, 1866; and March 3, 1866. This has been reproduced in Inghman, *The Northern Border Brigade,* 70–94. In the expanded account, Smith stated that Hedges's body had been stripped and pierced with bullets and arrows. See page 89.

10. The site of the skirmish is about ten miles southwest of present-day Gillette, Wyoming, in SE Section 28, T49R, R73W. See Doyle, *Journeys,* 358. For a discussion of Jarvis's adventure, see Corwin M. Lee, "C. M. Lee Diary, 1865," in Doyle, *Journeys,* 390; Albert M. Holman's Report, "Sawyers," 26. This report is the same as that found in Holman and Marks, *Pioneering the Northwest,* 12–50.

11. Hyde, *Life of George Bent,* 229–31.

12. Hyde, *Life of George Bent,* 232; Sandoz, *Crazy Horse,* 173; Grinnell, *The Fighting Cheyennes,* 209; Susan Badger Doyle, "Indian Perspectives of the Bozeman Trail," 62; Grenville Dodge to John Pope, Horse Shoe Station, September 15, 1865, Letters Sent, Department of the Missouri, Records of U.S. Army Commands, RG 393.

13. Dodge to Pope, Horse Shoe Station, September 15, 1865, Letters Sent, Department of the Missouri, RG 393.

14. Nelson was a farmer at Vermillion. He had joined Company B on September 11, 1862, when he was 18. See English, "Dakota's First Soldiers," 330.

15. John Rouse was a farmer at Bon Homme. He had enlisted in Yankton on September 8, 1862. See English, "Dakota's First Soldiers," 332.

16. Sawyers Report, 359; Smith in Inghman, *The Northern Border Brigade,* 89; "Lee Diary, 1865," in Doyle, *Journeys,* 394–95; Diary of John Colby

Griggs, in *Nebraska History* 70 (Summer 1989), 154–55. A slightly different version of this appeared in the *Missouri Republican,* October 30, 1865, as "Journal of Sawyers Wagon Road Expedition from Niobrara, Nebraska, to Virginia City, Montana Territory, by a Private of the Escort."

17. Letter from Capt. George Williford, Fort Connor, D.T., October 9, 1865, to Acting Assistant Gen. William Burn, Grenville Dodge Papers, Iowa Historical Society; Stanley Vestal, *New Sources of Indian History 1850–1891* (Norman: University of Oklahoma, 1934), 136.

18. "Report of Capt. George W. Williford, Fifth U. S. Volunteer Infantry," in "Sawyers," 49; *OR,* vol. 48, pt. 1, 388–89; Letter from Asst. Adj. Gen. George Price, Fort Laramie, September 3, 1865, to Maj. Gen. Grenville Dodge, Letters Sent, District of the Plains, RG 393.

19. Sawyers Report, 361; *Army and Navy Journal,* September 9, 1865, 33; Diary of John Colby Griggs, 156.

20. Sawyers Report, 361–62; *Montana Post,* October 14, 1865; Doyle, "The Evolution of the Bozeman Trail."

21. Sawyers Report, 362; Account of Albert M. Holman in Edwards, "A Fifteen Day Fight on Tongue River," 12–13. Holman prepared this abbreviated and more critical account for a talk at the Sheridan County Public Library in 1912. See George Kelley, Subject File 1189, S-620, Works Progress Administration Collection, Wyoming State Archives, Cheyenne.

22. "Lee Diary, 1865," in Doyle, *Journeys,* 400; Sawyers Report, 363.

23. Holman in Edwards, "A Fifteen Day Fight on Tongue River," 11.

24. Dr. D. W. Tingley's Report, 45; "Sawyers Report, 363; "Smith's Diary," 371, and "Lee Diary, 1865," 402, in Doyle, *Journeys*; Holman in Edwards, "A Fifteen Day Fight on Tongue River," 12–13;

25. Sawyers Report, 364, fn. 37; "Smith's Diary," in Doyle, *Journeys,* 377.

26. Holman in Edwards, "A Fifteen Day Fight," 12–13.

27. "Sawyers," 32.

28. Doyle, *Journeys,* 326, fn. 43.

29. Sawyers Report, 366; James Sawyers, "A Partial Account of the Book That Was Lost, 1865," n.d., W. C. Coutant Papers, File H74-9, Folder 64, Wyoming State Archives.

30. Sawyers, "Partial Account of the Book That Was Lost," Coutant Papers; Holman and Marks, *Pioneering the Northwest,* 9; *Montana Post,* October 14, 1865.

31. Dodge to Assistant Adjutant General Joseph Bell, Division of Missouri, November 1, 1865, Fort Leavenworth; *OR,* vol. 48, pt. 2, 340.

32. Doyle, *Journeys,* 351–52; Doyle, "The Evolution of the Bozeman Trail."

33. Holman and Marks, *Pioneering the Northwest,* 11; Inghman, *The Northern Border Brigade,* 70.

CHAPTER 9: COLE AND WALKER

1. Letter from Luther North, Columbus, Nebraska, November 16, 1928, to Robert Ellison, Folder 1 In2-bat-pre, American Heritage Center, Laramie, Wyoming; Charles H. Springer, *Soldiering in Sioux Country: 1865,* ed. Benjamin Frank Cooling III (San Diego, CA: Frontier Heritage Press, 1971), 36.

2. Report of Col. Nelson Cole, St. Louis, Missouri, February 10, 1867, to Gen. U. S. Grant, *OR,* Series I, volume 48, pt. 1, 366–67. This is an expanded report of the one he prepared on September 25, 1865, while near Fort Connor. The first report is also printed in *OR,* vol. 48, pt. 1, 380–83. The original is found in Miscellaneous File, Records of the Office of the Adjutant General, RG 94. See also William Devine, "Powder River Expedition '65," *Sheridan Post,* June 29, 1915; Palmer, "The Powder River Expedition," 7; Palmer, "Powder River Indian Expedition of 1865," 67; "Winning the West: Col. Nelson Cole's Expedition in the Powder River in Summer of 1865," *National Tribune,* August 5, 1920, 3; P. C. Stepps, "The Powder River Expedition," *National Tribune,* April 27, 1922, 3. Enlisted man Silas Hendrix seconded Cole's views of the mules and the teamsters. See Account of Silas Hendrix, "Wichita Warriors: The Expedition of 1866 [*sic*]," *Wichita Eagle,* January 7, 1906.

3. Lyman Bennett, "1865 Diary," entry for July 18, typescript, Wyoming State Archives, Cheyenne, Wyoming.

4. Bennett, "1865 Diary," entry for July 22; Springer, *Soldiering in Sioux Country,* 16; "The Indian Campaign," *Nebraska City News,* October 28, 1865, 1.

5. Springer, *Soldiering in Sioux Country,* 17.

6. Bennett, "1865 Diary," entry for August 14; Edward B. Heaton, "A Lost Army," *Cheyenne Daily Leader,* July 28, 1875.

7. Letter from George Price, July 31, 1865, to Connor, Letters Sent, District of the Plains, Records of U.S. Army Commands, RG 393; Palmer, "Powder River Indian Expedition of 1865," 66.

8. Report of Samuel Walker, Field Quarters, 16th V. C., Camp on Powder River, September 23, 1865, to Capt. George Price, Acting

Assistant Adjutant General, Department of the Plains, Miscellaneous File, Records of the Office of the Adjutant General, RG 94.

9. Palmer, "Powder River Indian Expedition of 1865," 66. Mutinies in the West were becoming common. The *Army and Navy Journal* for September 2 carried a story on the mutiny of the 6th West Virginia Cavalry at Leavenworth City. One hundred ninety men of the regiment refused to cross the plains. Three officers were sentenced to be shot, but the death sentence was commuted to imprisonment and hard labor. The remaining 150 soldiers went on to Fort Kearny. Men were especially anxious to return home, for they could expect a substantial payment upon discharge due to undrawn pay, partially paid bounties, and other claims. Final payment averaged about $250. See *Army and Navy Journal,* September 2, 1865, 18; Carl R. Fish, "Notes and Suggestions," *American Historical Review* 24 (April 1919), 436.

10. Springer, *Soldiering in Sioux Country,* 34. One observer reported, "We knew nothing of their whereabouts until they rode into camp; for a start six hundred miles apart, over different portions of the country, it was a close hit." See "The March of the Eastern Division in Montana Territory, Powder River, M.T., August 30, 1865," *Rocky Mountain News,* October 31, 1865.

11. At least two others who had been left behind in the hospital died of scurvy during the next month. See Report of Capt. Samuel Flagg, Battery E, Second Missouri Light Artillery, Fort Connor, September 20, 1865, *OR,* vol. 48, pt. 1, 385. For a discussion of the disease and its effect on frontier soldiers, see John D. McDermott, "No Small Potatoes: Problems of Food and Health at Fort Laramie," *Nebraska History* 79 (Winter, 1998), 162–70.

12. Letter from Luther North, Columbus, Nebraska, November 16, 1928, to Robert Ellison, Folder 1 In2-bat-pre, American Heritage Center. Lyman Bennett shared Cole's views of the guides: "The guides know no more about the country than I do and today lead us off our course and we performed at least five miles of additional travel in getting to the river to camp." See Bennett, "1865 Diary," entry for July 25.

13. "W.," Camp Near Ft. Laramie, October 6, 1865, in "The Indian Campaign," *Nebraska City News,* October 28, 1865, 1; Bruce, "The Powder River Expedition of 1865," 15; Bennett, "1865 Diary," entry for July 16; Report of Lt. William Rinne, Battery C, 2nd Missouri, Fort Connor, September 20, 1865, *OR,* 386.

14. Hyde, *Life of George Bent,* 235–37.

15. Indian sources put the number at 300 Minniconjous, Sans Arcs, Hunkpapas, and Blackfoot Sioux. See Hyde, *Life of George Bent,* 235–37.

16. Report of Capt. Edward S. Rowland, Battery K, 2nd Missouri, of Skirmish, September 1, In the Field, Montana Territory, September 2, 1865, *OR,* 387; Report of Lt. John H, Kendall, Battery L, 2nd Missouri, of Skirmish, September 2, In the Field, Montana Territory, September 4, 1865, *OR,* 387; Cole's Report, *OR,* 371; Bruce, "The Powder River Expedition of 1865," 15; Stepps, "The Powder River Expedition," 3.

17. P. C. Stepps remembered that "in the skirmish that followed, one of the men of Company C was wounded with a poisoned arrow, dying two or three days later in great agony." Although these occasions were rare, it was true that some warriors did doctor their arrows with various kinds of poisons. See Stepps, "The Powder River Expedition," 3; John D. McDermott, *A Guide to the Indian Wars of the West* (Lincoln: University of Nebraska Press, 1998), 53–54.

18. "W.," "The Indian Campaign," 1; Springer, *Soldiering in Sioux Country,* 45.

19. Letter from Commanding Officer, District of Nebraska, Fort Laramie, September 25, 1865, to General Dodge, Letters Sent, District of Nebraska, Entry 3191, RG 393; Springer, *Soldiering in Sioux Country,* 45.

20. Bennett, "1866 Diary," entry for September 3; "W.," "The Indian Campaign," 1; Springer, *Soldiering in Sioux Country,* 46; *Army and Navy Journal,* October 21, 1865, 130.

21. Letter from Commanding Officer, District of Nebraska, Fort Laramie, September 25, 1865, to Major General Dodge, Letters Sent, District of Nebraska, Entry 3191, RG 393; "The Indian War," *Yankton Union and Dakotaian,* October 21, 1865, p 2.

22. Cole's Report, *OR,* 373; Report of Col. Oliver Wells, 12th Missouri Cavalry, Fort Connor, September 20, 1865, *OR,* 383; Report of Maj. Clemens Landgraeber, 2nd Missouri Light Artillery, Fort Connor, September 20, 1865, *OR,* 385; Report of Capt. Samuel Flagg, Battery E, Second Missouri Light Artillery, Fort Connor, September 20, 1865, *OR,* 385; "The Indian Campaign," *Nebraska City News,* October 28, 1865, 1.

23. Described as being well over six feet in height and possessing great physical powers, Roman Nose (1830–1868) was the most famous Northern Cheyenne warrior of his time. Until his death, he steadfastly

remained a fighter, refusing to become a chief. In his youth, he was called Sautie or the Bat, later taking the name Woquni or Hook Nose, which whites translated as Roman Nose. He was a member of the Elk Soldiers or Elk-Horn Scrapers society. However, during his later years, he lived with the Dog Soldiers, a military society, to which he did not belong, but whose aggressiveness he admired. See John D. McDermott, "Roman Nose," in *American National Biography*, ed. John A. Garraty and Mark C. Carnes, vol. 18 (New York: University of Oxford Press, 1999), 794–95; Grinnell, *The Fighting Cheyennes*, 214; Anthony McGinnis, *Counting Coup and Cutting Horses: Intertribal Warfare on the Northern Plains, 1738–1889* (Denver: Coridillera Press, 1990), 114.

24. Bennett, "1865 Diary," entry for September 5; Report of Col. Oliver Wells, *OR*, 383.
25. Springer, *Soldiering in Sioux Country*, 49.
26. Ibid., 46–48.
27. *Army and Navy Journal*, October 21, 1865, 130.
28. Cole's Report, *OR*, 374; Bennett, "1865 Diary," entry for September 5. See also "The Indian War," *Yankton Union and Dakotaian*, October 21, 1865, 2; Letter from Commanding Officer, District of Nebraska, Fort Laramie, September 25, 1865, RG 393; "The Indian Campaign," *Nebraska City News*, 1.
29. Bennett, "1865 Diary," entry for September 7; Report of Col. Oliver Wells, *OR*, 383; Josepheus Rich, "He Was the Hero," *National Tribune*, June 9, 1910, 3; Hendrix, "Wichita Warriors."
30. Bennett, "1865 Diary," entry for September 7. Walker in his report describes the scene as follows: "The rest of the morning (Sept. 8th) about 10 o'clock we came to a tremendous gulch in our front, reaching from the bluffs which were here very high, all broken with deep ravines, to the river. While we were making a way to get around the gulch report came back that the advance guard under Lieut. Boardman was surrounded with the Indians. Advancing to the top of a butte I saw the whole valley in front of me covered with Indians and the guard dismounted holding their ground nobly. I ordered Maj. Reynolds forward with his battalion to their support until we could get out wagons, packs, & howitzers over the gulch. He was at once completely surrounded by at least one thousand (1000) Indians, but dismounting he soon drove them out of range with his carbines. We were now attacked from all sides front, rear, & flanks, but the Indians seemed to have but few fire arms. It was impossible to charge them over such ground. On

horse back we could drive them easily in any direction, but they could follow our men back." Walker's Report, Miscellaneous File, RG 94.

31. Report of Major Landgraeber, *OR,* 385.

32. Samuel Flagg estimated 2,000 to 3,000. See Report of Captain Flagg, *OR,* 385.

33. Springer, *Soldiering in Sioux Country,* 52.

34. Cole's Report, *OR,* 375; "The Indian War," *Yankton Union and Dakotaian,* 2; John McGaugh (16th Kansas), "Powder River Expedition," *National Tribune,* May 22, 1902, 2; "Our Indian Troubles," *New York Times,* September 27, 1865, 5; *Army and Navy Journal,* October 21, 1865, 130.

35. Springer, *Soldiering in Sioux Country,* 53.

36. Hollister, *Blackhawk Mining Journal,* October 20, 1865. See also "The Great Indian War," (Central City, Colorado) *Daily Miner's Register,* September 28, 1865, 2; Hendrix, "Wichita Warriors."

37. Stepps, "The Powder River Expedition," 3. See also newspaper reprint in the *Casper Tribune Herald,* August 24 and 31, 1930, and in "War Veteran Visits Scene of Indian Battle," unidentified newspaper, c. June 1925, File In2-bat-pre, American Heritage Center.

38. Walker's Report, Miscellaneous File, RG 94.

39. Report of Major Landgraeber, *OR,* 385; Report of Captain Flagg, *OR,* 385; Report of Lt. Lewis Holland, Battery E, Battery C, 2nd Missouri, Fort Connor, September 20, 1865, *OR,* 387.

40. Springer, *Soldiering in Sioux Country,* 55.

41. Cole's Report, *OR,* 376.

42. Walker's Report, Miscellaneous File, RG 94.

CHAPTER 10: RESCUE AND REVERSAL

1. "A Diary Kept by One of the Staff of General Connor," 16.

2. Ibid., 16; Palmer, "Powder River Indian Expedition of 1865," 87.

3. Statement of Henry E. Palmer in "Application for a Medal of Honor: Case of Charles L. Thomas," August 1894, Record and Pension Office, File 392759, Records of the Office of the Adjutant General, RG 94.

4. "A Diary Kept by One of the Staff of General Connor," 16–17.

5. Thomas enlisted June 22, 1863, in Company E, 11th Ohio, and was mustered out on July 14, 1866.

6. "A Diary Kept by One of the Staff of General Connor," inside cover.

7. Letter from C. L. Thomas, Dwight, Kansas, July 2, 1894, to Charles Curtis, in "Application for a Medal of Honor: Case of Charles L. Thomas."

8. Report of the Chief of the Record and Pension Office, and Statement of Palmer, in "Application for a Medal of Honor: Case of Charles L. Thomas"; Palmer, "Powder River Indian Expedition of 1865," p 88. Luther North claimed that his brother Frank was the first to find Cole: "He [Frank] always said he was the first, and as the Pawnees said he never told a lie. He told me that when he found them, and shook hands with Cole that he (Cole) held on to his hand and cried like a child. He became peeved at Frank afterward, when Frank criticized him for leaving the timber when the Indians attacked him. That was Frank's one fault, he was outspoken. He hewed to the line, and let the chips fall where they might." See Letter from Luther North, Columbus, Nebraska, November 16, 1928, to Ellison, Folder 1, In2-bat-pre, American Heritage Center, Laramie, Wyoming.

9. Statement of Palmer, in "Application for a Medal of Honor: Case of Charles L. Thomas"; Cole's Second Report, Fort Connor, Dakota Territory, September 25, 1865, *OR*, Series I, vol. 48, pt. 1, 382.

10. Statement of Ansel Steck, in "Application for a Medal of Honor: Case of Charles L. Thomas"; "The Great Indian War," *Miner's Register*, September 28, 1865, 2. See also McGaugh, "Powder River Expedition," 2; Lewis F. Crawford Interview of J. J. Freeze, Lewis F. Crawford Papers, North Dakota Historical Society, Bismarck, North Dakota; B. F. Hill (2nd Missouri Light Artillery), "Winning the West: Col. Nelson Cole's Expedition in the Powder River in Summer of 1865," *National Tribune*, August 5, 1920, 3.

11. Lewis F. Crawford Interview of J. J. Freeze.

12. Bennett, "1865 Diary," entries for September 9, 16, and 17; Lewis F. Crawford Interview of J. J. Freeze; Springer, *Soldiering in Sioux Country*, 57.

13. Springer, *Soldiering in Sioux Country*, 56.

14. Hollister, *Blackhawk Mining Journal*, October 20, 1865.

15. Bennett further criticized Connor and the command in this passage: "It seems that this Genl. in person, with 300 soldiers was compelled to beat a masterly retreat from 150 Arapahos and does to seem to again have attempted their destruction. One must naturally look out for his own safety even if it should be in flight. Comm[ander]. is heavy on bombast, and prosecuting does not seem to have been forgotten in the great Campaign." See Bennett, "1865 Diary," September 14, 17.

16. Cole's Second Report, *OR*; Bennett, "1865 Diary," entries for September 15 and 22; "The Indian Campaign," *Nebraska City News*, 1; Stepps, "The Powder River Expedition," 3.

17. Walker's Report, Miscellaneous File, RG 94.

18. Edward B. Heaton, "A Lost Army," *Cheyenne Daily Leader,* July 28, 1875; Capt. Luther North, "The Pawnee Battalion," *National Tribune,* April 27, 1922, 3; "The Powder River Expedition," *Army and Navy Journal,* October 7, 1865, 99; "Saved from Starvation," in *Deeds of Valor: How America's Heroes Won the Medal of Honor,* vol. 2 (Detroit, MI: The Perrien-Keydel Company, 1903), 121–31.

19. Palmer, "Powder River Indian Expedition of 1865," 92.

20. Springer, *Soldiering in Sioux Country,* 61.

21. Heaton, "A Lost Army."

22. Springer, *Soldiering in Sioux Country,* 57; Bennett, "1865 Diary," entry for September 20.

23. Walker's Report, Miscellaneous File, RG 94; Cole's Second Report, *OR,*; Letter from Commanding Officer, District of Nebraska, Fort Laramie, September 25, 1865, RG 393; "The Indian Campaign," *Nebraska City News,* 1; "The Indian War," *Rocky Mountain News,* September 27, 1865, 1.

24. Lyman G. Bennett, "The Powder River Expedition," *Cheyenne Daily Leader,* September 8, 1874.

25. Pope told Wheaton in a letter of instructions that it was "the purpose to return to a purely defensive arrangement for the security of the overland routes to Salt Lake." See *Omaha Republican,* September 29, 1865, 2; Palmer, "Powder River Indian Expedition of 1865," 92; Bruce, "The Powder River Expedition of 1865," 8.

26. Letter from General Dodge, Fort Laramie, August 31, 1865, to General Pope, in Grenville M. Dodge, *Battle of Atlanta and Other Campaigns* (Council Bluffs, IA: 1910), 96.

27. Letter from Dodge, Headquarters, United States Forces, Kansas and the Territories, Fort Leavenworth, November 4, 1865, Miscellaneous File, Entry 287, Records of the Office of the Adjutant General, RG 94; Alvin M. Josephy, *The Civil War in the American West* (New York: Vintage Books, 1993), 313–14.

28. *New York Times,* September 15, 1865, 1; *Army and Navy Journal,* September 9, 1865, 1.

29. *Report of the Secretary of Interior, 1865* (Washington, D.C., 1865), 582–83.

30. *Army and Navy Journal,* September 9, 1865, 1.

31. Bruce, "The Powder River Expedition of 1865," 8.

32. Burnett, "History of the Western Division of the Powder River Expedition," 576–78; Bennett, "1865 Diary," entry for September 26.

33. Letter from Captain and Acting District Commander Bailey, Headquarters, District of Nebraska, Fort Laramie, October 7, 1865, to Colonel Cole, Letters Sent, District of Nebraska, Entry 3187, Part II, RG 393.

34. Whitelaw Reid, *Ohio in the War: Her Statesmen, Her Generals, and Soldiers,* vol. 2 (New York: Moore, Wilstach & Baldwin, 1868), 819; Statement of Perrin J. Fitch, Portland, Oregon, December 6, 1904, C1654, Folder 4, Henry Clay Bretney Papers, Wyoming State Archives, Cheyenne.

35. Palmer, "Powder River Indian Expedition of 1865," 93; Young, "Journals of Will H. Young, 1865," 382.

36. Bennett, "1865 Diary," entry for September 30.

37. Letter from Commanding Officer, District of Nebraska, Fort Laramie, September 21, 1865, RG 393; "Particulars of the Recent Indian Attack," (Central City, Colorado) *Miner's Register,* October 8, 1865, 2; Letter from H. H. Heath, Headquarters, East Sub-District of Nebraska, Fort Kearny, N.T., October 31, 1865, to Lt. John Lewis, Acting Assistant Adjutant General, District of Nebraska, Entry 3198, Part II, RG 393.

38. Letter from General Dodge, Denver, Colorado, October 1, 1865, to General Connor, Letters Sent and Received, Department of the Missouri, Entry 2127, RG 393.

39. *Miner's Register,* October 27, 1865, 2; "Military Matters," *Rocky Mountain News,* September 18, 1865, 1; Letter from Henry E. Palmer, Omaha, Nebraska, June 3, 1898, to G. C. Coutant, Powder River Expedition Vertical File, In2-bat-pre, American Heritage Center.

40. Dodge to Assistant Adjutant General Joseph Bell, Division of Missouri, November 1, 1865, Fort Leavenworth; *OR,* vol. 48, pt. 2, 336-37.

41. O. J. Hollister, "Gen. P. Edward Connor," *The* (Salt Lake City) *Daily Tribune,* December 21, 1891; Chris Madsen, *Glory Hunter: A Biography of Patrick Edward Connor* (Salt Lake City: University of Utah Press, 1990), 152–59.

CHAPTER 11: PROSPECTS

1. *Washington Evening Star,* October 3, 1865, 1.

2. *Army and Navy Journal,* October 7, 1865, 99.

3. Hollister, *Blackhawk Mining Journal,* October 20, 1865.

4. To pass the time at Fort Laramie, Bridger entertained the troopers with Indian dances and stories of gold in the Black Hills. Several promised

to go with him to the goldfields in the spring. See Young, "Journals of Will H. Young, 1865," 382.

5. *Report of the Secretary of Interior, 1865,* 721–22.

6. "From Fort Sully," *Rocky Mountain News,* October 10, 1865, 4.

7. *Report of the Secretary of Interior, 1865,* 700–701.

8. 14 *Stat.* L. 703.

9. *Report of the Commissioner of Indian Affairs 1865* (Washington, D.C.: Government Printing Office, 1866), 192.

10. Young, "Journals of Will H. Young, 1865," 382. Big Ribs had been arrested in April, sent to Fort Laramie under guard in May, and returned to his band later in the summer, where he camped near Denver, living on government rations, until summoned by the military in October. See letter from Lt. Ewell Drake, Headquarters, Fort Collins, C.T., April 29, 1865, to Acting Assistant Adjutant General, District of the Plains; Letters from Col. C. H. Porter, Headquarters, South Sub District of the Plains, Denver, July 17 and July 18, 1865, to Capt. George Price, Acting Assistant Adjutant General, Fort Laramie, Letters Received, District of Colorado, Entry 3258, Part II, Records of U.S. Army Commands, RG 393; Josephine Clements, "Big Ribs Fate,"(Fort Collins, Colorado) *Triangle Review,* June 29, 1987.

11. Letter from General Upton, Commanding District of Colorado, Denver, October 3, 1865, to General Wheaton, Letters Received, District of Nebraska, Entry 3198, and Letter of Instructions from Brevet Major Commanding District of Nebraska, Fort Laramie, October 18, 1865, to Big Ribs, Letters Sent, District of Nebraska, Entry 3187, Part II, RG 393.

12. Memorandum of the Chiefs and Head-Men Whom Big Ribs Is to Visit, October 18, 1865, Letters Sent, District of Nebraska, RG 393.

13. Young, "Journals of Will H. Young, 1865," 382.

14. (Central City, Colorado) *Miner's Register,* October 18, 1865, 2; *Denver Journal,* October 20, 1865.

15. "Complimentary Supper to General Connor," *Rocky Mountain News,* October 16, 1865, 4.

16. Palmer, "Powder River Indian Expedition of 1865," 93.

17. Ovando [O. J. Hollister], "General Connor's Late Expedition," *Miner's Register,* October 22, 1865, 2. See also Hollister, "Gen. P. Edward Connor"; *General Laws and Joint Resolutions, Memorials and Private Acts, Passed at the Fifth Session of the Legislative Session of the Legislative Assembly of the Territory of Colorado* (Central City: David C. Collier, 1866), 180.

18. Hollister, "Gen. P. Edward Connor"; C. G. Coutant, *History of Wyoming,* 533; Palmer, "Powder River Indian Expedition of 1865," 95; "Gen. Connor," *Nebraska Republican,* March 30, 1866, 1.

19. "Another Indian Raid," *Miner's Register,* October 22, 2; J. D. Turner, "Indian Fight on Thursday," *Miner's Register,* October 24, 2.

20. *Rocky Mountain News,* October 16, 3, October 30, 1, and November 27, 1; "More Indian Depredations," *Miner's Register,* October 22, 1865, 2; Daniel S. Day, "Fort Sedgwick," *Colorado History* 42 (Fall, 1965), 32.

21. Telegram from Bvt. Maj. Gen. Frank Wheaton, Fort Laramie, October 28, 1865, Grenville Dodge Papers, Iowa Historical Society, Des Moines, Iowa.

22. Account of N. A. Rice, in "The Indian War," *Platsmouth* (Nebraska) *New Herald,* November 15, 1865, 2; "Indian Murder and Depredations," *Nebraska Republican,* November 17, 1865, 1; J. E. Richey to Dear Cope, Kearney House, November 15, 1865, in "From the First Nebraska," *Nebraska Republican,* December 1, 1865, 2; "From the Plains," *Oskaloosa* (Kansas) *Independent,* November 11, 1865, 3;

23. Bvt. Brig. Gen. H. H. Heath, Fort Kearney, November 12, in "A Fight with the Indians," *Nebraska Republican,* November 17, 1865, 2; J. E. Richey to Dear Cope, *Nebraska Republican,* December 1, 1865, 2; "E," to MESSRS. EDITORS, Fort Kearney, N.T., Nov. 12, 1865, in "Indian Expedition," *Nebraska Republican,* December 1, 1865; Grenville M. Dodge, "Diary," Grenville M. Dodge Papers, Iowa Historical Society, Des Moines, Iowa, 195–96.

24. "Indian Murders and Depredations," 1.

25. Emily Boynton O'Brien, "Army Life at Fort Sedgwick, Colorado," *Colorado Magazine* 6 (September 1929), 173.

26. "Indian Treaties," *New York Times,* November 12, 1865, 4.

27. This is the only instance in the Indian War of 1865 where whites reported witnessing torture.

28. Thomas R. Davis, "Massacre on the Smoky Hill Route," *Nebraska Republican,* December 15, 1865, 2.

29. Letter from Capt. George Williford, Fort Connor, November 26, 1865, Letters Sent, District of the Platte, Entry 6181, RG 393.

30. 11th Ohio Regimental Returns, December 1865–January 1866, Records of the 11th Ohio Volunteer Cavalry, RG 94; Telegram from Maj. A. J. Squires, Commanding Officer, Fort Caspar, to Col. Henry Maynadier, Telegrams Received; and Colonel Maynadier, January 11, 1866, to A. J. Squires, Letters Sent, Records of the District of the Platte, RG 393.

31. Letter from Maynadier, Fort Laramie, December 29, 1865, to General Wheaton, Letters Sent, District of Nebraska, RG 393.
32. Letter from Wheaton, Omaha, December 30, 1865, to Maynadier, Letters Sent, District of Nebraska, RG 393.
33. W. Cullum, *Biographical Register of the Officers and Graduates of the U.S. Military Academy at West Point,* 3rd ed. rev., vol. 2 (Boston and New York: Houghton Mifflin and Company, 1891), 452–53; Henry Maynadier File W375, Commissions Branch, Records of the Office of the Adjutant General, RG 94.

CHAPTER 12: SPOTTED TAIL'S DAUGHTER

1. The Management of Our Indian Affairs," *Rocky Mountain News,* December 1, 1865, 1.
2. George H. Holliday, *On the Plains in '65* (n. p., 1883), 90–91.
3. Maynadier reported the subsequent course of events in two similar letters. See Maynadier, Fort Laramie, March 9, 1866, to Acting Assistant Adjutant General, District of Nebraska, Letters Sent, West Sub-District of Nebraska, Records of the District of the Platte, Entry 614, Records of United States Army Continental Commands, RG 393, and Maynadier, Fort Laramie, March 9, 1866, to Hon. D. N. Cooley, Commissioner of Indian Affairs, Washington, D.C., Letters Received, Upper Platte Agency, Records of the Bureau of Indian Affairs, RG 75, National Archives. Hereafter cited as RG 75.
4. Eugene F. Ware wrote a detailed story about the girl, her love of white ways, and her tragic end in "The Daughter of Shan-Tag-A-Lisk," *The Agora* 2 (January 1893), 45–61, an early Kansas literary magazine, and included it as an appendix in *The Indian War of 1864.* See Ware, *Indian War of 1864,* 407–18. Ware identified the girl as Ah-ho-ap-pa (Fallen Leaf) as do others, but Maynadier and Reverend Wright referred to her as Monica. Indian sources named her as Mini-aku (Brings Water) and Hinzmwin (Yellow Girl or Yellow Buckskin Girl). See Statement by A. Wright in "Spotted Tail's Daughter," *New York Times,* July 15, 1877, 9; Letter from George W. Colhoff, Pine Ridge, October 28, 1898, to John Hunton, Item MP-98, Fort Laramie Collections, Fort Laramie National Historic Site, Wyoming; George E. Hyde, *Spotted Tail's Folk: A History of the Brule Sioux* (Norman: University of Oklahoma Press, 1961), 109. Over time rumors continued to grow that she had been in love with a white army officer. For example, see "An Indian Romance: The Love and Death of Spotted Tail's Daughter," *New Northwest,* July 23, 1875; "The Burial of Spotted Tail's Daughter," (Washington, D.C.)

Evening Star, July 22, 1876, 3; G. O. Hauser, *A Story of Fallen Leaf* (Guernsey, WY: *The Guernsey Gazette,* n.d.), 2; E. B. Wilson, *Cabin Days in Wyoming* (E. B. Wilson, 1939), 38–41; Grant L. Shumway, *History of Western Nebraska and Its People* (Lincoln: The Western Publishing & Engraving Company, 1921), 85–86; and L. G. Flannery, "The Story and Legend of Fallen Leaf," (Lingle, Wyoming) *Guide-Reivew,* November 3, 1960, 1.

5. "Mo Ni Ka Spotted Tail's Daughter," *The Liberty* (Missouri) *Tribune,* December 6, 1867, 1.

6. Ware, "The Daughter of Shan-Tag-A-Lisk," 57.

7. Letter from Maynadier, Fort Laramie, March 22, 1866, to Commissioner of Indian Affairs, Telegram Book, Fort Laramie Post Records, RG 393.

8. Letters of Maynadier, March 9, 1866, RG 75 and 393.

9. Ibid.

10. John Hunton, *Early Days in Wyoming: A Short History of Old Fort Laramie* (Torrington, WY: The Goshen News, 1928), 4–5.

11. "Mo Ni Ka," 1.

12. "Animal Painter of the Rocky Mountains: John D. Howland," *Rocky Mountain News,* July 27, 1902. Captain Howland was an eyewitness to the burial.

13. Statement of Wright in "Spotted Tail's Daughter," *New York Times,* July 15, 1877, 9. See also "Mo Ni Ka," 1; "Animal Painter Howland."

14. Henry B. Carrington, *The Indian Question* (Boston: DeWolfe & Fiske Company, 1909), 9.

15. Telegram from Col. Henry Maynadier, Fort Laramie, March 12, 1866, to General Wheaton, Telegram Book, Entry 618, Records of the District of the Platte, RG 393.

16. Letter from Maynadier, Fort Laramie, March 20, 1866, Letters Sent, West Sub-District of Nebraska, Records of the District of the Platte, RG 393.

17. Letter from Col. Henry Maynadier, Fort Laramie, March 22, 1866, to Commissioner of Indian Affairs, Telegram Book, District of the Platte, RG 393; *Official Roster of the Soldiers of the State of Ohio,* 548; Letter from Maynadier, Fort Laramie, March 20, 1866, to Acting Assistant Adjutant General J. Service, Letters Sent, West Sub-District of Nebraska, Records of the District of the Platte, Entry 614, RG 393; Hyde, *Spotted Tail's Folk,* 110–11.

18. In the fall of 1865, military authorities had negotiated treaties with some bands of Sioux and invited others to meet in the spring of 1866.

Councils were to be held at Fort Laramie (May 20), Fort Sully (May 20), Fort Rice (June 1), Fort Berthold (June 20), and Fort Union (July 5).

CHAPTER 13: CONCLUSIONS

1. Letter from Grenville Dodge, Fort Leavenworth, August 2, 1865, Letters Sent, Department of the Missouri, Entry 2081, Records of U.S. Army Commands, RG 393.

2. Hollister, "General Connor's Late Expedition," 2.

3. Letter from "M," February 26, 1865, in (Omaha) *Nebraska Republican,* March 7, 1865, 2.

4. Letter from Grenville Dodge, Fort Leavenworth, August 2, 1865, Letters Sent, Department of the Missouri, RG 393.

5. Ibid.; Richard N. Ellis, "Volunteer Soldiers in the West, 1865," *Military Affairs* 34 (April 1970), 54.

6. General Connor, Julesburg, Colorado, June 20, 1865, Letters Sent, District of the Plains, Entry 3254, RG 393.

7. Hollister, "General Connor's Late Expedition," 2. See also Hollister, "Gen. P. Edward Connor."

8. Fred Albert Shannon, *The Organization and Administration of the Union Army, 1861–1865* (Glouchester, MA: Peter Smith, 1965), chapter 2.

9. Afton et al., *Cheyenne Dog Soldiers,* 180; Letter from Col. William Collins, Fort Laramie, February 15, 1865, to John Pratt, Acting Assistant Adjutant General, District of Nebraska, William Collins Papers, FF5 Letters 51–59, Denver Public Library, Denver, Colorado. This also appears in *OR,* Series I, vol. 48, pt. 1, 92-98.

10. Dodge, Fort Leavenworth, November 1, 1865, to Assistant Adjutant General Joseph Bell, Division of Missouri, *OR,* vol. 48, pt. 2, 336; Bruce, "The Powder River Expedition of 1865," 7; *The American Annual Cyclopedia and Register of Important Events of the Year 1865* (New York: D. Appleton & Company, 1866), 180, noted that the grasshoppers were especially virulent that year.

11. Dodge, Fort Leavenworth, to Assistant Adjutant General Joseph Bell, Division of Missouri, *OR,* vol. 48, pt. 2, 336–37.

12. Hollister, "General Connor's Late Expedition," 2.

13. Ellis, "Volunteer Soldiers in the West," 54.

14. *Army and Navy Journal,* October 7, 1865, 99.

15. *Rocky Mountain News,* August 23, 1865, 1.

16. Letter from Major General Dodge, reproduced in William Devine, "The Powder River Expedition," typescript, Item In2-bat-pre, American Heritage Center, Laramie, Wyoming.

17. Asst. Adj. Gen. George Price, Denver, September 25, 1865, to Pope, Miscellaneous Files, Records of the Office of the Adjutant General, RG 94.

18. Letter from Dodge, Fort Leavenworth, November 1, 1865, to Asst. Adj. Gen. Joseph Bell, *OR,* vol. 48, pt. 2, 348.

19. "Our Indian Policy," *Nebraska Republican,* November 10, 1865, 1.

20. Letter from Dodge, Fort Leavenworth, August 2, 1865, Letters Sent, Department of the Missouri, RG 393.

21. Dodge to Bell, *OR,* vol. 48, pt. 2, 337.

22. Maurice Matloff, ed., *American Military History* (Washington, D.C.: Office of the Chief of Military History, 1969), 282; Pete Maslowski, "A Study of Morale in Civil War Soldiers," *Military Affairs* 34 (December 1970), 122–26.

23. Hollister, "General Connor's Late Expedition," 2.

24. Ellis, "Volunteer Soldiers in the West," 53–54.

25. Letter from Dodge, Fort Leavenworth, August 2, 1865.

26. For example, the *Army and Navy Journal,* October 7, 1865, reported that "about 300 men from the 14th, 15th, and 32nd Illinois regimens, comprising, it is said, some of the best soldiers in their regimens, deserted some time ago to avoid being sent to the plains. They returned a few days afterward." While the desire to return home may indeed have been an incentive to desert, the rate remained constant throughout the nineteenth century. See John D. McDermott, "Were They Really Rogues? Desertion in the Nineteenth-Century U.S. Army," *Nebraska History* 78 (Winter 1997), 165–74.

27. See letter from Dodge, Fort Leavenworth, August 2, 1865; Palmer, "Powder River Indian Expedition of 1865," 66; *Army and Navy Journal,* September 2, 1865, 18; Bennett, "1865 Diary," entry for July 18.

28. Springer, *Soldiering in Sioux Country,* 17.

29. Royal B. Hassrick, *The Sioux: Life and Customs of a Warrior Society* (Norman: University of Oklahoma Press, 1964), 33–34; Stanley Vestal, *New Sources of Indian History, 1850–1891* (Norman: University of Oklahoma Press, 1934), 139.

30. Grinnell, *The Fighting Cheyennes,* 9.

31. Afton et al., *Cheyenne Dog Soldiers,* xvii; Berthrong, *Southern Cheyennes,* 68–69; Grinnell, *The Fighting Cheyennes,* 14; James T. King, *War Eagle:*

Life of General Eugene A. Carr (Lincoln: University of Nebraska Press, 1963), 94–95.

32. H. D. Hampton, "The Powder River Expedition, 1865," *Montana* 14 (Autumn 1964), 7; *Report of the Special Indian Commissioners 1867* (Washington, D.C., 1868), 196; Alvin M. Josephy, *The Civil War in the American West* (New York: Vintage Books, 1993), 315.

33. Ware, *Indian War of 1864*, 353–54.

34. Palmer, "Powder River Indian Expedition of 1865," 85.

35. Letter from Major General Dodge, reproduced in William Devine, "The Powder River Expedition."

36. *Report of the Secretary of Interior, 1865*, 393.

37. William Devine, "The Connor Expedition."

38. Hubbard, "A Little Taste of Indian Warfare," 48.

39. Henry B. Carrington, *The Indian Question* (Boston: Wolfe & Fiske Company, 1909), 11.

40. Robert M. Utley, "The Contribution of the Frontier to the American Military Tradition," in *The Harmon Memorial Lectures in Military History, 1959–1987*, ed. Harry R. Borowski (Washington, D.C.: Office of Air Force History, 1988), 528.

41. Letter from Col. William Collins, Fort Laramie, February 15, 1865, to John Pratt, Acting Assistant Adjutant General, District of Nebraska, William Collins Papers, FF5 Letters 51–59, Denver Public Library. This is printed in *OR,* vol. 48, pt. 1, 92–98.

42. However, the appearance of the breech-loading weapon in the late 1860s began to change everything. It gave the Indian confidence in himself, enabling him to reload on horseback with great rapidity. He could fire several shots from behind his horse while troops advanced within 100 yards, and by the mid-1870s, a significant number of Sioux and Cheyennes had these weapons. "It was the breech-loading gun," declared Crook, "that caused the annihilation of General Custer and that part of his command." See "General Crook Set Right," *Army and Navy Register,* June 12, 1886, 373.

43. Grinnell, *The Fighting Cheyennes*, 213.

44. Letter from Dodge to Assistant Adjutant General Bell, Division of Missouri, November 1, 1865, Fort Leavenworth; *OR,* vol. 48, pt. 2, 344–45; John D. McDermott, *A Guide to the Indian Wars of the West* (Lincoln: University of Nebraska Press, 1998), 18.

45. Hyde, *Life of George Bent,* 222.

46. Hassrick, *The Sioux,* 225; Interviews of Good Seat (70–71), George Sword (99), Thomas Tyon, William Garnett, Thunder Bear, George

Sword, and John Blunt (106), and Short Feather (115), in James R. Walker, *Lakota Belief and Ritual,* ed. Raymond J. DeMallie and Elaine A. Jahner (Lincoln: University of Nebraska Press Bison Book, 1991); Carrington, *The Indian Question,* 9.

47. Testimony of Tenodore Ten Eyck, July 5, 1867, Special Commission to Investigate Indian Affairs, 1867, Records of the Office of Indian Affairs, RG 75. In considering the matter of mutilation, one clear-thinking soldier commented, "And why should we pride ourselves on not mutilating the dead, while we have no scruples as to the extent to which we mutilate the living?" See James Anson Farrar, *Military Manners and Customs* (London: Chatto & Winders, 1885), 158.

48. Letter from Connor to Cole, Fort Laramie, July 4, 1865, Letters Sent, District of the Plains, RG 393.

49. House Executive Document 5, 39th Congress, 2nd session, 1867, 1. *Letter from the Secretary of War.*

50. "The Indian Campaign," *New York Times,* March 31, 1865, 1.

51. Dodge to Pope, September 15, 1865, Horse Shoe Station, Letters Sent, Department of the Missouri, RG 393; Palmer, "Powder River Indian Expedition of 1865," 94–95.

52. Doyle, "The Evolution of the Bozeman Trail," 6–7.

53. *Montana Post,* October 14, 1865.

54. "Report of Col. James A. Sawyers," *South Dakota Historical Review* 2 (October 1936), 39–40.

55. It is common practice to accept Indian estimates of their dead and wounded at face value and characterize white estimates of enemy casualties as over inflated and self-serving. Yet, in some cases, reports by eyewitnesses from the field bear scrutiny. For example, General Dodge's representative with Cole informed his commander that he saw over 200 dead Indians that were killed in September fights. Also, Indian accounts rarely mention the deaths of those who may have died from wounds received in such battles. See Letter from Major General Dodge, reproduced in Devine, "The Powder River Expedition."

56. Cole's First Report; Bennett, "1865 Diary," entry for September 5; "The Indian War," *Yankton Union and Dakotaian,* 2; Letter from Commanding Officer, District of Nebraska, Fort Laramie, September 25, 1865, to General Dodge, Letters Sent, District of Nebraska, Entry 3191, RG 393; "The Indian Campaign," *Nebraska City News,* October 28, 1865, 1; Grinnell, *The Fighting Cheyennes,* 205.

57. Anthony McGinnis, "Strike and Retreat: Intertribal Warfare and the Powder River War, 1865–1868," *Montana* 30 (Autumn 1980), 34–35;

George E. Hyde, *Red Cloud's Folk: A History of the Oglala Sioux* (Norman: University of Oklahoma Press, 1976), 133.

58. Burnett, "History of the Western Division of the Powder River Expedition," 577–78.

59. Palmer, "Powder River Indian Expedition of 1865," 95.

60. Letter from Henry E. Palmer, Omaha, Nebraska, June 20, 1904, to Stephen H. Fairfield, Military History of the 11th Kansas, MS 617, Folder 12, Kansas Historical Society.

61. The Southern Cheyennes returned to their homeland in December 1865. See Grinnell, *The Fighting Cheyennes,* 236.

EPILOGUE

1. Maj. J. H. Evans, Fort Laramie, April 7, 1886, to Adjutant General, Washington D.C., Letter Sent, Fort Laramie Post Records, United States Army Commands, RG 393.

2. Special Orders No. 30, West Sub-District of Nebraska, March 16, 1866, and Special Orders No. 11, Fort Laramie, March 20, 1866, RG 393; Caspar Collins Military Service Record, Records of the Office of the Adjutant General, RG 94; "Funeral Obsequies," Caspar Collins Biographical File, B-C692-c-m, American Heritage Center, Laramie, Wyoming.

3. (Hillsboro, Ohio) *Highland News,* October 26, 1880; Elsie Johnson Ayers, *Highland Pioneer Sketches and Family Genealogies* (Springfield, OH: H. S. Skinner & Son, 1971), 452–53, 542–43.

4. Fairfield, "The Eleventh Kansas Regiment at Platte Bridge," 352–53.

5. Martin Anderson Military Service Record, RG 94; "Martin Anderson," in *The United States Biographical Dictionary,* Kansas Volume (Chicago and Kansas City: S. Lewis & Company, Publishers, 1879), 826-27; "Martin Anderson," in *Memorial Records, Lincoln Post No. 1, Department of Kansas G. A. R. Topeka, Kansas* (Topeka, Kansas, n. d.), 50; "Biographical Sketch Prepared from an Interview, April, 1897," Fort Caspar Collections, Fort Caspar; William E. Connelley, *History of Kansas* (Chicago: The American Historical Society, 1928), 844; "Martin Anderson, The First Republican," *Topeka Mail and Kansas Breeze,* May 22, 1896, 63.

6. Patrick Connor, File 4700 ACP 1887, Records of the Office of the Adjutant General, RG 94; Hollister, "Gen. P. Edward Connor"; "Patrick Connor," *Sacramento Union,* December 18, 1891; Wilson and Fiske, *Appletons' Cyclopedia of American Biography,* 2: 708–9; Leo P. Kibby, "Patrick Edward Connor, First Gentile of Utah," *Journal of the*

West, 425–33; Patrick Edward Rogen, "Edward Connor" (M.A. thesis, Department of History, Utah University, 1952); James F. Varley, *Brigham and the Brigadier: General Patrick Connor and His California Volunteers in Utah and along the Overland Trail* (Tucson, AZ: Westernlore Press, 1989); Charles C. Goodwin, "General P. E. Connor," in *As I Remember Them* (Salt Lake City: Salt Lake Commercial Club, 1913), 265–69.

7. Walter B. Stevens, *History of St. Louis, The Fourth City,* vol. 2 (St. Louis: The S. J. Clarke Publishing Company, 1909), 230–31; *In Memoriam, Nelson Cole* (Military Order of the Loyal Legion of the United States, Commandery of the State of Missouri, 1899); Palmer, "Powder River Indian Expedition of 1865," 108; Coutant, *History of Wyoming* (Laramie, WY: Chaplin, Spafford & Mathison, Printers, 1899), 540.

8. "Major General Grenville Mellen Dodge," typescript, Folder 87, Dodge Papers, Iowa Historical Society Des Moines, Iowa; "Builder of Union Pacific Railroad Dead," *Kansas City Journal,* January 4, 1916.

9. Nicholas O'Brien Pension File; Military Service Record, RG 94; (Cheyenne) *Wyoming Tribune,* November 28, 1874, 1, and September 24, 1944, 1; Nicholas O'Brien Vertical File, Wyoming State Archives, Cheyenne; Robert C. Morris, *Collections of the Wyoming Historical Society* (Cheyenne: Wyoming Historical Society, 1897), 172; "Demise of a Veteran," unidentified newspaper clipping, Nicholas J. O'Brien File B-Ob6-nj, American Heritage Center, Laramie; "Captain O'Brien, Pioneer, Dies," *Rocky Mountain News,* July 30, 1916, 4.

10. McDermott, "Introduction," in Ware, *Indian War of 1864,* iv–vii; "He Is Laid to Rest: The Remains of H. B. Ware Arrived This Morning," unidentified newspaper clipping, c. 1903, Eugene F. Ware Biographical File, Kansas State Historical Society, Topeka; *Ware Family Chronology* (n.p., 1906); James C. Malin, "Eugene F. Ware's Literary Chronology," *Kansas Historical Quarterly* 37 (Autumn 1971), 314; Charles S. Gleed, "Eugene Fitch Ware," 19–41, and J. S. West, "Eugene Ware," 65–71, *Kansas Historical Collections,* vol. 13 (Topeka: Kansas Historical Society, 1913–1914).

11. Copy of letter from Bretney to Lawrence Wilson in 1873; Henry Clay Bretney, Jr., "My Father"; Statement of Magnus J. Cohn (Company B, 2nd Cavalry), September 11, 1906; Letter from Mr. Dalton, Chief Board of Review, Bureau of Pensions, January 3, 1907, to Mary Bretney, in Bretney Pension File, Records of the Veterans Administration, RG 15; Case of Henry C. Bretney, File 3032, MM, Records of the

Advocate General, RG 153, National Archives; General Order No. 40, Headquarters, Department of the Missouri.

12. Henry Maynadier File W375, Commissions Branch, RG 94.

13. George E. Hyde, *Spotted Tail's Folk,* 301-2.

14. John D. McDermott, "Roman Nose," in *American National Biography,* ed. John A. Garraty and Mark C. Carnes, vol. 17 (New York: University of Oxford Press, 1999), 794–95; For an account of the battle in which Roman Nose died, see John Monnett, *The Battle of Beecher Island, and the Indian War of 1867–1869* (Miwot, CO: University of Colorado Press, 1992).

15. H. L. Lubers, "William Bent Family and the Indians of the Plains," *Colorado Magazine* 12 (January 1936), 19–22; Dan L. Thrapp, *Encyclopedia of Frontier Biography,* vol. 1 (Lincoln: University of Nebraska Press, 1988), 97–99; Hyde, *Life of George Bent;* George Bent, "Forty Years with the Cheyennes," ed. George E. Hyde, *The Frontier* (October 1905–February 1906).

16. "His Long Life Ended," *Denver Republican,* October 5, 1894; John Milton Chivington, Isabella widow, Pension File 41647, Records of the Veterans Administration, RG 15.

17. "A Chivington Card," *Omaha Weekly Herald,* June 10, 1868, 4.

18. Letter from Mrs. Sarah Chivington, Nebraska City, Nebraska, February 4, 1895, to Pension Examiner Sherman Williams, Chivington Pension File.

19. Deposition of Isabella Chivington, December 31, 1894, Chivington Pension File.

20. For example, see "The Battle of Sand Creek," *The Denver Times,* September 13, 1883, which is almost a verbatim account.

21. Ronald Becher, *Massacre along the Medicine Road: A Social History of the Indian War of 1864 in Nebraska Territory* (Caldwell, ID: Caxton Press, 1999), 407. See also Gary Roberts, "Sand Creek, Tragedy and Symbol" (Ph.D. dissertation, University of Oklahoma, 1984), 658–65.

22. *Omaha Daily Herald,* April 5, 1867.

23. Chivington Pension File.

24. "Pioneer Woman," *Denver Post,* March 11, 1910, 14.

PRIMARY SOURCES

National Archives Records

Record Group 15. Records of the Veteran's Administration. Pension Files: Henry Bretney, John Chivington, Anna Cole, Amos Custard, Winfield S. Davis, William Ellsworth, John Friend, John A. Harris, William H. Hartshorn, Oscar Jewett, R. R. Mitchell, Alonzo P. Richards, George Rowan, and James W. Shrader.

Record Group 75. Records of the Office of Indian Affairs.

Claims against Hostile Indians: Claim of Henry A. Bateman, no. 1084; John Richard, no. 1043; and James H Sutherland, no. 3367.

Special Commission to Investigate Indian Affairs, 1867.

Upper Platte Indian Agency, Letters Received.

Record Group 92. Records of the Office of the Quartermaster General.

Consolidated Correspondence File for Forts.

Consolidated Correspondence File, Department of the Platte.

Record Group 94. Records of the Office of the Adjutant General.

Appointment, Commission, and Personal Branch (ACP).

Commission Branch of the Adjutant General's Office.

Miscellaneous Files.

Military Service Records: Martin Anderson, William Brown, Nelson Cole, Caspar Collins, William Ellsworth, William Fouts, William Hall, John A. Harris, William H. Hartshorn, Nicholas J. O'Brien, Robert F. Patton, George Rowan, Samuel Walker, and Eugene F. Ware.

Records and Pension Office.

Chronological List of Battles with Data on the Disposition of the Wounded; Alphabetical Index to Causalities in Indian Fights.

Application for a Medal of Honor: Case of Charles L. Thomas, File 392759.

Records of the Surgeon General: "Classified Return of Wounded and Injuries Received in Action on 29th Day of August 1865, Battle of Tongue River, D.T."

Records of the 11th Ohio Volunteer Cavalry.

Records of the 11th Kansas Volunteer Cavalry.

Records of the 7th Iowa Volunteer Cavalry.

Record Group 123. Records of the United States Court of Claims.

Indian Depredation Claims: Claims of Joseph Bissonette, no. 1442; G. D. Connelly and E. D. Bulen, no. 2849; Samuel R. Darland, no. 366; William E. Dillon and John H. Maxon, no. 2850; Jules Ecoffey and Joseph Bissonette, no. 2208; Holan Godfrey, no. 2559; Louis Guinard, no. 1319, no. 7806, and no. 1319; William H. Harlow, no. 2990; Clement Lamoureaux and James Bordeaux, no. 732; John A. Morrow, no. 888; Louisa Pablo, no. 6133; and Leon F. Pallady, no. 8266.

Record Group 153. Records of the Judge Advocate General.

  Courts-Martial Files: Proceedings of a General Court-Martial for Henry Clay Bretney, September 1865, no. 3032.

Record Group 159. Records of the Inspector General.

  Letters Received.

Record Group 391. Records of United States Regular Army Mobile Units, 1821-1942.

Records of the 18th Infantry.

Record Group 393. Records of United States Army Continental Commands.

Records of the District of Colorado.

Records of the District of Nebraska.

Records of the Mountain District.

Records of the District of the Plains.

Records of the District of the Platte.

Records of the Department of Dakota.

Records of the Department of Kansas.

Records of the Department of the Missouri.

Records of the Department of the Platte.

Records of the Division of the Missouri.

Newspapers

Alma (Kansas) *Enterprise*

Army and Navy Journal

Army and Navy Register

Blackhawk (Colorado) *Mining Journal*

Buffalo (Wyoming) *Voice*
(Burlington, Kansas) *Osage County Chronicle*
Casper Star Tribune
(Central City, Colorado) *The Miner's Register*
Cheyenne (Wyoming) *Daily Leader*
Chicago Tribune
Dalton (Nebraska) *Delegate*
Denver Journal
Denver Post
Denver Republican
Denver Times
Eaton (Ohio) *Register*
Emporia (Kansas) *Gazette*
(Fort Collins, Colorado) *Beacon*
(Fort Collins, Colorado) *Triangle Review*
Fort Randall Independent
Greeley (Colorado) *News*
Helena (Montana) *Journal*
(Hillsboro, Ohio) *Highland Weekly News*
Kansas City Times
Lander (Wyoming) *Eagle*
The Laramie (Wyoming) *Republican Boomerang*
(Lawrence) *Kansas Weekly Tribune*
Leavenworth (Kansas) *Conservative*
The Liberty (Missouri) *Tribune*
Lincoln (Nebraska) *Republican*
Lincoln (Nebraska) *Star*
Montana Post
Natrona County (Wyoming) *Tribune*
Nebraska City News
New Northwest
New York Times
Omaha Bee
Omaha Daily Herald
Omaha Republican
(Omaha) *Nebraska [Daily] Republican*
(Omaha) *Nebraska Weekly Republican*
Oskaloosa (Kansas) *Independent*
Platsmouth (Nebrsaka) *New Herald*
Rapid City (South Dakota) *Journal*

Riley County (Manhattan, Kansas) *Democrat*
(Rawlins, Wyoming) *Carbon County Journal*
Rawlins (Wyoming) *Republican*
(Denver) *Rocky Mountain Herald*
(Denver) *Rocky Mountain News*
Sacramento (California) *Union*
(Salt Lake City) *Daily Tribune*
(Salt Lake City) *Union Vedette*
San Bruno (California) *Herald*
San Francisco Chronicle
Sheridan (Wyoming) *Post*
Sheridan (Wyoming) *Press*
Sioux City (Iowa) *Journal*
South Bend (Indiana) *Tribune*
Springfield (Massachusetts) *Republican*
St. Charles (Missouri) *Banner*
St. Charles (Missouri) *Journal*
St. Joseph (Missouri) *Gazette*
St. Louis Globe Democrat
Topeka (Kansas) *Daily Capital*
Topeka Mail and Kansas Breeze
(Washington, D.C.) *Evening Star*
(Washington, D.C.) *National Tribune*
Wichita (Kansas) *Beacon*
Wichita (Kansas) *Eagle*
Wyoming Derrick
The Wyoming Pioneer
Yankton (South Dakota) *Union and Dakotaian*

Manuscripts and Special Collections

American Heritage Center, Laramie, Wyoming.
  Fred Baum Collection.
  Grace Hebard Collection: Files for Caspar Collins, William Devine, Luther North, Nicholas O'Brien, and Powder River expedition.
  Paul Henderson Collection.
  Remi Nadeau Papers.
  "The Powder River Indian Expedition: A Diary Kept by One of the Staff of General Connor."
  J. W. Vaughn Collection.
  Frank Tubbs Collection.

Beinecke Rare Book and Manuscript Library, Yale University, New Haven, Connecticut.
  Thomas Moonlight Papers.
Brigham Young University, Provo, Utah.
  Robert S. Ellison Papers.
  W. M. Camp Papers.
Casper Community College, Casper, Wyoming.
  Finn Burnett Papers.
  Robert B. David Collection.
  Alfred J. Mokler Collection.
  Platte Bridge Vertical File.
Colorado State University Special Collections, Fort Collins, Colorado.
  William O. Collins Collection.
Denver Public Library, Denver, Colorado.
  George Bent Letters.
  W. M. Camp Papers.
  William O. Collins Family Papers.
  Robert S. Ellison Collection.
  William Henry Jackson Papers.
  Luther North Papers.
Fort Caspar Collections, Fort Caspar, Wyoming.
  L. C. Bishop Papers.
  John Maxon Collection: Letters and Statements of John H. Crumb, Robert S. Ellison, S. H. Fairfield, and John Furay.
  John Shrader Papers.
Fort Laramie National Historic Site Collections, Fort Laramie, Wyoming.
  Files on Ah-ho-ap-pa, William Fouts, Adolph Hannkamer, and George Walker.
Iowa Historical Society, Des Moines, Iowa.
  Grenville Dodge Papers.
Johnson County Public Library, Buffalo, Wyoming.
  Burton Hill, "Powder River Expedition of Major Patrick E. Connor, 1865, Johnson County Historical Society Meeting, May, 1964," typescript.
Kansas State Historical Society, Topeka, Kansas.
  William E. Connelley Collection: Letters of George M. Walker and George Drew.
  Indian Depredation and Battles (Clippings), Vol. 3.
  Kansas Scrap-Books, Biography E, Vol. 1.

Military History of the 11th Kansas Collection: Letters from Patrick Connor, Ferdinand Erhardt, Stephen H. Fairfield, Henry E. Palmer, James W. Shrader, and Charles Waring.

Preston Plumb Papers.

Eugene F. Ware Biographical File.

Library of Congress, Washington, D.C.

Manuscript Division:

Edwin R. Nash, "Diary."

Natrona County Public Library, Casper, Wyoming.

Fort Caspar Vertical File.

Nebraska Historical Society, Lincoln, Nebraska.

A. E. Sheldon Collection.

State Historic Preservation Office Files.

Newberry Library, Chicago, Illinois.

James E. Enos, "Recollections of the Plains."

North Dakota Historical Society, Bismarck, North Dakota.

Lewis F. Crawford Interview of J. J. Freeze, Lewis F. Crawford Papers.

Pioneer Museum, Douglas, Wyoming.

Peyton Scrapbooks.

Rawlins County Public Library, Pierre, South Dakota.

S.D. Sioux Indians Vertical File.

Sheridan County Fulmer Library, Sheridan, Wyoming.

Susan Badger Doyle, "The Evolution of the Bozeman Trail."

Southwest Museum, Los Angeles, California.

George Bird Grinnell Collection: Statements of White Bull and Big Rascal.

"Sioux, Cheyenne, Arapaho War Customs."

Archives and Manuscripts Section, West Virginia Collection, West Virginia University Library, Charlestown, West Virginia.

Andrew J. Squires Letters from Fort Caspar 1865.

Wyoming State Archives, State Parks and Cultural Resources Department, Cheyenne, Wyoming.

Lyman Bennett, "1865 Diary."

Henry Bretney Papers.

W. C. Coutant Papers.

Works Progress Administration (WPA) Collection.

Forts—General File.

File No. 1912, Vital Records Services.

John Hunton Papers.

William Jackson File.

Nicholas O'Brien Vertical File.

WPA Collection: George Kelley, Subject File 1189, S–620.

Articles and Books

Adams, Charles W. "Indian Campaign." *National Tribune,* February 11, 1898, 6.

Afton, Jean, David Fridtjof Halaas, and Andrew E. Masich, with Richard Ellis. *Cheyenne Dog Soldiers: A Ledgerbook History of Coups and Combat.* Denver: Colorado Historical Society and the University Press of Colorado, 1997. Contains ledgerbook art depicting incidents that occurred in 1865.

The American Annual Cyclopedia and Register of Important Events of the Year 1865. New York: D. Appleton & Company, 1866.

Anderson, Martin. "Martin Anderson." *Memorial Records, Lincoln Post No. 1, Department of Kansas G. A. R. Topeka, Kansas.* Topeka, KS: n.d.

Athearn, Robert G., ed. "From Illinois to Montana in 1866: The Diary of Perry A. Burgess." *Pacific Northwest Quarterly* 41 (January, 1950), 43–65.

Baylers, Robert. "Hanging of Two Face." *National Tribune,* January 26, 1911, 8.

———. "Soldiering on the Plains." *National Tribune,* March 3, 1910, 7.

Bettelyoun, Susan Bordeaux, and Josephine Waggoner. *With My Own Eyes: A Lakota Woman Tells Her People's History,* ed. and intro. by Emily Levine. Lincoln: University of Nebraska Press, 1999.

Bolton, Charles. "The Hanging of the Sioux." *National Tribune,* June 9, 1910, 3.

Brown, J. Willard. *The Signal Corps, U.S.A. in the War of the Rebellion.* Boston: U.S. Veteran Signal Corps Association, 1896.

Brown, Jesse. "The Freighter in Early Days." *Annals of Wyoming* 19 (July 1947), 112–16.

Brown, P. W. "The 11th Ohio Cav." *National Tribune,* March 31, 1910, 7.

———. "Fighting in the Indian Country in the 60's." *National Tribune,* June 6, 1910, 3.

Burnett, Finn G. "History of the Western Division of the Powder River Expedition." *Annals of Wyoming* 8 (January 1932), 570–79. This was reprinted in the *Sheridan Post,* February 23, 1936.

Burton, Richard F. *The City of the Saints and across the Rocky Mountains to California.* Niwot, CO: University Press of Colorado, 1990. Originally published in 1862 by Harper & Brothers Publishers, New York.

———. *Look of the Old West, 1860: Across the Plains to California.* Lincoln: University of Nebraska Press, 1963. This is a reprint of part of *City of the Saints.*

Carrington, Henry Bebee. *The Indian Question.* Boston: DeWolfe & Fiske Company, 1909.

Davis, John H. "Recitals and Reminiscences." *National Tribune,* June 5, 1905.

Deeds of Valor: How America's Heroes Won the Medal of Honor, 2 vols. Detroit, MI: The Perrien-Keydel Company, 1903, 121–31.

Dodge, Grenville M. *Battle of Atlanta and Other Campaigns.* Council Bluffs, IA: 1910.

Doyle, Bryan. "A Head Full of Swirling Dreams." *Atlantic Monthly* (November 2001), 147–50.

Doyle, Susan Badger, ed., *Journeys to the Land of Gold: Emigrant Diaries from the Bozeman Trail, 1863–1866,* 2 vols. Helena: Montana Historical Society, 2000.

Drake, Francis M. "Fighting the Sioux," *National Tribune,* November 28, 1898, 6.

E. C. "Recitals and Reminiscences." *National Tribune,* June 13, 1905.

Edmunds, Newton. "Governor's Message, December 7, 1864." *Council Journal of the Forth Session of the Legislative Assembly of the Territory of Dakota.* Yankton, SD: G. W. Kinsbury, Printer, 1865.

Edwards, Elsa Spear. "A Fifteen Day Fight on Tongue River, 1865." *Winners of the West* (December 1939), 12–13.

Erhardt, Ferdinand. "At Platte Bridge." *National Tribune,* July 11, 1918.

Fairfield, Stephen H. "The Eleventh Kansas Regiment at Platte Bridge" in *Transactions of the Kansas State Historical Society, 1903–1904.* Vol. 7. Topeka: Geo. A. Clark, State Printer, 1904.

Falbo, Ernest, ed. *California and Overland Diaries of Count Leonetto Cipriani from 1853 through 1871.* Portland, Oregon, 1962.

Fisher, Marcius Clay. "Recollections of the Experience of a Boy on the Bozeman Trail." *The Midwest Review* 7 (November 1925), 1–5, 30–33.

General Laws and Joint Resolutions, Memorials and Private Acts, Passed at the Fifth Session of the Legislative Session of the Legislative Assembly of the Territory of Colorado. Central City: David C. Collier, 1866.

Gray, John S. "Blazing the Bridger and Bozeman Trails." *Annals of Wyoming* 49 (Spring 1977), 23–51.

Hadley, C. B. "The Plains War in 1865." *Publications of the Nebraska Historical Society.* Vol. 5. Lincoln: Jacob North & Company, 1902, 278.

Hafen, LeRoy R., ed. *Powder River Campaigns and Sawyers' Expedition of 1865,* Far West and Rockies Series, vol. 12. Glendale, CA: Arthur H. Clark Company, 1961. Accounts of the expeditions include those of James A. Sawyers, Dr. D. W. Tingley, Capt. George W. Williford, Albert M. Holman, and Capt. B. F. Rockafellow.

————. *Relations with the Plains Indians*. Glendale, CA: Arthur H. Clark Co., 1959.

Hafen, LeRoy R., and Ann W. Hafen, eds. *The Diaries of William Henry Jackson, Frontier Photographer*. Glendale, CA: Arthur H. Clark Company, 1959.

Heaton, Edward B. "Among the Sioux." *National Tribune*, December 29, 1898, 2.

Holliday, George H. *On the Plains in '65*. n.p., 1883.

Hollingsworth, J. J. "The End of Old [*sic*] Crow." *National Tribune*, January 12, 1911, 8.

Hollon, W. Eugene. *Beyond the Cross Timbers: The Travels of Randolph B. Marcy, 1812–1887*. Norman: University of Oklahoma, 1955.

Holman, Albert H., and Constant R. Marks. *Pioneering the Northwest*. Sioux City, IA: Deitch & Lamar Co., 1924.

Hubbard, Josiah H. "A Little Taste of Indian Warfare." *The Army and Navy Club of Connecticut, Report of Twenty-Ninth Annual Meeting, Pequot House, June 21, 1907*. Case, Lockwood & Brainard Company, 1907.

Hughey, I. R. "Gen. Moonlight." *National Tribune*, August 1, 1907, 5.

Hyde, George E. *A Life of George Bent Written from His Letters*, ed. Savoie Lottinville. Norman: University of Oklahoma Press, 1968.

Inghman, Harvey. *The Northern Border Brigade: A Story of Military Beginnings*. n.p., 1926.

Jackson, William Henry. *Time Exposure: The Autobiography of William Henry Jackson*. New York: 1940.

Kuykendall, W. L. *Frontier Days: A True Narrative of Striking Events on the Western Frontier*. Rawlins, WY: J. M. and H. L. Kuykendall, 1917.

Latta, E. G. "Winning the West." *National Tribune*, December 22, 1921.

Lyon, Herman R. "Freighting in the 60's." *Nebraska Historical Society Publications*. Vol. 5. Lincoln: Nebraska State Historical Society, 1907, 265.

Marquis, Thomas B. "Red Ripe's Squaw." *Century Magazine* 118 (June 1929), 203–4.

Mattes, Merrill J, ed. "Joseph Rhodes and the California Gold Rush of 1850." *Annals of Wyoming* 23 (1951), 52–71.

————. *Platte River Road Narratives: A Descriptive Bibliography of Travel of the Great Central Overland Route to Oregon, California, Utah, Colorado, Montana, and Other Western States and Territories, 1812–1866*. Urbana and Chicago: University of Illinois Press, 1988. The author often quotes from diaries in his descriptions of them.

McGaugh, John. "Powder River Expedition." *National Tribune*, May 22, 1902, 2.

McGillen, George W. "Outwitting the Danites." *National Tribune*, February 6, 1910, 7.

A Military Manual of Military Telegraphy for the Signal-Service, United States Army, Embracing Permanent and Field Lines. Washington, D.C.: Government Printing Office, 1872.

Mixer, F. W. "An Indian Ambuscade." *National Tribune,* September 8, 1904, 3.

Moonlight, Thomas. "The Kansas Soldiery." *Leavenworth Daily Conservative,* December 12, 13, 15, 16, 17, 19, 20, 21, 22, and 27, 1865.

Mumey, Nole. *James Pierson Beckwourth, 1856–1866.* Denver: Old West Publishing Company, 1957.

Nelson, George W. "Recollections." *National Tribune,* February 6 and 8, 1865; May 1, 1890; and August 15, 1901.

"New America." *Chambers Journal* 4 (April 13, 1867), 23.

North, Luther H. "The Pawnee Battalion." *National Tribune,* April 27, 1922, 3.

O'Brien, Emily Boynton. "Army Life at Fort Sedgwick, Colorado." *Colorado Magazine* 6 (September 1929), 173.

Official Roster of the Soldiers of the State of Ohio in the War of the Rebellion, 1861–1866. Vol. 11. Akron: Werner PTG Litho. Co., 1891.

Olson, James C. "From Nebraska to Montana, 1866: Diary of Thomas Alfred Creigh." *Nebraska History* 29 (September 1948).

Pablo, Louise [Richard]. Statement of Louise Pablo [Louise Merivale Richard], n.d. Records of the United States Court of Claims. Record Group 123.

Palmer, Henry E. "Powder River Indian Expedition of 1865, With a Few Incidents Preceding the Same." In *Civil War Sketches and Incidents, Papers Read by Companions of the Commander of the State of Nebraska, Military Order of the Loyal Legion of the United States,* Vol. 1. Omaha: The Commandery, 1902. All or parts of Palmer's account have been published in various places. See *Transactions and Reports of the Nebraska State Historical Society,* vol. 2 (Lincoln, NE: Nebraska Historical Society, 1887); C. G. Coutant, *The History of Wyoming* (Laramie: Chaplin, Spafford & Mathison, Printers, 1899); Robert Bruce, "The Powder River Expedition," *The United States Army Recruiting News,* August 15, September 1, September 15, and October 1, 1928; and LeRoy R. Hafen, ed., *Powder River Campaigns and Sawyers' Expedition of 1865,* Far West and Rockies Series, vol. 12 (Glendale, CA: The Arthur H. Clark Company, 1961).

———. The Powder River Expedition." *National Tribune,* April 12, 1908, 7.

Paul, Eli R., ed. "A Galvanized Yankee along the Niobrara River." *Nebraska History* 70 (Summer, 1989).

Peck, David C. "In Indian Country." *National Tribune,* March 10, 1898, 8.

Peck, Robert Morris. "Rough Riding on the Plains." *National Tribune,* April 25, 1901, 1.

Pennock, Isaac. "Diary of Jake [sic] Pennock." *Annals of Wyoming* 33 (July 1951), 5 29. Part of the diary is reprinted in Mary Hurlbut Scott, *The Oregon Trail through Wyoming: A Century of History 1812–1912* (Aurora, CO: Powder River Publishers, 1959). It is also reprinted in "Diary of Isaac B. Pennick [sic]," in Grace Raymond Hebard and E. A. Brininstool, *The Bozeman Trail,* vol. 2, introduction by John D. McDermott (Lincoln: University of Nebraska Press, 1990), 160–72. A typed copy is found in the Kansas Historical Society, Topeka, Kansas.

Reagan, James. "Military Landmarks." *The United Service* (August 1880), 146–62.

Report of the Commissioner of Indian Affairs 1865. Washington, D.C.: Government Printing Office, 1866, 192.

Report of the Secretary of Interior, 1865. Washington, D.C., 1865.

Report of the Special Indian Commissioners 1867. Washington, D.C., 1868.

Rogers, Fred B. *Soldiers of the Overland: Being Some Account of the Services of General Patrick Edward Connor & His Volunteers in the Old West.* San Francisco: The Grabhorn Press, 1938.

Rowan, George W. "Fighting the Sioux." *National Tribune,* January 30, 1890.

Sawyers, James. "A Partial Account of the Book That Was Lost, 1865," n.d. W. C. Coutant Papers, File H74-9, Folder 64. Wyoming State Archives, Cheyenne, Wyoming.

———. "Wagon Road from Niobrara to Virginia City." House Executive Document 58, 10–36. 39th Congress, 1st session, 1865-1866, Serial 1256. Sawyers's report has been reprinted many times, including in "Report of Col. James A. Sawyers," *South Dakota Historical Review* 2 (October 1936), 3–46. The most recent reprinting is found in Susan Badger Doyle, ed., *Journeys to the Land of Gold: Emigrant Diaries from the Bozeman Trail, 1863–1866,* vol. 1 (Helena: Montana Historical Society, 2000), 357–70.

Second Biennial Report of the State Historian of the State of Wyoming for the period Ending September 30, 1922. Sheridan, WY: The Mills Co., 1923. Includes the story of the capture by Indians of Mrs. A. F. M. Cook.

Spring, Agnes Wright. *Caspar Collins: The Life and Exploits of an Indian Fighter of the Sixties.* Lincoln: University of Nebraska Press, 1969. Originally published by the Columbia University Press, 1927.

Springer, Charles H. *Soldiering in Sioux Country: 1865,* ed. Benjamin Frank Cooling III. San Diego, CA: Frontier Heritage Press, 1971.

Stepps, P. C. "The Powder River Expedition." *National Tribune,* April 27, 1922, 3.

Sullivan, John. "Fight at Platte River Bridge." *National Tribune,* March 15, 1928.

Tonganoxie, E. C. "Recitals and Reminiscences." *National Tribune,* June 13, 1905.

Towers, J. A. Letter in (Julesburg, Colorado) *Grit Advocate* 21 (October 1910).

U.S. Congress, Senate. *Testimony for the Claim of Ben Holladay for Losses and Damages.* Senate Miscellaneous Document 19. 46th Congress, 2nd session, 1880.

Unrau, William E., ed. *Tending the Talking Wire: A Buck Soldier's View of Indian Country, 1863–1866.* Salt Lake: University of Utah Press, 1979.

Walker, George Morton. "Eleventh Kansas Cavalry, 1865, and Battle of Platte Bridge." In *Kansas Historical Collections, 1915–1918.* Vol. 14. Topeka: Kansas Historical Society, 1918, 332–40.

Walker, James R. *Lakota Belief and Ritual,* ed. by Raymond J. DeMallie and Elaine A. Jahner. Lincoln: University of Nebraska Press Bison Book, 1991.

The War of the Rebellion: A Compilation of the Official Records of the Union and Confederate Armies. Series I and II, Vol. 48, Pt. 1. Washington, D.C.: Government Printing Office, 1898.

Ward, J. F. "The Massacre at Platte Bridge." *National Tribune,* December 12, 1907, 6.

Ware, Eugene F. "The Daughter of Shan-Tag-A-Lisk." *The Agora* 2 (January 1893), 45–61.

———. *The Indian War of 1864,* introduction by John D. McDermott. Lincoln: University of Nebraska Press, 1994.

Warren, Charles S. "The Territory of Montana." In *Contributions to the Historical Society of Montana.* Vol. 2. Helena: Montana Historical Society, 1896, 60–63.

Watkins, Albert, ed. *Nebraska State Historical Society Publications.* Vol. 20. Lincoln: Nebraska Historical Society, 1922.

"William D. Fouts." *Pfantz-Fouts Newsletter* 9 (March 1986).

Wilson, Charles William. "Army Life in the Rockies." *National Tribune,* June 22, 1899.

Young, Charles E. *Dangers of the Trail in 1865: A Narrative of Actual Events.* Geneva, NY: n.p., 1912.

Young, Frank C. *Across the Plains in '65.* Denver: Frank C. Young, 1905.

Young, Will H. "Journals of Will H. Young, 1865." *Annals of Wyoming* 7 (October 1930), 381.

Secondary Sources

Alter, Cecil. *Jim Bridger.* Norman: University of Oklahoma Press, 1962.

Andreas, Alfred T. *History of the State of Kansas.* Chicago: A. T. Andreas, 1883.

Annual Report of the Adjutant General of the State of Missouri. Jefferson City: S. P. Simpson, 1865.

Ault, Phil. *Wires West: The Story of the Talking Wires.* New York: Dodd, Mead & Company, 1974.

Ayers, Elsie Johnson. *Highland Pioneer Sketches and Family Genealogies.* Springfield, OH: H. S. Skinner & Son, 1971.

Becher, Ronald. *Massacre along the Medicine Road: A Social History of the Indian War of 1864 in Nebraska Territory.* Caldwell, ID: Caxton Press, 1999.

Bent, George. "Forty Years with the Cheyennes," ed. George E. Hyde. *The Frontier* (October 1905–February 1906).

Berthrong, Donald J. *The Southern Cheyennes.* Norman: University of Oklahoma Press, 1963.

Brown, Dee. *The Galvanized Yankees.* Urbana, IL: University of Illinois Press, 1963.

Brown, P. W. "The 11th Ohio Cav." *National Tribune,* March 31, 1900, 7.

Browne, J. Ross. *Resources of the Pacific Slope.* New York: D. Appleton and Co., 1869.

Bruce, Robert, ed. "The Powder River Expedition of 1865." *The United States Army Recruiting News* 10 (August 1928).

Burlingame, Merrill G. "John M. Bozeman, Montana Trailmaker." *Mississippi Valley Historical Review* 27 (March 1941), 547–48. This was revised, corrected, and reissued as *John M. Bozeman, Montana Trailmaker* (Bozeman, MT: Museum of the Rockies, 1983).

Byrans, Bill. *Deer Creek: Frontiers* [sic] *Crossroad in Pre-Territorial Wyoming.* Glenrock, WY: Glenrock Historical Commission, 1990.

Cabannis, Charles J., Jr. "The Eighteenth Regiment of Infantry." *Journal of the Military Service Institution* 12 (September 1891), 116–21

Castel, Albert. *A Frontier State at War.* Ithaca, NY: Cornell University Press, 1958.

Conkling, Roscoe P., and Margaret H. *The Butterfield Overland Mail, 1857–1859.* Glendale, CA: Arthur H. Clark Company, 1947.

Connelley, William Elsey. "Eleventh Kansas Volunteer Cavalry." In *History of Kansas.* Chicago: The American Historical Society, 1928.

———. *The Life of Preston B. Plumb, 1837–1891.* Chicago: Brown & Howell Company, 1913.

Conway, Cornelius. *The Utah Expedition.* Cincinnati: n.p., 1858.

Coutant, C. G. *The History of Wyoming.* Laramie, WY: Chaplin, Spafford & Mathison, Printers, 1899. Reprinted by Argonaut Press Ltd., New York, in 1966.

Cozzens, Peter. *General John Pope: A Life for the Nation.* Urbana and Chicago: University of Illinois Press, 2000.

Crane, Oliver. *Carrington: Biographical Sketch.* n.p., c. 1898.

Crawford, Samuel J. *Kansas in the Sixties.* Chicago: A. C. McClurg & Co., 1911.

Cullum, W. *Biographical Register of the Officers and Graduates of the U.S. Military Academy at West Point,* 3rd ed. rev. 3 Vols. Boston and New York: Houghton Mifflin and Company, 1891.

Cushman, Dan. *The Great Northern Trail: America's Route of the Ages.* New York: McGraw-Hill Book Co., 1966.

Danker, Donald F., ed. *Man of the Plains: The Recollections of Luther North.* Lincoln, NE: Nebraska Historical Society, 1961.

Day, Daniel S. "Fort Sedgwick." *Colorado History* 42 (Fall 1965), 19–20

Defendant's Brief on Their Motion for New Trial, Abraham T. Litchfield v. the United States and the Sioux, Cheyenne, and Arapahoe Indians, Filed September 14, 1891. Indian Depredations Claim, 366. Records of the United States Court of Claims. Record Group 123. National Archives.

Doyle, Susan Badger. "The Bozeman Trail, 1863–1868: The Evolution of Routes to Montana." *Overland Journal* 20 (Spring 2002), 10–11,

———. "John Bozeman." In *Civilian, Military, Native American Portraits of Fort Phil Kearny.* Banner, WY: Fort Phil Kearny/Bozeman Trail Association, 1993, 1–6.

———. "Indian Perspectives of the Bozeman Trail." *Montana* 40 (Winter 1990), 56–67.

Dunn, Ruth. *Indian Vengeance at Julesburg.* North Platte, NE: Ruth Dunn, 1972.

Dyer, Frederick H. *Compendium of the War of the Rebellion.* 3 Vols. New York: Thomas Yoselhoff, 1917.

Ellis, Richard N. *General Pope and U.S. Indian Policy.* Albuquerque: University of New Mexico, 1970.

———. "Volunteer Soldiers in the West, 1865." *Military Affairs* 34 (April 1970).

Ellison, Robert S., and A. B Ostrander. "The Platte Bridge Fight," *Winners of the West* 3 (March 15, 1926), 6–7.

English, A. M. "Dakota's First Soldiers: History of the First Dakota Cavalry, 1862–1865." In *South Dakota Historical Collection.* Vol. 9. Pierre, SD: 1918.

Erb, Louise, et. al. *The Overland Trail in Wyoming.* n.p., 1990.

"Eugene F. Ware." In *The National Cyclopedia of American Biography.* Vol. 12. New York: James T. White & Company, 1899, 202.

Federal Writers' Project. *Nebraska: A Guide to the Cornhusker State.* New York: Hastings House, 1939.

Fish, Carl R. "Notes and Suggestions."*American Historical Review* 24 (April 1919), 435–43.

Fowler, Loretta. *Arapahoe Politics, 1851–1978: Symbols in Crises of Authority.* Lincoln: University of Nebraska Press, 1982.

Gilbert, Hila. *Big Bat Pourier: Guide and Interpreter, Fort Laramie, 1870–1880.* Sheridan, WY: The Mills Company, 1968.

Gleed, Charles S. "Eugene Fitch Ware." In *Kansas Historical Collections.* Topeka, KS: 1913–1914.

Goodwin, Charles C. *As I Remember Them.* Salt Lake City: Salt Lake Commercial Club, 1913.

Granger, John T. *A Brief Biographical Sketch of Major-General Grenville M. Dodge.* Ayer Company, 1981.

Gray, John S. "Blazing the Bridger and Bozeman Trails." *Annals of Wyoming* 49 (Spring 1977), 30–47.

Greene, Jerome A. *Reconnaissance Survey of Indian-U.S. Army Battlefields of the Northern Plains.* Denver: National Park Service, 1997.

Greever, William S. *The Bonanza West: The Story of the Western Mining Rushes, 1848–1900.* Norman: University of Oklahoma Press, 1961.

Grinnell, George B. *The Cheyenne Indians: Their History and Ways of Life 1923.* 2 Vols. New Haven, CT: Yale University Press, 1923.

———. *The Fighting Cheyennes.* New York: Scribners, 1915. The second edition was printed by the University of Oklahoma Press in 1956.

———. *Two Great Scouts and Their Pawnee Battalion: The Experience of Frank J. North and Luther H. North.* Lincoln: University of Nebraska Press, 1973.

Hafen, LeRoy R. *The Overland Mail, 1849–1869: Promoter of Settlement, Precursor of Railroads.* Cleveland: Arthur H. Clark Company, 1926.

———. *Relations with the Plains Indians.* Glendale, CA: Arthur H. Clark Company, 1959.

Hafen, LeRoy R., and Francis Marion Young. *Fort Laramie and the Pageant of the West, 1834–1890.* Glendale, CA: Arthur H. Clark Company, 1938. Bison Book reprint in 1984.

Hampton, H. D. "The Powder River Expedition, 1865." *Montana* 14 (Autumn 1964), 2–15.

Hassrick, Royal B. *The Sioux: Life and Customs of a Warrior Society.* Norman: University of Oklahoma Press, 1964.

Hauser, G. O. *A Story of Fallen Leaf.* Guernsey, WY: *The Guernsey Gazette,* n.d.

Heitman, Francis B. *Historical Register and Dictionary of the United States Army.* 2 Vols. Washington, D.C: Government Printing Office, 1903.

Henderson, Paul. "The Story of Mud Springs." *Nebraska History* 32 (June 1951).

"Historical Sketch of Cheyenne County." *Nebraska Historical Society Publications,* ed. Albert Watkins. Vol. 18. Lincoln: Nebraska State Historical Society, 1920.

History of Cheyenne County, Nebraska, 1986. Dalton, TX: Curtis Media Corporation, 1987.

Hoig, Stan. *The Peace Chiefs of the Cheyennes.* Norman: University of Oklahoma Press, 1980.

———. *The Sand Creek Massacre.* Norman: University of Oklahoma Press, 1961.

Hooper, Byron G., Jr. "A Capsule History of the Julesburg Area." *The Denver Westerns Monthly Roundup* 19 (November 1961).

Hoopes, Alban W. *Indian Affairs and Their Administration, With Special Reference to the Far West, 1849–1860.* Philadelphia, 1932.

Hyde, George E. *Red Cloud's Folk: A History of the Oglala Sioux.* Norman: University of Oklahoma Press, 1976.

———. *A Sioux Chronicle.* Norman: University of Oklahoma Press, 1956.

———. *Spotted Tail's Folk: A History of the Brule Sioux.* Norman: University of Oklahoma Press, 1960.

"The Indian Version of the Platte Bridge Fight." *Annals of Wyoming* 32 (October 1960), 234–35.

In Memoriam, Nelson Cole. Military Order of the Loyal Legion of the United States, Commandery of the State of Missouri, 1899.

Jackson, W. Turrentine. *Wagons Road West: A Study of Federal Road Surveys and Construction in the Trans-Mississippi West, 1846–1869.* Berkeley and Los Angeles: University of California Press, 1964.

Johnson, Dorothy. "The Hanging of the Chiefs." *Montana Magazine* (Summer 1970), 60–69.

Josephy, Alvin. *The Civil War in the American West.* New York: Vintage Civil War Library, 1993.

Judge, Bill. "Fort Caspar." *Annals of Wyoming* 43 (Fall 1971), 281–83.

———. "I Am No Coward." *Frontier Times* (Summer 1979), 11, 24, 29.

Kibby, Leo P. "Patrick Edward Connor, First Gentile of Utah." *Journal of the West,* 425–33.

King, James T. *War Eagle: Life of General Eugene A. Carr.* Lincoln: University of Nebraska Press, 1963.

Klise, J. W. *State Centennial History of Highland County, Ohio.* 2 Vols. Owensboro, KY: Cook & McDowell Publications, 1980.

Knudsen, Dean. "Death at Horse Creek." *True West* 36 (March 1989), 14–21.

"Louis Philip Guinard Record of Death," File 1912. Vital Records Services, Division of Health and Medical Services. Wyoming Department of Health and Social Services. State Archives. Cheyenne, Wyoming.

Lowe, James. *The Bridger Trail.* Seattle, WA: Arthur H. Clark Company, 2000.

Lowry, Grace. "Life of Eugene Ware." M.S. thesis. Kansas State Teachers College, Pittsburg, Kansas, July 1936.

Lubers, H. L. "William Bent's Family and the Indians of the Plains." *Colorado Magazine* 12 (January 1936), 19–22.

Madsen, Chris. *Glory Hunter: A Biography of Patrick Edward Connor.* Salt Lake City: University of Utah Press, 1990.

Malin, James C. "Eugene F. Ware's Literary Chronology." *Kansas Historical Quarterly* 37 (Autumn 1971).

Marion, William L. "St. Mary's Stage Station." *Annals of Wyoming* 30 (April 1958), 40–41.

"Martin Anderson." *Memorial Records, Lincoln Post No. 1, Department of Kansas G. A. R., Topeka, Kansas.* Topeka, KS: n.d.

"Martin Anderson." *The United States Biographical Dictionary, Kansas Volume.* Chicago and Kansas City: S. Lewis & Co., Publishers, 1879.

Maslowski, Pete. "A Study of Morale in Civil War Soldiers." *Military Affairs* 34 (December 1970), 122–26.

Matloff, Maurice, ed. *American Military History.* Washington, D.C.: Office of the Chief of Military History, 1969.

Mattes, Merrill J. *The Great Platte River Road: The Covered Wagon Mainline via Fort Kearny to Fort Laramie.* Lincoln: Nebraska Historical Society, 1969.

Mattes, Merrill J., and Paul Henderson. *The Pony Express from St. Joseph to Fort Laramie.* St. Louis, MO: The Patrice Press, 1989.

McAuslan, Edward R. *The Overland Trail in Wyoming,* n.p., 1961.

McCann, Lloyd. *The Grattan Massacre.* Fort Laramie, WY: Fort Laramie Historical Association, 1966. Reprinted from *Nebraska History* 37 (March 1956), 1–25.

McDermott, John D. *Dangerous Duty: A History of Frontier Forts in Fremont County, Wyoming.* Lander, WY: Fremont County Historical Commission, 1993.

――――. *Frontier Crossroads: The History of Fort Caspar and the Upper Platte Crossing.* Casper, WY: 1999.

――――. *A Guide to the Indian Wars of the West.* Lincoln: University of Nebraska Press, 1998.

――――. "Guinard's Bridge and Its Place in History." *Town of Mills CLG Oregon Trail Sesquicentennial Newsletter* (Summer 1993).

――――. "Introduction." In reprint of Hebard, Grace and E. A. Brininstool. *The Bozeman Trail.* Vol. 1. Lincoln: University of Nebraska Press, 1990.

――――. "Introduction." In reprint of Hebard, Grace, and E. A. Brininstool. *The Bozeman Trail.* Vol. 2. Lincoln: University of Nebraska Press, 1990.

――――. "James Bordeaux." *French Fur Traders and Voyageurs in the American West,* ed. LeRoy R. Hafen, introduction by Janet LeCompte. Glendale, CA: Arthur H. Clark Company, 1995, 42–57.

――――. "John Baptiste Richard." *The Mountain Men and the Fur Trade of the Far West,* ed. LeRoy R. Hafen. Vol. 2. Glendale, CA: Arthur H. Clark Company, 1965, 289–303.

――――. "Joseph Bissonette." *The Mountain Men and the Fur Trade of the Far West,* ed. LeRoy Hafen. Vol. 4. Glendale, CA: Arthur H. Clark Company, 1967, 49–60.

――――. "No Small Potatoes: Problems of Food and Health at Fort Laramie." *Nebraska History* 79 (Winter 1998), 162–70.

――――. "Roman Nose." In *American National Biography,* ed. John A. Garraty and Mark C. Carnes. Vol. 18. New York: University of Oxford Press, 1999, 794–95.

――――. "'We Had a Terribly Hard Time Letting Them Go': The Battles of Mud Springs & Rush Creek, February, 1865." *Nebraska History* 77 (Summer 1996), 78–88.

McDermott, John D., and Gordon Chappell. "Military Command at Fort Laramie." *Annals of Wyoming* 38 (April 1966), 7–48.

McGinnis, Anthony. *Counting Coup and Cutting Horses: Intertribal Warfare on the Northern Plains, 1738–1889.* Denver: Coridillera Press, 1990.

――――. "Strike and Retreat: Intertribal Warfare and the Powder River War, 1865-1868." *Montana* 30 (Autumn 1980), 34–35.

McKusick, Marshall. *The Iowa Northern Border Brigade.* Iowa City: Office of State Archaeologist, University of Iowa, 1975.

"Military History of the Eleventh Kansas Volunteer Cavalry." *Report of the Adjutant General of the State of Kansas, 1861–1865*. Topeka, Kansas, 1896.

Mitchell, Robert. *Appletons' Cyclopedia of American Biography*, ed. James Grant Wilson and John Fiske. Vol. 4. New York: D. Appleton and Company, 1898, 346.

Mokler, Alfred James. "Chief Red Cloud in Natrona County Jail." *The Wyoming Pioneer* 3 (November-December 1942), 19–22.

———. *Fort Caspar (Platte Bridge Station)*. Casper, WY: The Prairie Publishing Company, 1939.

———. *Transitions of the West: Portrayal of the Indian Problem in the West and the Trials of the Pioneers Who Reclaimed This Country from Savagery to Civilization*. Chicago: R. R. Donnelly & Sons Company, 1927.

Monnett, John. *The Battle of Beecher Island, and the Indian War of 1867–1869*. Miwot, CO: University of Colorado Press, 1992.

Moody, Ralph. *Stagecoach West*. Burlingame, CA: Promontory Press, 1967.

Morgan, Violet. *Folklore of Highland County*. Greenfield, OH: The Greenfield Printing and Publishing Company, 1947.

Morris, Robert C. *Collections of the Wyoming Historical Society*. Cheyenne: Wyoming Historical Society, 1897.

Murphy, James C. "The Place of the Northern Arapahoes in the Relations between the United States and the Indians of the Plains, 1851–1879." *Annals of Wyoming* 41 (1969), 33–61, 203–59.

Murray, Robert A. *Army on Powder River*. Fort Collins, CO: Old Army Press, 1972.

———. *Bison Hunters to Black Gold: A Brief History of the Fort Caspar Area from Pre-historic Times to Oil Development*. Casper, WY: Wyoming Historic Press, 1986.

———. *Military Posts in the Powder River Country of Wyoming, 1865–1894*. Lincoln: University of Nebraska Press, 1968.

———. *Military Posts of Wyoming*. Fort Collins, CO: The Old Army Press, 1974.

Nadeau, Remi. *Fort Laramie and the Sioux Indians*. Englewood Cliffs, NJ: Prentice Hall, 1967.

National Park Service. *Sand Creek Massacre Project*. 2 Vols. Denver: National Park Service, Intermountain Region, 2000.

Nicholas, Thomas A. "Story of Sergeant Custard's Fight." *Annals of Wyoming* 43 (Fall 1971), 294–295.

Official Roster of the Soldiers of the State of Ohio in the War of the Rebellion, 1861–1866. Akron, OH: Werner PTG. & Litho. Co., 1891.

————. "Highlights on 'Big Bat' 14 Year Old Scout." *St. Charles* (Missouri) *Banner,* August 29, 1934.

————. Correspondence with Hila Gilbert, 1964–1966. St. Charles Historical Society. St. Charles, Missouri. On the life of Baptiste Pourier.

Olson, James C. "From Nebraska to Montana, 1866: Diary of Thomas Alfred Creigh." *Nebraska History* 29 (September 1948), 209.

————. *Red Cloud and the Sioux Problem.* Lincoln, NE: University of Nebraska Press, 1965.

Parker, C. F. "Old Julesburg and Fort Sedgwick." *Colorado Magazine* 7 (July 1930), 139–41.

Perkins, Jacob R. *Trails, Rails, and War: The Life of General G. M. Dodge.* Ayer Company, 1981.

Platte Bridge Vertical File. Wyoming State Archives, Cheyenne, Wyoming.

Portrait and Biographical Album of Washington, Clay, and Riley Counties, Kansas. Chicago: Chapman Bros., 1890.

Prucha, Francis Paul. *The Great Father: The United States Government and the American Indians.* Lincoln: University of Nebraska Press, 1984.

Rawlings, Charles. "General Conner's [*sic*] Tongue River Battle." *Annals of Wyoming* 36 (April 1964), 69–73.

Record of Service of Michigan Volunteers in the Civil War, 1861–1865. Lansing: Senate and the House of Representatives of the Michigan Legislature, n.d.

Reid, James D. *The Telegraph in America.* New York: Derby Brothers, 1879.

Reid, Whitelaw. *Ohio in the War: Her Statesmen, Her Generals, and Soldiers.* 2 Vols. New York: Moore, Wilstach & Baldwin, 1868.

Report of the Adjutant General of the State of Kansas, 1861–1865. Topeka, Kansas, reprint edition, 1896.

Report of the Secretary of Interior, 1865. Washington, D.C.: Government Printing Office, 1865.

Roberts, Gary. "Sand Creek, Tragedy and Symbol." Ph.D. dissertation. University of Oklahoma, 1984.

Robertson, John. *Michigan in the War.* Lansing, MI: W. S. George & Co., 1880.

Robrock, David P. "The Eleventh Ohio Volunteer Cavalry on the Central Plains, 1862–1866." *Arizona and the West* 25 (Spring 1983), 23–48.

"Rocky Ridge Attacked and Burned." *Wind River Mountaineer* 4 (October–November 1989), 9–11.

Rogen, Patrick Edward. "Edward Connor." M.A. thesis. Department of History, Utah University, 1952.

Root, Frank A., and William Connelley. *The Overland Mail.* Columbus: Longs, 1950.

————. *The Overland Stage to California.* Topeka, KS: 1901.

The Roster and Record of Iowa Soldiers in the War of the Rebellion. Vol. 6. State Printer of Iowa, 1910.

Sandoz, Mari. *Crazy Horse: Strange Man of the Oglalas.* New York: Hastings House, 1942. Reprinted as a University of Nebraska Bison Book in 1961.

Settle, Raymond W. *Empire on Wheels.* San Francisco, CA: Stanford University, 1949.

Settle, Raymond W., and Mary Lund Settle. *Saddles and Spurs: The Pony Express Saga.* Harrisburg, PA: The Stackpole Company, 1955.

————. *War Drums and Wagon Wheels.* Lincoln: University of Nebraska Press, 1966.

Shannon, Fred Albert. *The Organization and Administration of the Union Army, 1861–1865.* Gloucester, MA: Peter Smith, 1965. See chapter 2, "Feeding and Clothing the Volunteers."

Shumway, Grant L. *History of Western Nebraska and Its People.* Lincoln: The Western Publishing & Engraving Company, 1921.

Smith, Sherry L. *The Bozeman Trail.* Cheyenne, Wyoming Recreation Commission, 1981.

Stands in Timber, John, and Margot Liberty. *Cheyenne Memories,* 2nd ed. New Haven: Yale University Press, 1998.

Stevens, Walter B. *History of St. Louis, the Fourth City.* Vol. 2. St. Louis, MO: The S. J. Clarke Publishing Co., 1909, 230–31.

Stutheit, Ted. *The Pony Express on the Oregon Trail.* Lincoln: Nebraska Game and State Parks Commission, 1987.

Tate, Michael. "From Cooperation to Conflict: Sioux Relations with the Overland Emigrants, 1845–1865." *Overland Journal* 18 (Winter 2000–2001), 18–31.

Thain, Raphael P. *Notes Illustrating the Military Geography of the United States, 1813–1880.* Austin and London: University of Texas Press, 1979. Reprint of the 1881 edition published by the adjutant general's office.

Thompson, Robert Luther. *Wiring a Continent, the History of the Telegraph Industry in the United States, 1832–1866.* Princeton, NJ: Princeton University Press, 1947.

Thrapp, Dan L. *Encyclopedia of Frontier Biography.* 3 Vols. Lincoln: University of Nebraska Press, 1988.

Trenholm, Virginia Cole, and Maurine Carley. *The Shoshonis: Sentinels of the Rockies.* Norman: University of Oklahoma Press, 1964.

Tuttle, Charles R. *A New Centennial History of the State of Kansas.* Madison, WI, and Lawrence, KS: The Interstate Book Company, 1876.

Unruh, John D., Jr. *The Plains Across: The Overland Emigrants and the Trans-Mississippi West, 1840–1860.* Urbana: University of Illinois Press, 1982.

Utley, Robert M. "The Contribution of the Frontier to the American Military Tradition." In *The Harmon Memorial Lectures in Military History, 1959–1987,* ed. Harry R. Borowski. Washington, D.C.: Office of Air Force History, 1988.

————. *Frontiersmen in Blue: The United States Army and the Indian, 1848–1865.* New York: The Macmillan Company, 1967.

————. *Frontier Regulars: The United States Army and the Indian, 1866–1890.* New Haven, CT: Yale University Press, 1973

Varley, James F. *Brigham and the Brigadier: General Patrick Connor and His California Volunteers in Utah and along the Overland Trail.* Tucson, AZ: Westernlore Press, 1989.

Vaughn, J. W. *The Battle of Platte Bridge.* Norman: University of Oklahoma Press, 1963.

————. *Indian Fights: New Facts on Seven Encounters.* Norman: University of Oklahoma Press, 1966.

————. "Sergeant Custard's Wagon Train Fight." *Annals of Wyoming 32* (October 1960), 227–34.

Vestal, Stanley. *New Sources of Indian History.* Norman: University of Oklahoma Press, 1934.

Webb, Frances Seely. "The Indian Version of the Platte Bridge Fight." *Annals of Wyoming* 32 (October 1960), 235.

Werner, Fred H. *Heroic Fort Sedgwick and Julesburg: A Study in Courage.* Greeley, CO: Werner Publications, 1987.

West, J. S. "Eugene Ware." In *Kansas Historical Collections.* Vol. 13. Topeka, KS: 1913–1914, 65–71.

Willson, E. B. *Cabin Days in Wyoming.* E. B. Willson, 1939.

Wilson, James Grant, and John Fiske, eds. *Appletons' Cyclopedia of American Biography.* New York: D. Appleton and Company, 1898.

"Winning the West: Col. Nelson Cole's Expedition in the Powder River in Summer of 1865." *National Tribune,* August 5, 1920, 3.

INDEX

Note: Page numbers in *italics* indicate an illustration.

A

Abbot, Perry, wagon train, 110
Ackley's Ranch. *See* Gillette's Ranch
Adams, Major, 56
Adams, Pvt. Charles, 104–5, 224n
Ah-ho-ap-pa. *See* Spotted Tail's daughter
Alkali Station, 30, 34, 149
Alsop, Thomas, 82
American Fur Company, 223n
American Ranch, 22, 28
Anderson, John C., 51
Anderson, Maj. Martin, 79, 80, 88, *90*, 94, bio. 171
Andrews, Mr., 23
Antelope Stage Station, 29
Antram, Pvt. Jesse E., 98
Apaches, 43
Apt, Pvt. Jacob, 36
Arapahos, 6, 8, 13, 26, 32, 49, 54, 69, 78, 86, 97–98, 105, 111–16, 118, 121, 124–27, 139, 145, 146, 148, 151, 161, 163, 165, 167–69, 226n, 235n
Arkansas River, 6, 28, 75
Army and Navy Journal, 141–42, 145, 160, 231n, 243n

Army of Virginia, 10
Army of the Mississippi, 10
Ash Hollow, 35, 182n
Atchison, Kansas, 15, 50, 51, 203n

B

Back Wound (also Mischief Maker), 147
Bad Faces, 147
Baker, Pvt. Andrew, 93
Ballau, Pvt. James, 95, 98
Bancroft, Samuel D., 17
Bannock, Montana, 3
Barbarism, 165, 186n, 239n
Barnes, Asst. Adj. Gen. J. W., 82
Bat or Sautie. *See* Roman Nose
Baumer, Lt. Col. William, 57
Bear Butte, 82–83, 130
Bear River, Battle of, 8, 48
Bear That Looks Back, 147
Beatrice, Nebraska, 203n
Beauvais, Gemenier P., 70
Beaver Creek, 124
Beaver Creek Station, 27
Beckworth, James, 187n
Beecher Island, Battle of, 174

Bell Fourche, 130, 211n

Bellevue, Nebraska, 149

Beni, Jules, 15, 182n

Bennett, Maj. Lyman G. (Hill Climber), 129, 135, 139, 231n, 235n

Bent, Charles, 13, 17, 122

Bent, George, 43, 13, 17, 21, 22, 28, 39–40, 43, 93, 95, 106, 122, 150, 165–66, 174, *175*, bio. 175 and 181n, 216n

Bent, William, 13, 150, 181n

Bent's Fort, 181n

Biehn, Pvt. John, 193n

Big Crow, 17, 57, 201n

Big Head, 147

Big Horn Crossing, 121

Big Horn Mountains, 5, 44, 49, 77, 105, 108, 109, 110, 167, 220n

Big Horse, 93

Big Laramie River, 110

Big Mouth, 13, 55

Big Partisan, 147

Big Ribs, 146–47, 238n

Big Timber, 24

Bighorn River, 123, 126

Bissonette, Joseph, 34, 147

Blackfeet, 97

Black Bear (Arapaho), 111–12, 115, 124, 167, 226n 72

Black Bear (Sioux), 147

Black Bear's (Arapaho) children, 115–16

Black Bear's (Arapaho) wife, 115

Blackfeet Sioux, 150

Black Foot, 60–62, 70

Black Hills, 6, 39, 44, 49, 51, 70, 77, 82, 130, 162, 211n, 237n

Black Hills Mining Journal, 148

Black Kettle, 13, 25, 28, 146

Black Whetstone, 168

Black Wolf, 71

Bodine, Pvt. George, 68

Bogota, Columbia, 172

Bon Homme, South Dakota, 228n

Bone Pile Creek, 122

Bonwell, Pvt. William T., 68

Bordeaux, [Louis?], scout, 100

Bordeaux, James, 69, 70, 71, 157

Bordeaux's Ranch, 68

Border Brigade, Iowa State Militia, 120

Bordman, Captain, 134–35

Bounties, 231n

Bouyer, Mitch, scout, 69, 100, 109

Bowles, Mr., 2

Bowles, Samuel, 197n 12

Bozeman, Montana, 109

Bozeman, John M., 5

Bozeman Crossing, 69

Bozeman Trail, 6, 104, 120, 127, 144, 166–67, 178n

Bradbury, Cyrus A., 109

Bradshaw, Pvt. William, 134

Brannan, J. J., scout, 100

Brave Bear, 157

Brewer, 1st Lt. John S., 16, 27, 31–32, 102

Bretney, 1st Lt. and Capt. Henry, bio, 53 and 173–74, 54, 58, 67, 80, *89*, 89–91, 93–94, 142, 166, 198n, 199n

Bretney, Mary Elizabeth Jackman, 174

Brett, Pvt. Henry C. *See* Henry Bretney

Bridger, Jim, 5, 58, 100, *102*, 111–12, 118, 163, 237n

Bridger Pass, 9

Bridger Trail, 5

Bridger's Ferry, 104

Brings Water or Mini–aku. *See* Spotted Tails, daughter

Bross, Lieutenant Governor Illinois, 60

Brown, Capt. Albert, 73–74, 105, 110, 111, 126–27

Brown, Lt. J. Willard, 100

Brown, John, 12

Brown, Pvt. Moses, 93, 96

Brown, Pvt. P. W., 112

Brown, Lt. William, 39–43, 45, 159, bio. 193n, 195–96n

Brown, Pvt. William, 98

Brown's Creek, 39

Brown's Springs, 104

Brules, 7, 43, 51, 55, 69, 71, 86, 131, 146, 147, 153–57, 168–69. *See also* Red Cloud

Buchanan, citizen, 109

Buchanan, Pvt. John B., 98

Buckley, contractor, 81

Buena Vista, Battle of, 10

Buffalo Springs Ranch, 29

Bulen, E. D., 32

Bull Bear, 13, 122, 147

Bullock, Col. William, 62, 155

Burnett, Finn, teamster, 79, 104, 107, 119, 168, 200n, 222n, 221–22n 224n, 225n

Burnt Station. *See* South Pass Station

Burrows, N., 69

Burton, Richard, 1, 36

Buthton Station, 150–51

Butterfield, D. A., 118

Butterfield Overland Express, 50

C

Cache la Poudre, Colorado, 25

Caldwell, W. H., 68

Calico, 79

California Crossing, 15

California Hill, 182n

California Trail, 2, 51, 168

Camp, Pvt. George, 93

Camp Collins, 58, 78

Camp Cottonwood, 24, 27, 29

Camp Dennison, 53

Camp Dodge, 56, 79, 200n

Camp Douglas, 48

Camp Marshall, 57

Camp Rankin, 16–18, 24, 27, 29, 30–35, 67, 167

Cannon, 18, 21, 24, 31–32, 39, 41–42, 45, 68, 79, 88, 94, 115, 130, 133, 135, 159, 164–65, 195n

Cannon, James, 18

Cape Horn, 9

Carrington, Col. Henry B., 157, 164, 201n

Carson City, 8

Cascade, Colorado, 173

Casper, Wyoming, 79, 223n

Casper Creek, 212n, 217n

Causes, 2, 7, 10

Cavanaugh, James M., 147

Cedar Creek, 194n

Central City, 24, 28, 34, 148

Chalk Bluff's, 151

Chapell, Private, 94

Charleston, South Carolina, 174

Cherokee County, Kansas, 173

Cherokee Station, 69

Cherry Creek, 21, 22, 25, 28, 69, 185n

Cheyenne Dog Soldiers, 91, 93, 162. *See also* Roman Nose

Cheyenne Fork, 12

Cheyenne River, 77, 83, 130, 211n

Cheyenne Sioux, 162

Cheyennes, 6, 8, 12, 13, 14, 17, 21, 22, 24, 26, 28, 32, 33, 35, 38–44, 49, 51, 57–61, 63–64, 66, 68, 78,

79, 85, 86, 88, 91–93, 96–98, 100, 105–8, 111, 120–21, 128, 131–34, 139, 146–48, 150–51; fighting spirit, 162, 163, 165, 167–68, 194n, 201n, 215n, 217n, 232n, 244n

Chicago, Illinois, 174

Chicago Tribune, 60

Chivington, Isabella Arenzer, 176

Chivington, Col. John M., 13, *14*, 47, 51, 122, 146, 165, bio. 174–76, 181n

Chivington, Sarah, M., 174–76

Chivington, Thomas, M., 174

Chugwater River, 79

Cincinnati, Ohio, 176, 228n

Circleville, Kansas, 172

Civil War, 8, 9, 10, 46, 48, 50, 51, 55, 77, 100, 121, 159, 161, 164, 173, 183n, 185n, 192n, 219n, 220n

Clancy, Lieutenant, 90

Clark Brothers, 149

Clark's Fork, 69, 127

Clark's train, 23

Clear Fork of the Powder River, 108, 110, 111, 123

Cleve, Dick, 30

Cleve, Mrs. Dick, 30–31

Cleve's Ranch, 30

Cleveland, President Grover, 172

Clift, Mr., 30–31

Climatic conditions, 1, 159

Cold Springs Station, 143, 193n

Cole, Col. Nelson, bio. 77, 83, 118–19, 126–40, 142, 159, 161–65, 167–68, 172, 209n, 211n, 231n, 235n, 245n

Cole, Capt. Osmer, 124, 126, 145

Colfax, Sen. Schyler, 60, 78, 197n, 203n

Collins, 2nd Lt. Caspar, 1, 36, 44, bio.

53–54, 88, 90–91, 93, 94, 96, 97, 122, 161, 166, 167, 171–73, 199n, 214–15n, 215n, 217n, 222n

Collins, Catherine Weaver, 192n

Collins, Col. William Oliver, 12, 36–45, 53, 57, 159, 164, 171, bio. 172 and 192n, 195n

Colony, Oklahoma, 174, 181n

Colorado Historical Society, 32

Colorado Territory, 48

Columbus, Nebraska, 102, 129, 211n

Comanches, 28, 43, 97

Commissioner of Indian Affairs, 7, 103, 141, 156

Concord coaches, 182n

Confederate Army, 181n

Connelly, G. D., 32

Connor, Gen. Patrick Edward (Red Chief), 7–8, 47, bio. 48 and 172, 49, 56, 57, 58, 60, 61, 65–67, 74–75, 77–79, 81–85, 100, 102–4, 107, 109, 111–16, 120, 123, 124, 125, 126, 127, 128, 129, 130, 132, 133, 136, 138, 139, 141–47, 158–63, 165–66, 168, 208n, 209n, 209–10n, 210n, 211n, 220n, 222n, 223n, 224n, 225n, 235n

Connor Battle, 111–15, 145, 160, 164, 224n, 224n, 224n, 225n, 226n

Conrad, Capt. George, 73–74, 103, 105

Contractors, 74, 77–79, 145, 157, 159–60

Conway, Cornelieus, 1

Cook, C. B., 54

Cook's train, 23

Cooley, Sergeant, 110

Cooper's Creek Station, 110

Corn Band, 147

Corruption, 159

Cottonwood Springs Station, 15, 16, 24, 34, 58, 81, 159

Council Bluffs, Iowa, 46, 120, 141, 173

Court House Rock, 15, 35, 75, 182

Courtright, M., 69

Craven, Pvt. Harvey, 93

Crazy Head, 217n

Crazy Horse, 85

Crazy Woman's Fork of the Powder River, 106, 108, 123

Creighton, Ed, freighter, 82

Creighton, Sergeant, 58

Creighton & Hoel, 36

Crook, Brig. Gen. George, 164, 168

Crooked Lances, 122

Cross, Mr., 22, 23

Crow Dog, 174

Crows, 5, 6, 12, 109, 127

Crumb, Pvt. John, 217n

Culp, Pvt. Adam, 98

Curtis, Gen. Samuel R., 10, 22, 23, 34, 47, 76, 102 3

Custard, Sgt. Amos, 89–90, *92*, 94–95, 97–98, 167, 218n

Custard Fight. *See* Red Buttes, Battle of

Custard Hill, 98

Custer, Maj. Gen. George Armstrong, 100

Custer Battle, 44, 168, 194n

Cut Belly, 28

Cutler, Lieutenant, 149

D

Dalton (Nebraska) *Delegate*, 195n

Daugherty, Jim, scout, 100

Davis, Thomas R., 150

Davis, Col. Werter, 77

Davis, Winfield S., 36, 193n

Davis and Hyde's party, 109

Dead Man's Fork of Hat Creek, 73

Deep Holes Creek, 194n

Deer Creek Station, 9, 44, 53, 56, 57, 59, 78, 97, 98

Defond, Baptiste, 121, 123

Dennison's Ranch, 22, 23

Denver, 7, 12, 13, 15, 17, 23, 24–25, 26, 27, 34, 47, 48, 50, 59, 64, 78, 80, 81, 82, 111, 116–18, 127, 143, 145, 146, 165, 176, 188n, 238n

Department of Arkansas, 47

Department of Kansas, 10, 22, 46–47, 185n

Department of New Mexico, 47

Department of the Missouri, 46, 78, 82, 102, 143

Department of the Northwest, 10, 46–47

Desertion, 216n, 243n

Devil's Dive, 16, 18, 30, 167

Devil's Lake, North Dakota, 75, 162

Devil's Tower, 130–31

Devine, Pvt. William, 163

Dilleland, James, 125–26

District of Colorado, 23, 48, 55, 56

District of Nebraska, 48, 143, 185n

District of Upper Kansas, 75

District of Utah, 48, 141

District of the Plains, 48, 62, 64, 82, 83, 141

Dodge, Maj. Gen. Grenville M., 6, *11*, bio. 46, 48, 65, 74–75, 78, 82, 83, 103, 116, 141, 143, 146, 158, 162–63, 173, 208n, 223n

Dog feast, 70

Dog Soldiers, 122, 233n

Dole, William P., commissioner of Indian affairs, 103

Donjon, John, 56

Donnelly, J., 69
Doolittle, Sen. James, 76
Dorien, Paul, guide, 121
Double Head, 147
Douglas, Wyoming, 166
Downer, 151
Drake, Francis M., 45
Drew, Lt. William Y., 78, 90, 96, 215n, 216n, 218n
Dry Creek, 212n, 217n
Dry Fork Crossing, 167
Dry Fork of the Powder River, 104–5, 123
Ducker, Orlando, 68, 69
Dull Knife, 85, 86, 122, 147

E
Ecoffey, Jules, 34
Edmunds, Gov. Newton, 75–76, 141, 145
Edwards, Mr., 23
Elbert, Samuel, 34
11th Ohio Volunteer Cavalry, 8, 12, 36–45, 50, 51, 52–54, 56, 58, 67, 68, 69, 79, 80, 85–99, 102, 108, 111–12, 115, 118, 130, 142, 161, 179n, 192n, 194n
11th Kansas Volunteer Cavalry, 10, 49, 50, 53, 55, 56, 58, 59, 67, 68, 69, 77, 78, 79, 80, 81, 85–99, 161, 163, 208, 210n, 216n
Elk-Horn Scrapers. See Elk Soldiers
Elk Soldiers, 233n
Elkhorn Station, 67
Ellis, Richard, historian, 161
Elliston, Charles, 24, 32, 55, 60, 70
Ellsworth, William, 36–37, bio. 192n
Elm Creek Station, 59
Emmons, L. W., 73

Erhardt, Pvt. Ferdinand, 216n
Estes, Ben, guide, 121, 123
Eubank family, 12
Eubank, Lucinda, 12–13, 60–61, 70, 203n
Evans, Lieutenant, 111
Ewing, Thomas, Jr., 49

F
Fairfield, Sgt. Stephen, 10, 53, 98, 218n
Fast Bear, 150
Fetterman Disaster, 168
Ficklin's Springs, 36
15th Kansas Volunteer Cavalry, 83
5th United States Volunteer Infantry, 121, 152
Finch, Pvt. Perrin, 142
1st Battalion Dakota Cavalry, 121–23
1st Colorado Mounted Militia, 49
1st Colorado Volunteer Cavalry, 12, 51, 100, 110, 147
1st Michigan Volunteer Cavalry, 108
1st Nebraska Veteran Volunteer Cavalry, 24, 34, 58, 81, 149, 161
1st Nevada Volunteer Cavalry, 67
Flake Foot, 147
Fletcher, Jasper, 81
Fletcher, Lizzy, 81
Fletcher, Mary, 81
Fletcher, young Mary, 81
Food, 117–18, 147
Foolish Dogs military society, 86
Foote, Admiral, 10
Ford, J. W., 27
Ford, Gen. James, 49, 75
Fort Benton, 69
Fort Berthold, 242n
Fort Bridger, 9, 67

Fort Caspar, 9, 151

Fort Collins, 77, 97, 111

Fort Connor, 105–6, 108, 110, 123, 126, 127, 139–40, 142, 144, 151, 167

Fort Dodge, Iowa, town of, 121

Fort Douglas, 172

Fort Fetterman, 104

Fort Hall, 2, 5

Fort Halleck, 48, 49, 58, 77, 194n

Fort Kearny, 2, 12, 27, 47, 49, 50, 59, 60, 69, 70, 71, 74, 75, 77, 81, 98, 102, 103, 159, 160, 161, 165, 208n, 231n

Fort Laramie, 2, 6, 8, 9, 14, 15, 34, 35, 37, 43, 45, 49, 51, 54, 55, 56, 57, 59, 60–64, 67, 69, 70, 73, 75, 77, 78, 79, 80, 81, 82, 83, 88, 89, 94, 100, 102, 103, 105, 107, 108, 109, 111, 115, 120, 130, 131, 132, 141, 142–44, 146, 151, 153–57, 159, 160, 163, 166, 173–74, 193n, 194n, 201n, 219n, 223n, 237n, 238n, 242n

Fort Laramie Treaty of 1851, 6, 51, 70, 178n

Fort Leavenworth, 8, 10, 50, 55, 59, 77, 142, 161

Fort Lyon, 13, 181n

Fort McPherson National Cemetery, 184n

Fort Meade, 211n

Fort Mitchell, 36, 37, 43, 70

Fort Phil Kearny, 104, 111, 166

Fort Reno, 221n

Fort Rice, 75, 242n

Fort Riley, 49

Fort Scott Monitor, 173

Fort Scott National Cemetery, 173

Fort Sedgwick, 183n

Fort Sully, 146

Fort Wicked, 27

Foster, H. M., & Company, 29, 33

Foster, Sen. Lafayette S., 76, 81

4th Wisconsin Volunteer Cavalry, 69

Fouts, Charity, 70

Fouts children, 70

Fouts, Capt. William Davenport, 36–37, 40, bio. 70, *71*, 70–73

Fowler, Loretta, 226n

Fremont Orchard, Skirmish at, 12

Friday, 111

Furnay, Lt. John B., 102

G

Gallagher carbines, 159

Gallatin Valley, 5, 109

Galvanized Yankees, 8, 12, 49, 56, 59, 91, 121, 197n, 200n

Garden Creek, 79, 200n

Gaskill, Albert, 149

George, Milo, 49

Gillette, Wyoming, 228n

Gillette's Ranch, 28, 29, 33

Gillman's Ranch, 58

Gilpin, Hon. William, 147

Gittrell's Ranch, 27, 33, 189n

Goddard, Pvt. Benjamin P., 93

Godfrey, Holan, 27

Godfrey, John F., scout, 121, 123

Godfrey, William B., 59

Godfrey's Ranch

Gold, 3–4, 86, 108, 120, 237n

Gorton, Elijah, 149

Gorton, H. G., 149

Goose Creek, 124

Grand Army of the Republic, 173

Grant, Lt. Gen. Ulysses S., 10, 75

Grattan, 2nd Lt. John L., 51

Gray, Pvt. William D., 98
Gray Head, 147
Great Plains, 47
Great Platte River Road, 2
Great Salt Lake, 172
Great Sioux War of 1876–77, 165, 169
Green, Pvt. Martin, 98
Green River Station, 58, 60, 77
Greer, Capt. James, 79, 80, 88, 90, 94
Grimm, Cpl., Henry, 88, 93
Grinnell, George Bird, 162, 185n, 187n, 189n, 217n
Grote, Pvt. H., 133
Guernsey, Owen, 76, 141
Guides, 118, 121, 123, 130, 231n
Guinard, Louis, 68
Gwynn, Edgar W., 78

H
Hair Plait, 147
Hall, William, 37–38, bio. 191n
Halleck, Gen. Henry W., 47–48
Hamilton, Pvt. Rice B. 98
Hammond, Private, 79
Hanchett, Pvt. Alanson, 18
Hanging, Indian beliefs regarding, 201n
Hanging of the chiefs, 57, 60–64
Hankammer, Sgt. Adolph, 91, 93, 94
Harlan, Sec. of Interior James, 75–76, 127
Harlan, Theodore B., 36
Harlow, William, 29
Harlow's Ranch, 28, 148
Harney, Maj. Gen. William S., 156, 168
Harper's Weekly, 150
Harris, Pvt. John A., 42–43, bio. 194–95n

Hartshorn, Pvt. William H., 42–43, bio. 194n, 195n
Haymaker, Mrs. Edwin, 21
Haynes party, 23
Haywood, Dudley L., 36
Haywood, Pvt. William, 214–15n
Heath, Col. and Bvt. Brig. Gen. H. H., 81, 149, 161
Heart River, 6
Hedges, Charles, 120, 122
Hedges, Daniel, 120, 122
Hedges, Nathaniel, 122, 228n
Heil, Pvt. George, 98
Henry, Capt. Guy V., 48
Henshaw, Pvt. Henry, 78
Herndon Hotel, Omaha, 150
Herriman, John V., 37
Higbee, Congressman, 76
High Land Weekly News, 44
High-Backed Wolf, 88, 96
Hill, R. B., reporter, 76, 141
Hill, Pvt. Henry W., 93
Hillsboro, Ohio, 172, 192n
Hilty, Pvt. Joseph, 94, 98
Hoagland, Lt. A. S., 131
Hogan, Martin, 36
Holcomb, Philo, 32, 33
Holding, Sergeant, 79
Holladay, Ben, 15, 34, 47, 182n
Hollister, O. J., 148, 209n, 225n
Holman, Albert M., 124, 126
Holt, Sergeant, 131
Holton, Kansas, 172
Hook Nose or Woquni. *See* Roman Nose
Hoppe, Pvt. August, 98
Horse Black, 96
Horse Creek, 70
Horses, 137, 140, 158–59
Horseshoe Station, 9, 54, 56, 104, 143

Hubbard, Ashael Wheeling, congress-
man, 120–21
Hubbard, Pvt. Josiah, 80, 163–64
Hughes, Andrew, 30–31
Hughes, Gen. B. H., 147
Humphreville, Capt. Jacob H., 79, 102,
113, 119
Hunkpapa, 150, 169
Hutson, Pvt. J. G., 138
Hyde, George, 95, 174

I

Idlet, Sgt. William, 37, bio. 192n
Indian casualities, 245n
Indian populations, 7, 179n
The Indian War of 1864, 16
Intelligence, poor, 163
Interior Department, 76, 165
Iott, Sefroy, 70, 156

J

Jacobs, John M., 5
James, Private, 88
Janis, Antoine, scout, 100
Janis, Nick, scout, 100, 118
Jarvis, Private, 122
Jewett, Joe, 24
Jewett, Lt. Oscar, 100, 107, 114
Jocelyn, Capt. Stephen E., 200n
Jones, Lieutenant, 138
Johnson, Private, 114
Johnson, President Andrew, 101
Jules cutoff, 35
Julesburg, 2, 14, 15–18, 21–23, 27–34,
35, 36, 45, 48–50, 51, 64, 65, 67,
78, 81, 101, 148–49, 164, 169, 188n
Julesburg, Battles of, casualties named
184n, 17–21, 30–32

K

Kame, Pvt. William T., 54
Kay, John, 30
Kaycee, Wyoming, 110
Kehler, Pvt. Willie, 59
Keith's train, 23
Kelley, Mrs. Fanny, 12
Kellog, Capt. James, 126
Kennedy, J. J., 28
Kidd, Capt. James H., 100, bio. 102,
104–6, 123
Killdeer Mountain, Battle of, 7
Kimball, Colonel, 109
Kiowas, 26, 28, 43
Knox & Company, 109
Krumme, Captain, 149

L

La Bonte Station (Camp Marshall), 9,
53, 56, 97, 104
Laclede, Nissori, 203n
Lafferty, John, 53, 54, 198n
Lake DeSmet, 111, 123–24
Landscape, western, 1–3
LaPorte, Colorado, 9
La Prelle Creek, 45, 53, 56
La Prelle Station, 9, 80
Laramie County, Wyoming, 173
Laramie Loafers, 55
Laramie Peak, 67
Latham, Sgt. Charles M., 114–15
Laurant, Capt. J. C., 100
Lavin, T. W., 182n
Leach, Henry C., 147
Lean Bear, 13
Leavenworth, Kansas, 172, 231n
Leavenworth Daily Conservative, 56
Lebanon, Kentucky, 174
Le Due, Antoine, scout, 100

Left Hand, 13
Leg-in-the-Water, 13
Leighton, A. C., 79, 100, 113, 222n
Liberty Farm, 59
Lillian Springs Ranch, 28
Lincoln, President Abraham, 9, 56
Litchfield, Abraham, 32
Little Arkansas, 146
Little Bear, 23
Little Bear Wolf, 147
Little Bighorn, Battle of. *See* Custer Battle
Little Bighorn River, 127
Little Blue River, 12–13, 57, 59, 60, 61
Little Bull, 147
Little Dick, soldier, 224n
Little Laramie River, 110
Little Missouri River, 130, 140, 211n
Little Powder River, 136
Little Priest, 100, 103, 105, 116, 127, 151
Little Raven, 13, 28, 146
Little Robe, 13
Little Thunder, 55
Little Wolf, 13, 23, 85, 147
Livingston, Col. Robert R., 24, 34, 49, 50, 193n
Lodgepole Creek, 15, 16, 35, 43, 51, 182n
Lodgepole Creek Station, 43, 49
Lohans, Pvt. Frances W., 58
Long, Pvt. William B., 98
Long Soldier, 147
Lord, Private, 88
Loucerback, Pvt. Imry, 193n
Loup Fork, 77, 129, 211n
Low Horse, 146
Lull, John, 174,
Lull, Almira, 174

Lybe, Capt. A. Smyth, 89, 91, 94, 215–16n

M
Mackey, Major, 78
Maloney, John R., 36
Man Afraid of His Horses, 86, 147
Man That Stands in the Water, 147
Man That Steals the White Man's Horses, 147
Mankato, Minnesota, 7, 75
Mantel, Phillip, 110
Mantel Ranch, 110
Marcella, 5
Marsh, Mr., 23
Marshall, Captain, 108, 110, 118–19, 140
Marvin, Pvt. Fred, 200n
Matthews, Pvt. S. L., 108
May, George D., 93
Maynadier, Col. Henry, 151, bio. 152 and 174, 153–57, 240n
McCook, Maj. Gen. Alexander, 76
McCullough, Mr., 23
McCully, Pvt. George
McCune, Kansas, 203n
McDonald, Pvt. George W., 93, 97
McDougal, Sergeant, 94
McFayden, Mr., 102
McGillycuddy, Valentine, 179n
McGregor, Iowa, 150
McNasser, James, 118
Medicine Man, 111–12, 124, 167, 223n
Medicine River, 24
Merrill, E. G., 125–26
Merwin, stock tender, 150–51
Methodist Chuch, 174
Mexico, 10, 158

Mexican War, 10, 185n

Military Division of the Mississippi, 78

Military Division of the Missouri, 46–47, 49, 78, 140

Military Order of the loyal Legion, 172

Miller, Pvt. William H., 98

Miner's Register, 24, 34, 46, 54, 103, 158, 219n

Minnesota Uprising of 1862, 7

Minniconjous, 12, 14, 86, 131, 145–47, 150

Mischief Maker (also Back Wound), 147

Missouri River, 6, 14, 44, 78, 120, 145, 163, 167

Missouri River and Rocky Mountain Wagon Road Company, 69

Mitchell, Gen. Robert, 22, 24, 26–27, 28, 30, 34, 36, 50, 54, 163, bio. 185n

Monica. *See* Spotted Tails, daughter

Montana gold fields, routes to, 5–6

Montana Post, 5, 109, 127

Montgomery, Thomas J., 195n

Monterey, Battle of, 10

Monument, Dr., 151

Monument Station, 151

Moonlight, Col. Thomas, 25–26, 34, 49, 51, bio. 55–56, 57–58, 60, *61,* 62, 67, 70, 73–75, 81, 94, 165, 172, 208n

Mormon Trail, 2, 104

Morris, Pvt. James D., 133

Morrison, Mrs., 27

Morrow, John (Jack) A., 30, 31

Morrow's Ranch, 24, 30

Morton, Nancy, 13, 34

Mud Springs, Battle of, 35–36, 43, 45, 57, 61, 169, 193n

Mud Springs Station, 35–36, 49, 190n, 195n

Murie, Lt. Jimmy, 102, 225n

Murphy, John, 30

Mutilation, 165, 239n

Mutiny, 231n

Myers, Chief Q. M. Fred, 82

N

Nash, Capt. Edward, 100, 103, 111, 126

National Register of Historic Places, 190n

National Tribune, 44, 45

Nebraska City, Nebraska, 174–75

Nebraska City News, 174

Nebraska Republican, 29, 34, 50, 149, 158, 160

Nebraska Territory, 49

Nehring, Pvt. Sebastian, 93, 97

Nelson, Pvt. Anthony, 123, 228n

Nelson, George, 39, 45, 193n

New Madrid, 10

New York Times, 7, 23

New York Tribune, 60

Niobrara River, 6, 50, 120, 121, 127 130, 211n

Niobrara–Virginia City Wagon Road, 6, 120

North, Capt. Frank, 50, 100, 102–8, 111, 114–16, 118–19, 137, 139, 163, 222, 225n, 235n

North, Luther, 129, 235n

North Platte, Nebraska, 15

North Platte River, 6, 13, 14, 15, 29, 35, 39, 40, 42, 45, 60, 64, 68, 70, 71, 73, 104, 105, 110, 143, 148, 157, 163, 174, 182n, 194n, 212n, 223n

North Platte River Valley, 1–2, 6, 120, 148

O

O'Brien, Emily Boynton, 150
O'Brien, Capt. Nicholas J., 16–18, 22, 24, 27, 29–33, 79, 102, 108, 111, 114–15, 150, 156, 173
O'Fallon's Creek, 130, 143
O'Fallon's Bluff, 143
Office of Indian Affairs, 69, 146
Oglalas, 7, 13, 14, 28, 43, 51, 60, 61, 69, 86, 122, 131, 146, 147, 151, 157, 169, 223n. *See also* Red Cloud
Old Bear, 147
Old Bedlam, 155
Old Bull Hair, 96
Old Comanche (horse), 53
Old Crow, 17
Old Man Afraid of His Horses, 86
Old Smoke, 55, 154
Omaha, Nebraska, 8, 26, 55, 77, 120, 129, 150, 159, 164, 175, 211n
Omaha Daily Herald, 176
Omahas, 100, 103, 111, 114, 126
One Eye, 13
Oregon Trail, 2, 5, 9, 12, 14, 15, 50, 51, 57, 59, 64, 85, 86, 105, 111, 168, 192n, 200n
Oskaloosa Independent, 34, 210n
Otis, Mr., companion to Senator Colfax, 203n 60
Overland Stage Company, 15, 69
Overland Trail, 9, 58, 67, 68, 75, 107, 110, 111, 150, 168, 192n
Ovid, Colorado, 32
Owens, John, 110
Owl Woman, 181n
O Yoki ha pas, 147

P

Pacific Telegraph, 8–9, 15, 16, 32, 35, 36, 43, 51, 54, 59, 67, 78, 79, 80, 190n, 192n, 195n
Palladay, Leon, 24, 70
Palmer, Lieutenant and Captain Henry, 12, 60–61, 82, 100, 106, 107, 108–9, 113–14, 118, 140, 163, 209n, 211n, 224n
Panther Mountains, 77, 82, 131, 209n
Patton, James, 53, 199n
Patton, Robert F., 37, 41, bio. 194n
Pawnee Agency, 129
Pawnee Killer, 13, 51
Pawnee Scouts, 50, 102–8, 111, 114–16, 119, 137, 139–40, 163, 167, 225n, 235n
Pawnees, 6, 59, 71, 129
Peace Commission, 76, 141–42
Peace efforts, 75–76, 103, 145–46, 159–60
Peck, Pvt. David, 37–38, 193n
Pennock, Sgt. Isaac, 78, 95, 216n, 217n, 218n
Peno Creek, 111
Pierce, John M., 18
Pine Creek, 131
Pine Grove Station, 68
Piney Creek, 111, 123, 124
Planter's House, Denver, 116, 147
Platte Bridge Station, 9, 44, 54, 56, 67, 76, 78, 79, 80, 83, 85–99, 122, 144, 212n
Platte Bridge Station, Battle of, 85–99, 164, 167, 169, 172, 213n, 214n, 216n, 217n
Playford, Pvt. Jesse J., 93
Plumb, Col. Preston, 56, 58, 77
Plumb Creek, 13
Poison Creek, 54

Poison ivy, 130
Poisoned arrows, 232n
Pole Creek, 67
Pollock, Tom, freighter, 82
Pony Express, 36
Pope, Maj. Gen. John, bio. 10, *11*, 46–48, 75–76, 78, 82, 83, 121, 140, 141, 158, 165, 223n, 236n
Porter, Pvt. James A., 94, 98
Powder River, 5–6, 26, 28, 35, 44, 45, 49, 50, 51, 58, 75, 77, 81, 83, 86, 99, 100, 103, 104, 105, 106, 107, 109, 110, 111, 112, 119, 120, 121, 123, 129, 131, 132, 136, 137, 141, 143, 144, 160, 161, 162, 163, 166, 211
Powder River Expedition, 100–137, 143, 158–60, 162, 163, 167, 169, 220n
Powell, Pvt. Thomas, 98
Prairie Dog Creek, 111
Preston, Idaho, 8
Price, Asst. Adj. Gen. George, 62, 130, 147
Pryor's Fork, 126
Pumpkin Buttes, 106, 122, 167, 169
Pumpkin Buttes, Battle of, 122–23, 228n
Pumpkin Creek, 36

Q

Quartermaster Corps, 159, 161
Quinn, Richard, 21

R

Rawhide Creek, 130
Raymond, guide, 131
Raynolds, Capt. William, 5
Reynolds, Major, 233n
Reconstruction, 10, 158

Red and Black Foxes, 147
Red Buttes, 5, 6, 78, 85, 216n
Red Buttes, Battle of, 94–96, 122, 144, 165, 167, 169, 217n, 218n
Red Cloud, 7, 85, 86, 104, 122, 147, 151, 157, 164, 169
Red Cloud's War of 1866–68, 169
Red Leaf, 147
Reed, Henry R., 76
Reno, Gen. Jesse L., 221n
Republican National Committee, 173
Republican River, 22, 24, 28, 75
Rhodes, Pvt. Philip W., 54
Rich, Pvt. Josephus, 134
Richards, 2nd Lt. Alonzo, 100
Richards' Bridge, 5, 68, 223n
Richard, John, 5, 110, bio. 223n
Richard, Mary Gardiner, 223n
Richard, John, Jr., 100, 109
Richardson, A. D., 60
Rinehart, Capt. Levi M., 45, 53
Road Ranches, 2–3
Robbins, Capt. I. S. M., 147
Robbins, Capt. Samuel, 100, 105, 107
Rock Creek, 81, 110
Rock Creek Ranch, 110
Rocky Mountain News, 23, 29, 45, 56, 66, 73, 80, 81, 101, 116, 147, 153, 160
Rocky Ridge Station (St. Mary's), 9, 56, 67, 142, 151
Roman Nose, 86, 96, 133, 147, 166, bio. 174 and 232n
Roosevelt, President Theodore, 173
Roper, Laura, 13, 203n
Rosebud Reservation, 174
Rosebud River, 77, 83, 119 131, 209n, 211n
Ross, Lewis W., 76
Rouse, Pvt. John, 123, 228n
Rowan, Pvt. George, 44–45, bio. 196n

Rowland, Capt. Edward S., 131
Rubideaux, Louis, 70
Rulo, scout, 118
Rush Creek, 194n
Rush Creek, Battle of, 40–45, 57, 61,
    159, 164, 169, 195n
Ruth, Captain, 76, 141

S
Sage Creel Station, 68–69
St. Charles, Missouri, 223n
St. Clair, Pvt. Chavil, 67
St. Louis, 46, 65, 78, 141, 172
St. Mary's Station. *See* Rocky Ridge
    Station
Salt Lake City, 8, 15, 47, 81, 140, 143,
    148, 167, 172–73, 203n, 236n
Sanborn, Gen. J. B., 75, 146
Sand Creek Massacre, 13, 23, 76, 116,
    146, 153, 165, 174, 176, 181n
Sand Hill, chief, 13
San Francisco, 9, 13
Sandas, George, guide, 129
Sans Arcs, 14, 86, 150
Santa Fe Trail, 6
Santee Sioux, 7, 75
Savannah, Georgia, 174
Sawyers, James, bio. 120, 121–28,
    166–67
Sawyers expedition, 120–28
Schafer, Pvt. Ferdinand, 98
Scott's Bluff, 36
Scurvy, 130, 133
Sears, Charles W., scout, 121, 123
2nd California Volunteer Cavalry, 7, 73,
    79, 103, 105, 110, 111, 126, 127,
    130, 224n
2nd Missouri Light Artillery, 77, 83,
    102, 129, 131, 132–36, 161
2nd Nebraska Volunteer Cavalry, 50

2nd United States Cavalry, 173
Sedgwick, Maj. Gen. John, 183n
Selby, George W., 149
Seminole War, 55
7th Iowa Volunteer Cavalry, 16–18, 24,
    30, 32, 35–42, 44, 58, 70, 79, 102,
    108, 149, 159, 188n, 194n, 195n
7th Michigan Volunteer Cavalry, 107,
    110
Sheridan, Maj. Gen. Phillip, 209n
Sherman, Maj. Gen. William T., 46,
    78
Shoshonis, 6, 8, 47, 48, 68, 79, 93
Shrader, Cpl. James, 94–95, 216n
Shrike, D., 69
Sibley, Gen. Henry, 76
Sidney, Nebraska, 35, 190n
Signal Corps, 100, 109, 115
Single Crow, 147
Sioux, 3, 5, 6, 7, 12–14, 17, 21, 22,
    24, 26–29, 32, 33, 35, 38–44, 49,
    51, 57–59, 61, 63–65, 68, 69, 71,
    73, 79, 85, 93, 96–97, 103, 105,
    108, 111, 120, 128, 131, 133, 134,
    139, 140, 145–47, 149, 150–51,
    157, 162, 163, 165, 167–69, 201n,
    241n, 244n
Sioux City, Iowa, 5, 120, 127
Sitting Bear, 147
Sitting Bull, 169
16th Kansas Volunteer Cavalry, 50, 83,
    132, 134
6th Michigan Volunteer Cavalry, 85,
    98, 100, 102, 104–5, 123, 124, 126,
    140, 145, 219n
6th West Virginia Volunteer Cavalry,
    148–49, 161, 231n
Sade, Jack, 182n
Small, Lt. Charles, 50, 102, 111, 225n
Smiley, Lieutenant, 133
Smith, citizen killed, 109

Smith, Assistant Surgeon, 121
Smith, Colonel, 69
Smith, Pvt. Henry, 94
Smith, Lewis H., engineer, 121
Smith, S. R., 32, 33
Smith carbines, 88, 95
Smith's Station, 58
Smoky Hill River, 26, 75
Smoky Hill Road, 118
Smythe, Sergeant, 59
Snake Fork, 60
Snow Bird, 79
Snow Mountain, 69
Solomon Fork, 13
Song Face, 147
South Pass, 26
South Pass Station, 9, 54, 67, 80, 142, 151, 200n
South Platte River, 9, 12, 14, 15, 17, 22, 25, 28, 29, 32, 35, 188n
Southerland, James H., 29
Spanish American War, 172–73
Spearfish, South Dakota, 211n
Spencer carbines, 99, 129, 132, 138
Spotted Elk, 147
Spotted Tail, 7, 13, 51, 55, 147, 154–57, 169, 173
Spotted Tail's daughter, 154–57, 166
Spotted Wolf, 147, 194n
Spring Hill Station, 28, 129
Springer, 1st Lt. Charles, 130, 133–36
Springfield muskets, 88
Springfield rifles, 121
Sproul, Pvt. Samuel, 98
Squires, Maj. Andrew J., 151
Stage Stations, 2
Stahlkecker, Pvt. Tilman, 68
Standing Bear, 147
Standing Elk, 71, 147, 153, 157
Stanton, Sec. of War Edward M., 47, 69

Starving Elk, 17
Stead, Jack, 100
Steck, Pvt. Ansel, 139
Stepps, P. C., 135, 232n
Stewart, Perry, 68
Stinking Water Creek, 24
Stevenson, Robert Louis, 1
Stockton, Utah, 172
Stoddard, Pvt. Harley, 93
Storm, chief, 13
Strategy, military, 8–10, 25–28, 34, 44–51, 53, 58–59, 66, 69, 75–77, 89–65, 91, 102–3, 112, 120–21, 128, 131–32, 139–41, 143–44
Stray Horse, 96
Stroud, Captain, 151
Sulfur Springs Station, 68, 69, 81
Sully, Gen. Alfred, 7, 49, 75, 78, 121, 162–63
Summers, Pvt. Edwin, 95
Superintendent of Indian Affairs, 76
Supplies, 163
Swain, Pvt. Byron, 95
Sweetwater Bridge Station, 1, 9, 54, 59, 67, 78, 79, 80, 89, 142, 171
Swift Bear, 55, 147, 157

T
Tall Bear, 13
Tall Bull, 13, 147
Tall Indian, 147
Taylor, Supt. Edwin B., 76, 142
Temple, J. H., 143
"The Burning of Julesburg," sketch, 188n
Thick Ears, camp, 70
3rd Volunteer Colorado Cavalry, 13
3rd United States Volunteer Cavalry, 59, 88, 89–90, 200n
Thomas, Sgt. Charles, 137–38

Thomason, Pvt. Nicholas, 131
Thompson, Green, 21,
Thompson, Mrs. Green, 21
Thorton, Lieutenant, 148
Three Crossing Station, 9, 56, 59, 67, 142
Three Peaks, 82
Thunder Bear, 70
Timmons, Pvt. L. E., 57
Tingley, Dr. D. W., physician, 212
Todd, Sergeant, 98
Tongue River, 35, 86, 105, 108, 111, 112, 116, 118, 119, 123, 124, 125, 126, 128, 131, 137, 139, 145, 209n, 224n
Tongue River, Battle of. *See* Connor Battle
Topeka, Kansas, 172–73
Torture, 239n
Touching Cloud, 23
Transportation, 160, 163
Treasury Department, 166
Triggs, Lt. J. H., 70
Troy, New York, 175
Trunk, 147, 157
Tull, Pvt. Samuel, 98
Turnley, Q. M. Parmenas, 82
Twain, Mark, 1
12th Missouri Volunteer Cavalry, 77, 83, 129–36
Twyman, John, 59
Two Face, 28, 60–62
Two Kettle, 12
Two Kettle Sioux, 150
Two Thighs, 23
Tubbs, Capt. W. H., 100

U

United States Congress, 120, 142
United States Military Academy, 10

Union Pacific Railroad, 47, 128, 150, 173, 188n
Union Vedette, 172
Upper Platte Crossing, 56, 86
Upton, General, 147
Usher, J. P., 47

V

Valley City, 148
Valley Station, 22, 23, 27, 28, 34
Vandoren, Pvt. Bruce, 67
Van Kechten, carpenter, 151
Vermillion, South Dakota, 228n
Vaughn, J. W., 213n, 214n
Virginia City, Montana, 3, 6, 120, 127–28, 167
Virginia Dale Station, 9, 81
Volunteer troops, performance, 161

W

Wagon Box Fight, 165
Walker, 1st Lt. George M., 98, 216n
Walker, Lt. Col. Samuel, bio. 77, 83, 118–19, 129–40, 142, 161–65, 167–68, 209n, 211n, 233n
War Department, expenditures, 166, 76, 120, 143, 148, 165
Ware, 2nd Lt. Eugene F. (Ironquill), 1, 16, 27, 29–32, 102, 173, 181n, 240n
Ware, Noble, 32
Waring, Charles, 56, 216n
Warren, Gouvernor K., 121
Washakie, Chief, 79
Washington, D.C., 47, 100, 127, 141, 148, 156, 174–75
Washington Star, 145
Washington's Ranch, 28
Weapons, 88, 95, 99, 121, 132, 138, 159, 164, 244n. *See also* Cannon

Wentz, Asst. Surg. Julius

West, Mr., 81

West, Pvt. William, 98

Western Union, 8

Wheaton, Big. Gen. Frank, 143, 150, 151, 236n

Wheeling, Robert, train master, 100

Whiskey, 3, 110

White, Bob, 106

White Antelope, 13

White Bull, 86, 147

White Butte Creek, 28

White Clay, 147

White Earth River, 6

White Horse, 13

White Leaf, 23

White Man, 147

White Man's Fork, 22, 149, 187n

White Man's Fork, Battle of, 149

White Thunder, 71

Whiteley, Maj. S., 147

Wilcox, Lt. John, 43, 71–72

Williams, Sherman, 175

Williams, Pvt. T., 188n

Williamson, Pvt. James B., 91

Williford, Capt. George W., 121–23, 166

Willow Creek, 68, 89,

Willow Springs, 94, 105

Wilson, Pvt. William, 68, 98

Wind River Valley, 57–58

Windlass Hill, 182n

Winnebagos, 6, 100, 103, 105, 110, 115–16, 126, 140, 151

Wisconsin Ranch, 27

Wisely, Asst. Surgeon Joel F., 16–17, 33

Wolf Creek, 113–14, 124

Wolf Moccasin, 111

Wolf Tongue, 96

Wood, Lt. John R., 121

Wright, Wyoming, 121

Wright, Rev. A., 156

Y

Yankton, South Dakota 6

Yankton Sioux, 150

Yankton *Dakotaian*, 6

Yellow Bear, 70

Yellow Girl or Hinzmwin. *See* Spotted Tail's daughter

Yellow Nose, 41, 43, bio. 194n

Yellow Woman, 106

Yellowstone Canyon, 69

Yellowstone River, 5, 44, 69, 109, 127, 132

Young, Charles, 2

Young, Pvt. Thomas, 98

Young, Pvt. Will, 70, 78

Young Bear, 96

Young, Frank C., 186n

Young Wolf, 96

Youngest Old Man, 96

Z

Zeigler, Assistant Surgeon, 37

Zinn, Pvt. Jacob, 98

Zinn, Pvt. John R., 98